SHE-WOLVES

ALSO BY HELEN CASTOR

Blood and Roses: One Family's Struggle and Triumph During the Tumultuous Wars of the Roses

SHE-WOLVES

The Women Who Ruled
England Before Elizabeth

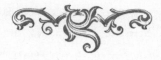

Helen Castor

HARPER

An Imprint of HarperCollins*Publishers*
www.harpercollins.com

HarperCollins books may be purchased for educational, business, or sales promotional use. For information, please write: Special Markets Department, HarperCollins Publishers, 10 East 53rd Street, New York, NY 10022.

FIRST EDITION

Maps © Martin Lubikowski
Designed by Nicola Ferguson

Library of Congress Cataloging-in-Publication Data has been applied for.

ISBN 978-0-06-143076-3

11 12 13 14 15   OV/RRD   10 9 8 7 6 5 4 3 2 1

For Helen Lenygon,
and in memory of Mary Yates

To promote a woman to bear rule, superiority, dominion or empire above any realm, nation or city is repugnant to nature, contumely to God, a thing most contrarious to his revealed will and approved ordinance, and finally it is the subversion of good order, of all equity and justice.

—John Knox, *The First Blast of the Trumpet
Against the Monstrous Regiment of Women*, 1558

I know I have the body of a weak and feeble woman, but I have the heart and stomach of a king, and of a king of England too.

—Queen Elizabeth I, 1588

CONTENTS

LIST OF ILLUSTRATIONS

Four kings of England: from the *Abbreviatio Chronicorum Angliae* of Matthew Paris, British Library MS Cotton Claudius D. VI. f. 9. © The British Library Board. All rights reserved .

The wedding feast of Matilda and Emperor Heinrich V: Corpus Christi College, Cambridge, MS 373 f. 95v, courtesy of the Master and Fellows of Corpus Christi College, Cambridge.

Effigies of Eleanor of Aquitaine and Henry II in Fontevraud Abbey: The Bridgeman Art Library.

Seal of Philippe II, from the Centre Historique des Archives Nationales, Paris: Giraudon/The Bridgeman Art Library.

Seal of King John, from the Centre Historique des Archives Nationales, Paris: Giraudon/The Bridgeman Art Library.

Isabella of France and her troops at Hereford (English School, 14th century, on vellum): The British Library/The Bridgeman Art Library.

Tomb effigy of Edward II in Gloucester Cathedral: Scala Images.

The earl of Shrewsbury presenting a book of romances to Margaret of Anjou: from the "Shrewsbury Book," British Library MS Royal 15 E. VI f. 2v. © The British Library Board. All rights reserved .

Edward VI, c. 1550, attributed to William Scrots. The Royal Collection © 2010 Her Majesty Queen Elizabeth II.

Lady Jane Grey, 1590s, by unknown artist. © National Portrait Gallery, London.

PREFACE

This is an attempt to write the kind of book I loved to read before history became my profession as well as my pleasure. It is about people, and about power. It is a work of storytelling, of biographical narrative rather than theory or cross-cultural comparison. I have sought to root it in the perspectives of the people whose lives and words are recounted here, rather than in historiographical debate, and to form my own sense, so far as the evidence allows, of their individual experiences. In the process, I hope their lives will also serve to illuminate a bigger story about the questions over which they fought and the dilemmas they faced—one that crosses the historical divide between "medieval" and "early modern," an artificial boundary that none of them would have recognised or understood.

What the evidence allows is, of course, very different as we look back from the sixteenth to the twelfth century. The face of Elizabeth I is almost as familiar as that of Elizabeth II, and the story of her life can be pieced together not only from the copious pronouncements of her government, but also from notes and letters in her own handwriting and from the private observations of courtiers and ambassadors, scholars and spies. Four hundred years earlier, with the significant exception of the Church, English culture was largely nonliterate. Memory and the spoken word were the repositories of learning for the many, the written word only for the clerical few. A historian, relying on the remarkable endurance of ink and parchment rather than on a vanished oral tradition, can never know Matilda, who so nearly took the throne in the 1140s, as closely or as well as her descendant Elizabeth. But we know a great deal, all the same, about what Matilda did, and how she did it; how she acted and re-acted amid the dramatic events of a turbulent life; and how she was seen by others, whether from the perspective of a battlefield or that of a monastic scriptorium. If the surviving sources cannot give us an intimate portrait suffused with private sentiment, they take us instead to the heart of the collision between personal relationships and public roles that made up the dynastic government of a hereditary monarchy.

These stories also trace the changing extent and configuration of the territories ruled by the English crown within a European context that was not a static bloc of interlocking nation-states, but an unpredictable arena in which frontiers ebbed and flowed with the shifting currents of warfare and diplomacy. That context lies behind one consistent inconsistency within these pages: I have used different linguistic forms to distinguish between contemporaries who shared the same name. I have chosen not to disturb the familiar identification of the main protagonists by their anglicised names, but I hope nevertheless that such differentiation might not only have the convenience of clarity, but also give a flavour of the multilingual world in which they lived.

All quotations from primary sources are given in modernised form; I have occasionally made my own minor adjustments to translations from non-English texts. I have chosen not to punctuate the narrative with footnote references, but details of the principal primary and secondary sources used and quoted in the text, along with suggestions for further reading, appear at the end of the book.

I owe many debts of thanks incurred in the writing of this book—first among them, to my agent, Patrick Walsh, and my editors, Walter Donohue at Faber and Terry Karten at HarperCollins in the United States. For their unfailing support and expert guidance, and for Walter's ever perceptive advice at critical moments, I am more than grateful. Three institutions provided a framework within which the book took shape: I am very lucky to count Sidney Sussex College, Cambridge, as my academic home; Ashmount Primary School is a community of which I feel privileged to be a part, for a few years at least; and Hornsey Library (and its café) offered a refuge without which I might never have finished writing. I hope it will be evident how much I have learned from other historians working in the field, many of them friends and colleagues, and among them all I should mention particularly John Watts, who found time to read a large section of the book to invaluable effect. I hope, too, that my friends and family know how much their generosity, support, and inspiration have meant: heartfelt thanks to all, and especially to Barbara Placido and Thalia Walters, the best of neighbours past and present. I owe more than I can say to Jo Marsh, Katie Brown, and Arabella Weir for their unstinting friendship and their strength and wisdom when I needed it most. My parents, Gwyneth and Grahame, and my sister Harriet have read every word of what follows with an insight and attention to detail of which I would be in awe if I weren't so busy thanking them, for that and so much else. And special thanks, with all my love, to my boys, Julian and Luca Ferraro.

The book is dedicated to two of the most inspiring history teachers I could ever have wished for.

PART I

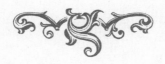

BEGINNINGS

THE TUDOR SUCCESSION

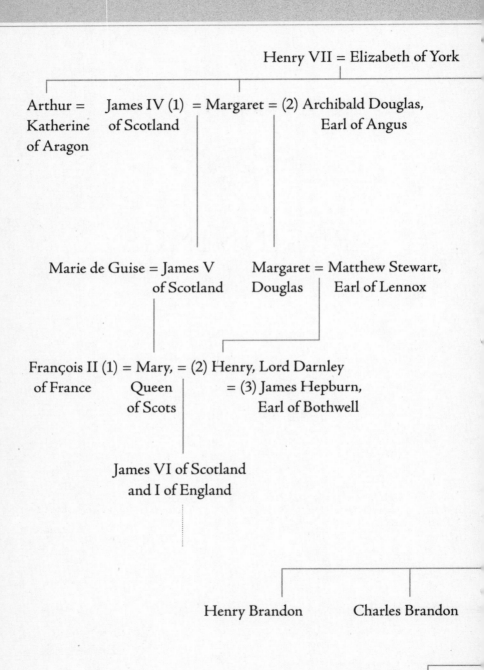

Henry VII = Elizabeth of York

Arthur =   James IV (1) = Margaret = (2) Archibald Douglas,
Katherine   of Scotland   Earl of Angus
of Aragon

Marie de Guise = James V   Margaret = Matthew Stewart,
           of Scotland   Douglas   Earl of Lennox

François II (1) = Mary, = (2) Henry, Lord Darnley
   of France   Queen   = (3) James Hepburn,
           of Scots   Earl of Bothwell

James VI of Scotland
and I of England

Henry Brandon   Charles Brandon

Guildford Dudley = Jane Grey

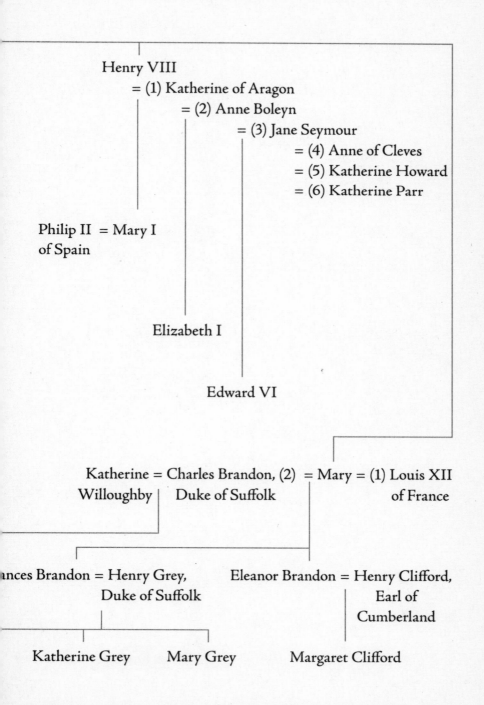

Henry VIII
= (1) Katherine of Aragon
= (2) Anne Boleyn
= (3) Jane Seymour
= (4) Anne of Cleves
= (5) Katherine Howard
= (6) Katherine Parr

Philip II = Mary I
of Spain

Elizabeth I

Edward VI

Katherine = Charles Brandon, (2) = Mary = (1) Louis XII
Willoughby | Duke of Suffolk | of France

ances Brandon = Henry Grey,   Eleanor Brandon = Henry Clifford,
Duke of Suffolk   Earl of
Cumberland

Katherine Grey   Mary Grey   Margaret Clifford

ONE

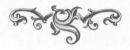

July 6, 1553:
The King Is Dead

The boy in the bed was just fifteen years old. He had been handsome, perhaps even recently; but now his face was swollen and disfigured by disease, and by the treatments his doctors had prescribed in the attempt to ward off its ravages. Their failure could no longer be mistaken. The hollow grey eyes were ringed with red, and the livid skin, once fashionably translucent, was blotched with sores. The harrowing, bloody cough, which for months had been exhaustingly relentless, suddenly seemed more frightening still by its absence: each shallow breath now exacted a perceptible physical cost. The few remaining wisps of fair hair clinging to the exposed scalp were damp with sweat, and the distended fingers convulsively clutching the fine linen sheets were nailless, gangrenous stumps. Edward VI, by the grace of God King of England, France, and Ireland, Defender of the Faith, and Supreme Head of the Church of England, was dying.

He was the youngest child of Henry VIII, that monstrously charismatic king whose obsessive quest for an heir had transformed the spiritual and political landscape of his kingdom. Of the boy's ten older siblings, seven had died in the womb or as newborn infants. One brother, a bastard named Henry Fitzroy—created Duke of Richmond and Somerset, Earl of Nottingham, Lord Admiral of England, and head of the Council of the North at the age of six by his doting father—reached his seventeenth birthday before succumbing to a pulmonary infection in the year before Edward's birth. His two surviving half-sisters, pale, pious Mary and black-eyed, sharp-witted Elizabeth, had each been welcomed into the world with feasts, bells, and bonfires as the heir to the Tudor throne; but they were declared illegitimate—Mary at seventeen, Elizabeth as a two-year-old toddler—when Henry repudiated each of their mothers in turn.

When Edward was born in the early hours of October 12, 1537, therefore, he was not simply the king's only son, but the only one of Henry's children whose legitimacy was undisputed. "England's Treasure," the panegyrists called him, and Henry lavished every care on the safekeeping of his "most precious jewel." By the age of eighteen months, the prince had his own household complete with chamberlain, vice chamberlain, steward, and cofferer, as well as a governess, nurse, and four "rockers" of the royal cradle, all sworn to maintain a meticulous regime of hygiene and security around their young charge. If the king could do nothing to alter the fact that Edward was motherless—Jane Seymour, Henry's third queen, had sat in state at her son's torchlit christening three days after his birth, but died less than a fortnight later—he did eventually provide him with a stepmother whose intelligence and kindness touched a deep chord within the boy. Katherine Parr, the king's sixth wife, was a clever, vivacious, and humane woman who befriended all three of the royal children. She was already close to Princess Mary, whom Katherine had previously served as a lady-in-waiting; and to nine-year-old Elizabeth and five-year-old Edward she brought a maternal warmth they had never before known, encouraging their intellectual development and enfolding them within a passable facsimile of functional family life. "*Mater carissima*," Edward called her, "my dearest mother," who held "the chief place in my heart."

But Henry died, a decaying, bloated hulk, in January 1547. Nor could Edward, king at nine, depend on the continuing support of his beloved stepmother. The bond of trust between them was broken only four months after his father's death by Katherine's impetuous remarriage to his maternal uncle, the dashing Thomas Seymour. She died little more than a year later after giving birth to her only child, a short-lived daughter named Mary. The young king now found his family fragmenting around him. Thomas Seymour, reckless and restlessly ambitious, was brought down by his own extravagant plotting six months after the loss of his wife. He was convicted of treason and executed in March 1549 on the authority of the protectorate regime led by his brother Edward, the Duke of Somerset. Just seven months later, Somerset himself fell from power, and was beheaded on Tower Hill in January 1552.

Edward had lost his father, his stepmother, and two uncles in the space of five years. He still had his half-sisters, but his dealings were straightforward with neither of them. He and Mary, twenty-one years his senior, were touchingly fond of one another; but they were irrevocably estranged as a result of the religious upheavals precipitated by their father's convoluted matrimonial history. In 1527 Henry had been implacably determined to annul his marriage to his first wife, Mary's mother, Katherine of Aragon. But the pope—at that moment barricaded within the Castel Sant'Angelo while Rome was sacked by the forces of Katherine's nephew, the Holy Roman Emperor Charles V—had been in no position to grant Henry the divorce he so urgently desired. And if papal authority would not sanction the dictates of Henry's conscience, then papal authority, Henry believed, could no longer be sanctioned by God. Convinced that the blessing of a son and heir had been denied him because his union with Katherine was tainted by her previous marriage to his brother Arthur—and intent on begetting such a blessing on the bewitching form of Anne Boleyn—Henry broke with Rome, and declared himself Supreme Head of the Church of England.

For the king, this was a matter of jurisdiction, not doctrine. In terms of the fundamental tenets of his faith, Henry remained a Catholic to the end of his life. But, with the ideas of Protestant reformers gaining currency across Europe, it proved impossible to hold the line that the new English Church was simply a form of orthodox Catholicism without the pope. Few of his subjects who shared Henry's doctrinal conservatism found it as easy as their king to discard the spiritual power of the "Bishop of Rome." Meanwhile, the most fervent support for the royal supremacy came from those who wished for more sweeping religious change. Thus it was that Edward's education was entrusted to Protestant sympathisers. Henry, of course, expected them to subscribe exactly to his own idiosyncratic brand of portmanteau theology, but their influence on a boy who later described the pope as "the true son of the devil, a bad man, an Antichrist and abominable tyrant" was unmistakable. Mary, on the other hand, had been brought up a generation earlier, when her father was still engaged in defending the faith of Rome against the challenge of the apostate Luther. The new religion espoused by her brother could be nothing but anathema to her, when vindication of her mother's honour and of her own legitimacy was inextricably bound up with adherence to papal authority. From 1550, their mutual intransigence embroiled them in a bitter wrangle over Mary's insistence on celebrating mass in her household, in open defiance of the proscriptions of Edward's Protestant government.

Between Edward and Elizabeth, there was no such spiritual breach. Elizabeth was the living embodiment of the Henrician Reformation—the baby born to Anne Boleyn after Henry had used his new powers as Supreme Head of his own Church to secure the divorce which the pope had refused him. Just as attachment to Rome was an indissoluble part of Mary's heritage, so separation from it was of Elizabeth's. And, like Edward, she had been exposed to the "new learning" both in her humanist-inspired education, and through the evangelical influences in Katherine Parr's lively household. Conforming to the Protestant Reformation instituted by Edward's ministers therefore presented Elizabeth with no crisis of conscience. The teenage princess adopted the plain, unadorned dress commended by the reformers with such austerity that Edward called her "my sweet sister Temperance." (More cynical observers noted not only the political expediency of this ostentatious godliness, but also how well the simple style suited her youth and striking looks—a conspicuous contrast to the unflattering effect of the heavily jewelled costumes favoured by thirty-five-year-old Mary.)

But Elizabeth's subtle intelligence was of a different stamp from the deeply felt, dogmatic piety of her brother and sister, albeit that this temperamental resemblance between Edward and Mary left them stranded on opposite sides of an unbridgeable religious divide. Elizabeth was cautious, pragmatic, and watchful, acutely aware of the threatening instability of a world in which her father had ordered the judicial murder of her mother before her third birthday. She had no memory of a time when her own status and security had not been at best unpredictable, and at worst explicitly precarious. As a result, she conducted her political relationships and religious devotions with diplomatic flexibility, rather than with the emotional absolutism of her siblings. ("This day," she said when told of the execution of Thomas Seymour, "died a man with much wit and very little judgement"—a shrewd and startlingly opaque response from a fifteen-year-old girl who had not been immune to Seymour's charms, and had only narrowly avoided fatal entanglement in his grandiose schemes.)

Despite their ostensible religious compatibility, then, Edward and Elizabeth were not close. They had been brought together in January 1547 to be told of their father's death—and clung to one another, sobbing at the news—but saw each other only rarely in the years that followed. Still, if the young king lacked the emotional and political support of immediate relatives at his court, it hardly mattered, given that Edward would one day surely marry and father a family of his own. He had been formally betrothed in 1543, at the age of five, to his seven-month-old cousin, Mary Stuart, the infant Queen of Scotland. But the Scots were unhappy about the implications of this matrimonial deal—which threatened to subject Scotland to English rule—for the same reason that the English were keen to pursue it. Unsurprisingly, the Scots resisted subsequent attempts to enforce the treaty through the "rough wooing" of an English army laying waste to the Scottish lowlands, and in 1548 Mary was instead taken to Paris to renew the "Auld Alliance" between Scotland and France by marrying the four-year-old dauphin, heir to the French throne.

A French bride—the dauphin's sister Elisabeth—was later proposed for Edward himself; but in the meantime he found friendship within his household, in the boys who shared his education. His closest companions were Henry Sidney, whose father was steward of Edward's household; Sidney's cousins Henry Brandon, the young Duke of Suffolk, and his brother Charles; and Barnaby Fitzpatrick, son and heir of an impoverished Irish lord. In 1551 Fitzpatrick was sent to France to complete his training as a courtier and a soldier, but Edward maintained an affectionate correspondence with his "dearest and most loving friend"—even if Barnaby failed to comply with some of the king's more serious-minded requests. "...to the intent we would see how you profit in the French," Edward wrote earnestly, "we would be glad to receive some letters from you in the French tongue, and we would write to you again therein."

The young king and his friends were taught by some of the finest humanist scholars in England. Edward mastered Latin before he reached his tenth birthday. Not only could he converse eloquently in the language and compose formal Latin prose, but he read and memorised volumes of classical and scriptural texts. In the years that followed, he acquired a fluent command of Greek and French, and at least a smattering of Italian and Spanish, through training which was not only linguistic but rhetorical, philosophical, and theological. His reading of Cicero, Plato, Aristotle, Plutarch, Herodotus, and Thucydides provided the intellectual basis for his weekly *oratio*, an essay in the form of a declamation, written alternately in Greek and Latin, which he was required to deliver in front of his tutors each Sunday. He studied mathematics and astronomy, cartography and navigation, politics and military strategy, and music, learning to play both the virginals and the lute.

His "towardness in learning" could not be denied, but his attempts to emulate the easy athleticism for which his ebullient father had been admired were less successful. As a young man, Henry had distinguished himself as an expert in the saddle and on the tournament field. He had been tall and well made, like his maternal grandfather, Edward IV: both stood over six feet, and were famed across Europe for their physical prowess and striking beauty (at least before the appetite for excess which they also shared transformed both their looks and their health). Edward VI, on the other hand, had inherited his mother's slight build along with her fair hair and grey eyes, with a tendency, by some reports, for his left shoulder to stand higher than his right. He rode well, and hunted regularly; but the surviving records of his first attempts in the tiltyard, where his father had so excelled, suggest that it was not an arena in which he immediately felt at home. In the spring of 1551, Edward led a group of friends dressed in team colours of black silk and white taffeta against challengers in yellow led by the young Earl of Hertford, in a sporting competition to "run at the ring"—that is, to tilt at a metal circlet hanging from a post, victory going to whichever rider succeeded in carrying it off on the point of his lance. "...the yellow band took it twice in 120 courses," the king noted disconsolately, "and my band touched often, which was counted as nothing, and took never, which seemed very strange, and so the prize was of my side lost."

But, unlikely though it seemed that he would rival his father's chivalric exploits, this slender, solemn boy was not noticeably frail. In his early childhood, policy rather than medical scrutiny had dictated the reports of Edward's health relayed by foreign ambassadors at his father's court. When a French marriage alliance was under consideration, François I's envoy told his royal master that four-year-old Edward was "handsome, strong, and marvellously big for his age." When the negotiations broke down, he observed that the prince had "a natural weakness" and would probably die young. In truth, Edward had suffered only two serious illnesses: malaria, contracted at Hampton Court Palace just after his fourth birthday in the autumn of 1541, from which he recovered completely in a matter of weeks; and an attack of what was diagnosed as measles and small-pox at the beginning of April 1552. Again, his recovery was rapid. By April 23 he was strong enough to shoulder the heavy ceremonial robes of the Order of the Garter on St. George's Day at Westminster Abbey, and on May 2 Edward wrote to his closest friend, Barnaby Fitzpatrick, to apologise for the break in their correspondence. He had been "a little troubled with the smallpox," he said, "...but now we have shaken that quite away."

He knew how lucky he was. A year earlier, he had ridden in full armour through the streets of London to dispel rumours that he had fallen victim to the epidemic of sweating sickness which had taken hold of southern England. But this defiant royal display could not protect his friends from the virulent disease. The mysterious "English Sweat" had arrived on English shores at the same time as the Tudor dynasty only a little more than half a century earlier, perhaps brought across the Channel by the French mercenaries who fought for Edward's grandfather, the future Henry VII, at Bosworth Field. It was now endemic—the outbreak of 1551 was the fifth since 1485—and deadly. That summer, the terrifying symptoms—fever, dizziness, intense headaches, rashes, pain in the limbs, and a drenching sweat—appeared in Cambridge, where Henry and Charles Brandon, the Duke of Suffolk and his brother, had been sent to study at St. John's College. They left the town as soon as they could, but it was already too late. Henry Brandon died on July 14. Charles inherited his brother's title on his sickbed; he was Duke of Suffolk for half an hour before he, too, perished. They were sixteen and fourteen years old.

Edward was already well aware of life's fragility, and he had his uncompromising faith to sustain him in his grief. Nonetheless, the deaths of the Brandon brothers cast a pall over the court that summer, despite the lavish reception laid on for three noble emissaries sent by the French king, Henri II, to invest Edward with the chivalric Order of St. Michael. The visit went well enough, but several onlookers, French and English, including Edward's principal tutor, John Cheke, expressed concern about the unremitting demands placed on the thirteen-year-old king by this elaborate diplomatic choreography, on top of the regular pressures imposed by his schooling and the daily meetings of his Privy Council.

Edward's illness the following spring intensified those worries, but he was robust enough by the summer of 1552 to undertake a stately progress through the southern counties of Sussex, Hampshire, Wiltshire, and Dorset, bestowing on some of his wealthiest subjects the costly honour of entertaining their king and his forbiddingly large entourage for days at a time. Throughout the trip, Edward sent regular bulletins to Barnaby Fitzpatrick, who was now serving with Henri II's army at Nancy in northeastern France. "...whereas you have all been occupied in killing of your enemies," he told his friend, "in long marchings, in pained journeys, in extreme heat, in sore skirmishings and divers assaults, we have been occupied in killing of wild beasts, in pleasant journeys, in good fare, in viewing of fair countries, and have rather sought how to fortify our own than to spoil another man's." It was apparent—however much Edward himself refused to admit it—that even these delightful diversions could now tax his stamina. But there still seemed no cause for serious concern about his well-being by Christmas 1552, when the court threw itself into extravagant festivities under the direction of the "Lord of Misrule," a gentleman of the royal household temporarily transformed into the anarchic ringleader of the season's entertainments.

By Easter 1553, however, the court pageants—and with them the king's health—had taken a more ominous turn. At the Palace of Westminster that April, the Master of the Revels presented a cavalcade of Greek Worthies wearing headpieces "moulded like lions' heads, the mouth devouring the man's head helmetwise," attended by torch-bearing satyrs, each equipped with a pair of "oxen's legs and counterfeit feet." But after the music and the tumbling, to the menacing beat of a single drum, came a "Masque of Death," a macabre parade of ghastly figures, each one "double visaged, the one side like a man and the other like death," bearing shields adorned with the heads of dead animals. And by then, as the players capered, the horrifying possibility was emerging that Edward might be watching a tableau of his own fate.

His physicians did not know it, but an attack of measles, such as the one from which the king had recovered a year earlier, serves to suppress the victim's resistance to tuberculosis. And at the beginning of February 1553—just two months before the Masque of Death stalked through Westminster's great hall—Edward had fallen ill with a feverish, chesty cold which he could not shake off. Six weeks later he was still confined to his chambers, Charles V's ambassador Jehan Scheyfve reported to the emperor in encrypted French, "and it appears that he is very weak and thin, besides which I learn from a good source that his doctors...are of the opinion that the slightest change might place his life in great danger." In April, Edward rallied enough to be allowed brief, carefully supervised outings in the spring sunshine in the gardens at Westminster, and after the Easter festivities he was parcelled up in velvet and furs to be transported seven miles down the Thames by river barge to his favourite palace at Greenwich, the great guns of the Tower of London booming in salute as the royal flotilla passed by. A fortnight later, however, Ambassador Scheyfve noted that the king had ventured outside only once since his arrival there. A "trustworthy source" had let slip that Edward was wasting away, and that his racking cough was now bringing up blood and alarmingly discoloured sputum.

In public, the king's councillors loudly maintained the fiction that his recovery was imminent. John Dudley, Duke of Northumberland, the ruthless politician who had supplanted Edward's uncle Edward Seymour, Protector Somerset, as his chief minister in 1549, announced firmly on May 7 that "our sovereign lord does begin very joyfully to increase and amend." But Scheyfve was in no doubt of the iron fist that lay beneath the surface of these velvet assurances. The royal doctors whose unhappy responsibility it was to preside over the king's slow decline had requested the benefit of a fresh medical opinion, and reinforcements to their ranks had been recruited; but all those who treated Edward were "strictly and expressly forbidden, under pain of death, to mention to anyone private details concerning the king's illness or condition," the ambassador reported. Meanwhile, gossip on the streets of the capital about his failing health was discouraged more forcibly: three Londoners who had been overheard to say that the king was dying had their ears cut off in punishment.

Edward himself was also pressed into service in the attempt to stem the flood of rumour and counter-rumour. He was now too weak to show himself in the open air, or even to stand unaided, but on May 20 he was held up at a window of Greenwich Palace to watch as three great ships set out from the Thames on a voyage of exploration masterminded by the Venetian cartographer Sebastian Cabot. Captained by Sir Hugh Willoughby and piloted by the talented navigator Richard Chancellor, the *Bona Esperanza*, *Bona Confidentia*, and *Edward Bonaventure* had been funded by a joint-stock company of merchants and courtiers to search for a passage through the northeastern seas to the trade routes of China. It was a glorious sight—the tall ships and their crews decked out in pale blue as they took their leave, while the cannon thundered and the crowds cheered. Propped up painfully behind Greenwich's ornate glass, Edward could not know that two of the three vessels setting off with such hope would never see England again. The small fleet was separated by a storm off the Norwegian coast little more than two months later. Richard Chancellor, at the helm of the *Edward Bonaventure*, reached the port of St. Nicholas on the White Sea and pressed on by sled to Moscow, where his overtures to the tsar, Ivan the Terrible, established English trading privileges so successfully that the China Company became the Muscovy Company immediately on his return. But

Hugh Willoughby—a distinguished soldier who had begged for this command despite his inexperience at sea—was not so fortunate. Lacking Chancellor's expert guidance, the *Bona Esperanza* and *Bona Confidentia* meandered up and down the Russian coast, hopelessly lost, until in September they dropped anchor in Arctic waters off the uninhabited shore of Lapland. The ice-bound ships, containing the frozen bodies of Willoughby and his men, were found by Russian fishermen the following summer.

Edward, whose black and gold desk was often heaped with maps and atlases beside his brass quadrant and astrolabe, had been excited by Cabot's ambitious plans; and the Duke of Northumberland, at the head of the young king's government, was a former Lord Admiral of England who had been instrumental in bringing Cabot from his Spanish home to London and assembling the wealthy syndicate to back Willoughby's mission. But in May 1553, as the three ships disappeared into the haze of the horizon, Northumberland had no time to savour the fruits of his labours. Despite the belligerent optimism of the duke's public pronouncements, it was obvious that Edward would not survive to see the return of the ship that bore his name. He was not seen again at the palace windows. Barely able to leave his bed, he was now running a constant fever. He coughed incessantly, and his face and legs began to swell. The noxious treatments administered by his anxious doctors became ever more oppressive: his head was shaved to permit the application of poultices to his scalp, and the stimulants prescribed as "restoratives" left him unable to rest without heavy draughts of opiates. Whispered conversations in the corridors at Greenwich and at Westminster no longer debated whether the king would die, but when. Everything now depended on who would succeed him—and that was a matter of terrifying uncertainty.

Henry VIII had moved heaven and earth—almost literally, given the convulsions he had precipitated in his subjects' spiritual lives—in his effort to secure a male heir. In the end, all his hopes had come to rest on the narrow shoulders of one boy, who had proved too fragile to sustain them. And, extraordinarily, there was no one left to claim the title of King of England. For the first time in the kingdom's history, all the contenders for the crown that Edward was about to relinquish were female.

This unprecedented lack of a king-in-waiting was in part the result of Tudor paranoia about the dilute solution of royal blood that flowed in the Tudor line itself. True, Henry VII, the first Tudor monarch, could trace his descent from Edward III, the mighty warrior-king who had ruled England in the fourteenth century. But that descent had come via the Beauforts, illegitimate offspring of Edward III's son John of Gaunt—a bastard family who had later been legitimised by an act of parliament but explicitly excluded from the royal succession. Henry VII's acquisition of the crown on the battlefield at Bosworth in 1485 therefore had everything to do with the unpredictable effects of civil war, and nothing to do with birthright.

Henry VIII's dynastic claims were less tenuous, thanks to his mother, Elizabeth of York, the eldest daughter of Edward IV and sister of the murdered princes in the Tower. But neither of the two Henrys would ever admit that her role had been more than that of a fitting consort for the "rightful" Tudor monarch. Meanwhile, both kings had engaged in a cull of the surviving representatives of the Plantagenet bloodline. Few of Elizabeth of York's remaining royal cousins died in their beds; some were cut down on the battlefield, others on the block. Violence had brought the Tudors to the throne, and violence now left them unchallenged in possession of it.

But this new dynasty was a young sapling compared to the Plantagenet family tree, and had produced few boys to fill its branches. Henry VII had been an only child, born to a thirteen-year-old mother who never conceived again. He fathered eight children: only four survived infancy, of whom the eldest, Arthur, died at fifteen, leaving one younger brother, the future Henry VIII, and two sisters, Margaret and Mary. Both of these Tudor princesses made glittering but short-lived diplomatic matches, Margaret to the King of Scotland and Mary to the King of France. Both then married again in widowhood, Margaret to Archibald Douglas, Earl of Angus, a

powerful Scottish lord, and Mary—in headstrong haste, only weeks
after the death of her first husband—to Charles Brandon, Duke of
Suffolk, the handsome best friend of her brother, King Henry.

By 1553 Henry VIII and his sisters, Margaret and Mary, were
dead. As Henry's son Edward hovered between fervent prayer and
feverish delirium, all eyes turned to his siblings and cousins, the possible contenders for his throne. The prospects were not reassuring.
There were Edward's two half-sisters, Mary and Elizabeth, both of
whom had been declared illegitimate more than fifteen years earlier. There was Mary Stuart, the ten-year-old Queen of Scots, granddaughter of Margaret Tudor by her first, royal marriage, who was
now living in Paris as the intended wife of the heir to the French
throne. Margaret's second marriage—a violently tempestuous relationship that ended in divorce—had left her with a single daughter, Margaret Douglas, whose legitimacy had also been brought into
question by her parents' separation. There was Frances, sole surviving child of the love match between Mary Tudor and her second husband, Charles Brandon; and Frances in her turn was now the mother
of three girls, Jane, Katherine, and Mary Grey. Frances's younger
sister Eleanor Brandon had died some years earlier, but she, too, had
left a daughter, Margaret Clifford. In these nine women—the oldest
nearly forty, the youngest not yet ten—were vested the remaining
hopes of the Tudor line.

Extraordinary though it might seem, their sex was the explicit
focus of little discussion in the fraught circumstances of May 1553.
It was, after all, what they had in common. What mattered now was
what separated them: the issues of principle—questions of birth and
faith—and the urgent political calculations that would identify the
next monarch from among their number. Henry VIII had been in no
doubt of the decisive factor in determining the succession, should the
worst ever happen to his only son: his own blood, he had declared,
should prevail. The rights of his eldest child, Mary, and then his
second daughter, Elizabeth, to inherit the crown after their brother
were upheld in the Act of Succession of 1544 and confirmed in their

father's last will, despite Henry's unwavering insistence, in other contexts, on their illegitimacy. It was a tribute to Henry's overwhelming personal authority that the tacit contradiction between his daughters' bastardy (which had been enshrined in statute law in the 1530s) and their standing as his heirs was not challenged in his lifetime.

By 1553, however, the old king had been dead for six years, and even his fearsome spirit could not compel obedience from beyond the grave. The force of Henry's commands had faded so much, in fact, that the impetus to set aside the claims of his bloodline sprang from the contentious process by which an equally fundamental embodiment of his rule—the Henrician Church of England—had also been abandoned. Since his death in 1547, the successive regimes led by the dukes of Somerset and Northumberland had dismantled the doctrinal conservatism of Henry's religious settlement in favour of the evangelical Protestantism in which their young king believed so ardently. For centuries, English church buildings had been infused with the sights, sounds, and smells of the Catholic liturgy, the notes of the Latin Mass echoing on air made visible by the scented smoke of candles and incense, while the intercessory presence of the saints took tangible form not only in carefully preserved fragments of flesh and bone, but in richly coloured images painted on plaster and worked in glass, stone, wood, and alabaster. Now, in only two years, parish churches had been transformed. By 1549, walls had been whitewashed, statues smashed, and shrines dismantled. Plain windows let the light shine in on places of worship dedicated to the word—and no longer the image—of God. Processions, pageants, and mystery plays were outlawed. Chantry chapels, founded to provide masses and prayers to speed the passage of sinful souls through Catholic purgatory, were dissolved. And worshippers in this new stripped-down Edwardian Church found the Latin Mass—the most fundamental expression of the Christian faith for as long as the kingdom of England had existed—replaced by the spoken English liturgy of a new Book of Common Prayer written by Edward's Archbishop of Canterbury, Thomas Cranmer.

Resistance to these drastic innovations took the frightening form of armed rebellion in the southwestern shires of Devon and Cornwall in the summer of 1549, and helped to bring down Protector Somerset's government that autumn. But the pace of religious change only increased under his successor, the Duke of Northumberland. Conservative bishops were deprived of their sees; bonfires of Catholic service books were lit; precious plate and vestments were summarily confiscated; and in 1552 Cranmer produced a second, radically revised and unequivocally Protestant prayer book. Only months later, however, the young king's rapidly deteriorating health threatened to undo the "godly reformation" over which he had presided. Should Edward die—a possibility that had to be faced by the spring of 1553—the Act of Succession would hand the crown to his elder sister Mary, whose devotion to the old faith had proved as resolutely immovable as Edward's allegiance to the new. It was a prospect that was wholly unacceptable to both the king and his chief minister: to Edward, because he could not countenance the idea that his own death might precipitate his subjects back into papist darkness; and to Northumberland, because his Protestant convictions were underpinned by the political certainty that his own career, and perhaps his life, would not long survive Mary's accession.

Edward was only fifteen, but he was a Tudor king who believed in his authority to command the future just as much as his father had done. Despite the troublesome technicality that, as a minor, he could not make a legally binding will—and that, even if he could have done so, a private document would have no power to overturn an act of parliament—Edward carefully composed what he called "my device for the succession." Drafting and redrafting in his own hand, he methodically set about excluding his Catholic sister's right to his throne. Religion was the essence of the issue, but—disquietingly for Edward—Mary's faith offered no formal justification for prohibiting her inheritance. The question of her legitimacy, however, proved to be more fertile ground. Their father's insistence that Mary was a bastard, even as he nominated her as her brother's heir, gave

Edward ample scope to argue (as letters patent drafted by his legal advisers later put it) that she was "clearly disabled to ask, claim, or challenge the said imperial crown." It was a tactic which would also strike a collateral target. If Mary was illegitimate, then so, too, was his younger sister Elizabeth, a committed believer in the reformed religion. But that, clearly, was an outcome Edward was prepared to accept, whether because he was convinced of his sisters' bastardy, or because he knew that Elizabeth's Protestantism was more politic and less full-hearted than his own.

The decision to set aside Mary and Elizabeth solved one problem—the intolerable possibility that Catholicism might be restored—but raised another: to whom could Edward entrust his crown and his legacy? The Act of Succession had already discounted the descendants of Henry VIII's elder sister Margaret, and Edward had no more reason than his father to restore them. Margaret's granddaughter and heir, Mary Stuart, was a staunch Catholic who, as Queen of Scotland and Dauphine of France, personified the traditional alliance between England's two most enduring enemies. Her proximity to the English throne had been a powerful element of her appeal as a prospective daughter-in-law to the French king, Henri II; but the threat of England being subsumed into a new Franco-British empire ruled from Paris was sufficiently alarming to undermine any chance that she might be seen as a viable claimant in London.

The lone remaining contenders, therefore, were the heirs of King Henry's younger sister, Mary, and her second husband, Charles Brandon, Duke of Suffolk. Edward, of course, knew the Brandon family well. His childhood friends Henry and Charles Brandon, whose loss he had felt so deeply in 1552, were not his blood relatives, but sons of the duke's remarriage to a fourteen-year-old heiress just three months after Mary Tudor's death. However, Tudor blood flowed in the veins of Mary's daughter Frances Brandon, whose husband, Henry Grey, the new Duke of Suffolk after the deaths of his wife's young half-brothers, was a member of Edward's Privy Council. In the early spring of 1553, the ailing king—"not doubting in the grace and goodness of God but to be shortly by his mighty power restored to our former health and strength"—still saw the claims to the throne of Frances Brandon and her three daughters as a safety net rather than an imminent political reality. The first draft of his "device" accordingly nominated as his successors any future sons to whom Frances might yet give birth, to be followed by the male heirs of her (as yet unmarried) daughters, Jane, Katherine, and Mary Grey.

By May, however, there could no longer be any question but that Edward was dying. If the king still laboured under any delusions about his prospects of recovery, Northumberland could not afford to indulge them, since the twin imperatives of safeguarding the fledgling Edwardian Church and securing the duke's political career were now matters of critical urgency. At the beginning of June, with Northumberland at his bedside, Edward once more took up his pen to amend his "device" for the succession. Where the original draft spoke of the crown descending to the unborn sons of Frances Brandon's eldest daughter—"the Lady Jane's heirs male"—the king now altered the text to read "the Lady Jane *and her* heirs male." With the addition of two small words, Jane Grey became the chosen heir to Edward's crown.

It seemed the perfect solution. Jane was fifteen years old, an exceptional scholar and a fiercely devout adherent of the same evangelical faith as Edward himself. She had also, on May 21, become Northumberland's daughter-in-law when she married his teenage son, Guildford Dudley, in a magnificent ceremony at the duke's London home. But Jane was an unwilling bride, forced into unhappy compliance out of duty to her ambitious parents, and it was far from clear whether her regal responsibilities would be any more welcome than her marital ones, either to Jane herself, or to the realm she now stood to inherit. Certainly, Edward's sister Mary, who had been dispossessed of so much in her thirty-seven years, would not stand quietly by while her rights as "Princess of England" were passed over in favour of a slip of a girl representing a church Mary hated. As so often before, she and her brother were evenly matched in the intensity of their convictions, Mary's determination to lead her people back to the true faith of Rome every inch the equal of Edward's resolve to save them from it. And in that campaign she would hope for the support of her cousin, the Holy Roman Emperor Charles V—whose ambassador, Jehan Scheyfve, continued to dispatch ominous reports of Edward's physical decline—as well as the backing of an as yet unknown number of her prospective subjects.

As a result, June 1553 was a month of mounting tension and barely suppressed fear. The Princesses Mary and Elizabeth, who had been prevented from seeing their brother since the early stages of his illness, were now kept in ignorance of the progress of the disease, beyond what they could glean of the speculation spreading from the capital to their homes twenty miles north, at Hunsdon and Hatfield. The Duke of Northumberland reinforced the garrison at the Tower of London and ordered royal warships into the Thames, and the king's lawyers and councillors were called in secret to his bedchamber to put their seals to Edward's "device" for Lady Jane's succession. The Chief Justice of the Court of Common Pleas, Sir Edward Montagu, apprehensively demurred on the grounds that the scheme was not only legally unenforceable but criminal, even treasonable, by the terms of the Act of Succession of 1544. But a combination of the fury of a dying boy and a promise that the plan would imminently be ratified by parliament brought the judges to heel. Their imprimatur persuaded those councillors who still hesitated, Archbishop Cranmer foremost among them, to append their signatures to the document. At the beginning of July, Princess Mary was at last summoned to the king's bedside. Northumberland planned to accommodate her in some suitably secure royal lodging—the Tower, say—on her arrival in the capital. It was hardly surprising that Mary fled in the opposite direction, taking refuge instead at her estates in Norfolk, which were reassuringly close to the coast should escape prove necessary, and surrounded by her loyal retainers.

Now, on the afternoon of July 6, the king lay in the great gilded bed, transformed by the extremity of his suffering into a figure of grotesque pathos. He was not alone: his personal physician, George Owen, who had been present at his birth fifteen years earlier, was in constant attendance, quietly assisted by Christopher Salmon, a favourite among Edward's valets. His devoted friend Barnaby Fitzpatrick had been unable to return as Edward had wanted, detained by family responsibilities in Ireland. Instead, two gentlemen of the king's chamber—Sir Thomas Wroth and Sir Henry Sidney, Edward's companion since childhood—kept vigil at his bedside. But he was beyond help. The imminent inevitability of his death had been reported to the royal courts of Europe for weeks, and time and again Edward had defied the rumours; but the stimulating effects of the powerful drugs his doctors had administered were fading as their toxins poisoned an already failing body. Now he lay still and silent, eyes closed in the swollen, darkened face, the disfigured hands motionless. For a moment it seemed as though the shallow breathing had stopped; but then Edward began to murmur to himself, the prayer inaudible but its purpose clear. Sidney took him in his arms, and held him until he died.

Outside, a summer storm raged. Later, it was said that the howling darkness that engulfed London was the wrath of Henry VIII, thundering from the grave at the thwarting of his will. His son was dead, and with him died Henry's vision of a glorious line of Tudor kings. Amid the chaos and confusion, one thing alone was certain: for the first time, a woman would sit upon the throne of England.

TWO

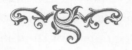

Long Live the Queen?

I cannot well guide nor rule soldiers, and also they set not by a woman as they should set by a man." So wrote Margaret Paston, a Norfolk gentlewoman contemplating the unhappy necessity of defending one of her properties against a rival claimant almost a century before Edward VI's death. She had her own reasons for emphasising her limitations: recently widowed and exhausted by years in the front line of similar disputes, she wanted to leave her grown-up sons in no doubt that they, not she, now bore responsibility for holding the family fort. Nevertheless, she was right, and about more than her own situation. In a few characteristically succinct and forthright words, she had identified the principal practical constraints on female rule in medieval England.

They were constraints that were evident in the most iconic image of power available to Margaret and her contemporaries. The great seal by which royal commands were authenticated was the physical manifestation of the crown's authority, a pictorial representation of England's ruler that was instantly recognisable to the vast majority of England's people who had neither set eyes on their monarch nor learned to read the documents from which the red wax hung. On one side of the seal the king sat in state to give justice to his people, orb and sceptre in his hands; on the other he rode a towering warhorse, his sword unsheathed in defence of his kingdom.

But a woman could not sit as a judge, nor could she lead an army. Physically, women were equipped for the differently hazardous work of childbearing, rather than wielding heavy steel on the battlefield. Culturally, they were by nature—that is, as designed by a divine creator—lesser than men. At their best, these softer, frailer beings might complement the sterner masculine virtues of their lords and masters with the feminine ones of mercy, mildness, and maternal nurture. At worst, they might lead men astray with their inconstancy, their irrationality, and their capacity—as whore rather than madonna—for sexual sin. Either way, it was in obedience, modesty, assistance, supplementarity, that a woman's place lay within the order of God's creation. And, as such, a woman was no more capable of leadership in peace than in war.

That, at least, was the theory. Experience, depending on individual capabilities, might be less absolute. Margaret Paston was intent on pointing out to her sons that they should not depend on her as captain of the family's defences precisely because—resourceful and indomitable as she was—she had had to play the role before, sending to her husband in London for crossbows and poleaxes as well as the sugar and almonds that usually made up her shopping lists. It was not ideal, then, but nor was it unthinkable that a woman might occupy a position of command or control. Supplementarity, after all, might mean that a wife or mother could be called upon to protect the interests of a husband or son if he were temporarily absent or hampered by youth or infirmity; and female assistance might be transmuted into influence or even guidance in the hands of a woman possessed of particular intelligence, charisma, or will.

Nevertheless, there were limits to what a woman could do. The power of a monarch, his authority instituted and sanctioned by God, was implicitly and inherently male. In practice, there were a number of ways in which such power might be acquired, but all of them reinforced that most basic identification. The dynasty that ruled Margaret Paston's England could trace its descent back to Duke William of Normandy, a warrior who had made himself a king on the battlefield in 1066. The Bayeux Tapestry, telling the story of that military conquest in elegantly enigmatic embroidery, depicts just three women within its narrative—one a nameless victim of war, another caught up in a now-unfathomable sexual scandal, and the third, Edith, wife of Edward the Confessor and sister of Harold Godwinson, an archetypal figure of female virtue at the deathbed of her royal husband. All are marginal figures in a masculine world, vastly outnumbered even by the horses and ships of the duke's invasion force, let alone by the men of his army. And William's forcible accession interrupted an older tradition whereby the Anglo-Saxon nobles chose their king from among the men of the royal bloodline. This opportunity for the judicious weighing up of personal qualities had the unfortunate habit of descending into a bloodbath, as candidates for the throne sought to demonstrate their own kingly ruthlessness and eliminate their rivals in one fell swoop—but, whether an Anglo-Saxon monarch was chosen by consensus or by violent competition, there was no doubt that he would be male.

It was only gradually, as new precedent and new custom began to be established in Norman England, that primogeniture emerged as the defining principle of the royal succession. Heredity, of course, risked bestowing the right to rule on daughters as well as sons. The developing common law within England, for example, allowed female heirs to inherit land, albeit not on the same terms as their male counterparts: an eldest son would succeed to an estate in its entirety, whereas, in the absence of a male heir, daughters would each receive an equal share. But a kingdom could not be divided in the same way as a smallholding, a manor, or even an earldom; and by the sixteenth century very little had been unequivocally resolved about the possibility of female succession to the English throne, other than the evident fact of its undesirability.

In some ways, the circumstances of 1553 appeared to offer more encouraging signs for the prospects of a female sovereign than had been the case even fifty years earlier. Tudor anxiety about the conspicuous vulnerability of the fledgling dynasty had combined with the personal frailties of the last two Tudor kings to diminish expectations of the monarch as warrior. Henry VIII had been at first too irreplaceable and then too incapacitated, and Edward VI simply too young, to lead an army into battle. Instead, the new model of the humanist prince, entering the fray on the intellectual rather than the military front line, offered a paradigm of government by brain rather than brawn from which women were less obviously excluded.

On the other hand, the very fact that the tumultuous upheavals in English life over the previous two decades had been fundamentally predicated on Henry VIII's desperate desire for a son had reinforced the manifest deficiencies of his rejected alternative, a female heir, in the minds of his subjects. And while the claim to the throne, such as it was, of the entire Tudor dynasty had come through a woman, Henry VII's mother had still been alive in 1485 to see her son crowned. Why, then, if women could indeed rule, had Westminster Abbey not rung with cheers at the coronation of Queen Margaret Beaufort? In fact, the protracted and bloody civil wars from which Henry Tudor had so unexpectedly emerged victorious had gone a long way toward suggesting that a combination of military force and plausible fitness for power was more likely to secure the crown than strict adherence to the hereditary principle. It seemed possible, therefore, that the lessons of recent history might count women out of contention altogether.

Certainly, that was the conclusion to which Edward VI had come when he first sat down to draft his "device for the succession." The young king had a methodical as well as a scholarly mind, and he had absorbed with every fibre of his being his father's conviction that a monarch could shape his kingdom by royal fiat in the form of statute and ordinance. Government now proceeded by the framing of detailed legislative regulation; and the original version of Edward's "device" therefore set out a logical plan for the institution of a new set of rules that would provide England with a legitimate, Protestant, and, crucially, male monarch to succeed him, should he fail to have a son of his own. His sisters were not legitimate; his Scottish cousins were not Protestant; which left his Grey cousins as the means by which the crown would pass, after the model of his great-grandmother Margaret Beaufort, through the female line to rest on the male head of one of their as yet unborn sons.

But life was too messy and unpredictable to be moulded even by the formidable will of a Tudor king. Edward had not planned to die at fifteen; and with his last illness his designs for the future of his kingdom fell apart. The nomination of Jane Grey as his successor abandoned logical principle in favour of pragmatic improvisation, since Jane was a female heir whose mother, from whom her claim derived, was still living. This, then, was no wholesale acceptance of female succession but an attempt to preserve the spirit of Edward's intentions through a lone anomaly—a legitimately born Protestant woman who would, by Edward's explicit specification, pass on the crown to her "heirs male." Should his scheme succeed, England's first queen regnant would also be its last. Should his father's will prevail, on the other hand, and his sister Mary inherit the crown, an entirely different precedent would be established.

In 1553, therefore, the future of female rule was about to be tested, in principle and in practice. But female rule in England also had a past. In 1153—exactly four hundred years before Edward's death, in a world as remote from Tudor England as the sixteenth century is from the twenty-first—a civil war that had raged for two decades was brought to an end with the sealing of a peace treaty at Winchester. That civil war had been caused by the claims of a woman who could—and, her supporters believed, should—have been the first queen to rule England in her own right. Matilda, daughter of Henry I and granddaughter of the Conqueror, came tantalisingly

close not only to establishing her right to the throne, but also to securing an unequivocal hold on power.

She did so in a political world where boundaries, laws, and precedents were drawn and redrawn with almost every generation—
partly because of the fluidity of an uninstitutionalised government,
and partly because newly Norman England was not bound by the
example of its Anglo-Saxon past. In one sense, then, this militarised
society—where monarchs were required to be soldiers, feudal lords
at the head of a personal following—offered little scope for female
leadership. But at the same time, there were few formal, explicitly
articulated obstacles standing in the way of female rule. And despite
contemporary assumptions about the limitations of her sex, Matilda
tested the presupposition of male sovereignty almost to destruction.

She did not succeed; nor did she unequivocally fail. Because her
challenge ended in concession and compromise, the precedent it set
was partial and complex. Women, it seemed, could not expect to exercise royal power in their own right; but Matilda both transmitted
her claim to her son and played an influential role in his councils.
The lesson of her failure to secure the throne—and the story of the
four centuries that elapsed before the claims of her female Tudor descendants—was therefore not straightforwardly that of the exclusion
of women from power in England. Instead, it appeared that the conventional roles of wife and mother might, in some unconventional
circumstances, offer opportunities for government to be guided by a
female hand.

Between the twelfth and the fifteenth centuries three more exceptional women—Eleanor of Aquitaine, Isabella of France, and Margaret of Anjou—discovered, as queens consort and dowager, how
much was possible if presumptions of male rule were not confronted
so explicitly. Eleanor governed England during the long absence of
her "most beloved son," Richard the Lionheart. Isabella challenged
her husband's misrule, championing the cause of legitimate government in the name of her young son, the future Edward III. Margaret
took up the standard of royal authority in defence of her infant son

and her incapacitated husband, Henry VI. All three had the freedom to act because their power was exercised under the legitimising mantle of a male monarchy.

But such freedom had limits. Eleanor found herself able to play the elder stateswoman only after she had spent fifteen years in custody for her involvement in a rebellion against her husband, Henry II. Isabella's failure to comprehend the responsibilities of power as well as its rewards resulted in her overthrow not long after that of her husband, Edward II. And Margaret's attempt to shoulder her husband's dead weight gradually collapsed, along with his government, as it became clear that the will animating this composite royal authority was not that of the king himself.

Freedom to act, in other words, did not mean freedom from censure and condemnation. The risk these queens ran was that their power would be perceived as a perversion of "good" womanhood, a distillation of all that was most to be feared in the unstable depths of female nature. The unease, if not outright denunciation, with which their rule was met has coalesced in the image of the she-wolf, a feral creature driven by instinct rather than reason, a sexual predator whose savagery matched that of her mate—or exceeded it, even, in the ferocity with which she defended her young. "She-wolf of France, but worse than wolves of France," Shakespeare famously dubbed Margaret of Anjou: "How ill-beseeming is it in thy sex / To triumph like an Amazonian trull / Upon their woes whom Fortune captivates!" And the appellation was later extended by Thomas Gray to Margaret's countrywoman, Edward II's queen Isabella ("She-wolf of France, with unrelenting fangs / That tear'st the bowels of thy mangled mate . . .").

The visceral force of this image drew on a characterisation of female power as grotesque and immoral that had surfaced with remarkable speed in a number of vituperatively explicit polemics once the prospect of a female sovereign became an imminent reality in 1553. Most resounding of all was the *First Blast of the Trumpet Against the Monstrous Regiment of Women*, unleashed in 1558 from his exile in the Swiss city of Geneva by the Protestant firebrand John Knox.

This tract, and others adopting a similar stance, were composed in reaction to the specific political and religious developments of the mid-1550s, but the arguments they made had deep roots within English political culture. Female "regiment"—or regimen, meaning rule or governance—was "monstrous"—that is, unnatural and abominable—because women were doubly subordinate to men, once by reason of Eve's creation from Adam's rib, and again because of her transgression in precipitating the fall from Eden. And therefore "to promote a woman to bear rule, superiority, dominion or empire above any realm, nation or city is repugnant to nature, contumely to God, a thing most contrarious to his revealed will and approved ordinance, and finally it is the subversion of good order, of all equity and justice," Knox ringingly declared, before elaborating several thousand words of largely circular variation on that pungent theme.

By this argument, then, any exercise of power by a woman was a manifestation of the female propensity for sin; and the Old Testament offered a ready identification of female rule as a sexualised tyranny in the infamous figure of Jezebel, wife of King Ahab, who exploited her hold over her husband and their two sons to turn Israel away from God and subject its people to immorality and injustice. "...such as ruled and were queens were for the most part wicked, ungodly, superstitious, and given to idolatry and to all filthy abominations, as we may see in the histories of Queen Jezebel...," wrote Thomas Becon, a Protestant preacher and homilist, in 1554. Knox, whose favoured rhetorical mode inclined markedly toward fire and brimstone, tackled the subject with obvious relish: "Jezebel may for a time sleep quietly in the bed of her fornication and whoredom, she may teach and deceive for a season; but neither shall she preserve herself, neither yet her adulterous children from great affliction, and from the sword of God's vengeance...." And Knox's blasting trumpet was directed not only at women who sought to rule in their own right, but also at those whose authority, like that of Jezebel herself, depended on their husbands and sons.

The example of the medieval queens who had exercised power

in England in previous centuries, therefore, was both complex and troubling, even for those who had no wish to emulate Knox and his colleagues in the articulation of polemical absolutes. A woman could not easily fit the role of a monarch, moulded as it was for a man. Nor could a wife or mother step forward to act in place of a husband or son without raising questions about the nature of her rule and its place in the right order of creation. But shedding the she-wolf's skin would come at a price: the "good woman" who acknowledged her duty of obedience and the primacy of her role as a helpmeet could not, after all, hope to offer sustained political leadership in any meaningful sense.

For the Tudor women confronting the succession crisis of 1553, then, the battle to secure the throne was only the first step on a hard road ahead. Their right to wear the crown would not go un-questioned, but that challenge was finite and graspable compared to the test which the exercise of power would present. In facing that greater test, they had every reason not to look back to their medi-eval forebears. Those earlier queens had been compromised by the provisional nature of their authority, and condemned by history for their unnatural self-assertion. No self-respecting Tudor monarch—self-evidently, of course, fit to rule by God-given right—would need to acknowledge such problematic exemplars. It was to kings, not queens, that Tudor sovereigns looked for example and warning. ("I am Richard II, know ye not that?" Elizabeth sharply remarked in re-sponse to Shakespeare's meditation on the nature of kingship.)

But that very identification with male sovereignty emphasises what the Tudor queens shared with the women who had held power in the centuries before them. In the lives of those women—in their ambitions and achievements, their frustrations and failures, the chal-lenges they faced and the compromises they made—were laid out the lineaments of the paradox which the female heirs to the Tudor throne had no choice but to negotiate. Man was the head of woman, and the king was the head of all. How, then, could royal power lie in female hands?

PART II

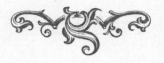

MATILDA

Lady of England

1102–1167

MATILDA

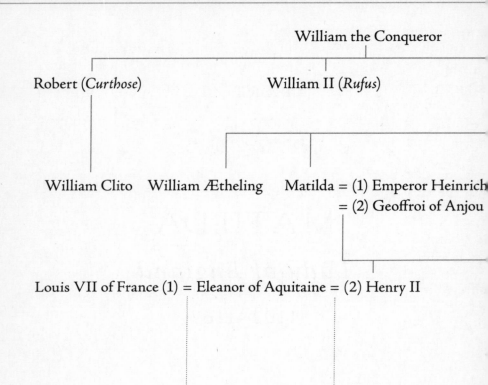

William the Conqueror

Robert (*Curthose*)   William II (*Rufus*)

William Clito   William Ætheling   Matilda = (1) Emperor Heinrich
                                              = (2) Geoffroi of Anjou

Louis VII of France (1) = Eleanor of Aquitaine = (2) Henry II

MATILDA

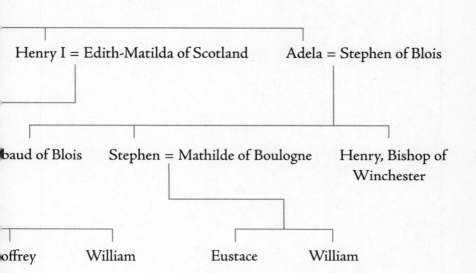

Henry I = Edith-Matilda of Scotland   Adela = Stephen of Blois

baud of Blois   Stephen = Mathilde of Boulogne   Henry, Bishop of
Winchester

offrey   William   Eustace   William

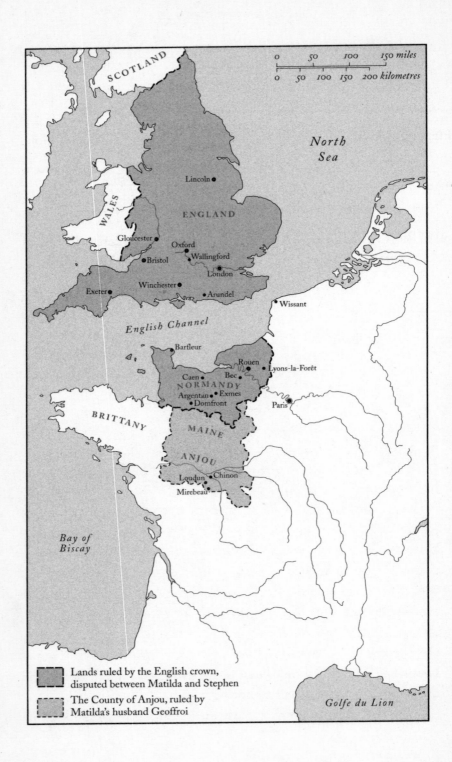

SCOTLAND

North
Sea

0   50   100   150 miles
0   50   100   150   200 kilometres

Lincoln •

ENGLAND

WALES

Gloucester •
Oxford •
Bristol •   • Wallingford
Winchester •   London •
Exeter •   • Arundel
                              • Wissant

English Channel

Barfleur •
                        Rouen •
                   Bec •   • Lyons-la-Forêt
Caen •
NORMANDY
Argentan • • Exmes
      • Domfront   Paris •

BRITTANY

MAINE

ANJOU

Loudun • • Chinon
  • Mirebeau

Bay of
Biscay

Golfe du Lion

Lands ruled by the English crown,
disputed between Matilda and Stephen

The County of Anjou, ruled by
Matilda's husband Geoffroi

THREE

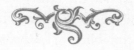

This Land Grew Dark

O n December 1, 1135, another King of England lay dying. Not a boy but a man of nearly seventy, Henry I had ruled the English people for more than half his lifetime. A bull-like figure, stocky and powerfully muscular, Henry was a commanding leader, "the greatest of kings," according to the chronicler Orderic Vitalis, who observed his rule admiringly from the cloisters of a Norman monastery. His greatness did not lie on the battlefield—a competent rather than exceptional soldier, Henry avoided all-out warfare where he could—but in his judgement, his charisma, and his acute political brain. Nor had age dimmed his relentless energy; he had spent the summer and autumn of 1135 on military patrol along the borders of his lands, and in November he rode to his lodge at Lyons-la-Forêt, thirty miles east of the Norman capital, Rouen, for the restorative pleasures of a hunting trip.

But while he was there, against his doctor's orders, the king in-

dulged in a dish of lampreys, an eel-like fish that was prized as a
delicacy, served in a pie powdered with spices or roasted with a sauce
of blood and wine infused with ginger, cinnamon, and cloves. Perhaps his physician was right about the indigestible richness of the
dish; perhaps the lampreys were dangerously unfresh; or perhaps the
illness by which Henry was struck that night was no more than unhappy coincidence. Whatever the cause, within a couple of days it
was clear that he was unlikely to survive. As in 1553, a king's mortal-
ity brought great men scrambling to his bedside, and the succession
to his throne became a matter of frantic political speculation.

The country whose rule Henry was about to relinquish would
not have been wholly familiar to his Tudor descendants. England
in 1135 was a young kingdom—or, rather, an old kingdom in the
upstart hands of a new royal dynasty. There had been a king of all
England for two hundred years, ever since the independent Anglo-
Saxon territories of Northumbria, Mercia, Wessex, and East Anglia
had first been united under Æthelstan, grandson of the great King
Alfred. Despite the repeated shockwaves of Viking assaults on this
newly unified land—assaults so successful that the English throne
was appropriated for a time by the Danish King Cnut—Anglo-Saxon
England had grown by the mid-eleventh century into a remarkably
powerful, wealthy, and sophisticated state. And then, on October
14, 1066, on a sloping field six miles north of Hastings, the flower of
the Saxon aristocracy was cut down by charging horsemen under the
command of Henry's father, William, Duke of Normandy.

William claimed to be the rightful heir of the Anglo-Saxon king
Edward the Confessor, but the Norman conquest of England that
followed the slaughter at Hastings was nothing less than a revolu-
tion. The Anglo-Saxon political caste was systematically eliminated,
as four or five thousand thegns—the great Anglo-Saxon landhold-
ers—were violently displaced by a new elite of fewer than two hundred Norman barons. French, not English, was now the language of
power in England. And this political year zero opened the way for
a new kind of kingship, too. The evolutionary intricacies of Anglo-

Saxon landholding were swept away by William's irruption into the political landscape. England was now the personal property of its conqueror, to be parcelled out at will among his loyal supporters through a chain of feudal relationships, where land was granted from lord to vassal in return for an oath of personal fidelity and a pledge of military service. Such relationships were the currency of politics throughout western Europe, but only in England, on a blank slate wiped clean by conquest, could the king create a feudal hierarchy depending directly on his own authority, untrammelled by customary rights and local tradition.

England, however, was only one part of the Conqueror's domains. After 1066 the Channel was no longer a frontier but a thoroughfare, carrying William and his most powerful subjects between the lands they now held on both sides of the sea. In England, he was a king, imposing his royal will on a vanquished people. In Normandy, on the other hand, he remained a duke—not a sovereign lord but a vassal of the King of France. In practice, Philippe I had little hold on his nominal liegeman: he could not come close to matching the military might that had enabled William to seize the English crown, nor could he escape the constraints of custom and precedent that William's invasion had obliterated on the other side of the Channel. Nevertheless, questions remained about how the new Norman kingdom of England might fit within a map of Europe which was composed not of neatly interlocking nation-states behind precisely defined borders, but of a constantly shifting web of overlapping jurisdictions, alliances, and allegiances.

Henry was the third Norman monarch to wield this double authority, after his formidable father and his dandified, overconfident brother William, known as "Rufus" because of his ruddy complexion. A child of the Conquest, born in Yorkshire two years after his father's triumph at Hastings, Henry personified the hybrid complexities of the Anglo-Norman world. He was educated in England, but—like the Conqueror, who briefly tried to learn English before giving it up as a bad job—Henry thought and spoke in Norman

French. The two greatest contemporary historians who recorded his exploits and revered his kingship, Orderic Vitalis and William of Malmesbury, were each the son of a Norman father and an English mother, one writing in the Norman monastery of Saint-Evroult, the other at Malmesbury Abbey in Wiltshire. And now, in December 1135, Henry's English birth would be followed by a Norman death, as he made his final confession and received the last rites at Lyons-la-Forêt.

Despite the hush of the room and the spiritual ministrations of the Archbishop of Rouen, the king's energetic mind could not find peace in his final hours. His overwhelming preoccupation, as it had been for the last fifteen years of his life, was the question of who should succeed him—and he had good reason to be anxious.

In the seventy years of its existence, Norman England had not yet settled on a means of determining the identity of a new king. Before 1066 the Anglo-Saxons had looked to the Witan, the great nobles of the realm, to choose the man best suited to lead them from among the Æthelings, direct royal descendants of the sixth-century warrior Cerdic, the first Saxon King of Wessex. In Normandy, meanwhile, the duke himself had traditionally nominated his own heir—in practice, almost always his eldest son—to whom his magnates then swore fidelity and allegiance.

That was the way in which the Conqueror had become Duke of Normandy, at the age of only seven; and he had followed Norman custom in designating as his successor there his eldest son, Robert, known as Curthose—"short shanks"—or, more contemptuously still, Gambaron—"fat legs"—because of his unimposing stature. In England, however, William was not bound by precedent, whether Norman or Anglo-Saxon. And for the last four years of his life, the king and his eldest son had been acrimoniously estranged. In September 1087, when William—now a corpulent but still powerfully imposing man of sixty—lay on his deathbed, he was grudgingly prepared to concede that Robert should rule in Normandy, as he had promised more than twenty years earlier. But in England, he intended that the crown should pass to his second and favourite son, William Rufus, who was dispatched from his father's bedside at Rouen across the Channel to Westminster. There Rufus was crowned king little more than two weeks after his father's death.

The result was war. Robert could not accept that his younger brother should supplant him in England, while Rufus set his sights on adding his elder brother's duchy to his new kingdom. Sporadic fighting and tension-filled truces left Rufus—who was a better soldier and a shrewder leader than his unimpressive brother—with the upper hand, until in 1096 Robert abandoned the struggle, pawning Normandy to Rufus for a cash payment of 10,000 silver marks to fund his departure on crusade.

Robert was still away, spending some time in southern Italy on a leisurely journey back from the Holy Land, when on August 2, 1100, William Rufus was killed, speared in the heart by a stray arrow during a hunting expedition in the New Forest. If Robert had hoped to succeed him as King of England—and he surely did, given that William had no children, and that each of the brothers had named the other his heir in a short-lived treaty of 1091—he was to be bitterly disappointed. Their clever, ambitious youngest brother, Henry, was with Rufus when he died in the dappled sunlight of the forest. Henry took only an instant to weigh up the opportunity with which the rogue arrow had unexpectedly presented him. Ruthlessly composed amid the panic and confusion, he spurred his horse twenty miles north to Winchester, the ancient capital of Wessex, where he seized control of the royal treasury and persuaded the barons who had reached the town in time for Rufus's hastily arranged burial the next morning to nominate him as their new king. He then rode full pelt for London, another sixty miles northeast, where he was crowned in Westminster Abbey on August 5, less than seventy-two hours after his brother's untimely death.

It was a brilliantly successful coup d'état. When Robert arrived home in Normandy a month later, he was unable to shake Henry's hold on England. Six years after that, when military tension broke into open warfare at Tinchebray in southwestern Normandy, Robert was defeated and captured by Henry's forces. The remaining three decades of his life were lived in captivity, where he abandoned any attempt to revitalise his cause in favour of a contemplative existence spent writing poetry and, from his comfortable quarters in Cardiff Castle, learning to speak Welsh.

Henry was now master of both England and Normandy—and the victory of this youngest of the Conqueror's three sons seemed to represent a conclusive defeat for the principle that eldest sons might expect to succeed their royal fathers. But Henry's perspective as a young pretender turned out to be very different from his scruples as an established and undisputed monarch. An archetypal poacher turned gamekeeper, Henry was adamant that his own offspring should never be ousted from power by a coup of the kind that he had masterminded to secure the throne for himself.

His campaign to establish the legitimacy of his line beyond all possible doubt began just three months after he became king, with his marriage to Edith, daughter of King Malcolm III of Scotland. Her father was dead, and Scotland was shaken by conflict over the succession; but the orphaned and exiled princess was a beautiful young woman whose "perfection of character," according to Orderic Vitalis, Henry had "long adored." Her particular political virtue as Henry's new queen, however, was that, through her mother, she had Anglo-Saxon royal blood in her veins. Edith herself was not an Ætheling, since only male heirs could claim that title. But any children of her marriage to Henry would have the unique distinction of tracing their descent from the house of Cerdic as well as from the Conqueror, and their right to rule would be affirmed twice over.

By the end of 1103, there were two royal infants: a girl called Matilda (the same Norman name that her mother had now adopted in place of the Anglo-Saxon Edith) and a boy named William. Despite the length and strength of their parents' marriage, which lasted until the queen's death in the spring of 1118, there would be no more children. The young Matilda was therefore dispatched to Germany for a magnificent diplomatic marriage to the Holy Roman Emperor, Heinrich V, and her brother—whom Orderic Vitalis called William Ætheling, in recognition of his doubly royal heritage—was educated as befitted a prince who would cement his father's success in binding England and Normandy together.

William was not, in fact, Henry's only son, since well-sown wild oats meant that the king had a growing family of illegitimate children, more than twenty in all, scattered around his English and French domains. "All his life he was completely free from fleshly lusts," the chronicler William of Malmesbury wrote with an impressively straight face, "indulging in the embraces of the female sex, as I have heard from those who know, from love of begetting children and not to gratify his passions...." But there could be no doubt that, among this large family, William was the apple of his father's eye, the boy on whose shoulders all Henry's hopes now rested.

William was only ten when he began to act as a formal witness of his father's royal edicts. By the age of sixteen, he was married to the daughter of Count Foulques of Anjou and Maine, territories immediately to the south of Normandy, and had ridden into battle with his father against the forces of the French king, Louis VI (known, thanks to his expanding girth, as Louis the Fat), on the plain of Brémule in eastern Normandy. Both his marriage and what turned out to be a stunning victory at Brémule were intended to secure his place in the succession against the one man who could challenge him: William Clito, the only legitimate son of Henry's older brother, the imprisoned Robert Curthose.

Like mirror images, these first cousins faced one another: two grandsons of the Conqueror, each named William in his honour, born within a year of each other, and each designated as a royal heir, "Clito" being the Latin equivalent of the Anglo-Saxon "Ætheling." But only one could succeed; and Henry's implacable determination that his son should be king made it certain that Louis the Fat would champion his rival. Both boys—at barely sixteen and seventeen, they were scarcely more—took their place amid the heat and dust of the

battlefield at Brémule in August 1119, but it was William Ætheling
who triumphed. William Clito fled with King Louis to the safety of
the French stronghold at Les Andelys where, the next day, Henry
returned the French king's captured warhorse and all its splendid
trappings, while William Ætheling sent back William Clito's pal-
frey with a selection of rich gifts for his defeated cousin in an exquisitely judged gesture of chivalric condescension. One year later, in the
summer of 1120, Louis finally bowed to the inevitable. He agreed to
accept the homage of William Ætheling as lawful successor to the
duchy of Normandy, thereby recognising the legitimacy of Henry's
rule on both sides of the Channel and of William's claims as his designated heir. William Clito's cause was lost, and William Ætheling's
future secure.

Fresh from this triumph, Henry and his magnates gathered at
Barfleur, the harbour at the northern tip of the Cotentin Peninsula
from where the Conqueror had launched his assault on England in
1066, and which was now the greatest port on the Norman coast. By
November 25, 1120, Henry's fleet was ready to sail. The voyage between England and Normandy was a familiar one to the king and his
court—Henry's father had crossed the Anglo-Norman sea seventeen times in the twenty-one years he ruled England—but it was not
to be taken lightly, especially in winter, when the risk of rough winds
and towering waves made the journey particularly hazardous. Henry
himself had never before sailed later in the year than September, but
there seemed no cause for concern as he surveyed the glassy water,
scarcely rippled by the southerly breeze that would billow gently in
the ships' sails on the way north to the English coast.

As the afternoon light began to fade, he embarked on the *esnecca*,
the king's great dragon-headed longship, named "serpent" in the ancient language of the Norsemen who had become "Normans" when
they settled in France two hundred years earlier. His son William,
however, was not with him. Instead, the seventeen-year-old prince
had taken passage on a newly refitted vessel named the *White Ship*,
piloted—propitiously, it seemed—by the son of the shipmaster who

had first brought the Conqueror from Barfleur to England fifty-four years earlier.

As the royal *esnecca* put to sea in the twilight, a glamorous company of ebullient young aristocrats assembled on the *White Ship*'s freshly scrubbed deck. Among them were two of William's illegitimate siblings: Richard, newly betrothed to a rich Norman heiress, and another Matilda, wife of the powerful Count of Perche. There, too, were the young Earl of Chester and his wife, along with the earl's illegitimate brother Othuer, who was the prince's tutor, and the king's favourite nephew, Stephen, Count of Mortain. Altogether the prince's entourage numbered more than two hundred people, from the cream of the Anglo-Norman nobility to the fifty rowers grasping the long oars that stretched down beneath the great square sail to the dark sea below.

And when at last the *White Ship* slipped out into the blackness of the quiet water, everyone on board was roaring drunk. Three casks of wine had already been emptied by the time the ship was ready to sail. As the party grew wilder and more raucous, the boisterous behaviour of the prince's companions had become so alarmingly reckless that Stephen, Count of Mortain—who alone was still sober because of a stomach upset—asked to be put ashore. He was safely back on land when the ship left the quayside, its oars pulling violently through the water as the inebriated crew raced to overtake the *esnecca*, somewhere ahead in the pitch-dark night, with the clamorous encouragement of the drunken passengers.

No one saw the rock at the mouth of the harbour. There was no warning: just the heart-stopping jolt of a brutal impact; the sickening crunch of splintering wood; and sudden screaming panic as the ship began to list. With freezing water pouring in through the shattered hull, it took only minutes for the *White Ship* to go down. The frantic cries of hundreds of terrified voices carried faintly to the shore, but on a moonless night, in perishing temperatures, there was no hope of rescue.

As the voices fell gradually, chillingly silent, two men were left alone in the darkness, clinging to a spar. One was a young nobleman named Geoffrey FitzGilbert; the other, a butcher named Berold, a native of Rouen, who had set foot on board only to reclaim some debts he was owed by the careless aristocrats of the prince's court. They prayed together, trying to keep up each other's spirits despite the shock and the biting cold. Eventually FitzGilbert could hold on no longer. His numbed and stiffened fingers lost their grip on the wet wood, and he slipped quietly away into the depths of the sea. But the butcher clung on, his rough sheepskin jacket—so unlike the waterlogged silks and furs that had dragged the drowning courtiers down—still preserving the last traces of his body's warmth. At dawn, he was found by three fishermen. He was the *White Ship*'s only survivor.

It was two days before anyone dared break the news to King Henry, waiting anxiously in England for his son's arrival. When a stuttering boy was finally pushed forward to tell him of the wreck, this bull of a man collapsed in anguish. It was a personal tragedy: Henry had lost kinsmen, friends, and servants, and, most terrible of all, three of his beloved children. But, for a king, the personal was always political, and all Henry's hopes for his country's future had been swallowed by the sea along with his drowned son. "No ship that ever sailed brought England such disaster," William of Malmesbury wrote grimly.

Overwhelming grief cast a long shadow over the rest of Henry's life, but it did not incapacitate him for long. Just two months after the horror at Barfleur he married for a second time, to Adeliza, a beautiful girl the same age as his dead son. Politically, it was a promising alliance—Adeliza was the daughter of Godfrey, Count of Leuven and Duke of Lower Lorraine—but the raison d'être of the match was the need to resolve the sudden crisis over the succession. In that, however, it failed. Despite the fact that Henry's ability to father children had been energetically demonstrated over the course of thirty years, and that Adeliza would eventually go on to have seven of her own when she married again after Henry's death, this royal coupling produced no new heirs.

By 1125 it was already becoming clear that the fifty-seven-year-old king could not rely solely on the dwindling likelihood that his young wife might give him another son. But Henry did have one surviving legitimate child: his daughter, Matilda. He had not seen her for fifteen years, ever since she had left England as an eight-year-old girl to travel to Germany to join the court of her future husband, the Holy Roman Emperor Heinrich V. But in May 1125 the emperor succumbed to cancer at the age of just thirty-eight, and his young and childless widow was suddenly free to rejoin her father.

Henry lost no time in taking advantage of Matilda's abrupt liberation from her imperial duties. At Christmas 1126 he presented his newly returned daughter to his magnates at a great gathering of the court held at Windsor and Westminster. There the nobles were required to swear a solemn oath that they would uphold her right, and that of any sons she might one day have, to succeed to her father's throne. They did so without demur, in public at least; but Henry could not rest content with this formal acceptance of his daughter's title, and in 1131 he demanded that his leading subjects repeat their pledges, reiterating their commitment to Matilda as ruler-in-waiting.

By that time, Henry had also sought to bolster her position, as he had done that of his dead son, through an alliance with Anjou, Normandy's southern neighbour. In 1128 Matilda therefore married Geoffroi, heir to the county of Anjou, whose sister had once been the wife of her drowned brother. And by the time Henry made his last, fateful journey to Lyons-la-Forêt, his daughter's second marriage had given him two healthy grandsons, two-year-old Henry and one-year-old Geoffrey, in whose chubby hands lay the future of the Anglo-Norman realm.

The king had done all he could, but he could not be sure that it was enough. Earls, counts, and bishops crowded at his bedside as he roused himself to insist again, with a dying man's desperate urgency, that all of his lands, on both sides of the sea, should pass to his daughter. At last, on the night of December 1, 1135, Henry I died.

"He was a good man, and was held in great awe," wrote the author of the Anglo-Saxon Chronicle. "In his time no man dared do wrong against another; he made peace for man and beast." It was a mercy, perhaps, that the sightless eyes of the Lion of Justice would not see the darkness that followed his passing.

FOUR

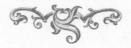

Mathilda Imperatrix

I t is a measure of the peculiarity of Matilda's position in 1135 that we know so little about her. Her contemporaries, whether friends, enemies, or neutral observers, struggled to decide how to handle or to judge her, how to place her within a political narrative that expected its chief protagonists to be male. As a result, she is an insubstantial, inconsistent presence in the chronicles, rarely seen in more than two dimensions, often disconcertingly portrayed as a marginal figure in her own story.

We can only guess what she looked like. Her father, Henry, William of Malmesbury tells us, was "more than short and less than tall," a vigorous, thickset man with receding black hair, a steady gaze, and an unfortunate tendency to snore. Her mother, Edith-Matilda of Scotland, meanwhile, was "a woman of exceptional holiness, and by no means negligible beauty." Although William puts no specific features to these royal good looks, he shows us the pious queen walking

barefoot in church during Lent in penitential humility, and wearing a haircloth shift under her elaborate gowns. But, master of the
thumbnail portrait though he was, William of Malmesbury's sketch
of Matilda herself is uncharacteristically opaque, a somewhat imper-
sonal coupling of her parents' most striking qualities: she "displayed
her father's courage and her mother's piety; holiness in her found its
equal in energy, and it would be hard to say which was more admi-
rable."

In part, of course, this arm's-length treatment of Matilda's character stems from the fact that she was an unknown quantity in England when she crossed the Channel at her father's side in September
1126 for the first time in more than sixteen years. She was English-
born, probably in February 1102 at Sutton Courtenay, a manor
house near the ancient town and abbey of Abingdon in Oxfordshire,
and seems to have lived in England for the first eight years of her
life, although reliable information about her upbringing is almost entirely lacking. We know that her intelligent, capable mother rarely
accompanied the king to Normandy, instead spending most of her
time at the royal Palace of Westminster, a mile and a half westward
along the Thames from London's city walls, where Matilda's flamboyant uncle, William Rufus, had built the largest great hall England had ever seen to house his marble throne. We cannot take it for
granted that Matilda lived at Westminster with her mother—royal
children rarely spent all or even most of their time in close proximity
to their parents—but it seems likely that the queen's cultured household, with its profound religious sensibility, provided the defining
context for Matilda's education.

Matilda's mother tongue, like that of her parents and her peers,
was Norman French, but she learned to read in Latin, the language
of the Church, of international diplomacy, and of literate culture in
England after the Conquest had obliterated Old English literary traditions. We might also hope, for her sake, that she was well prepared
for her future as a royal bride, since it was a role she was expected to
take up, in public at least, when she was no more than a child.

She was only six years old when the most eminent king in western Europe, Heinrich V of Germany, sought her hand in marriage. The kingdom of Germany was an agglomeration of states under the rule of a monarch chosen by a select group of the most powerful German noblemen and archbishops (albeit that, as in England, the hereditary principle proved hard to resist, so that Heinrich was the fourth heir of the Salian dynasty in direct succession to wear this supposedly elective crown). The German ruler was known not only as *Rex Teutonicorum*—King of the Germans—but also as *Rex Romanorum*—King of the Romans—in recognition of the fact that his power extended over what remained of the Western Roman Empire after its split from the Byzantine East, lands which included not only Germany but northern Italy, Burgundy, Austria, and Bohemia. And the man who was elected King of the Romans could claim the right to be crowned by the pope in a ceremony which would elevate him from a mere king to the status of emperor, a title conferring on its holder a unique authority within western Christendom.

For Matilda's father, King Henry, whose family had held the crown of England for less than fifty years and whose own controversial claim to the throne was not yet established beyond all challenge, this alliance with a monarch who would follow in Charlemagne's footsteps as ruler of the Western Roman Empire was an enticing prospect—one for which he was more than prepared to send his small daughter overseas, and with her a large amount of money. And it was England's wealth that made the match so appealing for Heinrich, whose authority over lands stretching from the Baltic to the Adriatic was not matched by his cash flow. The deal was done in the summer of 1109: seven-year-old Matilda was betrothed to the German king by proxy at a magnificent meeting of her father's court; and it was agreed that, along with the hand of his child-bride, Heinrich would receive 10,000 silver marks, the same immense amount for which Robert Curthose had pawned the duchy of Normandy to William Rufus just thirteen years before.

Matilda had only a few months left to enjoy the familiarity of life in England. She had just passed her eighth birthday in February 1110 when she said goodbye to her parents, her brother, and her home, and set sail for the northern French county of Boulogne, accompanied by a distinguished retinue of aristocrats and clergymen. They rode beside her carriage—its embroidered cushions doing little to ease the jolting of the wooden chassis on the wheel-axles—two hundred miles eastward, over the flat plain of Flanders and across the western borders of her future husband's empire into the duchy of Lower Lorraine. There, in Liège, a great city ruled by a powerful prince-bishop, Matilda for the first time met the man to whom she was promised in marriage.

Heinrich was twenty-four years old. It was four years since he had become King of Germany in succession to his father, Heinrich IV, whose reign had been blighted by bloody conflict over the extent of his royal authority, both with the nobility of Saxony and with the pope. He had been excommunicated in the course of this struggle, and as a result his corpse still lay unburied in an unconsecrated side-chapel of the imperial cathedral at Speyer, awaiting reconciliation in death with the papacy against which he had fought so bitterly in life.

But the start of his son's rule was not marred by such battles. The new young king had allied himself with his father's enemies two years before the old king's death, and, with their support, his accession brought a temporary peace to the Empire. The task that Heinrich now faced was to rebuild the power of his crown. In theory, his authority reached from Hamburg in the north to Rome in the south, from Lyons in the west to Vienna in the east. In practice, however, he needed to ride to Rome at the head of an ostentatiously imposing entourage—a retinue which might, as circumstances dictated, take on the form of an army—to stamp his rule on his Italian territories and to secure his coronation as emperor at the hands of the pope. For that, he needed money; and so his little bride, who would bring him such a great dowry, was graciously and warmly received.

For the next few months Matilda accompanied her future husband on imperial progress, first of all to the graceful city of Utrecht in the Netherlands, more than a hundred miles north of Liège. There, at Easter, the royal couple were formally betrothed once again, in person this time, and Heinrich endowed his wife-to-be with rich gifts and lands reflecting her status as his consort. The court then moved along the valley of the Rhine to Cologne, Speyer, and Worms, before arriving at Mainz, the foremost archiepiscopal see of all Germany, where preparations were under way for Matilda's coronation. At eight, she was too young to become a wife, but not to be recognised as a queen: a solemn betrothal was as binding in the sight of the Church as the marriage vows to which she had committed herself for the future, so that contemporaries saw no incongruity in the fact that Matilda would receive her crown some years before her wedding ring.

Mainz, like Speyer and Worms, was home to one of the three great *Kaiserdome*, imperial churches built in monumental red sandstone on an awe-inspiring scale. The Romanesque cathedral at Mainz had an inauspicious history: fire had gutted the building on the day of its inauguration almost exactly a century earlier, and in 1081 another devastating blaze had undone the painstaking repairs. But, thanks to Heinrich IV, a new octagonal tower now soared over the nave as his small daughter-in-law arrived in ceremonial procession on July 25—the feast day of St. James the Apostle, whose mummified hand was preserved among the priceless relics in the royal chapel—to be crowned Germany's queen. A new archbishop had not yet been appointed to the see of Mainz after the death of the last incumbent in 1109, so it was the Archbishop of Trier who carried Matilda delicately in his arms while the Archbishop of Cologne anointed her with holy chrism and placed a crown (which was almost certainly too large, as well as too heavy, for a child) on her young head.

The ritual was designed to impress all those present, the eight-year-old girl at its centre as well as the assembled onlookers, with its potent blend of the sacred and the majestic. It was therefore with a powerful sense of her royal duty and dignity that Matilda left Mainz for Trier, a little less than a hundred miles westward, to learn what it was to be a German queen. Her education there was overseen by the prelate who had held her during her coronation, Archbishop Bruno, one of her future husband's closest and most trusted counsellors, a man described by the French statesman and chronicler Abbot Suger of Saint-Denis as "elegant and agreeable, full of eloquence and wisdom." Trier was a Roman city, the oldest in Germany, lying in the valley of the Mosel River between low wooded hills, and its cosmopolitan Franco-German culture provided the ideal setting for this Norman princess to learn the language, laws, and customs of her newly adopted home.

While Matilda studied under Archbishop Bruno's careful guardianship, Heinrich put the treasure she had brought as her dowry to immediate and productive use. The royal couple's betrothal at Utrecht in April had doubled as an opportunity for the king to begin the process of assembling forces for his planned expedition to Rome, and in August he crossed the Alps at the head of a vast following—Abbot Suger and Orderic Vitalis suggest a figure of thirty thousand knights, which, even allowing for evocative exaggeration, implies an exceptionally intimidating host—that was equipped and provisioned by Matilda's silver.

Relations between Heinrich and Pope Paschal II had deteriorated badly since the king's accession, over the bitterly contested question of investiture—the competition between Church and state for control of the creation of bishops, a running battle that was the focal point of a broader war over the relative powers of spiritual and temporal authority. Despite Paschal's initial hopes, Heinrich had proved no more willing to yield to claims of a papal monopoly on investiture than his excommunicated father had been, and the pope therefore refused to crown him emperor unless he changed his mind. Heinrich had a ready answer: his soldiers seized Paschal and sixteen of his cardinals and held them all in close confinement for two months until they capitulated. Under this peculiarly irresistible form of persuasion, Paschal confirmed his royal enemy's right to invest bishops with the ring and crozier of episcopal office; and on April 13, 1111, in the echoing basilica of St. Peter in Rome, the pope's unwilling hands placed the imperial crown—an octagonal diadem of gold studded with jewels and cloisonné enamelwork, enclosed by a golden arch and surmounted by a jewelled cross—on the new emperor's head.

The conflict was far from over. Once Heinrich and his army had returned to Germany, the papal council lost no time in repudiating the concessions he had extorted by force. The imperial coronation was a sacred rite that could not be undone, but, while hostilities continued, it was abundantly clear that the emperor's bride could not hope to be crowned in her turn as his empress.

She could, however, expect to become his wife. In January 1114, just before her twelfth birthday—twelve being the canonical age at which girls were permitted to enter into the sacrament of marriage—Matilda and Heinrich finally took their vows in the towering cathedral at Worms on the western bank of the Rhine. The sheer grandeur of the celebrations, the most opulent gathering of the German court in a generation, defied the descriptive powers of the chroniclers. Five archbishops, thirty bishops, and five dukes witnessed the ceremony, each attended by an ostentatious entourage; "as for the counts and abbots and provosts," one well-informed but anonymous commentator continued, "no one present could tell their numbers, though many observant men were there. So numerous were the wedding gifts which various kings and primates sent to the emperor, and the gifts which the emperor from his own store gave to the innumerable throngs of jesters and jongleurs and people of all kinds, that not one of his chamberlains who received or distributed them could count them."

Matilda's performance on this intimidatingly magnificent occasion was immaculate. She was "a girl of noble character," the anonymous chronicler remarked, "distinguished and beautiful, who was held to bring glory and honour to both the Roman Empire and the English realm." It was also the beginning of her public life at her imperial husband's side. It seemed an unlikely partnership: a girl scarcely on the brink of adulthood, married to a man of twenty-eight,

a monarch who was not only able and astute but ruthlessly and re-
lentlessly hard-headed. But observers were in no doubt of how well
the relationship worked. "The emperor loved his noble wife deeply,"
wrote Orderic Vitalis; and, even if we choose to be a little more
cynical than the conventions of courtesy allowed in describing the
emotional dynamics of this dynastic alliance, it remains clear that
Matilda won the trust and the respect of her powerful husband.

Her own family supplied the best of models for a royal consort.
Her mother, Edith-Matilda, had been a devoted and skilful partner
in Henry I's regime, while her maternal grandmother, Margaret of
Scotland, was so widely revered for her piety that she was later declared a saint. But Matilda had never known her grandmother, and
had not seen her mother since she was eight years old, and her success as Heinrich's queen owed as much to the resilient intelligence of
her own response to the role as it did to her genes or the training of
her earliest years.

A complex task lay ahead of her. To be the consort of a ruler was
not to be a mere appendage; she was not simply a decorative ornament to his court, or the passive embodiment of a political treaty.
A crowned queen shared in her husband's majesty—she, too, had
been anointed by God, her authority given divine sanction—and, if
she was necessarily a satellite of his power, she nevertheless had an
influential part to play in his government. She might emphasise the
spiritual dimensions of his rule rather than the worldly preoccupa-
tions that took the lion's share of a king's attention: the saintly Margaret of Scotland, for example, was unusual only in the extent, not
the fact, of her religious devotion. She might serve as his representative when he could not be physically present, as Edith-Matilda had
done with distinction in England during the years King Henry spent
across the Channel in Normandy. And she might temper his justice
with mercy, her intercession enabling her husband to moderate the
harshness of the punishments he inflicted without compromising the
respect in which his judgements were held.

This, in fact, was the first formal queenly role which the eight-year-old Matilda had been called upon to play, in ritual form, on her arrival from England in 1110, when she was asked at Liège to intercede for a disgraced nobleman, Godfrey, Count of Leuven and Duke of Lower Lorraine (whose daughter Adeliza would become her stepmother ten years later). And from 1114, when she left her schoolbooks behind after the extravagant spectacle of her wedding to take her place at her husband's side, she fulfilled her duties as a sponsor of petitions and supplications with a dignity and grace that would later inspire her German subjects to remember her as "the good Matilda."

But she could not be insulated for long from the Empire's dangerous instability. Her husband, like his father before him, faced armed rebellion in Saxony and the Rhineland, while conflict with the Church now loomed menacingly on German soil. Archbishop Friedrich of Cologne—the man who had touched holy oil to Matilda's forehead at her coronation, and hitherto one of Heinrich's most loyal ecclesiastical supporters—finally abandoned the emperor in 1114, his theological conscience finding common cause with his territorial ambition. Pope Paschal had already sanctioned the emperor's excommunication three years earlier, but now, in April 1115, the archbishop formally pronounced the dread sentence of anathema at Cologne, where imperial forces had been defeated by a rebel army only a few months before. A formidable faction within the German Church now held that their emperor had been excluded from the community of the faithful. All those who had sworn homage and fealty to him, they declared, were no longer bound by their oaths.

If Heinrich had any doubt about the need to return to Italy to tackle the poisonous conflict between the Holy Roman Empire and the Holy See at its source, it was dispelled three months later, when news came of the death of Matilde of Tuscany, Countess of Canossa. *La gran contessa*, at almost seventy, had become a legend, "the daughter of Peter and the faithful handmaid of Christ," according to the great reforming pope Gregory VII. Heir to vast estates in northern Italy stretching across the Lombard plain from the Apennines to the Alps, the countess had been the pope's most devoted ally through forty years of violent struggle between the papacy and the Empire. From her impregnable fortress at Canossa, perched high on a spur of the north face of the Apennines looking over the plain to her nearby cities of Reggio and Modena, she had ridden with her troops against Emperor Heinrich IV, standing in her stirrups with her father's sword in her hand, the war cry "For St. Peter and Matilde!" ringing around her.

Heinrich V had learned the lesson of his father's inability to defeat Matilde, opting for conciliation instead of confrontation. He visited her respectfully at Bianello, the castle in the foothills to the northeast of Canossa that stood sentinel for the fortress, and appointed her his lieutenant in Liguria, swearing that "in the whole earth there could not be found a princess her equal." His strategy paid off in 1115 when the dying countess—who, though twice married, had no children—named him her heir. This was an unprecedented opportunity to impose imperial rule in Italy; but it would have to be taken swiftly, before the pope, to whom Matilde had previously promised her lands, could act to stop him.

By the end of February 1116 the emperor's forces were ready. When he left Augsburg at the head of his army, his fourteen-year-old wife was with him. Soldiers, horses, carts loaded with arms and provisions, and carriages for Matilda and her ladies travelled more than three hundred miles across the Alps, over the Brenner Pass, a prehistoric pathway that had become a regularised road when the Roman Empire expanded inexorably northward through the mountains. It was the lowest and easiest of the eight major Alpine passes, and an expedition that included the might of an imperial army had no need to fear the bandits who lay in wait by the roadside to relieve merchants and pilgrims of their possessions. But low and easy were relative terms in an Alpine crossing, and strength in numbers offered no cushion against the implacable landscape. Even swaddled in furs, Matilda could not escape the rawness of the thin air as she gazed up at the massive snow-covered peaks that overshadowed their labouring convoy.

There could have been no greater contrast between the wildness of the mountains and the comfort of their reception in Italy: a forty-eight-hour stay amid the sumptuous luxury of the doge's palazzo in Venice, behind crenellated walls and colossal towers that proclaimed *La Serenissima*'s mastery of the sea. From there, the emperor and his queen travelled southwest to Padua and Mantua before arriving outside the forbidding ramparts of Countess Matilde's Apennine fortress at Canossa. Heinrich was shrewd enough to recognise that generosity and compromise were the surest ways to win support from those who had suffered under the harsh inflexibility of the countess's rule, and he was welcomed inside Canossa's gates, his young wife warmly greeted as a noble successor to her formidable namesake.

It was a whole year before the emperor felt confident enough of his hold on the regions of Emilia-Romagna and Tuscany to move toward Rome. But despite Heinrich's efforts at diplomacy, Pope Paschal could not contemplate a second encounter with an imperial army with equilibrium. He withdrew the papal curia eighty miles to the southeast, to the magnificent abbey at Montecassino first founded by St. Benedict almost six hundred years earlier, leaving Heinrich to take control of the holy city just before Easter 1117. It was a hollow victory: the emperor staged a triumphal procession through the Roman streets, but could not convince a single cardinal to participate in the elaborate ceremonies of crown-wearing that, by custom, marked the emperor's presence in Rome on a great feast day of the Church.

Heinrich turned instead to Maurice Bourdin, the French-born archbishop of the Portuguese see of Braga, whom Paschal had sent to him as an envoy. A controversial and fiercely ambitious man, Bourdin lost no time in abandoning his allegiance to the pope in order to seize the chance of becoming indispensable to the emperor. Despite the fact that the only bridge over the Tiber was controlled by Pope Paschal's supporters from their vantage point in the immense circular stronghold of the Castel Sant'Angelo, the imperial entourage managed to cross the river by boat to reach St. Peter's Basilica.

There, perhaps on Easter Sunday, and certainly again at Pentecost seven weeks later, Archbishop Bourdin placed an imperial crown on fifteen-year-old Matilda's head as she sat in state at her husband's side.

This was not an imperial coronation. Bourdin was not the pope—indeed, he had been excommunicated before the Pentecost ceremony for his abandonment of the papal cause—and Matilda was not anointed as an empress. Officially, she remained *Regina Romanorum*, the Queen of the Romans; but, despite its irregularities, this ceremonial confirmation of her imperial status left a lasting mark. She had not been crowned by the pope, but she had been given a crown in the pope's church at the side of her husband the emperor; and for the rest of her life she would be known to contemporaries as the Empress Matilda, *Mathilda Imperatrix*.

Her experiences in Italy shaped not only her sense of her own political standing, but her political education, too. In 1118, when Heinrich was forced to return north to deal with rebellion in Germany, he left Matilda, at just sixteen, to rule his Italian territories in his stead. Now her task was not to mitigate the terrible majesty of her husband's authority, but to embody it. Very few details have survived of her actions as regent, save for one cameo in a court at Castrocaro, set amid gently rolling hills thirty miles south of the city of Ravenna, when she sat in judgement over the conflicting claims to a local church of a bishop and an abbey from the neighbouring towns of Forlì and Faenza. The climactic moment of the case came when the young queen rose to declare her decision in favour of the monastery, and to pronounce an imperial prohibition on anyone who dared challenge her ruling.

If we cannot re-create more details of her government in Italy in 1118–1119, we can at least decipher its place among the formative influences of Matilda's young life. Since crossing the Alps, she had had the opportunity to witness at close quarters a vicious political game, played on a European stage for the highest possible stakes in this world and the next. She had also, at Pentecost in St. Peter's, acquired a plausible claim to share in her husband's unique imperial status. And she had now, for the first time, stood alone to exercise the royal authority in which she shared through her marriage. It was hardly surprising if, in the process, she absorbed a deeply felt sense of her own regality, together with an understanding that ruthlessness and reconciliation could each be vital weapons in a ruler's armoury. All were, of course, entirely proper to her role as consort to the most exalted ruler in western Europe. But it was only a year after her return from Italy to Germany in the autumn of 1119 that the first hint came of what would prove to be a dramatically different future.

The drowning of her brother William in the wreck of the *White Ship* in November 1120 can hardly have been a devastating emotional blow. Eighteen months younger than Matilda, he had been only six when she left England, and, immersed in her new life in the Empire, she had not seen him or their parents for a decade. Nor did his death precipitate any immediate transformation in her position. Her father, King Henry, married again within a matter of weeks and kept his young bride at his side as he travelled through his domains, in the hope that she would give him a new heir. Even as the months went by without any sign that Queen Adeliza might have conceived, there remained the constant possibility of an imminent pregnancy. And certainly there was no public suggestion that Matilda, who was already a queen in a distant land, might figure in Henry's plans for the succession.

But there are signs that both Matilda's husband and her father were well aware of her potential importance in Anglo-Norman affairs, should Henry's hopes of a son be disappointed. When the bitterly destructive conflict between the Empire and the papacy was finally ended by a concordat agreed at Worms in 1122 (which distinguished between the spiritual and temporal investiture of bishops, assigning the former to the pope and the latter to the emperor), the settlement owed a great deal to the precedent of the English agreement over the same issue that King Henry had reached with the papacy in 1106. And in the years after 1122, the priority which

Heinrich gave to the closeness of his contact with his father-in-law is striking.

Matilda had hoped to visit Henry in England that summer for the first time in twelve years, but, with the king waiting in Kent for her arrival, she had to abandon her journey when she was refused safe passage by the Count of Flanders, a vassal of the French king who had every reason to fear being caught in a vise by closer cooperation between the Anglo-Norman realm on one side and the Holy Roman Empire on the other. Thereafter, despite the ongoing threat of unrest in the northern duchy of Saxony, the emperor threw himself into a hard-fought battle to wrest control of Utrecht from its bishop. He had previously visited the city only once, in 1110, for his formal betrothal to his child-bride. Now, however, his repeated presence there—in 1123 at the head of an army—indicated the strategic significance of its location less than forty miles from a point on the North Sea coast where neither the Count of Flanders nor the King of France could impede imperial communications with England.

Perhaps Heinrich envisaged a future in which England and Normandy might become the western limits of an extended empire over which he and Matilda would rule together before uniting their territorial claims in the person of their son and heir. But no such child had yet been born when that dream was shattered. In the spring of 1125, visiting Utrecht for the third time in three years, the emperor was overwhelmed by an agonising and desperate illness that he had struggled to conceal. On May 23, at the age of thirty-eight—"in the very flower of his age and victories," wrote William of Malmesbury—Heinrich died. To this energetic, bold, ruthless man, Matilda had been a devoted wife and a trusted consort; the little Norman princess had become a German queen in quietly triumphant style. Now, at twenty-three, she was his widow, trusted in death, as she had been in life, when he bequeathed into her keeping the priceless crown, lance, and sword that made up the imperial insignia.

But Matilda had no further part to play in the government of the Empire. Successful though her marriage had been in personal and political terms, it had failed as a vehicle for dynastic ambition. Had she had a son, she might have ruled in his name until he came of age, as her husband's grandmother, the redoubtable Empress Agnes, had done for six years during the minority of Heinrich IV. But when the body of Heinrich V was solemnly conveyed three hundred miles along the Rhine to be buried beside his father, grandfather, and great-grandfather at Speyer Cathedral, it was as the last emperor of the Salian line. Matilda handed over the imperial insignia to the Archbishop of Mainz, who would preside over the election of the next King of Germany, and made her way to join her father in Normandy. In doing so, she abandoned the German lands with which her dead husband had endowed her, and turned her back on offers of marriage from among the ranks of the German princes. Instead, she returned, a German-speaking woman, to the Anglo-Norman court she had left as a French-speaking child a decade and a half earlier. She brought with her an imperial title, as well as more tangible riches from the imperial treasury, including two jewelled crowns of solid gold—one of them so heavy that it could only be worn when supported by two silver rods—and the mummified hand of the apostle St. James, on whose feast day she had been crowned at Mainz Cathedral.

Some Anglo-Norman observers, orbiting around the gravitational fields of Rouen and Westminster, would later remark that the adult Matilda who returned to her childhood home was haughty and full of amour propre. Certainly—and unsurprisingly, given the nature of the surviving sources—they betray no sign of sympathy for a young woman who had lost her husband, her guiding influence since childhood, in a bereavement that abruptly uprooted her from everything that was familiar in her life for the second time in fifteen years. Nor is there any acknowledgement that there might be other, less censorious ways of describing the grandeur of a widowed queen who had been the consort of the greatest monarch in Europe for almost as long as she could remember, and had received an imperial crown in the papal basilica along the way. Now, it seemed, she might wear a crown in her own right as her father's only surviving heir. Whatever view her countrymen might take of Matilda's deportment, the crucial question was this: could a woman rule?

The simple answer was that there was no formal prohibition to prevent her from doing so. The very fact that the principles governing royal inheritance in the Anglo-Norman realm were so fluid, that precedents had scarcely had time or opportunity to take root since the violent upheavals of 1066, and that realpolitik rather than theoretical right had triumphed in the contested successions of 1087 and 1100, meant that there were few incontrovertible rules by which candidates for the throne might be either selected or excluded. One of those few rules, thanks to the Church's increasingly strict control over the sacrament of marriage, was that illegitimate children no longer stood alongside their legitimate half-siblings in the line of succession. Despite the fact that King Henry's father, the great Conqueror himself, had been bastard-born, neither Henry nor any of his nobles seems to have given serious consideration to the possibility that the eldest of his large illegitimate brood, Robert, Earl of Gloucester, might claim the throne, even though the charismatic earl was already a proven leader on the battlefield and at his father's court.

Bastardy, then, was a clear disqualification; being female, however, was not. There is no record of a single word of protest from any of the Anglo-Norman nobles when Henry required them to swear that they would support his daughter as his successor, should he die without a male heir. The only controversy that erupted in January 1127 was the result not of dissent spilling over but of eagerness to demonstrate loyalty, in the form of a squabble over who should be first in line to take the oath. That honour went to David, King of Scots, the younger brother of Henry's first queen and Matilda's maternal uncle, who had been brought up at the English court and held rich estates in England as well as the Scottish throne. Once the Scots king had sworn, however, there was a tussle for precedence between Robert of Gloucester, Henry's illegitimate son, and the king's favourite nephew, Stephen of Mortain, who had so narrowly escaped a watery grave in the wreck of the *White Ship*—"a noteworthy contest," William of Malmesbury reported, from which Stephen, the son of Henry's sister Adela, emerged victorious.

But a pledge of future allegiance imposed by a present and irresistibly formidable king did not guarantee that Matilda's rule would ultimately be accepted. Within the unpredictable arena of European politics, where frontiers between rival territories were shaped and reshaped not only by the treacherous currents of international diplomacy but by the constant friction of war, a monarch was by definition a soldier, a feudal lord riding with sword unsheathed at the head of steel-clad knights. Despite the extraordinary exploits of Matilde of Canossa, that was a role for which no woman was trained, or could hope to inhabit without challenge. At the same time, a king's duty to protect his lands and his people also required that he should be a judge and a lawgiver—and, while women might appear in court as litigants or witnesses, there was no official public place for a woman in the process of making or enforcing the law.

Though Matilda was not explicitly barred from inheriting her father's throne, the idea of what it meant to be a monarch remained inescapably male. That assumption was embedded even in the language of regality: a queen's very title, from the Anglo-Saxon word *cwén*, meant the wife of a king, not his female equivalent. In Latin, meanwhile, a *regina* or *imperatrix*—a queen or an empress—was a female adjunct to a *rex* or *imperator*, derivative words representing a derivative form of authority.

Reality did not, of course, always conform so neatly to linguistic etymology or political theory. Matilda's contemporaries in England hardly had far to look to find instances of women taking a lead in government, whether it was Queen Edith-Matilda presiding over meetings of her absent husband's council, the Empress Agnes holding the German Empire together in the name of her little son, or Matilda herself pronouncing judgement in her husband's stead in the court at Castrocaro. True, women might be excluded from formal public office in normal circumstances, but a queen was by definition exceptional, sharing in her husband's unique authority through the sacrament of marriage and the consecration of her crowning.

But what made such manifestations of female rule fundamentally unthreatening to the maleness of kingship was the fact that this queenly authority was exercised in the name of a husband or son. And, for all that Matilda stood centre stage as the nobles swore their oaths in 1127, it was clear that the capacity of royal women to act as vessels for the transmission of kingly power lay at the heart of Henry's plans for his daughter. She might still be supplanted in the succession if he and his young wife had a new son; but, if they did not, Matilda stood ready, a woman young and strong enough to replenish Henry's lineage with sons of her own. Her destiny might yet lie in her role as the daughter and mother of kings, rather than as a monarch in her own right.

For that, however, she would need a new husband, and quickly—a requirement that became acute in the spring of 1127 with a spectacular revival in the fortunes of Henry's exiled nephew, William Clito, once the rival of William Ætheling, now a threat to the drowned prince's sister, Matilda. In March, Count Charles of Flanders—the man who had blocked Matilda's path between the Empire and England five years earlier—was brutally murdered while he prayed before the altar of a Bruges church; and King Louis of France seized upon this unexpected chance to install William Clito in his place as ruler of the wealthy and strategically vital lowlands that lay between Boulogne and Antwerp. Matilda's marriage was now a matter of critical importance defensively as well as dynastically, and the identity of her prospective bridegroom clear: Geoffroi, the son and heir of Count Foulques of Anjou, whose lands, immediately to the south of Normandy, might either protect or threaten its borders.

A week before the wedding in June 1128, Geoffroi was knighted by his bride's royal father in Rouen. He cut a gorgeous figure: fifteen years old and nicknamed "*le Bel*" ("the Fair"), he was lithe and athletic, his face "glowing like the flower of a lily, with rosy flush," dressed in the finest armour with golden spurs and a sparkling gem-studded helmet, golden lions rearing proudly on his shield. Matilda, however, was hardly likely to be dazzled by a beautiful boy. Eleven years his senior, and with fifteen years' experience of imperial politics under the belt of her silken gown, she angrily disdained the idea that she should marry an untested teenager whose status was so vastly inferior to her own. If, as seems entirely possible, her grief for the dead emperor was heartfelt, then the contrast between this arrogant adolescent and the father-figure that Heinrich had been can only have deepened her revulsion at the match. Hildebert of Lavardin, the learned and deeply pious Archbishop of Tours, wrote to her in sorrow soon after the alliance was proposed to seek reassurance that she would no longer distress her father with her disobedience. But in the end, as the archbishop had foreseen, Henry was immovable, and, for Matilda, unhappy duty prevailed.

The unwilling bride endured three weeks of extravagant cele-brations, from the wedding ceremony in the glorious new cathe-dral at Le Mans on June 17 until the couple's tumultuous arrival in Angers, the capital of her new husband's *comté*, where they were greeted by cheering crowds and a cacophony of bells. By that time it had at least been arranged that Matilda's new title would be that of a countess, rather than a countess-in-waiting. Her father-in-law, Count Foulques, left immediately after the wedding to embark on the long journey to the Holy Land, abandoning Anjou to his son in favour of a crown of his own, acquired through a new marriage to Melisende, heiress to the recently established Latin kingdom of Je-rusalem. However, Matilda remained unimpressed. Whenever she could, she avoided calling herself "countess," preferring the overrid-ing magnificence of her personal style as "empress, and daughter of the king of the English."

Vows, however reluctantly taken, could not be forsworn. Never-theless, within a year it seemed that the relationship might founder. Matilda's personal antipathy to the match had not been enough to outweigh the political logic of an Angevin alliance to counter the threat of William Clito's menacing presence in Flanders; but less than six weeks after the wedding, that threat abruptly vanished when Clito was killed in a skirmish with a Flemish rival. It is possible that this welcome reversal of fortune prompted King Henry to reconsider the calculations he had made about his daughter's future and the usefulness of her new husband—and, if Matilda's prospects as a female heir remained profoundly uncertain, her husband's position was more nebulous still. Did Geoffroi expect in time to become a king in right of his wife, as his father was about to do far away in Jerusalem? Certainly the young count, whose golden good looks concealed a will and temper to match Matilda's own, was antagonised by Henry's refusal to elucidate his plans for his new son-in-law. By the end of 1129 the couple were living apart. Matilda had left Anjou to return to her father's city of Rouen in Normandy, and Geoffroi was loudly threatening to turn his back on the whole fiasco by departing on pilgrimage to the shrine of St. James at Compostela in northwestern Spain.

Still, reservations or no, Henry decided that he could not allow the marriage to disintegrate before it had served its purpose in providing him with a grandson. In the late summer of 1131 he brokered—or perhaps imposed—a reconciliation. A great council was held at Northampton on September 8; there the Anglo-Norman nobles renewed their solemn oaths of allegiance to Matilda, who then returned with all honour to her husband in Anjou. Nothing had been clarified, but personal discontent had been suppressed, for the time being, under the pressure of an irresistible political imperative. And to good effect: on March 5, 1133, thirty-one-year-old Matilda gave birth at Le Mans to her first child, a healthy boy, Henry, who inherited his Angevin father's red-gold hair and the vigorously stocky physique of the royal grandfather for whom he was named.

Little more than a year later, at Rouen in June 1134, the difficult birth of a second son, Geoffrey, almost cost Matilda her life. King Henry was at her bedside as she prepared for death by arranging her bequests and burial. Characteristically, she found the strength even in this extremity of illness to insist that her own wishes should be respected in the planning of her tomb, forcing her father to agree that she should be interred not, as he wanted, in the ancestral vault of the dukes of Normandy at Rouen Cathedral, but at the abbey of Bec in the peaceful valley of the Risle thirty miles southwest of the city, a spiritual home to which she had developed a particular devotion. Slowly, however, she recovered; and thereafter she and her husband found a way to work together as political partners united, if not by affection, then by their shared interest in their sons' inheritance.

While Henry delighted in his sturdy grandsons, the dynastic triumph of their birth encouraged another attempt at self-assertion by their ambitious father. Geoffroi had succeeded in providing Henry's daughter with legitimate male heirs, but he had received little encouragement to hope that the king envisaged him ruling England and Normandy at Matilda's side. He had been granted no Anglo-Norman lands; he had not been invited to attend Henry's court since his wedding; and he had not stood beside his royal wife as she received the oaths of the Anglo-Norman magnates in 1131. Four years later, it was beginning to grate heavily that he had not yet even taken possession of the castles along the border between Normandy and Anjou which he had been promised as a dowry along with Matilda's hand. Henry, it seemed, had no intention of ceding control there to his son-in-law before his death. For Geoffroi, however, this royal refusal to hand over the fortresses was not only a slap in the face in terms of his already uncertain standing as Matilda's husband, but a strategic blunder that might compromise his ability to make good her claim to Normandy and England whenever the time came to do so.

As relations deteriorated between these two tenaciously wilful men, Matilda found herself caught in the middle. This time, as the mother of two young sons—and perhaps with a sense that her powerful father might even now be keeping open his plans for the succession—she stood shoulder to shoulder with her once-despised husband. In the summer of 1135, as political disagreement escalated into the flexing of military muscle, she remained with Geoffroi in

Anjou while Henry prowled the southern frontiers of Normandy,
soldiers at his back. Father and daughter were still estranged in November when the king retired for a few days to his lodge at Lyons-la-
Forêt to enjoy the hunt. It would prove to be his last journey.

The bitter conflict of his last months had been rooted in Henry's
refusal to surrender any of his territories to his presumptuous son-
in-law while his grip on government, even at the age of sixty-seven,
remained as strong as ever. But that did not mean that his commitment to the succession of his own bloodline had wavered. Now, when
he suddenly found himself facing the unanswerable reality of death,
he spent his final hours insisting on his daughter's right to his throne.
But the unexpectedness of his illness allowed no time for remorse or
reconciliation, and Matilda was not at his side when he died during
the night of December 1.

The next morning, his body was carried to Rouen, where it was
reverently received into the hushed cathedral. An expert embalmer
set to work on the corpse ("lest it should rot with lapse of time
and offend the nostrils of those who sat or stood by it," William of
Malmesbury explained), removing the internal organs, which were
placed in an urn and buried at the nearby church of Notre-Dame-
du-Pré, before filling the body with aromatic balsam, covering it with
salt, and sewing it into layers of ox-hide. It was then transported west
to Caen, just twenty miles from the Norman coast, to lie in state
in the austerely beautiful abbey church of Saint-Étienne, which had
been founded sixty years earlier by Henry's father, the Conqueror,
and now housed his tomb. There the bier rested for four weeks, until
in January 1136 favourable winds at last allowed the monks of Saint-
Étienne to escort the body across the Channel to Henry's own foundation, the great Cluniac abbey at Reading, for burial before the high
altar of the still uncompleted church.

Matilda was not among the noble mourners at the funeral who
made precious offerings and distributed alms for the good of her father's soul. By then, her claims as his heir had already been dealt an
unexpected and desperate blow.

FIVE

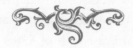

Lady of England

The chroniclers who described the events of the winter of 1135–1136 made little mention of Matilda. They had dutifully reported the oaths to support her that had been taken by the Anglo-Norman nobility in 1127 and again in 1131, and William of Malmesbury—the most sympathetic to Matilda's cause—recounted Henry's deathbed declaration of her right to succeed him. But she is conspicuous by her absence from most contemporary narratives of the aftermath of her father's last illness.

That historiographical absence reflects a physical one. Henry's strategic plan for Matilda's marriage left her stranded on the sidelines, with her husband in Anjou, rather than at the centre of the action precipitated by his sudden death. It was not that she was slow to react. In the first week of December, as soon as the shocking news came from Lyons-la-Forêt, Matilda rode north to seize control of the disputed border castles of Domfront, Exmes, and Argentan that she had been promised as her dowry. She was so successful in her mission that her grip on this frontier territory was never shaken, and it was from these fortresses that her campaign to claim Normandy and England would be launched. For the moment, however, she could reach no further. Geoffroi was detained by rebellion in Anjou, while Matilda, it seems, was immobilised by a pregnancy that had begun only a few weeks before her father's death. She established her household at Argentan, the four-towered castle that King Henry had built forty miles south of Caen to serve as a garrison, a treasury, and a favourite lodge from which he could hunt in the nearby Gouffern forest. She gave birth there to her third son, William, on July 22, 1136.

By that time, however, events in England had moved decisively beyond her grasp. Had Matilda stood at the centre of the Anglo-Norman political stage when her father died, at Lyons-la-Forêt or Rouen, Westminster or Winchester, she would have been poised to assert her claim to his throne as his only legitimate child, born in the purple (that is, born to a reigning king just as her father had been, a circumstance of which Henry himself had made much in pressing his own right to the throne thirty-five years earlier), her title validated by Henry's designation and the barons' oaths of loyalty. As it was, she was barely even in the wings. At her dying father's side, she might have made a credible figurehead for unity, taking on Henry's weighty mantle as bringer of peace to his people. Instead, in her absence, the nobles had more than enough reason to look elsewhere for leadership.

For all of Henry's attempts to bind the future to his will, the only precedents so far established for the succession of the Norman kings of England favoured might over right. William Rufus in 1087 and Henry himself in 1100 had won the throne by acting swiftly to seize the crown, and then fighting to retain it. The legitimacy of their rule was born of their hold on power, not the other way round. In theory, Matilda's claim to be her father's heir was unanswerable, but in practice she was hampered by multiple disadvantages: she was female;

her husband, whose status in relation to her claim to the crown remained deeply ambiguous, was a distrusted outsider among the powerful men she now sought to rule; and she was not there in person to counter escalating doubts and uncertainties. Meanwhile, the barons who had accompanied Henry's corpse from Rouen to Caen went into conclave during the uncertain weeks while they waited for the wind to change for the long Channel crossing, and emerged with a proposal that the crown should go to an alternative candidate: Thibaud, Count of Blois, son of Henry's formidably able sister, Adela.

Plausible though Thibaud might have been as a ruler—at forty-five, he was a seasoned soldier and experienced politician as well as a royal nephew—the magnates had overlooked the fact that the precedents of the half century since the Conquest offered no more convincing support to the idea of a king chosen by election than they did to the prospect of the hereditary principle handing the crown to a king's daughter. Someone else, however, had been paying much closer attention to the lessons of recent history. While the Norman barons debated and Matilda settled into her stronghold at Argentan, Thibaud's younger brother Stephen, Count of Mortain, left his wife's county of Boulogne at speed with the smallest of retinues and took ship across the shortest stretch of the Channel from Wissant, Boulogne's main port, to Dover. Without pausing to gather support or supplies, he rode the eighty miles to London as hard as he could. He was welcomed into the city before turning seventy miles southwest to Winchester, the historic capital of Anglo-Saxon England, where his youngest brother, Henry, was bishop. There Stephen took control of the heaped silver and gold in the royal treasury; and on December 22, just three weeks after King Henry's death, he was crowned King of England in the vast Romanesque cathedral by the hastily summoned Archbishop of Canterbury.

It was 1100 all over again. The blueprint of Henry's own coup d'état after his brother Rufus's death in the New Forest could scarcely have been followed more assiduously. Speed and implacable resolve had won Henry the throne; and now Stephen had taken the crown for himself before the nobles at Caen or Matilda at Argentan had an inkling of what was happening.

In principle, Stephen's credentials as a potential king were questionable. He was not even the senior male heir within his own family—his elder brother, Thibaud, had inherited their father's lands and title as Count of Blois—and his royal blood came in the female line from his mother, Adela, which suggested no hereditary grounds on which Matilda's claim, or that of her young sons, should be disbarred in favour of his own. Moreover, he had made great play of his loyal support of King Henry's wishes over the succession, vying with his illegitimate cousin Robert of Gloucester to be first among the magnates to swear allegiance to Matilda as Henry's heir in 1127. His victory in that precedence dispute, and his prominence among the noble oath takers, now left him vulnerable to dangerous accusations of perjury, something of which his apologists among the chroniclers were all too well aware. (Chief among them, the anonymous author of the *Gesta Stephani*—The Deeds of Stephen—put into the mouth of the dying King Henry a conscience-wracked acknowledgement that the oath had been extorted from his barons, as a basis from which to argue that "any forcible exaction of an oath from anyone has made it impossible for the breaking of that oath to constitute a perjury.")

But, while legalistic theorising might cast a shadow over Stephen's pretensions, they were much more plausible in pragmatic and empirical terms. After all, King Henry himself had defied the hereditary claims of an older brother; and Stephen's character and experience suggested that he might be capable of emulating his royal uncle in more ways than one. By now in his early forties, a decade older than his cousin Matilda, Stephen had made his career at Henry's court. His uncle's favour had made him a rich man—the king had given him the Norman county of Mortain in the southwest of the duchy as well as valuable lands in England that made him one of the greatest of the Anglo-Norman nobility—but Stephen had had to work for his rewards. Mortain was a frontier lordship, while his

English estates had been seized from magnates who had opposed Henry in the name of Robert Curthose and his son, William Clito. Stephen's personal interests—now inseparable from his loyalty to his uncle—therefore threw him into the fight against Clito and his followers.

Years of campaigning in Normandy and Flanders had established Stephen's reputation as an energetic and effective soldier, while his presence at Henry's court as the king's most favoured nephew made his name as a man of courtesy, generosity, and charming good nature. The possibility that he might one day come closer still to the throne may even have been in Henry's mind during the unsettling years between the wreck of the *White Ship*—in which Stephen had so nearly died—and Matilda's unforeseen return from Germany as an imperial widow. Certainly, in early 1125 his power and wealth were exponentially increased when Henry arranged his marriage to Mathilde, heiress to the county of Boulogne, an alliance which brought him control of the vital cross-Channel trading route to the Low Countries, as well as vast estates in the southeast of England.

If the thought that his nephew might succeed him had indeed occurred to Henry, it was summarily discarded after his daughter's return. But Stephen had not been so quick to relinquish the idea. Beyond that, we cannot know for certain what he was thinking on his lightning dash across ice-cold water and frozen roads to snatch the crown for himself—what form his ambition took, or how he justified his actions, beyond the likelihood that he sought to keep the Count of Anjou, a neighbour and bitter enemy of the counts of Blois, from taking power in his royal wife's name. Nor can we be sure why Matilda made no greater effort, no more expansive move, to stake her claim. William of Malmesbury offers only the maddeningly opaque observation that she delayed any attempt to return to England "for certain reasons." Was her health badly compromised by her pregnancy even in its earliest stages? Did she think the nobles who had knelt before her to swear their loyalty would simply rally to her cause, leaving her waiting at Argentan for acclamation that never came? Or was it the reverse, a belief that her position could only be made good by more military might than she so far had at her disposal?

What we do know is that, amid the paralysing confusion that followed Henry's death—news, after all, could travel only as fast as a horse could gallop, and might already be dangerously old when it arrived—it was Stephen who seized the moment. This apparently easy-going man tapped into a vein of implacable single-mindedness to offer decisive leadership at a moment when England and Normandy were teetering on the brink of chaos. (There was "no one else at hand," the *Gesta Stephani* declared, "who could take the king's place and put an end to the great dangers threatening the kingdom.") And fortune smiled on a man who found himself in the right place at the right time. His home in Boulogne was within striking distance of the English coast; its strategic importance to the English wool trade, together with Stephen's own experience of the wealthy cloth towns of Flanders, won him a warm welcome in the city of London; and his formidable brother Henry, as Bishop of Winchester, was on hand to broker his acceptance by the Church and to smooth his path into the ancient seat of royal government.

Above all, the key to Stephen's coup was the solemn ceremony that took place in the incense-clouded cathedral at Winchester on December 22. A coronation was not merely—or not at all, in Stephen's case—a pageant for public display; the service at Winchester was a hurried affair in the presence of scarcely any noblemen and only three prelates. Instead, it was a sacramental rite, which changed forever the man at its centre. Stephen entered the cathedral a claimant to the throne; he left it a king. Some might think him a wrongful king and oppose his rule on those grounds—but they could not deny his kingship, which had taken effect at the moment when the archbishop had touched his head, breast, shoulders, and arms with holy oil. At that instant, the interregnum that had begun when Henry took his last breath at Lyons-la-Forêt was ended.

In that instant, too, lay the seeds of civil war. Matilda was the only surviving child of her father's marriage, and had been named his heir and received oaths of loyalty from his nobles. Stephen, meanwhile, had been anointed and crowned as Henry's successor. Two distinct forms of royal legitimacy now stood in direct opposition to one another, embodied in two different people. And it was clear that these rival claims could be reconciled only in victory for one, and defeat for the other.

By the spring of 1136, it seemed as though Stephen had already won the fight with a single blow. Matilda, weighed down by her pregnancy at Argentan, her husband entangled in home-grown revolt in Anjou, was an irrelevance. In January, her cousin had stood in her place as chief mourner at her father's lavish burial. Later that month, his control of the riches of the royal treasury, combined with his contacts in the fertile recruiting ground of Flanders, enabled him to mobilise an army of mercenaries with astonishing speed against King David of Scotland, Matilda's maternal uncle, who had overrun the English frontier from Carlisle to Newcastle as soon as he heard of Stephen's coup. The menacing size of Stephen's forces—"greater than any in living memory," according to the chronicler Henry of Huntingdon—rapidly persuaded David to come to terms; and the new king's success in seeing off the Scots helped to convince the Anglo-Norman nobility that they should rally to Stephen's standard.

What the country needed, in the words of the *Gesta Stephani*, was "a king who, with a view to re-establishing peace for the common benefit, would meet the insurgents of the kingdom in arms and would justly administer the enactments of the laws." The oath Stephen had sworn at his coronation had promised his new subjects justice; now he had taken up arms against a hostile invasion to imposing effect. There could be no doubt that it was Stephen—not his cousin Matilda, nor his elder brother, Thibaud, whose candidacy for the throne had withered in the bud once word of Stephen's coronation began to spread—who offered the best chance of maintaining "peace for the common benefit" across England and Normandy. Here perception and reality blurred and merged: the more pledges of allegiance the new king secured from among the nobles, the more unhesitatingly he could bring to heel those who resisted him; and the more effectively opposition was crushed, the more magnates would be driven to pledge him their support.

At Easter, the irresistible logic of this virtuous circle was played out when Stephen staged a spectacular gathering of his court, "more splendid for its throng and size, for gold, silver, jewels, robes, and every kind of sumptuousness, than any that had ever been held in England," Henry of Huntingdon reported admiringly. This theatrical demonstration of the magnificence of his kingship and his mastery of the kingdom—now reinforced by a papal letter approving his coronation and excusing the violation of his oath of loyalty to Matilda—secured the attendance, and with it the service, of all but a small handful of the bishops and nobles of England and Normandy. It was an occasion which combined promise and threat to overwhelming effect, and its glittering success was confirmed by the belated arrival of Robert of Gloucester, Matilda's illegitimate half-brother, who had so far held himself aloof from Stephen's nascent regime.

Gloucester was one of the greatest noblemen in the country, powerful, charismatic, and intensely proud. He had been at his father's bedside when he died and had received from him an extraordinary cash legacy of £60,000 from which to distribute wages and rewards to Henry's troops and household. He might therefore have hoped to be a kingmaker, even if his bastardy meant that he could not be a king; and certainly the idea that he should now be compelled to swear allegiance to a man with whom he had once competed for influence at his father's court cannot have been easy to swallow. But by the end of April it was clear that the alternative to accepting the new King Stephen was impotent and ultimately dangerous isolation. ("If he were to resist," William of Malmesbury argued on his behalf, "it would bring no advantage to his sister or nephews, and would certainly do enormous harm to himself.") Gloucester's homage—which was performed in return for confirmation of his title to his lands, and ostentatiously warm demonstrations of royal favour—therefore acknowledged Stephen's triumph, and, in doing so, made that triumph complete.

Or so it seemed. The winter of 1136 was a bitter one for Matilda. She had played her part in her father's plans, entering into a distasteful marriage so that she and her sons would be ready to inherit his throne, only to discover that it was the precedent of Henry's actions rather than the pronouncement of his intentions which determined the identity of his successor. She, who had once presided in majesty over the imperial court, now found herself embattled with her three boys in the frontier fortresses that remained her only foothold in her father's lands. Perhaps it was a relief, in personal terms, that her partnership with her unloved husband could now function at a distance, as the political alliance it was, rather than in unwanted intimacy. But, for Matilda, the demands of duty and the exercise of power had always come before sentiment or personal satisfaction. The very concept of private happiness, in fact, can scarcely have made sense to a woman who had left her home as a child of eight to live out a public destiny. Any relief, therefore, at a separation made necessary by their joint campaign to press her claim—with Geoffroi now launching regular raids into Normandy from his base in Anjou—can only have been overshadowed by frustration at their failure to make any meaningful headway.

On the other hand, they were not, at least, being driven back from the Norman frontiers, and that in itself might cause Stephen problems. Normandy had been disintegrating into chaos ever since King Henry's death. The duchy would always be more difficult to control than England since it lacked the centralised administration that allowed English government to regulate itself in the king's absence. It was no accident that Henry had spent more than half of his time on the Norman side of the Channel; and the wisdom of that decision was confirmed once his commanding presence was removed, when disputes between belligerent rival landowners sprang bloodily into life. "...stubborn Normandy, an unhappy mother country, suffered wretchedly from her viper brood," Orderic Vitalis lamented from his cloisters at Saint-Evroult. "For on the very same day that the Normans heard that their firm ruler had died…, they rushed out hungrily like ravening wolves to plunder and ravage mercilessly."

Such lawlessness did not in itself help Matilda's cause, since, if the Norman barons loathed each other, they despised the Angevins more. In one raid lasting only thirteen days, Orderic reported, Geoffroi's forces "made themselves hated forever by their brutality," burning homes, crops, and churches, plundering and slaughtering as they went. And, for as long as the army that fought in her name was led by her husband and recruited in Anjou, Matilda would struggle to be seen as the daughter of the King of England rather than the wife of the Angevin count. But, at the same time, the first cracks were beginning to appear in the façade of Stephen's victory; and the longer Normandy was left to implode into violence, the wider those cracks might become.

Questions were first raised over Stephen's judgement in the summer of 1136, when he faced the task of extinguishing what should have been the last few embers of resistance in England. A lord named Baldwin de Revières, who had given devoted service to King Henry and his family, refused to recognise Stephen as king and fortified the southwestern castle of Exeter against him. With characteristic energy and speed, Stephen raced westward to pin Baldwin and his small garrison within the looming walls of the fortress, built on the Conqueror's orders three-quarters of a century earlier. There could have been no better opportunity to display the military muscle that lay behind the theatrical splendour of the Easter Court, and Stephen's army therefore included not only his formidable Flemish mercenaries but an imposing show of the baronial forces that were now at the king's command.

As the siege tightened in the stifling heat of an exceptionally hot summer's sun, the castle's well ran dry. Its defenders survived for a while by eking out their supplies of wine, but when the wine barrels, too, were empty Baldwin was forced to plead for the lives of his followers. The garrison's desperation was obvious and pitiful. Baldwin's wife came to Stephen as a supplicant, barefoot, her long hair hanging loose, weeping in grief and fear; and the dreadful effects of dehydration were shockingly evident, according to the *Gesta Stephani*, in her companions' "sagging and wasted skin, the look of torpor on their faces, drained of the normal supply of blood, and their lips drawn back from gaping mouths." It was a churchman, Stephen's brother Henry of Winchester, who argued that kingship rather than humanity should dictate his response to their pleas. Baldwin was a rebel and a traitor, and his destruction was not only warranted but necessary to demonstrate the terrible power of Stephen's rule.

Others within the royal camp, however, led by Earl Robert of Gloucester, pressed for mercy. To the acute eyes of Bishop Henry, it was clear that the earl's enthusiasm for leniency was closely related to his reluctance to join Stephen in the first place, and that his covert agenda was to undermine rather than reinforce the king's authority. But, despite Stephen's instinctive talent for rapid and decisive action, his royal uncle's ruthlessness did not come so naturally to him. All his life, his easy, unpretentious charm and generous good nature had inspired genuine affection in those around him; but now he was about to discover the disadvantages, to a king, of being loved rather than feared. At Gloucester's urging, Stephen allowed Baldwin and his garrison to go free. As a result, the very public moral of the siege of Exeter was that resistance to Stephen need be neither futile nor fatal.

It was a lesson reinforced eight months later by the king's belated attempt to take control of the spreading anarchy in Normandy. Stephen's regime could not hope to endure without challenge if he failed to establish an unshakeable grip on Normandy as well as England. His most powerful subjects held lands on both sides of the Channel, and they looked to their king to protect their interests on French as well as English soil. But it took Stephen more than a year even to take ship for the Norman coast; and he was still twenty-five miles from the walls of Matilda's fortress at Argentan when his army suddenly disintegrated. Simmering hostility between Stephen's Flemish mercenaries and his Norman barons erupted into violence, while the deep mutual suspicion between the king and Robert of Gloucester was laid bare when Gloucester accused Stephen of plotting to ambush and kill him. The king and his closest supporters retreated to England after nine fruitless months, leaving Normandy neither at peace nor protected from Angevin assault, with Gloucester now ensconced in his Norman power base around Caen and Bayeux. Seven months after that, in June 1138, the disaffected earl publicly renounced his allegiance to Stephen, and declared for his sister, Matilda.

Gloucester's decision to set himself up as his sister's champion transformed Matilda's position beyond recognition. Until the summer of 1138, hers had been a lost cause, supported only by the forces of her Angevin husband, who was a hated outsider in Normandy, while England itself remained completely beyond her reach. Now, at a stroke, the support of her half-brother gave her a foothold, and potentially an army, at the heart of her cousin's kingdom. And Stephen's regime—which had once seemed, in the absence of any viable opposition, so tightly woven as to be unassailable—began to fray so badly that it was possible for the first time to imagine it unravelling altogether.

Initially, it appeared that the king might be doing enough to contain the damage. In Normandy, the joint forces of Earl Robert and Count Geoffroi were held off by Count Waleran of Meulan, the elder of two noble brothers, the Beaumont twins, who were fast becoming Stephen's right-hand men. Meanwhile, Stephen himself sped through England at the head of his troops, seizing castles and territory that belonged to Gloucester and his followers. Once again, he failed to press home a siege, this time at the southwestern port of Bristol, where Gloucester's supporters were holed up within the earl's massive fortress, a bastion built of creamy-pale limestone quarried from his lands near Caen. But, if the king's decision to turn away from this daunting stronghold in favour of softer targets gave renewed suggestions of an unwillingness to strike the killer blow, that hardly seemed to matter once the men of Yorkshire had rallied at

Northallerton around the standard of their archbishop to defend the kingdom against Matilda's uncle, David of Scotland, whose forces had overrun the north once more in the spring and summer of 1138. Mustered around a ship's mast hung with the banners of the patron saints of the great Yorkshire cathedrals, St. Peter of York, St. John of Beverley, and St. Wilfred of Ripon, topped with a gleaming silver pyx containing the consecrated host, the English army routed the Scots in less than two hours.

It was a terrible and bloody triumph, with thousands of Scots cut down by English arrows that "buzzed like bees and flew like rain." And it was a wounding blow for Matilda, given that her cause in England, as in Normandy, was now identified with an invading enemy beaten back by forces loyal to King Stephen. There could be no mistaking, if there had been any doubt before, that Matilda herself would have to stand at the centre of the campaign to secure her inheritance. She needed her husband for the sons he had given her and for the troops he now led, and her half-brother as an Anglo-Norman magnate who could take her fight into the heart of Stephen's kingdom. But the legitimacy of her cause depended on Matilda alone. Her uniquely royal blood—despite the female body in which it was housed—represented the only hope of challenging the sanctity of Stephen's coronation.

In the spring of 1139, therefore, Matilda at last decided to stake her claim as publicly and explicitly as she could in direct defiance of Stephen's hold on her father's crown. Her first step was to send to Rome, in the hope that Pope Innocent II could be convinced to throw the moral and political support of the Holy See behind her campaign. In April, Bishop Ulger of Angers crossed the Alps to the Holy City, as Matilda herself had done before him, to attend the Second Lateran Council, a great gathering of almost a thousand prelates from across western Christendom. There, he presented her case: Stephen, he said, had usurped the throne of England, which was Matilda's by right, thanks to her hereditary title and the oaths of loyalty sworn to her by the spiritual and temporal peers of the kingdom.

In response, Stephen's representative, a smoothly fluent lawyer named Arnulf, archdeacon of the Norman diocese of Sées, made no attempt to engage with the substance of Matilda's claim, instead trying to sweep it aside in its entirety by arguing that she was not, in fact, her father's legitimate heir. Her mother, Queen Edith-Matilda, Arnulf declared, had not simply been educated in a convent but had made profession as a nun; her marriage to King Henry had therefore been invalid, and Matilda was no more than one of Henry's many bastards. It was a specious argument as well as an insulting one, since Edith had taken no vows, and her freedom to marry had been confirmed by the saintly Anselm, then Archbishop of Canterbury, almost forty years before. But it served Stephen's purpose, for the time being at least. Pope Innocent had only just returned to Rome after nearly a decade of schism within the Church caused by disputes over his own election, and he had more pressing problems at hand than England's distant troubles. He had heard enough. Refusing to engage any further with the lawyers' bickering, he halted the hearing by reiterating the position he had taken three years earlier, recognising the fait accompli of Stephen's coronation and therefore his status as king.

The edifice of Stephen's rule was still holding, despite public argument in the papal curia and the threat of more noble defections in the wake of Gloucester's defiance. But the strain was more and more apparent, with Stephen himself constantly on the move in the effort to stamp out resistance before it could spread out of control, while doling out ever more lavish rewards from the depleted royal treasury to magnates in whose loyalty he could trust less and less. "...the king hastened, always armed, always accompanied by a host, to deal with various anxieties and tasks of many kinds which continually dragged him hither and thither all over England," the author of the *Gesta Stephani* reported despairingly. "It was like what we read of the fabled hydra of Hercules; when one head was cut off, two or more grew in its place." And in June 1139, tensions within the regime at last reached breaking point.

The backing of his younger brother, Henry, Bishop of Winchester, had been crucial to the success of Stephen's coup, and Henry—whose unwavering commitment to the interests of the Church coincided happily with his flamboyant personal ambition—had expected that his own eminence in spiritual and temporal affairs would in due course be recognised by his election as Archbishop of Canterbury after the death of the elderly William of Corbeil in 1136. But in December 1138, Henry found himself passed over in favour of a much more obscure candidate, Abbot Theobald of Bec, whose principal qualification appeared to be his association with the Beaumont twins, Waleran of Meulan and Robert of Leicester, the young noblemen whose influence over Stephen was obvious and growing. Having shoved aside the pretensions of the king's brother, the Beaumonts next turned their sights on Bishop Roger of Salisbury, King Henry's former chief minister, who, along with a pair of episcopal nephews, Bishop Alexander of Lincoln and Bishop Nigel of Ely, still controlled the chancery and the exchequer, the administrative institutions through which England was governed. The bishops had at their disposal not only the substantial powers of pen and parchment but knights and castles strategically placed across their dioceses—and, in the fear-filled summer of 1139, it was not difficult to persuade the increasingly paranoid king of the threat their power might now represent.

More difficult was the question of how to bring the three bishops down. Mere suspicion was insufficient grounds for the arrest of a peer of the realm, but suspicion was all there was. In the absence of any concrete evidence that they were engaged in treasonable conspiracy, Waleran of Meulan came up with a ploy by which the bishops might be disarmed. When the court arrived in Oxford in June, one of the Beaumonts' noble allies was persuaded to pick a fight with the Bishop of Salisbury's men over the rooms they had been allocated, a domestic dispute which turned violently ugly, as happened all too readily when steel blades were a part of everyday dress. But bloodshed within the bounds of the royal court, contrived though it was in this instance, constituted a breach of the king's peace, for which Bishop Roger and his nephews were summarily arrested. They were removed from their offices in the royal administration, to be replaced by Beaumont nominees, and their castle strongholds were seized into the king's hands along with the treasure and the weapons stockpiled there.

The ruse was clear and—thought Stephen's brother Henry—outrageous. Bishop Henry was a stalwart defender of ecclesiastical rights, with lavishly appointed and massively fortified castles of his own. He had also spent the months since he had been denied the archbishopric of Canterbury working furiously behind the scenes to secure his own nomination as the pope's legate in England, a role which gave him even greater authority than he would have had as archbishop. He therefore had both motive and means to strike back against his brother's betrayal, and against the Beaumont brothers, his hated rivals who seemed now to be pulling the strings of royal policy. As a result, on August 29, England witnessed the extraordinary spectacle of a king being summoned by his own brother to appear before a specially convened ecclesiastical council on charges that he had ridden roughshod over Church liberties. Although the council broke up after three days of argument and counterargument without formal conclusion, it was now abundantly clear that, with every move the mistrustful king made to tighten his grip on power, more of the country would slip through his fingers.

Twenty-nine days later, for the first time in eight years, Matilda herself at last set foot on English soil. It had been apparent for some time that she would have to take the fight to Stephen, rather than inching forward from the safety of her base at Argentan. Normandy mattered, but the crown belonged to England, and she could not hope to succeed if her claim was not made a reality there. The difficulty was how to achieve that goal. Her brother's defection from Stephen's cause meant that she could now, for the first time, reach the Norman coast—only fifty miles from Argentan, but fifty miles too far if the terrain was hostile—via his fortress at Caen. But the south coast of England offered no welcoming haven, since its harbours were under Stephen's control. One of Gloucester's men had tried to hold a gateway open by securing the earl's castle at Dover against the king during the previous year, but he had soon been overwhelmed by an intimidating fleet sent by Stephen's queen, Mathilde, from her port at Boulogne. Meanwhile, the voyage around Land's End to Gloucester's stronghold at Bristol was too dangerously uncertain to provide a realistic alternative.

But during the summer of 1139 it emerged that there was a chink in Stephen's apparently impenetrable defences. The towering castle at Arundel, overlooking its own port on the navigable river Arun just five miles from the sea, was the home of the dowager queen, King Henry's widow, Adeliza. She was now remarried to William d'Aubigny, whom she had come to know as one of Henry's most trusted household attendants, and, after the barren years of her first marriage, the happy couple were on the way to amassing a brood of seven children. Outwardly, she and her new husband were loyal subjects of King Stephen; but, privately, Adeliza's sympathies lay with her stepdaughter. Respect for her dead husband's chosen heir was reinforced by a personal relationship—the two women were almost exactly the same age, and had spent a significant amount of time in each other's company after Matilda's return from Germany—and by an old debt of gratitude for Matilda's part in the political rehabilitation of Adeliza's father almost thirty years earlier, when the eight-year-old princess had performed her first formal act of intercession as the emperor's bride-to-be at Liège.

Old debts were about to be repaid. On September 30, 1139, a ship slipped quietly into the port of Arundel. A handful of its passengers—Robert, Earl of Gloucester, and a small, heavily armed bodyguard of loyal knights—disappeared almost immediately, hooded and cloaked, to ride 120 miles westward to the safety of the earl's fortress at Bristol, moving under cover of night and across open country to avoid Stephen's troops and spies. The rest of the party—Matilda, with a much larger military escort of her own—was spirited inside the impregnable walls of Arundel Castle. At last, she had taken the decision that she should abandon the battle for Normandy to her husband, and leave her three sons in safety under his supervision. Now she hoped that support for her cause in England, which had so far achieved some piecemeal disintegration of Stephen's hold on the realm, might take more threatening shape around the rallying point of her presence.

That, at least, was the theory. In practice, news of her arrival spread quickly, and Stephen—who was only ninety miles away, ruing his decision to allow Baldwin de Revières to go free, since he was now having to besiege him again at Corfe Castle in Dorset—immediately marched east to surround the ex-queen Adeliza and her royal guest at Arundel. Matilda, it seemed, was at her cousin's mercy. But her decision to expose herself to this danger was more finely calibrated than it appeared. By arriving at the head of a knightly escort rather than an army, she and her half-brother had used Stephen's weapons of speed and surprise against him to make landfall in England before the king could be warned of what was happening. It was Robert of Gloucester who had openly defied Stephen's authority, and against whom the king might legitimately take reprisals; but, by travelling fast with the bare minimum of protection, the earl was able to reach his power base at Bristol before Stephen could cut him off, a manoeuvre that would have been impossible had Matilda—who, however great her strength of character, was not used to the physical demands of a soldier's life—ridden with him.

Meanwhile, Matilda herself was left vulnerable to Stephen's advancing troops; but here it suddenly became clear that her sex could, for once, be used to her benefit rather than her disadvantage. Matilda was the daughter of a king, the widow of an emperor, and Stephen's own cousin, who had been welcomed into the hospitality of his predecessor's queen. Were Stephen to wage war on two women of such exalted status, he risked not only opprobrium but open rebellion from a far greater number of his subjects than he had so far faced. Even if he were to decide that this was a risk worth taking, the mighty fortifications of Adeliza's castle could not easily be overrun; and, if Stephen were pinned down by another lengthy siege, Robert of Gloucester would be free to strike against him at will. Meanwhile, even should he succeed in taking Arundel, it was far from clear that it would be either legally or politically tenable to hold Matilda captive.

Much better, the king's brother Bishop Henry argued, to allow her to join Gloucester in Bristol, since Stephen would then be able to fight without restraint against an enemy hemmed into a single place, well away from the crucial administrative and economic centres of the southeast. Reluctantly, Stephen stood down his preparations for a siege, and gave orders that Matilda should be delivered into her half-brother's care at a prearranged place within reach of Bristol by the uneasy pairing of Bishop Henry himself and his rival Waleran of Meulan—a noble escort "which it is not the custom of honourable knights to refuse to anyone," William of Malmesbury pointed out, "even their bitterest enemy."

Bishop Henry's advice was strategically sound, although a less transparent character than Stephen might perhaps have hesitated before allowing his disaffected brother to ride a hundred miles in the company of the cousin who was claiming his throne. The opportunity to parley in private with the bishop was an unexpected bonus for Matilda, whose risky tactics had paid off handsomely. Despite Stephen's best attempts to secure his kingdom against her, she had slipped, wraithlike, through his defences to reach the safety of her half-brother's citadel at Bristol. Her situation there could not be said to be strong—especially given that Stephen and his soldiers were now heading westward toward them with their usual menacing speed—but it was infinitely better than it had been when she was cooped up at Argentan, able to do little more than worry away at the fringes of her cousin's power.

Now she could begin to exploit the momentum of her advance, recruiting to her cause men who had been waiting to declare themselves until opposition to Stephen was no longer a do-or-die mission for principled loners, but an unmistakably viable political movement.

Chief among them were Brien Fitzcount and Miles of Gloucester, two of the "new men" who had risen high in the service of her father. Fitzcount, as his name suggested, was an illegitimate son of the Count of Brittany, and his service to King Henry had been rewarded with grants of land in Wales and the strategically valuable lordship of Wallingford in the Thames Valley, fifty miles west of London. Miles of Gloucester, meanwhile, had acquired his toponymic by following in the footsteps of his father and grandfather as sheriff of the western county of Gloucestershire and keeper of the king's castle at Glouces-ter itself. Four years earlier, in 1135, both men had concluded that discretion was the better part of valour and acknowledged Stephen as king; but both now lost no time in committing themselves to the newly arrived Matilda.

Fitzcount, who had been brought up in King Henry's household, knew Matilda and her half-brother well. Indeed, he and Robert of Gloucester—two bastard-born magnates, one the king's natural son, the other almost an adopted one—had been at Matilda's side more than a decade earlier when she travelled to Rouen for the un-happy betrothal that preceded her second marriage. As an illegiti-mate child with no offspring of his own, Fitzcount's family loyalties were focused exclusively on the royal dynasty that had welcomed and nurtured him, and the allegiance he now offered to Matilda was heartfelt and unshakeable. Just as well, given that it was only a matter of days before his resolve was brutally tested by the arrival of Stephen's troops outside the walls of Wallingford Castle. The king was making impressive headway as he pushed westward across coun-try from Arundel toward Bristol, seizing castles as he went. He set a siege in train at Wallingford as he passed, and Fitzcount—though his garrison was well provisioned and protected behind the castle's walls and double moat—was left isolated and exposed, cut off from his allies in the west country, and facing two hastily constructed forts on the opposite side of the river full of soldiers intent on starving him out, however long it might take.

If Brien Fitzcount was Matilda's chivalric champion, her most passionately loyal supporter, then Miles of Gloucester brought to her cause a razor-sharp military brain. As Stephen advanced on Bristol, Miles led a contingent of troops around behind the king's army and marched on Wallingford. Suddenly, the soldiers Stephen had left there found the tables violently turned. Miles's men smashed their way into the besiegers' forts, killing those who resisted and taking prisoner anyone willing to surrender. With the siege successfully lifted and Fitzcount liberated, Miles was poised—potentially at least—to march on London. When the news reached the king, Stephen turned his army about and raced back to protect his capital, while Miles—to whom the advantages of guerrilla strikes were becoming increasingly apparent—wheeled north to attack Worcester, of which Waleran of Meulan was the new earl. By the time Stephen and his right-hand man heard what had happened there and came to the aid of the devastated city, three weeks had passed and Miles was long gone.

A pattern had been set. Matilda's supporters could not strike a decisive blow against Stephen's much larger army, but they could keep the king on the back foot with feints and lightning strikes, darting just out of his reach while exhausting him in the pursuit. And this brutal dance bought Matilda time to consolidate her west country power base. She moved from her half-brother's castle at Bristol to the royal fortress at Gloucester, where her most gifted commander, Miles (who, the *Gesta Stephani* said, "always behaved to her like a father in deed and counsel"), was in charge of her safety. Here, she was a ruler at the head of her own royal household, not a client in her brother's establishment. She did not yet have much that was tangible to offer in the way of privilege and patronage, but she could give royal promises of future preferment to those nobles who were prepared to cast off their allegiance to her rival.

There were increasing numbers of such men as the months wore on, but fewer who would support her cause with the unswerving ferocity of the triumvirate of Miles of Gloucester, Brien Fitzcount, and her brother Earl Robert. As the magnates hesitated—some of them confusing not only the chroniclers but Stephen and Matilda, too, about where their loyalties lay—there was a terrible price to pay for the country. The network of Norman castles that had been constructed with intimidating speed little more than half a century earlier to pin down the population of a newly conquered land was now atomised, each fortification a closely defended island amid a sea of devastation, the surrounding countryside plundered to supply local garrisons, or reduced to blackened earth by hostile troops. It was "a dreadful thing," said William of Malmesbury in quiet anguish, "that England, once the noblest nurse of peace, the peculiar habitation of tranquillity, had sunk to such wretchedness."

Matilda had done well—if at a heavy cost—to make her challenge so potent a reality on English soil, and she had undoubtedly damaged Stephen's kingship; but her own claim to rule was still a long way from universal acceptance. And the risk was that this increasing anarchy might become a form of violent stalemate. Bishop Henry, who saw the danger that the future might hold little but mutually assured destruction, threw himself into the search for peace, presiding over a meeting near Bristol between Matilda's brother Robert and Stephen's queen, Mathilde, before sailing across the Channel to consult both Louis VII of France and his own and Stephen's elder brother, Thibaud of Blois. With what proposals he returned we do not know, but, whatever they were, Matilda—who had been schooled in the hard-headed politics of the Empire, and knew that hers was still the weaker hand—was prepared to accept them.

Stephen, however, preferred to fight. Perhaps he believed that war gave him an unanswerable advantage over an opponent who could not lead her own troops, and that his own presence on the battlefield would serve to remind his kingdom that he was not only a king but a warrior, something that Matilda could never be. But, if her sex denied her the benefits of military leadership, it also protected her from the dangers of war. However great Stephen's triumphs, Matilda was one enemy who would never be killed or captured in combat. Stephen himself, meanwhile, was about to learn at first hand the perils that awaited a king who stood in his army's front line.

The man who brought the cat-and-mouse conflict at last to the point of open confrontation was Ranulf, Earl of Chester, Robert of Gloucester's son-in-law, who had until now, despite his marriage, remained at least superficially Stephen's man. The polar opposite of the loyalists Brien Fitzcount and Miles of Gloucester, Ranulf made a principle only of his own territorial interests. In 1140, however, that meant seizing the opportunity to grab the castle of Lincoln, 120 miles north of London, from the harried king. The earl took the fortress by bare-faced trickery: he sent his wife on a social call to the castellan's lady, and then arrived himself, all smiles, to escort her home—but, once welcomed inside, he and his knightly attendants ambushed the guard and barred the gates to all but the detachment of troops he had stationed nearby. Stephen had lost the fortress to a sucker punch, and only a lengthy siege could now retrieve it.

Wearily, the king decided to tolerate this provocation rather than confront a magnate who had not yet explicitly defected to Matilda's side. But when the citizens sent a surreptitious message complaining about the earl's cruel and unjust behaviour, and pointing out that Ranulf and his family were spending Christmas at the castle with only perfunctory protection, Stephen could not resist committing himself to another of the lightning assaults that were his speciality. He marched a strike force from London to Lincoln before Twelfth Night had marked the end of the Christmas festivities, and besieged the castle with the help of the disgruntled townspeople. But, despite Stephen's speed, Earl Ranulf had already slipped away. As he made for his estates in the northwest, he sent importunate messages to Matilda's camp, offering his allegiance and appealing for help from his father-in-law.

Robert of Gloucester had so far been unimpressed by his son-in-law's self-interested manoeuvring, but his daughter, Ranulf's countess, remained under siege in the castle, and it had to be said that her unlovely husband's defection was a godsend to Matilda's cause. Gloucester did not hesitate—and, this time, it was Stephen's turn to be taken by surprise. Earl Robert and Earl Ranulf were almost outside Lincoln's walls when the king realised that his small force was about to be attacked by a much larger army. His advisers urged him to retreat and regroup; but Stephen was a brave man, and the prospect of running away was repugnant to him. His father's life had been blighted by a humiliating accusation of cowardice after he fled from a siege at Antioch while on crusade in the Holy Land forty years earlier, and Stephen was adamant that he would not risk the same fate. Instead, he readied his troops for battle.

The chroniclers laced their accounts of his preparations with portents of impending disaster. On the night before the armies met, a storm howled around the city, hailstones lashing down, thunder rolling around the blackness of the skies. At dawn the next morning, Sunday, February 2, when Stephen went to Lincoln's immense cathedral to celebrate the feast of Candlemas, the flame of his elaborate candle suddenly flickered and died, and the wax broke in his hands. Mass had not yet ended when the pyx containing the consecrated host fell from the chain that supported it and plunged onto the altar. "This," Henry of Huntingdon wrote with the implacable certainty of hindsight, "was a sign of the king's downfall."

Stephen was not so convinced that he faced inevitable defeat as he drew up his soldiers outside the west walls of the city. But it took only minutes, once the massed cavalry of Robert of Gloucester and Ranulf of Chester began to charge, for his hopes to be trampled into the freezing mud. The king stood firm at the head of his infantry in the centre of the field, but the earls who led what little cavalry he had quickly decided to save themselves and their men, rather than stay to face annihilation. Their receding hoofbeats drummed under the din of battle as Stephen laid about him with his great sword, steel striking on steel and slicing into flesh. When the weapon shattered in his grip, he fought on with a battle-axe, Matilda's men pressing ever closer, until at last a rock struck his head and he fell to the ground. God, who had blessed his kingship in the hush of Winchester Cathedral five years earlier, had clearly now changed his mind.

Divine protection had not, however, abandoned him altogether.

He was not dead—merely concussed, and distraught at the desertion of magnates who had sworn him their fidelity. He was also a prisoner. Stephen was first taken under guard 140 miles southwest to face Matilda at Gloucester Castle, and then on to her half-brother's fortress at Bristol. There he was initially treated with honour, until his tendency to wander from his quarters—"especially at night, outside his appointed place of custody, after deceiving or winning over his guards," as William of Malmesbury pointedly explained—persuaded Earl Robert to keep the king humiliatingly and uncomfortably chained in irons.

A little more than five years after her father's death, Matilda found herself at last within reach of his throne. She had come face to face with the cousin who had usurped her crown—but the chroniclers remain tantalisingly silent about the details of this fraught meeting, as they did so often with climactic events in her life. The author of the *Gesta Stephani* (possibly Robert of Lewes, the Bishop of Bath, but, whoever he was, certainly a partisan of Stephen's with close ties to the king's brother Bishop Henry) was so hostile to Matilda that he could barely bring himself to name her. Where he did so, it was as "the Countess of Anjou," the disparaging title she herself spurned, while elsewhere in his text she appears obliquely as "King Henry's daughter" or "the Earl of Gloucester's sister." William of Malmesbury was much more sympathetic to Matilda's cause, although the hero of his narrative is not Matilda herself but her half-brother Earl Robert, "who," William tells us admiringly, "for his steadfast loyalty and distinguished merit, has pre-eminently deserved that the recollection of him shall live for all time." Neither writer was willing—or, probably, able—to give any sense of Matilda's own experience of this violent turn of fortune's wheel. It seems likely that this was the first time the cousins had met since Stephen had knelt before Matilda ten years earlier to renew his oath to recognise her as her father's heir. But whether she greeted the captive king with cold disdain or blazing anger—anything in between seems less easily imaginable, given her forceful temperament—we cannot know.

What is clear is the chain reaction triggered by Matilda's triumph. Her husband, Geoffroi of Anjou, advanced into Normandy and, through a well-judged mix of negotiation and military manoeuvring, began an apparently inexorable annexation of the duchy on her behalf. In England, meanwhile, Stephen's support was crumbling. Some loyalists were driven from their castles at swordpoint by Matilda's resurgent supporters, but more made the calculated decision to throw in their lot with her cause. Just as a virtuous circle of pragmatic political logic had allowed Stephen to establish his kingship in the wake of his coup, so Matilda now appeared to carry all before her. The battle of Lincoln had reversed the polarity of politics; there seemed no prospect that Stephen—like Robert Curthose before him—would ever emerge from his prison, and magnates with territorial and dynastic interests to defend on either side of the Channel therefore had to face the reality of her victory.

Matilda herself proceeded with deliberation. Stephen was safely in chains, but he was still an anointed king, and to vindicate the legitimacy of her rule she would need the backing of the Church if her own prospective coronation were to supersede his. Above all, there was one man whose support she needed: Bishop Henry of Winchester, her own cousin, Stephen's brother, and the pope's legate in England. The ground may already have been laid during their long ride together from Arundel to the outskirts of Bristol after Matilda's arrival in England sixteen months earlier. Certainly, agreement was quickly reached when the two met again on March 2—exactly a month after the battle at Lincoln—on open ground near the bishop's city of Winchester. Matilda promised that she would consult him on all important matters of government; and in return, Bishop Henry offered her his oath of allegiance, and surrendered the much-depleted royal treasury at Winchester into her hands. The next day, he received her in ceremonial procession into his cathedral, where a dozen bishops and abbots had gathered to welcome her into the sacred place where Stephen had been crowned.

Four weeks later, while Matilda waited behind the fifty-foot walls of Oxford Castle, her new ally Bishop Henry rose to speak before a specially convened council of the Church at Winchester. William of Malmesbury, who was there, gives a first-hand account of the address. The great King Henry, the bishop declared, had left England and Normandy to his daughter Matilda. However, when he died, "because it seemed tedious to wait for the lady, who made delays in coming to England since her residence was in Normandy," Bishop Henry continued, in a startlingly smooth piece of historical revisionism, "provision was made for the peace of the country and my brother allowed to reign." But Stephen, he explained, had failed in his office: "No justice was enforced upon transgressors, and peace was at once brought entirely to an end, almost in that very year; bishops were arrested and compelled to surrender their property; abbacies were sold and churches despoiled of their treasure; the advice of the wicked was hearkened to, that of the good either not put into effect or altogether disregarded." As so often, Bishop Henry's genuine concern for peace and for the interests of the Church dovetailed seamlessly with the certainty that his own influence—"the advice of the good," as he modestly put it—should prevail.

And that advice was now clear. God had spoken, and Stephen was a prisoner. After sober consultation among the ranks of the assembled clergy, England's Church pronounced its judgement in the voice of Bishop Henry himself: "We choose as lady of England and Normandy the daughter of a king who was a peacemaker, a glorious king, a wealthy king, a good king, without peer in our time, and we promise her faith and support."

"Lady of England" was a nebulous, ambiguous title, but also a telling one. To be England's lady—*domina*, in the Latin spoken by Bishop Henry and his ecclesiastical colleagues—was to exercise *dominium*, that is, power or lordship, of the kind that her royal father had enjoyed. All that remained was to proceed to Westminster, to take command of her capital, and to be anointed as a new kind of queen—one who would rule in her own right, not as her husband's helpmeet. The crown, it seemed, was finally hers.

SIX

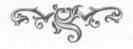

Greatest in Her Offspring

 ow, at last, Matilda stood at the heart of politics, and the chroniclers could no longer keep her at the margins of the stories they told. But they did not like what they saw. "She was lifted up into an insufferable arrogance," Henry of Huntingdon declared censoriously, "...and she alienated the hearts of almost everyone." The author of the *Gesta Stephani*, who had until now treated her with disdain, also reacted with withering disapproval: "She had brought the greater part of the kingdom under her sway, and on this account...she was mightily puffed up and exalted in spirit."

These words have become the defining account of the difficulties Matilda faced at this, the crucial moment when the kingdom lay within her hands. More than eight hundred years later, historians have had no hesitation in endorsing the same damning verdict. "All chroniclers agree that in her hour of victory she displayed an intolerable pride and wilfulness," one of the most perceptive writers on the period remarks; while another, more gently but no less categorically, explains that "here for the first time an aspect of her character, which had not so far been apparent, was to let her down."

But it is striking that *not* all the chroniclers did in fact join this critical chorus. William of Malmesbury, for example, did not choose to contrast his eulogising account of the Earl of Gloucester's "restraint and wisdom" with any explicit criticism of "that formidable lady," his hero's half-sister. And another source gives us an altogether different portrait of Matilda's approach to her royal destiny. The Abbot of Gloucester, a renowned scholar named Gilbert Foliot, supplied Brien Fitzcount with a sophisticated legal and theological defence of Matilda's claim, in the course of which he penned an elegant sketch of the former empress as a devoted royal daughter. "... in accordance with her father's wishes she crossed the sea, passed over mountains, penetrated into unknown regions, married there at her father's command, and remained there carrying out the duties of imperial rule virtuously and piously until, after her husband's death, not through any desperate need or feminine levity but in response to a summons from her father, she returned to him. And though she had attained such high rank that, it is reported, she had the title and status of Queen of the Romans, she was in no way puffed up with pride, but meekly submitted in all things to her father's will ..."

Foliot's approving description of a modestly dutiful woman in the years before 1135 is, of course, a partisan portrayal in pursuit of a political argument—but the same is also true of the hostile *Gesta Stephani*, the chief witness for the prosecution in the years after King Henry's death. And closer examination of the *Gesta's* account of Matilda's conduct after the battle of Lincoln demonstrates that criticism of the "intolerable pride" with which she responded to her rival's defeat cannot for a moment be taken as the product of coolly neutral observation. "... she at once put on an extremely arrogant demeanour instead of the modest gait and bearing proper to the gentle sex," the *Gesta's* author complained, "began to walk and speak and do all things more stiffly and more haughtily than she had been wont, to such a point that soon, in the capital of the land subject to her, she actually made herself queen of all England and gloried in being so called."

The *Gesta's* support for Stephen's cause is unmistakable here—but so is the extent to which the writer is troubled by the very idea of a woman holding power in her own right. Matilda was facing the challenge of becoming Queen of England (a title which, despite the *Gesta's* affronted protests, she did not yet have)—not in the conventional sense of a king's partner, but in the unprecedented form of a female king. And kings did not deport themselves with a "modest gait and bearing." Instead, they were—and were required to be—supremely commanding and authoritative, as her father and her first husband had been. William of Malmesbury's admiring description of King Henry had made the point insistently: "The standard of his justice was inflexible; he kept his subjects in order without disturbance and his nobles without loss of dignity ... If any of the more important lords, forgetting their oath of allegiance, swerved from the narrow path of loyalty, he used at once to recall the strays by prudent counsel and unremitting efforts, bringing the rebellious back to toeing the line by the severity of the wounds he inflicted on them. Nor could I easily recount the long-continued labours he expended on such people, leaving no action unpunished which could not be committed by the disaffected without some impairment of his royal dignity."

In such circumstances, it is hard to imagine quite what Henry would have had to do to be accused of acting with "insufferable arrogance." The expectation of unquestioning obedience, and the punishment of those who did not comply with his commands, were indissoluble elements of his kingship. He believed in his own authority, and there could be no suggestion of unwonted pride in the fact that he required others to acknowledge it. How, then, could Matilda achieve a "royal dignity" to match her father's if she could employ only the "modest gait and bearing proper to the gentle sex" to command her kingdom?

We could perhaps argue that the context of violence, division, and turmoil within which Matilda was forced to assert herself meant that she needed to tread particularly carefully, to avoid alienating those who did not yet share the unwavering loyalty of her innermost coterie. But her father had also had to fight for his throne against the pressing claims of a rival; and for both Henry and Stephen, too, in equally troubled circumstances, it was clear that acting like a king—inhabiting the role with absolute conviction—was essential if the kingdom were to be convinced that the crown was on the right man's head. In fact, those elements of Stephen's character that were less than imperious served to raise questions about his authority rather than reinforcing it: his affable generosity, for example ("such a kindly and gentle disposition that he commonly forgot a king's exalted rank," the *Gesta* noted), or his light voice, so soft that he had had to depute someone else to rouse his troops with a battlefield speech before the fighting at Lincoln.

The truth of the matter was that Matilda found herself trapped. She urgently needed to show that she was a credible ruler. Her sex had already prevented her from leading her own army into battle, but this, at last, was her chance to prove that being a woman (and a woman standing alone, given that the man to whom she was married was neither present in England nor a political asset there) need not constrain her command in the council chamber. But when she sought to emulate her formidable father and her first husband, the two great kings whose rule she knew best, she encountered not awestruck obedience, but resentment of a "haughtiness and insolence" that was deemed unnatural and unfeminine.

That much is clear from the *Gesta*'s specific objections to her conduct on what should have been her triumphal approach to London. First, the *Gesta* claimed, she failed to show due deference to "the chief men of the whole kingdom," the chronicler's patron Bishop Henry of Winchester prominent among them. "...she did not rise respectfully, as she should have, when they bowed before her, or agree to what they asked, but repeatedly sent them away with contumely, rebuffing them by an arrogant answer and refusing to hearken to their words; and by this time she no longer relied on their advice, as she should have, and had promised them, but arranged everything as she herself thought fit and according to her own arbitrary will." What this boils down to, when issues of style and substance are disentangled, is that Matilda did not do exactly what her advisers told her—and one can only guess what King Henry would have said to the suggestion that his counsellors should have the last word in his government.

Secondly, she summoned the richest of London's citizens and asked them for a large sum of money as a contribution to her royal expenses, a request made "not with unassuming gentleness, but with a voice of authority," the *Gesta* explained disapprovingly. When they begged to be excused, pleading poverty, "she, with a grim look, her forehead wrinkled into a frown, every trace of a woman's gentleness removed from her face, blazed into unbearable fury," declaring that the Londoners had lavished their wealth on Stephen's cause, "and therefore it was not just to spare them in any respect or make the smallest reduction in the money demanded." The citizens—here portrayed as innocents abashed by her rage—returned in anxious gloom to their homes.

Both of these incidents also appear in William of Malmesbury's more sympathetic account—but in strikingly different form. William omits any mention of Matilda's financial demands on the citizens of London, explaining instead that the inhabitants of the capital, "who had always been under suspicion and in a state of secret indignation, then gave vent to expressions of unconcealed hatred" toward her. Meanwhile, Matilda's supposedly high-handed treatment of her advisers here becomes a specific dispute with Bishop Henry, the most recent convert to her cause, and one whose support was predicated on his hopes of imposing his own influence on her rule. The bishop wanted Stephen's personal estates, the rich and strategically vital counties of Mortain and Boulogne (the latter including vast tracts of land in the southeast of England), to be committed to Stephen's twelve-year-old son, Eustace, for as long as his father remained in prison. Matilda understandably refused, unwilling to hand over such power to a boy who would inevitably see her as the usurper of his royal inheritance—at which the bishop, "enraged by this affront," left her court and began at once to plot against her.

Between claim and counter-claim, it is clear that Matilda faced two pressing and intractable problems: her relationship with Bishop Henry, without whom she would not have been recognised as "Lady of England," but who expected as the price of his backing a degree of control over royal policy that no monarch could tolerate; and the attitude of the Londoners, whose overwhelming economic interest in the trade route through Boulogne predisposed them to support Stephen's claim to the crown, an alliance which Stephen himself had cemented with expansive promises of royal favour. But the minute Matilda tried to tackle those problems with what her father would have recognised as kingly authority, she was accused of acting with a headstrong arrogance unbecoming to her sex.

That is not to say that her decisions and her behaviour were beyond reproach. It is not difficult to imagine that the daughter of the domineering King Henry—a woman who had been raised in imperial splendour and was now for the first time wielding power that she believed had been stolen from her—might have been less than subtle in her treatment of former opponents. At the same time, it is not easy, even with hindsight, to decide whether confrontation or conciliation was the better way of dealing with those of her subjects whose professions of newfound loyalty seemed likely to be the thinnest of political veneers. But we can be more confident in rejecting the suggestion that "an aspect of her character, which had not so far been apparent, . . . let her down." Matilda's fledgling regime was not crippled by the sudden revelation of previously undetected personal flaws. Instead, she was taking her first steps in the new persona of a female monarch—and found herself stumbling over the implicit contradictions between being a woman and being a king.

Could any woman have kept her footing? It seems unlikely. As Matilda made preparations at Westminster for the coronation she hoped would transform her from England's lady to its reigning queen, she faced resistance led by an enemy who showed that, in the exercise of female power, context was everything. Stephen himself was doing little from his prison cell in Bristol Castle to stiffen the resolve of those who still hesitated to accept Matilda's victory. (His characteristic mildness was such that, when visited by the Archbishop of Canterbury, a consummate political pragmatist who "thought it unbefitting his reputation and position" to transfer his allegiance to Matilda "without consulting the king," Stephen gave him "a courteous permission to change over as the times required.") But his cause was kept alive by his queen, Mathilde, a woman every inch as formidable as Matilda herself, but one who—acting as she was in the name of her incarcerated husband—escaped any kind of censure.

Mathilde began by adopting the classic pose of the queen consort as intercessor, begging Bishop Henry's council at Winchester not to recognise Matilda's claim, and, when that intervention failed, writing to Matilda herself to ask "for her husband's release from his filthy dungeon." Once it became clear, however, that graceful pleading would get her nowhere, she did not hesitate to resort to brute force—uncompromisingly gritty and resolute behaviour for which she was not castigated but lauded. The author of the *Gesta Stephani* had scarcely taken a breath after berating Matilda for abandoning "the modest gait and bearing proper to the gentle sex" when he launched into a paean of praise to Stephen's queen: "...forgetting the weakness of her sex and a woman's softness," he wrote with obvious admiration, "she bore herself with the valour of a man." In the circumstances, Matilda could have been forgiven for despairing at the double standard by which she was dubbed an unnatural virago and her opponent a paragon of amazonian virtue.

Mathilde's strategy was one of violent confrontation. She mustered her husband's Flemish mercenaries under their able commander, William of Ypres, and marched them from her lands in Kent to the south bank of the Thames, separated only by a narrow stretch of river from London's city walls and from Matilda's residence in the Palace of Westminster, which lay a mile and a half outside the capital to the west. There Stephen's queen ordered that this "magnificent body of troops" should "rage most furiously around the city with plunder and arson, violence and the sword." The Londoners looked on in horror, the *Gesta Stephani* reported with a touch of bathos, as "their land was stripped before their eyes and reduced by the enemy's ravages to a habitation for the hedgehog."

Queen Mathilde was demonstrating with single-minded aggression that the would-be Queen Matilda could not protect her capital from the depredations of an army loyal to her rival. As a result, Matilda's triumph suddenly began to seem more illusory than real. And that in turn undermined the Londoners' reluctant rationale for deserting a king whose territorial power dovetailed with their own trading interests, and who had wooed them with promises of privileged self-government. While Matilda remained preoccupied with her planned coronation, the decisive moment at which she would at last become England's anointed ruler, the citizens of her capital dispatched envoys to parley in secret with Stephen's queen—and the result, for Matilda, was nothing short of catastrophic. On June 24, 1141, just as she was about to sit down to a banquet designed as a precursor to her ceremonial entry into London, the city's bells began to toll in hideous cacophony, its western gates swung open, and thousands of Londoners swarmed across the fields toward Westminster with weapons in their hands. In shock, Matilda and her attendants ran for their horses and fled westward, making for the safety of her castle at Oxford, while the mob ransacked her lodgings and trampled the uneaten feast into the dirt. She had lost England's capital—and with it her chance to be crowned England's queen.

It was, said the *Gesta Stephani*, as though Stephen's supporters were "bathed in the light of a new dawn." Among those soaking up its rays was Bishop Henry of Winchester, who just two months earlier had proclaimed Matilda "Lady of England" and "cursed all who cursed her, blessed those who blessed her, excommunicated those who were against her, and absolved those who supported her." Now, having left her court and retreated to his episcopal palace at Winchester, he summarily retracted this anathema, and complained to anyone who would listen about Matilda's disgracefully assertive conduct—"that she had wished to arrest him; that she had disregarded everything she had sworn to him; that all the barons of England had kept their faith with her but she had broken hers, being unable to show restraint in the enjoyment of what she had gained." Queen Mathilde, it turned out, had played her part in encouraging her brother-in-law's defection as well as that of the Londoners, although in the bishop's case she had shrewdly taken on the ego-massaging persona of humble petitioner rather than avenging amazon. (Bishop Henry had been moved, the *Gesta Stephani* solemnly explained, "by the woman's tearful supplications, which she pressed on him with great earnestness....")

Matilda soon learned of his betrayal, and, once she had rallied her forces after her chaotic flight from London, she made for Winchester at the head of her army, intending to secure the city and its treasury, and demanding that Bishop Henry appear before her to explain himself. But the bishop managed to slip away from his episcopal palace in the southeast of the city just as Matilda arrived at the royal castle in the west. Her forces, led by her brother Robert of Gloucester and her right-hand men Miles of Gloucester and Brien Fitzcount, had to content themselves with besieging the garrison the bishop had left behind. As they settled into the city for what promised to be a lengthy blockade, they had no inkling that Bishop Henry had appealed for help to Queen Mathilde, and that William of Ypres's mercenaries were even at that moment advancing on the city and would soon encircle it.

It was Lincoln all over again: a great nobleman had slipped the net of a siege laid against him and summoned an army to besiege the besiegers. But this time the roles were reversed. This time it was Matilda's forces, laying siege to a small garrison within a city fortress, who were ambushed by their enemy's sudden arrival. As the violence intensified—with the city engulfed in flames after Bishop Henry's men threw burning brands into the streets, while William of Ypres tightened his stranglehold on the surrounding countryside—the urgent need to secure Matilda's safety became starkly apparent. On Sunday, September 14, Robert and Miles of Gloucester rallied their troops for a final stand, hoping against hope to fight their way out, but intent at all costs on winning time for Matilda's escape. In that, they succeeded: Matilda fled forty miles northeast to Devizes, riding astride her horse like a man for greater speed, the devoted Brien Fitzcount at her side. Her prostration after two unrelenting days in the saddle was such that she had to be carried the rest of the way to Gloucester on a litter tied between two horses ("as though she was a corpse," one chronicler remarked—an observation which would later spawn wild rumours that she had been smuggled out of Winchester in a coffin).

But the price of her escape was high. Soon after she had reached the refuge of her own impregnable castle, Miles of Gloucester arrived at its gates, no longer the proud castellan but a lone fugitive, exhausted, alone, and half-naked, his armour discarded in his flight. And he bore bad news. Matilda's brother Robert had tried to hold out too long, and had been surrounded and captured. With his imprisonment, the last traces of Matilda's triumph at Lincoln were stripped away. Her brother was indispensable to her cause because of the men he commanded and the land he controlled—and now his freedom could only be secured by giving up the biggest prize of all: Stephen, who was still languishing in confinement at Bristol Castle.

Elaborate arrangements were put in place for the exchange of prisoners. Stephen was set free on the arrival at Bristol of his wife, Mathilde, and younger son, William, who were to be held there with all honour as surety for Earl Robert's safety. Two days later, once Stephen had ridden to Winchester and been welcomed by his supporters there, Earl Robert set out in the opposite direction, leaving behind his own son as a guarantee of the queen's well-being. When the earl had been safely received within the walls of his fortress at Bristol, Mathilde and her son were allowed to return to Stephen's side, and Robert's son was then released in his turn. With this stately diplomatic pavane along the road between Bristol and Winchester, the two sides once again took up the positions they had occupied eight months earlier, and Bishop Henry called yet another Church council to rubber-stamp his latest about-turn ("saying that he had received the empress not of his own will but under compulsion...however, God in his mercy had given affairs a different course from what she had hoped, so that he might avoid destruction himself and rescue his brother from bondage..."). It was almost as though Matilda's moment of triumph had never happened.

But not quite. The dramatic reverses that took place between February and November 1141 left permanent scars on the political landscape, the profound significance of which only gradually became apparent. While Stephen's supporters had been occupied in the fight to secure his freedom in England, across the water Matilda's husband, Geoffroi of Anjou, had seized the opportunity to advance steadily into central Normandy, and his presence in the duchy was now so strong that many magnates whose estates lay principally on the Norman side of the Channel saw no option but to recognise his authority. There could be no clearer demonstration of the new reality of Geoffroi's power than the defection from Stephen's cause of the king's favourite, Waleran of Meulan, who had fought in Stephen's army in the rout at Lincoln but came to terms with Geoffroi in Normandy only six months later. From this point on, Waleran and his twin brother, Robert of Leicester, would play a delicate game in order to safeguard their family's lands on both sides of the sea—Waleran in Normandy with Matilda's husband, and Robert in England with Stephen, each brother, from supposedly opposite sides, doing his utmost to minimise risk to the family's interests. Despite Stephen's resurgence in England, therefore, it was clear that, unless he could find some way to halt Geoffroi's seemingly unstoppable momentum in Normandy, ultimate victory would always elude him.

At the same time, Matilda had discovered quite how deep resistance ran to the idea that she might rule for herself. It was one thing for the magnates to acknowledge that the line of legitimate succession might deposit the crown on a female head; quite another, it turned out, for them to accept that a woman should exercise power like any other king. Her husband's military successes undoubtedly meant that Stephen would struggle to obliterate Matilda's claims completely; but on the other hand, she, too, would have no chance of winning a decisive victory if the greatest strength of those claims—the theoretical legitimacy of her personal rule—could not in fact be put into practice.

For the moment, however, the implications of this stalemate remained unexamined, as the two sides manoeuvred for the best new foothold in the old terrain on which they now found themselves. Stephen set out on yet another military sweep across his kingdom, but was halted at the midland city of Northampton in May by a bout of serious illness. Matilda, meanwhile, took advantage of this lull in hostilities to send her brother Earl Robert to Normandy to solicit military help from her husband; but Geoffroi—whose principal concern was the conquest of Normandy rather than the pursuit of his wife's royal title in distant England—found the earl's presence so useful, as a commander and as a legitimising Norman presence in his Angevin army, that he repeatedly delayed Robert's return.

Matilda had no way of knowing that Stephen's health was already beginning to improve even as she dispatched her brother to her husband's side. As a result, Geoffroi's ruthless prioritisation of his own interests placed his wife in grave danger. While she waited at Oxford for her brother's return, Stephen gathered his troops and marched to Wareham, the Dorset port from which Earl Robert had sailed. There the rejuvenated king seized the castle and garrisoned it to block the earl's gateway back into England, before marching north and then east toward Oxford. When Stephen's army forded the deep waters of the river and stormed into the city, Matilda and her supporters were taken by surprise, horror-struck within the castle's massive walls to find themselves once again under siege.

And this time, Stephen would not be deflected. Earl Robert—

who raced to his ships when news of Matilda's plight reached Normandy, incandescent with fury that he had been detained to help his brother-in-law at his sister's expense—hurled his knights into an attack on Wareham as soon as his fleet reached the coast, taking the harbour and the town and pressing hard to force his way into the fortress. But Stephen decided to let the port go if it kept Robert out of the way while he tightened his grip on Oxford, "thinking," as the *Gesta Stephani* put it, "he could easily put an end to the strife in the kingdom if he forcibly overcame her through whom it began to be at strife."

By the middle of December 1142, after three months trapped inside a burned and blackened city, Matilda and her small garrison were cold, starving, and almost bereft of hope. Just before Christmas, she decided to risk everything on one last effort to escape. It was not the first time she had to call on her reserves of physical strength or her unbending will; and she had twice before succeeded in slipping through Stephen's outstretched fingers, once in spiriting herself into Arundel Castle on her arrival in England, and then in securing a perilous route out of the besieged city of Winchester. This, though, was the most dangerous challenge she had yet faced, and she met it with undaunted courage. In the still of the night, with a bodyguard of just three trusted soldiers, she left Oxford Castle by a small side gate. The frozen terrain that confronted her seemed impossibly forbidding: a heavy fall of snow shrouded the ground stretching ahead into the darkness, and the shouts of the watch Stephen had set to encircle the castle echoed on the cold air.

But the bitter winter proved to be a welcome ally. Wrapped in white cloaks as camouflage against the snowy landscape, Matilda and her knights walked silently across the river, its treacherous current now muffled under a layer of ice thick enough to bear their weight with ease. No one saw them pass; and no one challenged them as they trudged seven miles through the cold and dark, feet numb and freezing in the drifting snow. Fear and necessity kept exhaustion at bay until they reached the town of Abingdon, where they found horses to carry them just a few miles more to the safe haven of Brien Fitzcount's castle at Wallingford.

When news of her daring escape began to spread ("a manifest miracle of God," William of Malmesbury called it), Stephen accepted the surrender of the beleaguered garrison she had left behind and allowed them to go free, his customary generosity of spirit perhaps reinforced by a rueful admiration of his rival's bravery. Even the author of the *Gesta Stephani*, who was sometimes venomous in his hostility to Matilda, seemed reluctantly impressed by the good fortune her courage had brought: "I do not know whether it was to heighten the greatness of her fame in time to come, or by God's judgement to increase more vehemently the disturbance of the kingdom, but never have I read of another woman so luckily rescued from so many mortal foes and from the threat of dangers so great," he wrote.

But if Matilda's escape had kept her cause alive—and raised doubts yet again about God's verdict on Stephen's claims—it also marked the end of her hopes that she might one day rule the kingdom her father had bequeathed to her in person. England found itself once more carved up into rival networks of fortresses (Matilda now making her base at the Bishop of Salisbury's massive citadel of Devizes in Wiltshire), with the countryside in between left plundered and desolate by the passing of troops from one armoured island to another. Given that her husband had made it abundantly clear that he could not and would not pause in his conquest of Normandy to send an army that might turn the tide decisively in England, it seemed that the kingdom was condemned to endure a war of attrition between evenly matched enemies, neither of whom had the strength to destroy the other. In the midst of this destructive deadlock, however, one small step pointed a way forward: when Robert of Gloucester had returned from Normandy to England, too late to rescue his sister from the siege of Oxford, Geoffroi of Anjou sent with him Matilda's eldest son, nine-year-old Henry.

This visit to England, Henry's first, was relatively brief—two years spent in training with sword and schoolbooks in his uncle's household at Bristol Castle—but it was significant nonetheless. Henry was the ace in Matilda's hand, even at the same time as his presence sounded the death knell for her prospects of standing alone as England's monarch. Her sex had proved to be a stumbling block which she simply could not transcend. That she could not command troops on the battlefield had served to compromise her leadership— though it had also protected her from danger—but the fatal flaw in her campaign for the throne was not her own inability to fight, nor any theoretical limitation to her authority, but the inability of her most powerful subjects to accept the reality of a woman ruling by and for herself. Matilda's son, as he grew toward adulthood, was an entirely different prospect: a male heir who embodied all the hereditary right of Matilda's claim, but who could also promise the uncomplicatedly powerful kingship of his grandfather and namesake.

Ensconced in her west country power base after all the dramas and dangers of 1142, Matilda recognised that the battle she now faced was to win the crown for her son, rather than to wear it herself. The decision to fight for her son's rights rather than her own was born of tough-minded political pragmatism, as well as fierce maternal and dynastic ambition, and in it there was no trace of the intolerable personal pride of which she had been accused during the months when the throne had seemed to be hers for the taking. Either that arrogance had disappeared as suddenly as it had supposedly appeared or it had never in fact existed in the form that her enemies alleged.

Our view of Matilda during these years of dogged struggle is even more elusive than before because of the loss of the two greatest chroniclers among the ranks of her contemporaries: Orderic Vitalis, who died in 1142, lamenting the disintegration of his Anglo-Norman homelands, and William of Malmesbury, whose humane and inexhaustible curiosity was finally extinguished just after he had noted his intention to discover more details of Matilda's audacious escape from Oxford at the end of that year. (The last sentence of his *Historia Novella* poignantly reads, "I am disposed to go into this more thoroughly if ever by the gift of God I learn the truth from those who were present....") As a result, we have no way of knowing how Matilda coped with six years of relentless attrition during which she endured bereavements of her own. Miles of Gloucester, her ablest general, was killed by a misdirected arrow on a Christmas Eve hunting trip in the Forest of Dean in 1143. Four years later, her greatest lieutenant, her brother Robert, Earl of Gloucester, succumbed to a fever at his castle at Bristol; and two years after that the staunchly faithful Brien Fitzcount died, having already retreated from the political world into a life of religious contemplation.

Despite these losses, Matilda could still rely on the west country strongholds of which her brother's earldom of Gloucester formed the heart, while Stephen dominated much larger swathes of territory across the midlands and the east. Some lords offered loyalty to one side or the other, while others, striving to protect their own interests, hovered between the two—though it is worth noting that, in the case of Robert of Gloucester's powerful son-in-law, Ranulf of Chester, it was Matilda's quietly steadfast treatment of her supporters, rather than Stephen's suspicious unreliability, that won such allegiance as this serial turncoat was ultimately prepared to offer. Still other magnates, Waleran of Meulan among them, abandoned altogether the dark ambiguities of internecine conflict to pursue a war that offered instead the glorious certainties of faith and salvation, joining the crusade that set out from Europe for the Holy Land in 1147.

In 1148, Matilda herself left England to return to Normandy. This was not a surrender, but a recognition of where the long-term power of her position now lay. While she and Stephen had been locked in violent stand-off in England, her husband had advanced through Normandy with methodical ruthlessness, finally sweeping into the capital, Rouen, at the beginning of 1144. That summer, he was formally invested as Duke of Normandy—his claim to the title justified by his wife's inheritance and his own military success— amid the solemn grandeur of Rouen's great cathedral. By the end of the year, he had secured recognition as duke from Louis VII of France, and controlled every castle in the duchy save one, the fortress of Arques, just outside the port of Dieppe. A few months later, when Arques finally capitulated, Geoffroi's conquest was complete. Stephen no longer held a single Norman stronghold, and all hope that he might one day retrieve his position there was extinguished.

From that point on, though Stephen unquestionably had the upper hand in England, it was increasingly apparent that the foundations of his power were crumbling away. No magnate with a claim to estates in Normandy could now afford to commit himself irretrievably to Stephen, however great the short-term advantage on the English side of the Channel. The king, too, was getting older—he turned fifty probably in 1142—and, because the legitimacy of his rule depended on the personal sanction of his coronation rather than on hereditary right, it could not be assumed that his teenage son, Eustace, had any certain claim to succeed him.

Stephen pressed hard in the attempt to persuade Archbishop Theobald of Canterbury to crown his son during his own lifetime, a custom previously adopted by the kings of France in an attempt to reinforce the practice of hereditary succession. But the days were gone when his brother, Bishop Henry, stood ready and able to swing the weight of the Church behind Stephen's cause. The new reformist pope, Eugenius III, elected in 1145, refused to renew the worldly bishop's status as papal legate. (Only a year earlier, Eugenius's spiritual mentor, Bernard of Clairvaux, had vituperatively denounced Bishop Henry as "the man who walks before Satan, the son of perdition, the man who disrupts all rights and laws.") And Stephen's determination to take a stand on his royal authority over episcopal appointments in England antagonised Eugenius enough for the pope to reject any suggestion that Eustace should be pre-emptively crowned.

Matilda, meanwhile—who knew from her years of experience in Germany and Italy just how destructive conflict with the papacy could be—handled her relations with the Church with skilful diplomacy, something which contributed to the growing perception that, as the *Gesta Stephani* now began to suggest, it was her son, not

Stephen's, who was "*iustus regni Anglorum heres et appetitor*"—"the lawful heir and claimant to the kingdom of England." Strikingly, the *Gesta*'s author speaks of Stephen as "the king" and Henry as "the lawful heir" as if there were no incompatibility between the two. And, from one increasingly influential point of view, there was none: it was possible to accept that Stephen was king with God's blessing as manifested through his anointing, and at the same time to argue that the hereditary right to succeed to Henry I's throne had passed through Matilda to his grandson.

Young Henry had returned to Normandy in 1144 in the wake of his father's conquest of Rouen, to continue his political education in the duchy where, as Geoffroi soon astutely declared, he would take over the reins of government once he reached adulthood. Three years later—now almost fourteen, with his grandfather's restless energy and a temperament as fiery as his flame-coloured hair—Henry made another impromptu appearance in England. He recruited a small company of mercenaries, hired on credit because he had no ready cash, and sailed across the Channel in an impulsive attempt to relieve his mother's hemmed-in military position. News of his unexpected arrival sparked panic among Stephen's supporters: rumour had it that he stood at the head of an army of thousands, with more troops to come. But soon more accurate reports, of a tiny band led by an inexperienced boy, began to spread; and, after a failed attempt to seize Purton Castle near the Wiltshire town of Cricklade, Henry's unpaid soldiers began to desert him. Neither Matilda nor Robert of Gloucester, hard pressed as they were, had the funds to bail him out of the hole he had dug for himself; so the chastened teenager appealed for help instead to Stephen himself, who—"ever full of pity and compassion," the *Gesta Stephani* reported—sent him the money for his return crossing to Normandy.

Stephen's magnanimity to his young cousin might seem extraordinary—and it certainly appeared so to the *Gesta*'s author, who could explain it only in terms of a "profound and prudent" belief that "the more kindly and humanely a man behaves to an enemy, the feebler he makes him and the more he weakens him." It was not the first time that the king had conducted himself with unusual mildness, a quality that might variously be lauded as generosity or condemned as weakness. In this case, however, his lack of a killer instinct dovetailed neatly with the inescapable political conclusion that it was entirely in Stephen's interests for Matilda's son to be removed from English soil as quickly as possible—an achievement for which a limited amount of cash clearly seemed a small price to pay. As for Henry, safely back in Normandy by the end of May 1147, it had been a hot-headed and in some ways foolish escapade; but it had also put down a marker of his utter determination to fight for his inheritance.

A year later, when Matilda at last gave up her personal leadership of the struggle in England to return to Normandy in the summer of 1148, her decision seems to have been precipitated by the need to tread carefully in relation to the Church. Her strategically vital stronghold at Devizes Castle, thirty miles east of Bristol, had belonged to Bishop Roger of Salisbury before Stephen had confiscated it when the bishop fell from power, and Matilda's troops had then captured it from Stephen's forces. But the new bishop, Jocelin de Bohun, now demanded its return with the vigorous support of Pope Eugenius, who threatened excommunication against anyone unjustly withholding the fortress from ecclesiastical hands. Matilda was determined neither to risk the kind of bitter confrontation with the papacy that was damaging her rival's cause, nor simply to abdicate control of a castle that formed one of the keys to her territorial position. It made sense, therefore, to remove herself from the firing line; and in June 1148 she travelled to Falaise, twenty miles south of Caen, to make her personal peace with Bishop Jocelin, while at the same time leaving the fortress itself safely in the hands of a loyal garrison.

But she was able to leave England secure in the knowledge that her son was poised to take her place. The developing partnership between mother and son was obvious from their seamless manoeuvring over Devizes: Matilda wrote to Henry explaining her pious decision to observe the dictates of the Church, and handing over the responsibility for implementing that decision to him; sixteen-year-old Henry, arriving at Devizes in the spring of 1149, then dutifully restored the outlying properties to the bishop, but explained that he needed to hold on to the castle for just a little longer, until God had brought victory to his cause. Between them, they had smoothly managed to pacify the Church, while leaving their troops undisturbed behind the walls of the bishop's castle.

By the end of that year Henry had been knighted at the northern outpost of Carlisle by his great-uncle David, King of Scots, a solemn moment which publicly signalled his emergence into adulthood. He had also demonstrated his developing credentials as a military leader not only by seizing the harbour of Bridport on the south coast, but, more important, by evading Stephen's best attempts to capture him. And, on his return to Normandy at the beginning of 1150, Henry's father, Geoffroi, true to his word, handed over the government of the duchy into the hands of its new young duke.

Stephen now found himself in unfamiliar and deeply unnerving territory. He had succeeded for years in defending his crown against a rival whose claim raised as many questions as it answered, simply because she was female. Whatever arguments Matilda might make on the grounds of hereditary right or broken oaths of fealty, Stephen had on his side the fact of his kingship, a role which—as had become clear at the gates of London in 1141—she could not hope to inhabit in any straightforward way. That fact, however, offered Stephen little defence against the charismatic new Duke of Normandy, his revered grandfather's namesake and every inch his heir. Meanwhile, Stephen himself could no longer lean on the mighty weight of the Church, which had done so much to underpin his acceptance as king; and the magnates, too, on both sides of the partisan divide, increasingly saw in Henry the only hope of reuniting the dismembered Anglo-Norman realm.

Stephen's powerlessness was now exposed with merciless clarity. A king who had won his throne by taking his chances without fear or hesitation suddenly found that he had no more moments left to seize. He could not force Henry onto the battlefield, because his nobles did not want to fight. The earls of Chester and Leicester, the former in Henry's camp and the latter in Stephen's, went so far as to sign a private treaty of mutual protection: if they were forced to go to war against each other, they declared, they would lead no more than twenty knights into battle, and any property each captured from the other would be returned. They were not alone in seeking an insurance policy of this kind; and the *Gesta Stephani* reported that, when Henry returned to England in 1153, Stephen found to his despair that a number of the magnates in his camp "had already sent envoys by stealth and made a compact with the duke." The *Gesta*'s author had, of course, come to exactly the same political conclusion himself: he describes Stephen (who is clearly by this point no longer the hero of the narrative that bears his name) as "gloomy and depressed" in the face of this betrayal, before recounting with breathless admiration how Henry "attacked the king's party with determination and spirit everywhere ... Nor did he fail of splendid success, rather did it come to him more abundantly the more eagerly he strove for loftier aims."

Henry was twenty years old, already a proven leader, who had spent the last three years consolidating his hold on Normandy, and on Anjou, too, after the sudden death in 1151 of his father, Geoffroi, at the age of just thirty-eight. Remarkably, he had succeeded in doing so despite incurring the wrath of Louis VII of France. The pope's mentor, Bernard of Clairvaux, Stephen's implacable enemy, had prevailed upon the French king to recognise Henry as Duke of Normandy in the summer of 1151; but this uneasy alliance was shattered in May 1152, when Henry shocked Europe by marrying the king's newly divorced wife, Eleanor of Aquitaine. Louis was incensed by this provocation, and declared war on Normandy, only for his troops to be beaten back with humiliatingly imperious ease by Henry's forces. When Henry set foot on the English coast in January 1153, he did so, therefore, as master of lands in France which stretched, thanks to his new wife's duchy of Aquitaine, all the way from Dieppe in the north to the Pyrenees in the south.

Stephen, at last, had no choice but to confront the reality of Henry's triumph. He was past sixty; his indomitable wife, Mathilde, on whom he had relied so heavily, had died in the spring of 1152; his son Eustace could find no support from the Church or among the Anglo-Norman lords; and his nobles, disillusioned by the conflict and desperate to defend their own interests in a war-ravaged land, were in no mood to take up arms yet again on his behalf. He could no longer hold out against a settlement that had become both necessary and irresistible. If the king clung to any hope that God might still vindicate his possession of the crown as a dynastic rather than a personal right, it was crushed in August 1153 when twenty-four-year-old Eustace died suddenly, only a few weeks after withdrawing from his father's court in furious protest at his own imminent disinheritance. Stephen had a second son, William; but even the grieving king himself now realised that any attempt to advance William's claim in his brother's place would be doomed to abject failure.

The painstaking diplomacy that brought Stephen and Henry to the conference table was conducted by Archbishop Theobald of Canterbury and the king's brother Henry, Bishop of Winchester. Superficially, they were an odd couple—the archbishop was a man of low-key subtlety, while the bishop wore his ego on his richly embroidered sleeve—but they were both skilful politicians, and both now convinced of the desperate need for a permanent peace. The treaty they drafted was formally ratified on November 6, 1153, when Stephen and Henry came face to face—weary resignation meeting restless self-assurance—at Winchester, the ancient city where Stephen had first become king eighteen years earlier. There, surrounded by the lords and bishops of England and Normandy, Stephen recognised Matilda's son as the lawful heir to his kingdom; and in return Henry "generously conceded," a Norman chronicler wrote, "that the king should hold the kingdom for the rest of his life, if he wished." In order to cement this accommodation between Stephen's de facto kingship and Henry's hereditary right, and to smooth over the apparent contradictions between the two, Stephen then "adopted"

Henry, solemnly swearing to maintain him "as my son and heir in all things."

The war was over, and the cause for which Matilda had fought so hard was won. The cost of that victory was her own eclipse. The author of the *Gesta Stephani*, ever hostile, seized on the opportunity to write her out of his story completely, while the charter enacting the terms of the treaty mentioned her only in passing as "the mother of the duke," who, along with Henry's wife and his younger brothers, had committed themselves to observe its terms. It would be less than a year, however, before Matilda reaped the reward of this self-denial. Stephen had spent the summer of 1154 on progress in the north, masking the destruction of all his hopes in the trappings of royal splendour. But on October 25, after conducting a meeting with the Count of Flanders, the king "was suddenly seized with a violent pain in his gut, accompanied by a flow of blood." It had happened before; but this time he could not be saved. He died later that night—if not a broken man, then one reduced to a shadow of himself. He was buried, as he had wished, at his own foundation of Faversham Abbey in Kent, next to the new graves of his steadfast wife and his ill-fated son.

The death of an enemy who was also a cousin, and a generous man as well as an unremitting opponent, could hardly be a cause for unalloyed jubilation. Matilda's triumph lay elsewhere: in the fact that, for the very first time since the Conquest, the accession of a new king did not take the form of a race for the coronation chair. Henry was in Normandy when news came of Stephen's death, and he remained there until December 7, putting his affairs in order and waiting for favourable winds, before he set sail for his new kingdom. For six long weeks England patiently awaited his arrival, with no sign of conflict or resistance: "by God's protecting grace she did not lack peace," Henry of Huntingdon incisively observed, "through either love or fear of the king who was on his way." And then, on December 19, 1154—almost exactly nineteen years since Henry I had breathed his last—Henry II was crowned in majesty at Westminster Abbey. After two decades of bitter conflict, the competing imperatives of hereditary right, divine sanction, and political pragmatism were united at last in Matilda's son, now the undisputed successor to her father's throne.

Matilda herself observed these dramatic events from a distance. She had settled her household at Rouen—"a fair city set among murmuring streams and smiling meadows," Orderic Vitalis had called it—in a residence her father had built on the south side of the Seine amid the green of his park at Quevilly, beside the priory of Notre-Dame-du-Pré, an offshoot of her beloved abbey of Bec. Here she established a routine reminiscent of the life led by her mother, Edith-Matilda, at Westminster. Matilda was in Normandy, not in England, and the king was her son, not her husband; but, like Edith-Matilda before her, she acted as counsellor, confidante, and royal deputy when Henry was absent, as he often was, on his constant travels around his vast dominions. Like her mother, she became increasingly preoccupied with spiritual concerns, under the guidance of the monks alongside whom she lived; but she did not retreat from the world. Her son's trust in her judgement, and the authority she exercised on his behalf, are unmistakable: "If you do not do this," declared one royal mandate dispatched from England to the justices of Normandy in the later 1150s, "let my lady and mother the empress see that it is done."

The surviving sources give us only a few glimpses of her influence at work in her son's government, but it was there nonetheless. In the autumn of 1155, less than a year after his accession, Henry was contemplating an attempt to conquer Ireland, a territory he intended to bestow on his younger brother William; but the overambitious plan was shelved, according to the Norman chronicler Robert of Torigni, when Matilda made clear that she was not convinced of its merits. However daring and impulsive the new king might be, he recognised his mother's acumen and the wisdom of listening to her words of caution. Walter Map, a writer who knew Henry's court well, thought Matilda's advice ill-founded and deleterious, but the specific examples he cites serve only to reinforce the impression of tough lessons

learnt by an incisive political brain, rather than his own more scath-
ing assessment. "I have heard that his mother's teaching was to this
effect," Map wrote, "that he should spin out the affairs of everyone,
hold long in his own hand all posts that fell in, take the revenues
of them, and keep the aspirants to them hanging on in hope; and
she supported this advice by an unkind analogy: an unruly hawk, if
meat is often offered to it and then snatched away or hid, becomes
keener and more inclinably obedient and attentive. He ought also
to be much in his own chamber and little in public: he should never
confer anything on anyone at the recommendation of any person,
unless he had seen and learnt about it."

Henry was not one to hide himself away or to disguise himself
behind an inscrutable royal mask: his life was lived in full view of his
court and at breakneck speed. Nor, perhaps, was the capricious withholding of rewards necessarily the best way to inculcate unshakeable
loyalty—understandable though an obsession with control might be
for a woman who had never enjoyed unquestioned command. But
Matilda's insistence on the vital importance of personal knowledge
and personal experience was recognisable at the heart of Henry's
rule. The tireless energy of his government was founded on his sharp
intelligence and his extraordinary recall of facts and faces; "he had at
his fingertips an almost complete knowledge of history, and a great
store of practical wisdom," noted his chaplain, Gerald of Wales.

And the king also knew the value of his mother's experience,
which came to the fore in 1157 during negotiations with the Holy
Roman Emperor, Friedrich Barbarossa, over the fate of the mummified hand of St. James, brought from Germany to England thirty-
two years earlier by Matilda herself. The emperor insisted that this
sacred relic should now be restored to the imperial treasury, while
Henry was equally determined that it should remain as the focus of a
developing cult at Reading Abbey, his royal grandfather's foundation
and final resting place. The result was a tense exchange of elaborate
diplomatic courtesies, at the end of which the hand remained safely
untouched within its jewelled reliquary at Reading while Friedrich

received instead a dazzling array of mollifying gifts, including not only four great falcons but a vast tent of extraordinary workmanship, so huge that a mechanism was required to raise it. There is no direct evidence to put Matilda's role in this delicate diplomacy beyond doubt; but it is impossible to imagine that her long-ago experience of crossing the Alps with the German court was not brought to bear on the selection of a gift which combined exquisite luxury with such practical good sense. The emperor spent the next four years on campaign in Italy, just as Matilda and her first husband had done before him; and an awestruck visitor to his camp outside Milan remarked admiringly on the lavish imperial pavilion, which was big enough, he said, to stage a coronation.

Not all of Matilda's interventions were so successful. In 1156 she had to endure the bitterest of divisions among her children, when her second son, twenty-two-year-old Geoffrey, rose in rebellion against his elder brother, complaining that their father had intended him to rule Anjou if Henry succeeded to the throne of England. Matilda presided over a strained family conference that gathered at Rouen in February, but Henry was immovable, and Geoffrey withdrew to prepare for war. He could not resist his brother's might for long, however; it took less than six months under siege at his castles of Chinon, Mirebeau, and Loudun, just south of the Loire River between Angers and Tours, before he was forced to cede his claim to Anjou and settle for an annuity in lieu of the power to which he had aspired.

There is no sign that Matilda held any brief for her younger son's demands; she had fought too long and too hard for Henry's inheritance to see it put at risk in his moment of triumph. But she cannot have relished the fragmentation of her family, nor the subsequent and unexpected loss of her two younger children: Geoffrey died, disappointed and humiliated, in 1158, and William at her side in Rouen six years later. By then Matilda, at sixty-two, was no longer the political force she had once been. She had been seriously ill in 1160; and, though she recovered, her influence with Henry began to falter after 1162, when she counselled fruitlessly against the appointment of his close friend Thomas Becket as the new Archbishop of Canterbury. Henry would have plenty of time to regret that he did not follow her shrewd advice, but Matilda did not live to see the volatile relationship between king and archbishop reach its violent end. As late as the summer of 1167 she was still playing her now-accustomed role as elder stateswoman, writing to Louis VII of France in the attempt to defuse escalating hostilities between him and her son. As she had hoped, a truce was agreed in August, and Henry immediately availed himself of the opportunity to launch an invasion of the independent duchy of Brittany. It was only a matter of weeks, however, before he was racing back to Normandy, recalled by the devastating news of his mother's death.

Matilda died on September 10, 1167, surrounded by the devoted monks of Bec who had become her spiritual family. She was buried in their midst, her body sewn into an ox-hide and laid to rest before the high altar in the abbey church, her tomb bathed in light from a magnificent seven-branched candlestick and a halo of lamps above. Her deep faith was reflected not only in the luminous ceremonial of her funeral rites, but in the priceless treasures she bestowed on the abbey. She had already given into the monks' keeping the two crowns of solid gold she had brought from Germany (the heavier of which, supported by its silver rods, her son had worn at his coronation), as well as portable altars of marble and silver, precious relics housed in an ebony chest, rich plate and vestments, and her own imperial cloak, spangled with gold. Now she left them the contents of her private chapel: ornaments of gold and silver, chasubles and copes, and two silver boxes in the shape of eggs gripped in a griffin's claws.

They were the glittering traces of an extraordinary life; six decades that had taken her from the quiet of an English childhood across Europe and back again, from the brutality of civil war to the tranquillity of Bec's echoing cloisters. And it was a life lived by a remarkable woman. Matilda inherited her father's commanding temperament, his ability to inspire loyalty, and his political intelligence—but the role she played and the qualities she possessed have been much obscured, then and now, by the preconceptions of the lords she sought to lead and the clerics who wrote her story. "Haughty" and "intolerably proud" are the adjectives indelibly associated with her name, phrases coined in those few months of her life when she tried to exercise power as a monarch in her own right, and repeated by historians ever since. Strikingly, they were never used to describe any male member of her fearsomely domineering family; and they do not fit well with what we know of Matilda in the decades before and after that brief moment in 1141. Certainly, her demeanour was unflinchingly regal, and she was driven by a resolute belief in her own capacity to rule, but in the end the defining stamp of her political career was her acutely judged pragmatism in securing the succession of her son at the expense of her own claim to the crown.

The implications of that decision are clear in the Latin verses later inscribed on her grave: "Great by birth, greater by marriage, greatest in her offspring, here lies the daughter, wife, and mother of Henry." Her son's triumph was the vindication of everything she had done; but the price to be paid for that victory was her disappearance between the lines of her own epitaph—a tacit acceptance that a female heir to England's throne, unlike her male counterpart, could not expect to rule for herself. The question would not arise again for four hundred years, until the agonising death of a fragile boy in 1553; and in the meantime any woman who aspired to the exercise of power in England—most immediately Matilda's formidable daughter-in-law, Eleanor of Aquitaine—could hope to achieve it only by negotiating the roles of daughter, wife, and mother that, etched into Matilda's tomb, came to define her career in retrospect.

But, if Matilda's last resting place framed her achievements only in relation to her father, husband, and son, one of those men was unwilling to do the same. Her son would become one of the most exceptional rulers in medieval Europe; and throughout his turbulent life, this volatile, powerful monarch acknowledged the political legacy of his courageous and controversial mother by calling himself "Henry FitzEmpress."

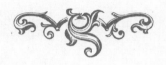

PART III

ELEANOR

An Incomparable Woman

1124–1204

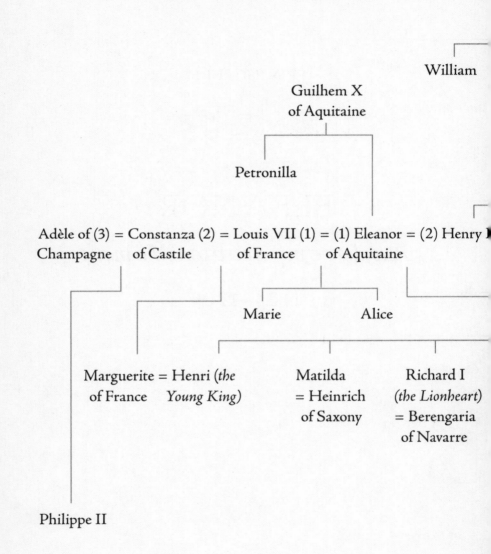

William

Guilhem X
of Aquitaine

Petronilla

Adèle of (3) = Constanza (2) = Louis VII (1) = (1) Eleanor = (2) Henry]
Champagne   of Castile   of France   of Aquitaine

Marie   Alice

Marguerite = Henri (*the*   Matilda   Richard I
of France   *Young King*)   = Heinrich   (*the Lionheart*)
                                   of Saxony   = Berengaria
                                                    of Navarre

Philippe II

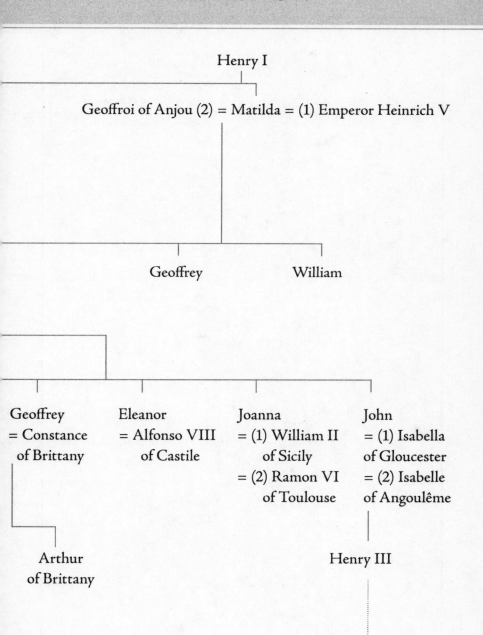

Henry I

Geoffroi of Anjou (2) = Matilda = (1) Emperor Heinrich V

Geoffrey   William

Geoffrey
= Constance
of Brittany

Eleanor
= Alfonso VIII
of Castile

Joanna
= (1) William II
of Sicily
= (2) Ramon VI
of Toulouse

John
= (1) Isabella
of Gloucester
= (2) Isabelle
of Angoulême

Arthur
of Brittany

Henry III

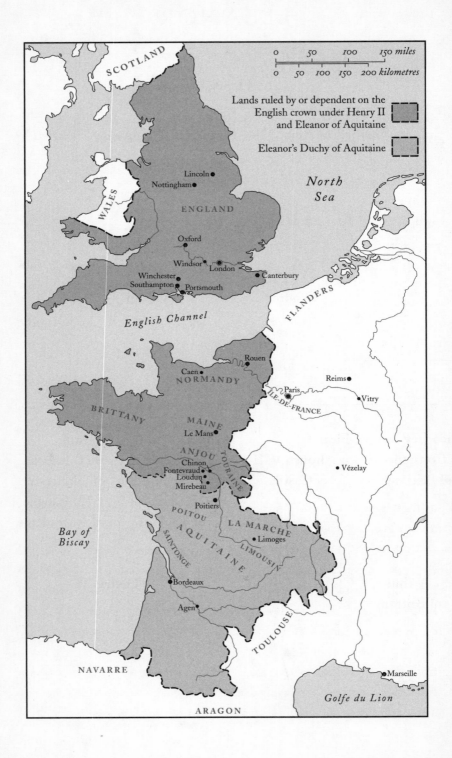

SCOTLAND

0   50   100   150 *miles*
0   50   100   150   200 *kilometres*

Lands ruled by or dependent on the
English crown under Henry II
and Eleanor of Aquitaine

Eleanor's Duchy of Aquitaine

Lincoln •
Nottingham •

*North
Sea*

WALES

ENGLAND

Oxford •
Windsor • • London
Winchester •
Southampton • • Canterbury
• Portsmouth

FLANDERS

English Channel

Rouen •

Caen •
NORMANDY

Paris •
ÎLE-DE-FRANCE

Reims •
• Vitry

BRITTANY

MAINE
Le Mans •

ANJOU
Chinon •
Fontevraud •
Loudun •
Mirebeau •

TOURAINE

• Vézelay

• Poitiers

POITOU

AQUITAINE

LA MARCHE

LIMOUSIN
• Limoges

*Bay of
Biscay*

SAINTONGE

• Bordeaux

• Agen

TOULOUSE

NAVARRE

• Marseille

Golfe du Lion

ARAGON

SEVEN

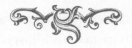

An Incomparable Woman

A casual observer at Henry II's court in September 1166 might have been forgiven for thinking that Eleanor of Aquitaine was the most conventional of queens. A great heiress, famed for her beauty and her agile mind, she had brought her royal husband a rich inheritance that stretched from the green valleys of the Vienne River, where soft light danced on stately water as it flowed toward the Loire, to the foothills of the Pyrenees, where a stronger sun struck towering crags of granite and limestone.

And, along with the landscape and liegemen of her vast duchy of Aquitaine, Eleanor had given her husband a large brood of heirs to inherit his growing empire. Seven months pregnant now with the king's eighth child, she had played to perfection the role of dutiful consort, spending enough time with her husband to ensure a succession of pregnancies—she gave birth five times in the first six years of their marriage alone—while also, so far as her repeated confinements allowed, providing a figurehead for his government in England during his long and frequent travels through his lands in France.

If her role as royal wife and mother was utterly conventional, so, too, is the fact that the chroniclers recorded no pen-portrait of Eleanor to match their detailed descriptions of her husband and king. Henry exerted a particular fascination on the men who recorded the events of his reign. In part at least, this is because a significant number of the contemporary writers whose works have survived—Walter Map, Gerald of Wales, Herbert of Bosham, Roger of Howden, and Peter of Blois—served in one capacity or another as clerks at his court, and therefore observed his charisma, his idiosyncrasies, and his extraordinary capabilities at close range. It remains clear, however, that the sheer magnetic force of his personality reached far beyond the confines of his household.

He had inherited the sturdy physicality of his royal grandfather and namesake, Henry I: he was neither tall nor unusually short, but broad and stockily muscular, thick-necked and square-chested. The solidity of his powerful frame blurred easily into fat, which he held at bay not only by the frugality with which he ate and drank, but also by virtue of the relentless energy that had been so marked in his grandfather, a quality which, in the younger man, became an almost pathological restlessness. He was a "human chariot dragging all after him," wrote Herbert of Bosham, a cultured dandy whose personal style had little in common with that of his strenuous king. On his frequent military campaigns Henry scarcely paused to eat or sleep, his bowed legs and hoarse voice testifying to the hours he spent in the saddle. But times of truce did not bring peace to his household. Instead, he rose before dawn to satisfy his compulsive obsession with hunting, returning dusty and blood-smeared from the kill to spend his evenings still on his feet, reducing his courtiers—who were not permitted to sit while their king remained standing—to a state of exasperated exhaustion.

His leonine colouring—red-gold hair and ruddy, freckled face, offset by expressive blue-grey eyes—was a legacy from his Angevin father, although he did not share the physical beauty for which Geoffroi had been celebrated in his youth. Henry's bulk, his closely shorn hair and his plain, practical clothes, gave him a physical appeal that derived from his commanding vitality rather than any more obvious glamour. He was driven and ambitious, like his father; but his quick, scholarly mind seems more likely to have come from his remarkable mother, Matilda. Like her, this man of tireless action was entirely at home among intellectuals and academics. "...with the King of England," wrote Peter of Blois, "it is school every day, constant conversation with the best scholars and discussion of intellectual problems." He read voraciously, his memory was prodigious, and, though he expressed himself only in French and Latin, he knew something, Walter Map reported, of "all tongues spoken from the coast of France to the river Jordan."

However, where Matilda's public life was shaped by her self-control and carefully considered pragmatism, Henry was passionately emotional, a character of extremes and contradictions. He was unpretentious, patient, and approachable, and possessed of unearthly calm in the face of crisis, yet capable of the most violent fits of rage. Court gossip (reported in 1166 to Archbishop Thomas Becket, once the king's closest friend, now estranged and in exile) described one outburst of ferocious temper that left Henry screaming on the floor, thrashing wildly and tearing at the straw stuffing of his mattress with his teeth. He loathed betrayal in others, but was notorious for his willingness to break his own word without a second thought. He could be fierce or gentle, harsh or generous; and he contrived (without apparent contrivance) to be simultaneously an immovable object and an irresistible force.

The first hint that our observer of Henry's court might get that Eleanor of Aquitaine was no conventional queen was the fact that she was a match, in personal as well as political terms, for this overwhelming, brilliant, bloody-minded king. Before she ever took her place at Henry's side, she had had another life full of incident and experience. And the eventful prehistory of England's queen was more than enough to show that the serene, swollen-bellied madonna of the autumn of 1166 was only one persona among many in the repertoire of an exceptional, unpredictable woman.

Eleanor was born probably in 1124, the first daughter of Guilhem, heir to the great duchy of Aquitaine. The court over which her family presided was dramatically different in style from the sober piety of the Anglo-Norman and German royal households in which Matilda had spent her childhood. At its head was Eleanor's grandfather, Duke Guilhem IX, crusader, womaniser, and poet of love and lust—the first of the troubadours, writing in Aquitaine's native *langue d'oc*, whose verses have survived. William of Malmesbury, hundreds of miles away in England, recounted scandalous rumours of the duke's provocative exploits and his sardonic wit: he ordered that his mistress's portrait should be painted on his shield, William reported with some relish, declaring that "it was his will to bear her in battle as she had borne him in bed."

Such tales probably had their roots in garbled elaborations of Duke Guilhem's songs, fiction turning into breathlessly reported fact as it travelled northward. But the truth needed little such embellishment. The duke's long-suffering duchess, Philippa of Toulouse, eventually left him for a religious life at Fontevraud Abbey—a new double monastery founded in 1101 by the ascetic preacher Robert d'Arbrissel, where both monks and nuns lived under the direction, unusually, of an abbess—fifty miles north of the duke's city of Poitiers. In Philippa's place at his side, Guilhem installed the woman whose notoriety had reached as far as the cloisters at Malmesbury— she of the supposed shield-portrait, the wife of the lord of nearby Châtellerault, though her name is not known—and arranged a marriage between his lover's daughter and his own eldest son.

That son and heir, who became Duke Guilhem X when his father died in 1127, was a less flamboyantly talented character, famous for his insatiable love of food rather than his poetry. He spent ten turbulent years at the helm of Aquitaine's affairs before deciding, in 1137, to invoke the spiritual support of St. James the Apostle by making a pilgrimage to his Galician shrine. (The saint's hand, thanks to Matilda, was now an object of veneration at Reading Abbey, but his body was believed to lie beneath the great granite cathedral newly built in his honour at Compostela in northwestern Spain.) If the saint responded to the duke's prayers, however, it was to secure the welfare of his soul rather than his duchy. Guilhem was already seriously ill when he arrived at Compostela, and he died there on Good Friday 1137. His body was buried before the cathedral's high altar, his pilgrimage transmuted into a permanent resting place.

His death left his children orphans. His wife, Anor of Châtellerault, had died several years earlier, along with their only son, another Guilhem. Two daughters remained: Petronilla, the younger, and her elder sister, Eleanor, who had been named after their mother—hence Aliénor, "another" (in Latin, *alia*) Anor. The girls had been left at Aquitaine's port city of Bordeaux under the distant guardianship of the French king, Louis the Fat, who was the duke's nominal overlord. When reports arrived from Spain of Duke Guilhem's death, Louis lay sick at his hunting lodge at Béthisy, northeast of Paris, exhausted by encroaching age and the physical strain of his obesity. But ill health had not compromised his instincts as a king, and he responded with alacrity to the news that the fate of Aquitaine now rested on the slender shoulders of a thirteen-year-old girl. Eleanor should marry his son, the king declared; and he immediately dispatched the prospective bridegroom, seventeen-year-old Louis, to Bordeaux with an imposing retinue which included the greatest noblemen in France as well as the king's chief minister, Abbot Suger of Saint-Denis, and hundreds of well-armed knights.

It was an abrupt and forceful courtship, but the political imperatives that lay behind it were too compelling to be ignored. For 150 years, it had been the ambition of the Capetian kings to turn their theoretical sovereignty over the great feudal lords of France—the dukes of Aquitaine prominent among them—into the reality of power. But old freedoms could not be so easily curtailed; and, despite three decades of King Louis's shrewd and commanding rule, the area under the crown's direct control remained limited to the Île-de-France, the "island" around Paris bounded by the rivers Seine, Marne, Oise, and Beuvronne. Now, however, marriage vows rather than military force promised to deliver Aquitaine into royal hands. And, for Eleanor and those who advised her, the prospect of a husband who would be King of France as well as Duke of Aquitaine offered protection for her rights as the duchy's heir, rights which would otherwise be rendered acutely vulnerable by her youth and her sex.

And so, just three months after her father's death, Eleanor married Louis, the heir to the French throne, in Bordeaux's magnificent cathedral. In accordance with Capetian custom, her young husband had already been crowned king at Reims six years earlier (by Pope Innocent II, no less, for whom the French court was temporarily providing refuge from the challenge of a schismatic rival in Rome). This consecration in childhood was designed to safeguard the prince's right to succeed his father; and it was therefore for the second time that Louis was crowned alongside his bride in Bordeaux, in the course of a specially devised coronation ceremony which emphasised that the people of Aquitaine were now numbered among the subjects of the French king. Only days later, Eleanor became queen in fact as well as in name. Louis the Fat died on August 1, 1137—killed by an attack of dysentery in the intense heat of an oppressive summer—and on August 8 the young Louis VII and his new wife were crowned yet again, definitively this time, amid cheering crowds in Eleanor's city of Poitiers.

The repeated coronations were intended, in part, to counteract the fact that the young man Eleanor had married had not been born to be king. Louis the Fat's namesake and successor was his second son, who had been destined from an early age for a life in the Church. But in 1131 the boy's elder brother, Philippe—a fifteen-year-old whose response to his own coronation-in-advance had been to defy his father with adolescent arrogance—tripped over a stray pig while riding through a Parisian street. The sudden, catastrophic fall of horse and rider left the young man bloodied and broken, in a coma from which he did not recover. He was buried in the abbey church of Saint-Denis, the Parisian necropolis of the French monarchy; and it was from the cloisters of Saint-Denis that eleven-year-old Louis emerged, wide-eyed, to find his future transformed.

His gaze was scarcely less innocent at seventeen, when he acquired his queen and his kingdom at almost exactly the same time. According to later gossip, Eleanor would one day remark that her husband was more monk than king—a judgement that captures Louis's assiduous piety, and a certain unworldliness that remained from his years in the cloisters, but conveys little of his enthusiasm for either his bride or the business of ruling. Possession of Eleanor's vast domains gave Louis more hope than any of his predecessors had of extending his authority across the length and breadth of France, and soon he set about pressing her claim, inherited from her grandmother Philippa, to the *comté* of Toulouse beyond Aquitaine's southeastern borders. He was also, by all accounts, besotted with his wife, offering her an infatuated, puppyish devotion.

Eleanor herself was much less impressed. From the start, this union between a boy raised by monks (even monks under the acute eye of Abbot Suger) and the granddaughter of a licentious troubadour was not a meeting of minds. We have only scraps of information with which to piece together the royal couple's relationship, but the overwhelming impression is that the young queen had worldly, sophisticated tastes, a sharp wit, and an appreciation of the subtle ambiguities of politics, while her gauche husband conducted himself with an awkward combination of self-denying religiosity and judgmental inflexibility. Certainly, too, Eleanor in Paris was a stranger in a strange land: not as obviously and manifestly far from home as eight-year-old Matilda had been in Germany, but nevertheless an orphaned teenager housed within a forbidding fortress in a crowded, jostling city whose inhabitants spoke with the unfamiliarly rounded tones of the *langue d'oïl*, the language of the French north, rather than in the hybrid frontier dialect of Poitou or with the lively musicality of Occitan itself.

Of course, this cultural isolation was the eternal condition of a royal bride, transported miles from her homeland as the incarnation of an alliance or treaty, a weaver of peace or a conduit of power. But the knowledge that Eleanor was not alone in her fate offered little in the way of comfort. The contrast in style between north and south in France was all too apparent forty years later to the troubadour Bertran de Born, lord of Hautefort in the Limousin, who professed himself unimpressed by his stay at the English king's court in Normandy: "a court where no one laughs or jokes is never complete; a court without gifts is just a paddock-full of barons. And the boredom and vulgarity of Argentan nearly killed me...." Paris was not Argentan, but neither was it Poitiers or Bordeaux. And if Eleanor felt any of the alienation expressed in her countryman's song, it can only have been compounded by the effects of her failure to perform the eternal function of a royal bride: the provision of a male heir to safeguard the succession of the dynasty into which she had married.

However much the fault lay at Louis's door—and the suspicion was that the monkish king was not a frequent visitor to his wife's bed—the blame, in contemporary eyes, rested only with the queen. By 1144, after seven years of marriage, it is possible that Eleanor had had one miscarriage, but it is certain that she had produced no living heir. She was not a woman to be cowed by unhappy circumstance, and her position was protected from serious threat by Louis's devotion, by her youth, and by the power of the lands she brought to the French crown. But something of her frustration, as well as her fiery temperament, may be apparent in her fraught relationship with some of her husband's closest advisers. One in particular, a eunuch named Thierry Galeran, she hated so much (according to John of Salisbury, the future Bishop of Chartres who was then a student in Paris) that she subjected him to relentless mockery and ridicule.

At least Eleanor had the support of her sister, Petronilla, a companion who shared her language, her culture, and her memories of their former life in Aquitaine. But Petronilla's presence at her side precipitated the most horrifying incident of Louis's kingship, one that cast a long shadow, and set in motion a chain of events that would ultimately lead Eleanor away from Paris forever. It began in 1142, when a husband was found for Petronilla from among the great noblemen of France. The king's cousin Raoul, Count of Vermandois, forty and one-eyed, was a champion of the French crown, his battle-damaged sight a badge of the devoted service he had given Louis's father. He was the perfect political match for the queen's sister in every way but one: he was already married. That, it seemed, was a minor inconvenience, and his wife of twenty years, Éléonore of Champagne, was rapidly put aside.

But the repudiated countess had two brothers, who might not be content to see her so publicly humiliated. One, Stephen, was otherwise engaged across the Channel in the battle to retain his hold on the English crown; but the other, Thibaud of Blois and Champagne, was one of the most powerful magnates in France, who had ridden alongside Raoul of Vermandois in the young king's retinue on the road to Bordeaux to meet his queen five years earlier. Raoul's matrimonial rearrangements now set him on a collision course with his former brother-in-law; and massing ominously in support of the insulted Thibaud was the collective might of the Church. Despite his ostentatious piety, King Louis, like many another monarch, had already clashed with the pope over the vexed question of the right to elect and invest bishops. Now—in spite of the fact that three tame French bishops had been found to annul Raoul's first wedding and sanction his second—Pope Innocent II decided to act to defend the sacrament of marriage from the vagaries of royal whim and political convenience. By the end of 1142, both Louis and his cousin Raoul had been excommunicated and their lands placed under interdict, and Innocent had witheringly denounced the young king as "a boy in need of instruction."

For Louis, the need to demonstrate that he was no longer the child whom Innocent had crowned at Reims won out over religious obedience or political judgement. He blamed Count Thibaud for the reverses he had suffered, and in January 1143 he marched into

Champagne at the head of an army, determined to bring his vassal to heel. At Vitry, a poorly defended town a hundred miles east of Paris, the king watched with grim satisfaction as the inhabitants fled in terror before the onslaught of his troops. Thirteen hundred men, women, and children barricaded themselves into their church while their homes were torched around them. And then, as they prayed desperately for salvation, the flames spread to the roof timbers of their sanctuary. Before Louis's gaze, the building was engulfed. Amid unbearable heat and the deafening uproar of fire and falling masonry, the air filled with acrid smoke and the nauseating, cloying stench of burning flesh. From the holocaust of Vitry, no one emerged alive.

It was a massacre of innocents, and visceral in its horror. Even this, however, could not immediately check Louis's obstinacy, and his army continued its advance across Thibaud's lands. But the conflagration did plant seeds of doubt in the king's mind about the justice of his cause, uncertainty that was rapidly compounded by the strictures of Bernard of Clairvaux, the most venerated and uncompromising of Europe's spiritual leaders. At fifty-two, Bernard's influence was felt far beyond the walls of the abbey he had founded in a densely wooded valley only fifty miles from Vitry. His example was the driving force behind the rapid spread of the new Cistercian order, an austere re-imagining of the Benedictine rule, which Bernard embraced with such single-minded asceticism from his tiny cell in the angle of the roof at Clairvaux that he pushed himself to the brink of his physical endurance, existing on the barest minimum of food and sleep. But from his gaunt frame issued a voice that thundered across Europe.

His spiritual standing was such that in 1130, when Innocent II was driven into French exile after the contested election of a rival pope, Louis the Fat had given the arbitration of Innocent's claims to the Holy See into Bernard's hands. The stern judgement of the Abbot of Clairvaux not only decided French support for Innocent but, as he travelled indefatigably on a scrawny donkey at the pope's side, secured the backing of Germany, Spain, and England for Innocent's eventual restoration to Rome. Now neither rank nor birth, wealth nor power, offered a shield against Abbot Bernard's critical gaze. Kings and bishops, noblewomen and nuns—all could be judged and found wanting, the cure for their errors contained in excoriating letters dispatched from a pen that scarcely seemed to rest.

Abbot Suger, the king's greatest confidant and counsellor, had felt compelled to lay aside the luxurious trappings of power, adopting a simple woollen habit and taking up residence in a single small room in Saint-Denis's cloister, after a rebuke from Abbot Bernard some years earlier. After Vitry, it was Louis's turn to feel the stinging lash of Bernard's tongue. "... from whom but the devil can I say that this counsel comes which adds fire to fire and slaughter to slaughter; which lifts the cry of the poor, the groaning of captives, the blood of the slain to the ears of the Father of the fatherless and the Judge of widows?" The abbot, as always, spoke with the assurance of absolute spiritual certainty, and he left the king in no doubt of the reckoning he faced: "... provoked by the constant excesses you commit almost daily, I am beginning to regret having stupidly favoured your youth more than I should have done, and I am determined that in future, to the best of my limited ability, I will expose the whole truth about you.... I speak harshly, because I fear harsher things for you."

Louis had no matching certainty of his own, and he crumbled before the abbot's assault. By 1144 the king had collapsed into a state of wretched penitence, and was ready to make terms with both the pope and Count Thibaud. The royal army withdrew from Champagne, and the interdict was lifted. Meanwhile, Abbot Suger saw an opportunity to cement this fragile peace in the ceremony to consecrate the extraordinary new choir he had built for the basilica at Saint-Denis, a breathtaking confection of soaring arches and gorgeously coloured light. Abbot Bernard, for his part, deplored lavish ornament in church architecture, as in everything else: a misuse of earthly riches, he said, that could better be used to succour the poor, and a worldly distraction from the contemplative inwardness of the soul's quest for God. But, in that at least, he had not persuaded

Abbot Suger to follow him. For Suger, the overwhelming beauty of his building was a path to grace, a radiant, transcendent space that gave earth-mired sinners a glimpse of heaven.

On June 11, 1144, therefore, a uniquely powerful congregation of sinners passed through the gilded bronze doors of Suger's church to see the bones of St. Denis, France's patron saint, placed in a golden shrine at the centre of the choir. King Louis was there, contrite and remorseful. Abbot Bernard had swallowed his revulsion at the opulence of his surroundings to be present in the cause of peace. And there, too, weighed down by heavily embroidered robes amid the press of the crowd, was Louis's wife, Eleanor.

It seems unlikely that Bernard was much impressed by this encounter with France's queen. He had known her father—who had been a supporter of the schismatic anti-pope in the days when Abbot Bernard was Pope Innocent's chief hope of regaining the throne of St. Peter—and had brought the duke to his knees, literally, it was said, in a confrontation at Parthenay, just west of Poitiers. It was for the sake of Eleanor's sister that Louis had watched more than a thousand souls burn at Vitry. And now here she stood, a woman—her sex in itself a source of anxiety and repugnance from the perspective of the ascetic Cistercian ideal—decked out in the kind of superficial magnificence that the abbot deplored.

But neither was Eleanor overawed by the emaciated figure dressed in the coarse white wool of the Cistercian habit. Throughout her life she would display a judicious piety, conventional in form and expression; but she was not about to bow her head to a spiritual philosophy by which she herself would be written off as an embodiment of worldly vanity. Instead, this unlikely pair recognised, each in the other, a formidable will and an imposing personality. The result was a bargain. Eleanor would do what she could to steer her husband in the ways of peace; and in return Abbot Bernard would petition the Queen of Heaven on behalf of the Queen of France, in the hope that Eleanor might conceive an heir to her husband's throne.

Heaven, it seemed, was listening to the saintly abbot, if not quite as carefully as were the crowned heads of Europe. In 1145, the year after the great and the good had gathered at Saint-Denis, Eleanor at long last gave birth for the first time. The baby was strong and healthy, and perfect in every way except for its sex: it was not the longed-for boy, but a girl, named Marie in thanks to the Virgin for this blessing bestowed, and in hope of better to come.

Meanwhile, Abbot Bernard could have no cause for complaint about Eleanor's side of their deal. By the end of 1145 Louis was not only penitent, and reconciled with the Church in France and in Rome, but committed to a greater goal even than peace itself: he planned to wage a holy war, to defend Christendom against the infidel. That summer, news had reached France that the city of Edessa had fallen to Muslim forces commanded by the emir of Aleppo, Imad ad-Din Zengi. For the Latin states of the Levant, founded half a century earlier in the wake of the victorious First Crusade, the loss of Edessa represented both a spiritual affront—the city housed the graves of the apostles Thomas and Thaddeus as well as thousands of Christian inhabitants—and a profound strategic threat.

Louis did not hesitate. At Christmas 1145, with his court gathered around him at Bourges for the annual royal ceremony of crown-wearing, he declared his intention to embark on a crusade. In the same month, the new pope, Eugenius III—the first Cistercian to be elected to the Holy See, and himself a disciple of Bernard of Clair-vaux—published a bull urging the faithful to come to the aid of Edessa and confirming the remission of sins for all who joined the campaign. Three months later, the crusade was formally launched amid extraordinary scenes at Vézelay in northern Burgundy.

Many roads led to Vézelay: lying between Paris and the great motherhouses of the Cluniac and Cistercian orders, it was one of the chief staging posts for pilgrims travelling south to Santiago de Compostela. And it was itself a place of pilgrimage, its newly rebuilt hilltop abbey dedicated to St. Mary Magdalene, the patron of penitents, whose bones, contemporaries believed, rested there in a gilded shrine. Little wonder that it seemed the perfect place for a king to begin a journey that was, in part at least, one of pilgrimage and expiation.

But even Vézelay, its church freshly extended to cope with the thronging crowds it regularly had to accommodate, had never seen anything like the gathering of Easter Sunday 1146. So many people had packed into the town that the church had to be abandoned altogether, and a makeshift stage hastily constructed on the hillside beyond. There Louis sat in state, wearing stitched to the shoulder of his mantle a crusader's cross sent especially by Pope Eugenius, who had been unable to leave Italy because of the dangerous uncertainty of Roman politics. In his place, however, the pope had dispatched the frail but luminously charismatic figure of Abbot Bernard. Amid a reverent hush, the great man spoke fervently, with indomitable energy and urgent rhetoric, exhorting the Christians of the west to help their fellows in the east.

Then it was Louis's turn to address his subjects, telling them of his "great devotion to this war," before kneeling in tears at the abbot's feet to take the cross for all to see. Behind him pressed the magnates of France, including Henri, heir to the king's old enemy Thibaud of Champagne, along with so many others that the heap of fabric crosses Bernard had brought with him to confer upon would-be crusaders was quickly exhausted, and the abbot was forced to improvise replenishments by tearing strips from his own white robe as the crowd clamoured to reach him.

It was a profoundly stirring spectacle, unprecedented in substance as well as style. The First Crusade had been a speculative, self-consciously pioneering expedition, its lordly leaders venturing into the unknown to seek new spheres of influence as well as eternal salvation. But its triumph in the face of towering odds—capturing the holy city of Jerusalem, and establishing Christian states there and further north at Tripoli, Antioch, and Edessa—meant that expectations, and the stakes that went with them, were now far higher. Never before had a crowned king undertaken to lead a crusade in person—a military campaign that would take him thousands of miles away from the lands it was his sacred duty to rule, and would keep him away for a matter of years rather than months, even supposing that he returned at all. He would spend untold sums, prised from the pockets of his subjects left behind. He would face the manifold dangers of landscape, climate, disease, and a terrifying enemy. And he would do it all, it emerged, with his wife by his side.

Eleanor, too, had sat, dressed in a crusader's robe, on the platform at Vézelay; had knelt before Abbot Bernard to receive the cross; and had pledged her vassals of Aquitaine to join the campaign. She, too, received the blessing of Pope Eugenius himself at Saint-Denis on June 11, 1147, during an elaborately staged send-off for the crusaders where the queen, almost fainting on a suffocatingly hot day, watched her husband take possession of the *oriflamme*, a banner of fire-red silk on a golden lance that hung above the abbey's altar until the king should have need of it to lead his troops in battle. And she, too, joined the French army when it assembled at Metz in the far east of France to embark on the long journey across Europe to rendezvous with the crusading forces of the German king, Conrad III, in Asia Minor.

The presence of the French queen and her attendants alongside the soldiers and the waggons full of arms was itself an indication of the confidence with which the expedition set out. Eleanor travelled in style, despite Eugenius's instruction to his crusaders to deport themselves with sober simplicity. (His papal bull forbade them to bring hawks and hounds, to employ minstrels, or to wear "multi-coloured clothes or minivers or gilded and silver arms.") But no silken pillow or upholstered saddle could disguise the fact that this was a journey beside which Matilda's wintry crossing of the Alps thirty years earlier paled into insignificance.

From Metz the French army, with the queen's elegant entourage in its midst, travelled a hundred miles northeast to Worms, where ships were waiting to ferry them all—nobles, ladies, bishops, troops, horses, arms, and baggage—across the Rhine. They moved at speed, covering between ten and twenty miles a day as they pressed on another two hundred miles eastward to the Bavarian city of Regensburg, at the northernmost bend in the Danube, where a German fleet had assembled to carry them downriver through the lands of the King of Hungary. When they reached Bulgaria, they left their boats, instead turning southward by road—and, despite being sporadically held up by the frustrating unwieldiness of their four-horse baggage-carts, they were still making good time as they entered the territories of the Byzantine Emperor, Manuel Komnenos. By October 4, they had reached Constantinople, capital of the Eastern Empire and the greatest Christian city in the world.

Relations between the Christians of west and east were far from easy, and the arrival of the French king at the head of his army, less than a month after the German king had passed by at the head of his, was hardly welcome to the emperor. Indeed, having expressed diplomatic joy at news of the crusaders' plans a year earlier, Manuel had now concluded that the security of his empire was better served by agreeing to a twelve-year truce with the Turks. But he was eager to see the French leave his capital as peacefully as they had come, and the royal couple were received with grace and extraordinary magnificence into this most brilliant of cities. Eleanor was entertained by the Empress Eirene, formerly Bertha of Sulzbach, a Bavarian noblewoman turned Byzantine consort whose pious disdain for the elaborate clothes and painted faces of court fashion contrasted sharply with the gilded intricacy of the imperial palaces and churches in which the two women met. We have no way of knowing whether queen and empress found common ground; there was, at least, a suggestion that one of Eleanor's ladies should consider taking a Greek husband. Either way, her stay was brief. Manuel made rapid arrangements for the French to cross the Bosphorus in Byzantine ships, and soon they were once again on the move, this time tracing a path around the coast of Asia Minor.

But they were about to learn that grand plans and a sense of entitlement could not guarantee the success of a military expedition on this wildly ambitious scale so far from home. The first unwelcome surprise had been the sheer expense of keeping such a vast contingent in the field, and Louis had been writing home to Abbot Suger in Paris with instructions to send more money (instructions that were far easier, of course, to dispatch than to fulfil) ever since they had reached Hungary.

Now it began to be clear that much worse was to come. Any illusion that divine sanction would guarantee the crusaders' victory, irrespective of unfamiliar terrain and hostile climate, evaporated in an instant when news arrived of the humiliating retreat of the German king's forces, who had taken a more direct but much more dangerous route across the Anatolian plateau. In that empty, arid landscape, the German crusaders had run desperately short of food and water. Starving and incapacitated by thirst, they found themselves harried on all sides by Turkish raids. The Seljuk archers moved fast, their horses fresh and strong, and let fly dense volleys of arrows with deadly accuracy before melting back into the barren hills. Under this remorseless assault, the wretched remains of Conrad's once-proud army turned tail and struggled back to the Byzantine city of Nicaea in the far northwest of Anatolia, carrying their shaken and wounded king with them.

In the circumstances, their rendezvous with the French in November 1147 was a far cry from the moment of triumph that either Louis or Conrad had anticipated. The combined forces of the crusade—the Germans nursing their wounds and the French discomfited by their allies' plight—made their way down the coastal road, struggling through fords and over mountains, to spend an unhappy Christmas at Ephesus. Conrad and his men then limped back to Constantinople, where Manuel had offered the services of his imperial doctors to nurse the injured king back to health, while Louis and his cavalcade headed onward, despite heavy falls of rain and snow.

But on the steep slopes of Mount Cadmus, the French army became dangerously overstretched. The vanguard—which included Eleanor and her ladies, and was commanded by Geoffroi de Rancon, a nobleman from the queen's county of Poitou—made the ascent with unexpected ease, and decided, without consultation, to press on to pitch camp on the plain below. In doing so, they left the forces behind them stranded on the mountainside. The footsoldiers and baggage train, who were expecting to meet them at the summit, found no one there, while the king and his bodyguard, bringing up the rear, had not yet even begun the climb. And while the baggage train hesitated, strung out on narrow rocky paths edged by fearful drops, the Turks seized their moment.

The whine of an arrow in flight was the first sign of the slaughter to come. As the Seljuks closed in, firing from all sides, terror and panic spread among the French ranks. There was nowhere to turn: death rained from the sky in a hail of Turkish steel, while men and horses stumbled and fell, their bodies breaking on the rocks below. Messengers fled to tell the king of the unfolding massacre, and Louis and his knights rode as hard as they could to the rescue. But they could not strike a decisive blow against an enemy that was hidden on the hillside all around them. All they could do—at the cost of many more lives—was to shepherd what remained of the baggage train to the safety of camp.

Recriminations began at once. Eleanor's vassal Geoffroi de Rancon was blamed for his impulsive leadership of the van, and was dismissed, to return home to Poitou. But Louis's command of his army had been exposed, in this first major military encounter, as complacent at best, and deeply flawed at worst. It was a bruised, reduced, and dispirited company that struggled onward to the port of Adalia to take ship for the Christian principality of Antioch.

We know nothing of Eleanor's experience of these alarming events. But the very fact that there is so little mention of the queen in the principal sources for this part of the crusade (which include an eyewitness account by the king's chaplain, Odo of Deuil) nevertheless suggests some plausible, if limited, conclusions. Eleanor, it seems, was physically strong. It was an arduous journey, and, whatever the privileged conditions in which the queen travelled, they could not have been enough to shield her completely from the privations of life with an army that had lost much of its equipment in raids and skirmishes and was running disastrously short of provisions. Yet there is no suggestion of urgent concern about the well-being of the queen and her ladies, nor any proposal that they—like the wounded King of Germany—should turn back to take refuge under the protection of the Byzantine Emperor at Constantinople. By the same token, it also seems reasonable to conclude that she was undaunted by the dangers she faced. And, certainly, her behaviour once she reached the haven of Antioch was anything but fearful.

It rapidly became clear, once the exhausted French contingent had landed at Antioch's port of St. Simeon on the eastern Mediterranean shore, that the crusade had wrought no greater transformation on the royal couple's marriage than it had on the king's abilities as a general. Eleanor and Louis, it appears, had spent little time together since leaving France. The queen seems to have been kept away from the king's pavilion by considerations of propriety and safety, and, in all likelihood, by Louis's determination to undertake the holy work of a crusader in the chaste condition of a pilgrim. But, after months as a camp follower, in Antioch Eleanor found herself once again a queen at the centre of a court—and one that offered attractions of beguiling familiarity.

The ruler of Antioch was Eleanor's uncle, Ramon of Poitiers, her father's younger brother, who had acquired his principality along with the hand in marriage of its ten-year-old heiress in 1136. Ramon was "the handsomest of the princes of the earth," according to the later chronicler William of Tyre—urbane and charming, and the most attentive and generous of hosts. That generosity could not, however, be mistaken for disinterested kindness. Antioch was caught between the twin threats of Muslim and Byzantine expansionism, and the crusaders' arrival seemed to offer Ramon the chance to strengthen his own hand in relation to those two looming predators. His plan was to persuade Louis to help him capture the great Muslim-held trading city of Aleppo in northern Syria, just beyond the eastern border of his principality—and he enlisted his niece, Eleanor, as an ally in his diplomatic offensive.

Louis, however, had other priorities. The crusade had originally been intended to liberate Edessa, which lay northeast of both Antioch and Aleppo. But now—almost a year and two thousand miles after he had first set out on his mission—Louis heard the devastating news that Edessa was no longer there to be saved. An Armenian-led revolt had been crushed with such vehemence by its Muslim captors that the city lay deserted, its walls in ruins. As a result, an alternative target would have to be found for a crusade that had been intended as a triumph, but threatened now to descend into farce. For Ramon of Antioch, who confidently presented his plans to the French king at a council convened for the purpose in May 1148, Aleppo was the obvious answer; but Louis declared his intention instead to ride three hundred miles south to rendezvous once more with the German king, Conrad, who was now healed of his wounds and had just arrived in the holy city of Jerusalem.

Ramon was appalled and incredulous. Having come so far, how could Louis now turn his back on the enemy he had set out to confront? And as the political relationship between Antioch and its French visitors collapsed into recrimination, so, too, did Louis and Eleanor's marriage. The young queen had revelled not only in the comforts of her handsome uncle's court, but in the charms of his company. She sympathised with his plans, and had undertaken to press his case with her husband. But the long, laughing conversations between uncle and niece—their intimacy compounded by the fact that the French struggled to understand the Poitevin or Occitan dialect in which Ramon and Eleanor could choose to speak privately—sparked scandalised whispers that the relationship had gone further than could be explained away by the politics of queenly intercession or the joy of a family reunion.

It was a dangerous moment for Eleanor. The wife of a king was the means by which his bloodline would be propagated, and, if the legitimacy of his heirs were to go unquestioned, she herself needed to be beyond reproach. But strikingly, and remarkably, Eleanor was unabashed by the currents of gossip and rumour that swirled around

Antioch and soon raced across Europe. She knew her own strength, as heiress to the vast duchy that had transformed her husband's power within his own kingdom, and she showed no fear for either her position or her reputation. There is no way of knowing, now, whether her affection for her glamorous uncle had grown into a full-blown affair—a relationship which, in the minds of shocked contemporaries, would constitute not only adultery but incest. Almost nine centuries later and with limited and partial evidence, we cannot with any confidence sift fact from speculation and innuendo. But speculation and innuendo there certainly were. And not only did Eleanor do nothing to distance herself from Ramon and his court, but when Louis declared his plans to leave Antioch for Jerusalem, she—astonishingly—refused to go with him.

It was an extraordinary public breach between France's royal couple, and an unexpected and damaging crisis for a military campaign that already seemed destined for humiliation rather than victory. There could be no possible doubt, now, of how independent-minded Eleanor was; how brave—or perhaps reckless—in the face of convention; and how unhappy she had become with her husband. And when Louis tried to insist that she remember her duty, she showed just how far she was prepared to go to escape him. "When the king made haste to tear her away," wrote John of Salisbury, a well-informed source who was then a clerk at the papal curia, "she mentioned their kinship, saying it was not lawful for them to remain together as man and wife, since they were related in the fourth and fifth degrees."

It was true that Louis and Eleanor were related within the degrees of consanguinity prohibited by the Church—that is, they shared an ancestor within their families' last seven generations. But then, so did almost everyone else within the royal and noble houses of Europe. The Church—faced with the need to choose between the extinction of the ruling classes for want of suitable marriage partners, and the prospect of turning a blind eye to the enforcement of ecclesiastical rules—had opted for the latter; and consanguinity had therefore become a prohibition to be invoked at the convenience, rather than for the discipline, of the aristocracy. Usually, it was an instrument wielded by powerful men to rid themselves of wives who were no longer politically convenient, and Eleanor had seen how useful it could be when Raoul of Vermandois had discarded Éléonore of Blois in order to marry her sister. But Eleanor also, it now appeared, saw no reason why this escape route should not be open to a troubled queen just as well as to an inconvenienced nobleman.

What Louis thought of his wife's disaffection is much less clear. "…the king was deeply moved," John of Salisbury later remarked, "and although he loved the queen almost beyond reason he consented to divorce her if his counsellors and the French nobility would allow it." There are profoundly mixed messages here: Louis, by this account, was all but immobilised by the conflicting impulses of piety, passion, and politics. And further confusion is added by the only strictly contemporaneous evidence we have. "Concerning the queen your wife," Abbot Suger wrote to Louis from Paris in 1149, "we venture to congratulate you, if we may, upon the extent to which you suppress your anger, if there be anger, until with God's will you return to your own kingdom and see to these matters and others."

If Louis was angry—and it seems, at the very least, a plausible reaction to such a dramatic affront—he did not express it publicly. What we can be sure of is that Eleanor wanted a way out of her marriage, and that her behaviour was the talk of Europe, while her husband—susceptible though he might be to suggestions that their union was sinful—did not want to let her go, whether because he loved her, because he needed her lands, or because he could ill afford the embarrassment of being deserted by his wife in the course of a crusade that was already shaping up to be a humiliating failure. And, despite her uncle's support, Eleanor was unable to hold out in the face of her husband's insistence that she stay by his side. When the French army left Antioch by night, at speed and with none of the fanfare that had greeted their arrival, the queen, however reluctantly, was with them.

The rumours that sprang from Eleanor's self-assertion in Antioch pursued her for the rest of her life. Later, sympathetic chroniclers would find themselves unable to resist alluding to the scandal with an unmistakable frisson of excitement, even as they ostentatiously drew a veil over the episode. "Many know what I would that none of us knew...," wrote Richard of Devizes forty years later. "Let no one say any more about it; I too know it well. Keep silent..."

But, while the whispers about Eleanor and her uncle persisted, silence descended instead over the queen's experiences for a year after her enforced removal from his court. The French marched south to Tripoli and then south again to Jerusalem, where Louis and his army were welcomed with cheers and the singing of hymns. A few weeks later, at the end of June 1148, a magnificent gathering of the kings and nobles of France, Germany, and Jerusalem took the decision that their thwarted crusade should now besiege Damascus, the great Muslim city almost 150 miles to the northeast; but only a month later, after a promising attack through the walled orchards that made up the city's outer defences, their combined forces were driven off by impassable blockades and the imminent prospect of starvation. Riven by argument about who was to blame for the fiasco, they trailed disconsolately home. And of the French queen's whereabouts during this damp squib of a campaign, the chroniclers recorded nothing at all.

We do know that, when Louis decided to remain in Jerusalem while his nobles made the long journey home in the autumn of 1148, Eleanor stayed with him. If he had fallen short as a crusader, he was determined that he would not fail as a pilgrim, and the king and queen made an elaborate tour of the Holy Land's most sacred sites, culminating in the celebration of the Christian calendar's holiest feast at Easter 1149. Shortly afterward, the royal couple at last set sail from the port of Acre on the kingdom of Jerusalem's Mediterranean shore.

Eleanor, it had to be said, did not make as likely a pilgrim as the monkish Louis, and she had already made it clear that she no longer welcomed his company. Whatever her mood after their long sojourn in the east, it was unlikely to have been improved by their voyage home. They took ship in two Sicilian vessels, one carrying the king and his household, the other the queen and hers. But, by taking passage as guests of one ally, Roger II, the Norman King of Sicily, they fell foul of another. Roger was engaged in protracted hostilities with the forces of Byzantium, since Emperor Manuel Komnenos saw him as the usurper of lands in southern Italy that should by rights be in Byzantine hands. And, as Eleanor gazed out from the deck of her Sicilian ship across the brilliant blue waters of the Mediterranean, a Byzantine fleet hove menacingly into view.

She had wished for a separation from her husband, but not in this frightening form. As the little Sicilian convoy scattered under the Byzantine attack, enemy ships closed round the queen's vessel to corner and capture it. Eleanor's time as a prisoner of the Greeks was brief, since rescue was close at hand in the form of Sicilian reinforcements; but by then the king's galley was far out of sight, while storms drove Eleanor's ship south toward North Africa. It was two long months before either made landfall again, Louis on the shore of Calabria in southern Italy, and Eleanor at Palermo in Sicily. There, finally, her health gave way under the strain of an already gruelling voyage compounded by the debilitating effects of isolation and uncertainty. It took three weeks before she was well enough to leave her bed and join her husband on the Italian mainland. And her convalescence can hardly have been helped by the arrival of the horrifying news that Ramon of Antioch, to whom she had said goodbye so unwillingly, had lost his life a few weeks earlier in battle with Nur ad-Din, the new ruler of Aleppo. Ramon's head was hacked from his body, his good looks finally obliterated by this butchery, and sent in a silver box as a trophy for the caliph of Baghdad.

Weary, grieving, and despondent, Eleanor made her way north at her husband's side to Tusculum, a hill town fifteen miles southeast of Rome, to accept the hospitality of the pope en route home to Paris. Eugenius III had last seen the couple in the glorious setting of Saint-

Denis, at the ceremony to launch the crusade toward inevitable and triumphant victory. Now it seemed as though their marriage, just like the crusaders' hopes, was fractured beyond repair. But the pope was determined to save this, if nothing else, from the ruins of the campaign. He issued a stern prohibition on any mention of the issue of consanguinity as a threat to the legitimacy of their marriage, confirming the validity of their union "by word and writing," and threatening anathema against anyone who sought to dissolve it. And he sweetened compulsion with encouragement, ordering that the bed prepared for Eleanor and Louis to share should be protected from the autumnal air by some of his own priceless hangings.

Louis was delighted by this papal blessing, since (John of Salisbury reported) "he loved the queen exceedingly, in an almost boyish fashion." The reaction of Eleanor—about whom there was no longer anything girlish, and whose affection for her husband had long since been exhausted—is not recorded. There could be no doubt, however, that the pope's pronouncement had closed the door on any hope that she might imminently escape her marriage. And Eleanor did not waste her energy by struggling further. It seems clear that she had resigned herself for the time being to her future in France: she became pregnant soon after their return to Paris, and gave birth in 1150 to a second daughter, Alice.

For two years thereafter, the chroniclers paid little attention to France's newly domesticised queen. While Louis threw himself into war against Duke Henry of Normandy, the seventeen-year-old son of the Empress Matilda, Eleanor remained in the background; and she stayed there when this fiery young man arrived at the French court at the end of August 1151 to confirm a peace brokered by the doughty Bernard of Clairvaux.

But only seven months after Henry's visit, Eleanor found herself again the talk of Europe when—despite the pope's prohibition—her marriage was once again dragged into the glare of public scrutiny. On March 21, 1152, having given the matter their formal consideration, an august assembly of French bishops declared that the impediment

of consanguinity rendered the marriage of their king and queen null
and void. This was the same blood relationship that Eleanor had first
raised in Antioch as a reason for separating from her husband, and
which the pope had so sweepingly dismissed in confirming the legitimacy of their relationship. Something, clearly, had changed.

Most contemporaries, and historians since, have looked for
the answer to Louis, who until now had refused to accept that he
might part from his wife, whom he loved, and who had brought him
such powerful territories as her dowry. The king, it is usually assumed, must have tired of Eleanor's coldness toward him, or suddenly become overwhelmed by doubt about her ability to bear him a
male heir. But that conclusion perhaps underestimates the strength
of the cards Eleanor held in her hand, or the way she chose to play
them. She had been forced to acquiesce in the rapprochement brokered by Pope Eugenius in 1149, but there is no mistaking that her
disenchantment with her marriage endured nonetheless. Certainly,
the bishops' pronouncement came as no surprise to her: she uttered
no word of protest at the annulment, instead riding immediately to
her own city of Poitiers, and leaving forever her two daughters, the
younger of whom was not yet two.

In fact, Alice's birth in 1150 had, in retrospect, been a lucky break
for Eleanor. Her status as the mother of girls has usually been seen
as a position of weakness; it was mothers of boys, so the assumption
goes, who could hope to assert their own power in their sons' names.
But, for Eleanor in 1152, the exact reverse was true. If she still wanted
to escape her husband—and there is no reason to suppose that papal
blandishments had done anything to change her mind—it was essential that she should not give birth to a son. If she bore Louis a boy,
then the uncontested legitimacy of the heir to the kingdom of France
would depend on the validity of his parents' marriage. Escape, at that
point, would be near-impossible (unless perhaps to a convent, which
Eleanor had so far shown no sign of finding an attractive prospect).
And, even if she could find some acceptable way of extricating herself
without casting any hint of a shadow over her offspring, any son she

had with Louis would be the heir not only to France but to Aquitaine as well—a fact that would undermine her chances of regaining control of her own duchy, as well as radically reducing her appeal to potential new suitors once she was free.

Without a son, however, Eleanor had an ace to play. Louis needed a legitimate male heir to inherit his kingdom (a necessity demonstrated only too convincingly by the bitter conflict still festering between Stephen and Matilda on the other side of the Channel). And if his wife refused him access to her bed, he stood no chance of fathering one. The odds are that this is what Eleanor did, once their enforced reunion between papal sheets was over. The king and queen were still young—thirty-two and twenty-eight, respectively—and baby Alice provided very recent proof of their fertility. But less than two years after Alice's birth, Louis was prepared to let Eleanor go, and Aquitaine with her—a huge political and territorial sacrifice that was worth making only if he saw no other way of securing the future of his dynasty.

Louis made a last-ditch attempt to cling to what he had lost, politically if not personally, by continuing to style himself "Duke of the Aquitainians" for two years after Eleanor had left. But by then, the success of Eleanor's strategy was clear for all to see, since, whatever he might call himself, her former husband no longer held any semblance of power in her lands. And it also transpired that the timing of her departure from the French court—seven months after the visit of the young Duke of Normandy—had not been entirely coincidental. No one, in March 1152, could mistake the fact that the newly divorced Duchess of Aquitaine was once again a great catch for the unmarried magnates of Europe; she had plenty of childbearing years still ahead of her, and whoever fathered her sons would add Aquitaine to his family's lands in perpetuity. A chronicler from Tours reports that Eleanor narrowly evaded two ambushes on her journey to Poitiers as a free woman, both laid by ambitious young noblemen intent on winning her hand by kidnap rather than diplomacy: one was Thibaud, the new Count of Blois after the death of his father and namesake; and the other Geoffrey of Anjou, teenage son of the Empress Matilda. But once Eleanor eluded their grasp, it emerged that her hand had already, secretly, been taken—and that the man who would become her second husband was Geoffrey's older brother, Duke Henry of Normandy, whom she had met in Paris the previous summer.

That, at least, is the most plausible conclusion to be drawn from the speed with which Eleanor and Henry married. Only eight weeks and two days after the bishops had proclaimed her divorce, Eleanor, at twenty-eight, made new vows to a nineteen-year-old whose boundless energy and charisma as a soldier and a leader marked him out, in personal terms, as the polar opposite of her first husband. Politically, though, the two men had more in common: each had stood to gain immeasurably from the addition of her lands to his own; and Henry, no less than Louis, could offer her a crown. The diadem was not yet quite in his hands in the spring of 1152, since, across the Channel in England, King Stephen still clung to the hope that his own son Eustace might succeed him. And Henry's chance to press his claim to the throne on English soil was further delayed by the need to defend his French possessions against Louis's furious reaction to the news of this provocative wedding. A French army swarmed across the Norman frontier; but Henry set in motion a counterattack that was swift, violent, and irresistible. In little more than two months, Normandy was secure. A year later, with Eustace dead and Stephen's resistance finally extinguished, Henry was formally recognised as the heir to the English throne. One more year after that, on December 19, 1154, Eleanor sat by Henry's side in Westminster Abbey as they were crowned King and Queen of England.

Eleanor had effected an extraordinary transformation. For fifteen years she had been Queen of France—a focus of personal loyalty for her Aquitainian vassals, but afforded no place in the formation of royal policy, dominated as her husband's government was by the monastic influence of Abbot Suger. Nor, on the other hand, had she fulfilled the expected role of a royal consort. In fifteen years perhaps three pregnancies had produced only two daughters, not the male heir France needed; and when she had accompanied her husband on crusade, her incautious behaviour had scandalised Europe.

Now she had a second chance to be a queen, beside a very different man, in a very different realm. And one of the most striking aspects of this transfiguration was how much it owed to Eleanor's own agency. Admittedly, Louis was following in the footsteps of his father and grandfather, who had both separated from their first wives. (His father's short-lived first marriage was annulled on the predictable grounds of consanguinity, for political reasons, it seems; his grandfather, on the other hand, repudiated the mother of his eldest son to pursue an outrageously irregular union with the wife of the then Count of Anjou, and was excommunicated for his pains.) But neither had risked losing territory on the immense scale of the duchy of Aquitaine as a result of divorce. And, crucially, it was Eleanor who had first raised questions about the validity of her marriage; Eleanor who, in all likelihood, had brought the issue to a head in 1152; and Eleanor who, before she had even left the French king's side, had found herself a new husband whose power could rival Louis's own.

She had done so with determination, fearlessness, and an utter lack of concern for the world's verdict on her conduct. After the reverses she had suffered at Antioch, she had played her hand with acuity and skill. In leaving her first husband, and marrying her second, she had decisively shifted the balance of power in France. Together, Eleanor of Aquitaine and Henry of Normandy and Anjou now ruled lands that stretched from Barfleur in the north to the Pyrenees in the south—a territorial realignment that relegated Louis in Paris to the sidelines, and helped to overwhelm Stephen's resistance to Henry's claims in England. Henry could offer his bride the prospect of a crown, but there is no doubt that she helped him to secure it for her.

While he was doing so, Eleanor immersed herself in those elements of a royal wife's role that she had so signally failed to fulfil at her first attempt. Within six months of marrying Henry she was pregnant, and in August 1153—adding insult to injury for her ex-husband—she gave birth to a son, William, a name that conveniently celebrated the dukes of Aquitaine and the Norman conqueror of England simultaneously. Within a year she had conceived again, and was heavily pregnant when she was anointed and crowned at Westminster in December 1154, two weeks after enduring a stormy Channel crossing to set foot in her new kingdom for the first time. Her second son, named Henri after his father, was born in London in February 1155. Three more babies followed in the next three years: Matilda in 1156, Richard in 1157, and Geoffrey in 1158. Thereafter the rate at which she produced more children slowed, but it did not stop altogether. Eleanor, her own namesake, was born in 1161, and Joanna in 1165; and by the autumn of 1166 she was pregnant again for what was to prove the last time.

For the first fifteen years of her second marriage, then, she was almost constantly occupied with the physically demanding business of childbearing. The royal household was well equipped with wet nurses, attendants, and tutors to wait on the royal children's every practical need; Eleanor's days were hardly consumed by the minutiae of motherhood. But repeated pregnancies, combined with her formal responsibilities as the consort of a king who never stopped moving around his vast territories, meant that she had little scope for political initiative at the highest level. She appeared at Henry's side at ceremonial gatherings of the court throughout his empire, and she embodied one facet of his authority, at the head of a government managed with increasing administrative sophistication, when he was absent on campaign with his army. But the main female influence in Henry's counsels during these years was that of his mother, the Empress Matilda, an experienced and astute presence at her home in Rouen. Eleanor, meanwhile, was absorbed in the vitally important but altogether less cerebral task of stocking the royal nursery.

All that was to change in 1167. In September of that year, Matilda died. Nine months earlier, Eleanor had given birth to her last child, a boy named John. Her years as a silent madonna were over. She was ready to step into her mother-in-law's place as a political force to be reckoned with. And Henry, like Louis before him, was about to discover that loyalty to her spouse was not the foremost of his wife's many qualities.

EIGHT

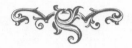

The War Without Love

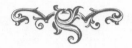n 1167 the Norman conquest of England was a century old. The wider empire of which Normandy and England were now part, on the other hand, had been in existence for less than a decade and a half. Henry had welded his disparate territories together through a characteristically overwhelming combination of brute force and sharp political judgement. He had overpowered a rebellion led by his own brother Geoffrey in Anjou, and extended his influence westward into the independent duchy of Brittany, as well as consolidating his power in England, Normandy, and Aquitaine. He had set his government in order, so that in England, for example, the chaotic aftereffects of civil war, played out in disputes over landholding and inheritance, could finally be put to rest in his law courts without the need for his constant presence. And he had gathered around himself a group of able advisers, of whom only one had proved anything less than an asset to the regime: Thomas Becket, once his closest friend, whom Henry had promoted to the see of Canterbury only to find that his new archbishop took his

duties to the Church, rather than the crown, much more seriously than the king had anticipated.

By 1167 his breach with Becket over the relative powers of ecclesiastical and royal authority had become overt and irretrievable. The archbishop had escaped into exile in France, where Louis, always delighted by any opportunity to make trouble for Henry, gave him sanctuary. But, despite this increasingly bitter and, for Henry, profoundly irritating dispute, there could be no mistaking that the King of England was now the most powerful man in western Europe. He ruled a great deal more land and commanded more men and money than his nearest rival, Louis of France. Louis had grown a little into his own authority since his desertion by his first wife and the deaths of his mentors, Abbot Suger and the venerated Bernard of Clairvaux, in the early 1150s. He had also, at last, after the births of two more daughters by his second wife, fathered a son by his third. But, as he lightheartedly remarked to Henry's clerk Walter Map, "Your lord the King of England, who lacks nothing, has men, horses, gold, silk, jewels, fruits, game and everything else. We in France have nothing but bread and wine and gaiety...." And, however much Louis's political standing had developed, the joke remained too close to the truth for French comfort.

Having so comprehensively mastered the present, Henry was now confronted with the challenge of the future. How was his empire, bound together for the moment by the sheer force of his own dynamism, to be managed when he was gone? And how was his growing family of sons to be accommodated within the territories he had amassed? Henry sought to answer both questions at once in early 1169 when he concluded a comprehensive peace treaty with Louis at the border town of Montmirail, between his own city of Le Mans and the French king's capital at Paris.

Henry's lands would be divided, he declared, between three of his sons. The eldest of Henry and Eleanor's children, William, had survived for only three years, dying in December 1156. But the rest of their large brood had proved as hardy as their unstoppable parents, and their second son, Henri, was now a strapping fourteen-year-old, tall, blond, charming, and charismatic. In the usual manner of international diplomacy, the complex pre-history of the kings of France and England and the queen who had married each of them in turn had been swept to one side when the young prince's marriage was arranged: at the age of just six, the son of Eleanor and Henry had made his vows to Marguerite, the toddler daughter of Louis of France by his second wife, Constanza of Castile. And at Montmirail, for the first time, King Henry confirmed what inheritance the now-teenage couple would one day rule. Young Henri would shoulder his father's mantle, taking over the territories that made up the king's personal inheritance—the cross-Channel realm composed of the kingdom of England, the duchy of Normandy, and the county of Anjou.

His mother's duchy of Aquitaine, meanwhile, would go to his eleven-year-old brother, Richard, who—as the junior partner in this double marriage alliance—was betrothed to Marguerite's younger sister Alix. Aquitaine would therefore retain its independence from the kingdom of England, an arrangement explicitly confirmed by the fact that Richard would do homage for his duchy to his French father-in-law, Louis, rather than to his own father or brother. And for ten-year-old Geoffrey, Henry and Eleanor's third son, there was Brittany, where the exhausted and browbeaten duke, Conan IV, finally abandoned all attempts to hold off Angevin domination. Conan's only daughter and heir, Constance, had already been betrothed to Geoffrey in yet another dynastic alliance forged in the nursery. Now it was confirmed that the young man would one day rule Brittany in the name of his wife, and that the duchy would be formally subjected to Angevin overlordship, since Geoffrey, it was agreed, would perform homage as duke to his elder brother Henri.

The territorial settlement at Montmirail left many questions unanswered—not least in making no provision for the youngest of Henry and Eleanor's sons, John, who was not yet three. There would be time enough later, it seemed, to consider the claims of the baby of the family, although the treaty meant that as he grew into boy-

hood he was already known as *Jean Sans Terre*—John Lackland—
in sympathy for his limited prospects. But the Montmirail agreement did sketch out an understanding of what share of their father's
empire each of his elder brothers should expect to rule, and a basis
on which the kings of France and England might find a way to act in
co-operative tandem rather than at destructive loggerheads.

The accord was given ceremonial confirmation at Westminster
Abbey eighteen months later, when young Henri was crowned King
of England in his father's presence—a calculated deployment of the
same stratagem of coronation-in-advance with which the French
kings had traditionally sought to guarantee their sons' succession,
and which Stephen had failed to secure for the ill-fated Eustace
before Henry himself had taken the throne. Only the fact that the
young man was anointed by the Archbishop of York rather than the
Archbishop of Canterbury (Thomas Becket's rift with his king being
one of the few issues left unresolved and festering by the diplomacy
at Montmirail) cast a pall over the lavish celebrations. But preceding
all of these carefully calibrated dispositions—and laying the foundation for them, in fact—had been a telling change in the royal family's political and domestic arrangements. In 1168, Eleanor had come
home to Aquitaine.

It was not that, during the previous fifteen years, she had either
been constantly at her husband's side, or totally estranged from her
native land. Far from it: the hours that Henry regularly spent in the
saddle as he rode at punishing speed around his domains meant that
the couple were frequently separated. Meanwhile, Eleanor's more
stately travels had taken her to Aquitaine's cities of Poitiers and Bordeaux as well as to London and Oxford, Argentan and Angers. But
her move in 1168 was qualitatively different. Between 1156—when
Henry did homage to Louis VII for his new wife's duchy and received
that of the Aquitainian barons in his turn—and 1167, not a single
surviving charter produced by the ducal administration of Aquitaine
had mentioned its duchess. Eleanor, it seems, had been too busy pro-
ducing heirs, and too firmly sidelined by a husband intent on dem-

onstrating the overriding force of his own will, to play more than a
decorative role in the government of her people.

Now that was changing. Henry's thoughts were turning to the
possibility that the future of his empire might lie in delegation rather
than centralisation. And, in the case of Aquitaine, his mind was con-
centrated by the particular challenges the duchy posed to its rulers—
challenges that were multiplied many times over if those rulers came
from beyond its northern frontier. Aquitaine was huge in size, covering an area larger than Normandy and Anjou put together, and,
for northerners travelling south, its territories became ever more
alien as their journey progressed, not only in language but in culture,
customs, and climate. It had to be said that Anglo-Normans and
Angevins themselves were not the easiest of bedfellows, but the tensions between them were born of proximity and long experience, of
similarity rather than difference. Aquitaine was another matter. For
inhabitants of Normandy and Anjou alike, the peoples of the south
could appear disconcertingly foreign, whether foppishly refined to
the point of degeneracy, or disgustingly uncivilised in their habits
and dress. Either way, clearly, they were not to be trusted.

Henry's countrymen, therefore, whether in England, Normandy,
or Anjou, were all too likely to assume that Aquitaine was virtually
ungovernable. The truth, however, seen through less prejudiced eyes,
was more heartening. The duchy was a region not only of extraordinary cultural sophistication—its poetry and music matched by
the exquisitely carved stonework of its churches—but of extraordinary wealth. Besides its agricultural riches, its golden fields and dark
forests, coiling rivers and open coasts, Aquitaine plied a profitable
export trade in two of twelfth-century Europe's most valued com-
modities: salt, essential for food preservation, which was distilled
from sea water all along the duchy's Atlantic shore; and wine, produced to a superb standard in Bordeaux and Saintonge, and shipped
to markets across Europe. That trade filled the Duke of Aquitaine's
coffers with revenue from customs and tolls, and—although power
was in essence a matter of land and loyalty rather than of commer-

cial transactions—ready cash flow would more than help to raise an army or keep it in the field.

From his cities of Poitiers, built on a great promontory overlooking streams surrounding it on three sides, and Bordeaux, the bustling port on the west bank of the Garonne where the river meanders to the sea, the duke therefore stood every chance of dominating vast tracts of his duchy. The regions from Poitiers west and southward down the coast to La Rochelle, Saintes, and Bordeaux, and then east and south again to Agen, were prosperous and peaceful. But there was no denying that the lands of Poitou and the Limousin in the centre and east of the duchy—and particularly the castle-studded territories south of Poitiers belonging to the counts of Angoulême and the great Lusignan family—had the potential to be profoundly troublesome. Either of these vassals of the duke could use the strategically crucial location of their estates to disrupt communications between the key cities that owed allegiance to their overlord. The challenge of managing ambitious and aggressive men with such widespread scope to cause conflict had been a familiar one to Eleanor's father and grandfather; and, if Henry needed a reminder to keep his eye on the region, he got it in 1168 when Geoffroi de Lusignan rose in rebellion against him.

The threat was manifest: the Lusignans were bullish and intransigent, and support from Louis of France would always be forthcoming for those in Aquitaine who sought to throw off his rival's yoke. And the violence had alarming consequences. The Earl of Salisbury, an experienced soldier dispatched with Queen Eleanor to hold Poitou while Henry was engaged in urgent diplomacy with Louis, was killed in action: an unfortunate casualty of unlucky fate, said the Lusignans; stabbed in the back while unarmed and defenceless, protested the earl's outraged men. Either way, the killing—rather than the more usual imprisonment and ransom—of a trusted noble lieutenant was, for Henry, both shocking and sobering.

The Lusignans' revolt was suppressed by a combination of the treaty agreed with Louis at Montmirail in the following year, and a virulent campaign of repression waged by Henry in its wake. But the need to find a long-term strategy for the rule of Aquitaine, and Poitou in particular, was left in stark relief. And that circumstance lent a great weight of significance to Eleanor's return to the turreted palace at Poitiers in which she had spent so much of her childhood. She was the hereditary Duchess of Aquitaine, freed now from the labours of childbearing to take up the reins of government among her vassals, who had sworn allegiance to her long before they had bowed the knee to the second of her husbands. For Henry, who had learned much from his gifted mother, this was a deliberate decision to deploy the skills and charisma of his equally, if very differently, gifted wife—Eleanor's fearlessness marking a counterpoint to Matilda's shrewd caution. For Aquitaine, it was the restoration of a measure of native rule (which, however tempestuous the politics of the duchy under Eleanor's father and grandfather, remained infinitely preferable to domination from the north). And, for Eleanor, it was not only a homecoming but, at the age of forty-four, her first clear chance at sustained political autonomy on a public stage.

Her new role as Aquitaine's duchess was founded on her own hereditary rights, but it was reinforced and amplified by her functions as wife and mother. She was her husband's lieutenant in this part of his empire, even if his right to rule there originated with her. She was also serving as guardian of the duchy during the adolescence of her son Richard, who had been named as Aquitaine's future duke in the settlement of 1169. Richard was an exceptionally able boy and, it emerged, his mother's favourite—a bond that was established decisively in these years when he was immersed, with her, in the culture and landscape of her own girlhood. And, just as his older brother Henri's position as heir to England and Normandy had been ritually confirmed by his coronation at Westminster two years earlier, in June 1172 fourteen-year-old Richard was formally enthroned as Duke of Aquitaine.

In the cool interior of the Romanesque church of Saint Hilaire at Poitiers, watched by the painted gallery of bishops, martyrs, and saints on the richly coloured walls, Richard sat in the abbot's chair—

by tradition, an honorific right of the counts of Poitou—to take possession of the sacred lance and banner that symbolised the authority of the dukes of Aquitaine. Because that authority reached further than Poitou, the ceremony was then repeated seventy-five miles to the southeast at Limoges, chief city of the Limousin. There Richard received the ring of St. Valérie, a virgin martyr of the early Church whose rapidly developing twelfth-century cult identified her as the symbolic embodiment of Aquitaine itself. It was the young duke who wore the saint's ring, but the ritual personification of the duchy as a woman could not help but focus attention on the woman who ruled with and for him.

We cannot now reconstruct many of the details of Eleanor's government in Aquitaine, but the fact of her role is unmistakable. In 1168 and 1171 she held great Christmas courts of her own, as she had never done before, gathering her vassals around her in Aquitaine in the absence of her husband, but with her young son by her side. And, after a decade in which she had appeared in not a single extant ducal charter, in five years she now issued fifteen surviving charters in her own right and on her own authority, sometimes in association with her husband or son—"I and Richard my son," some acts began, while others were addressed by the queen-duchess to "the king's faithful followers and hers"—but never dependent on them. Meanwhile, Henry neither issued any charters of his own for Aquitaine during these years, nor saw any need to confirm or otherwise validate those of his wife.

It seemed, therefore, as though the delegation of power within Henry's empire, of which Eleanor's rule in Aquitaine formed a key part, was working. Certainly, it survived two major shocks in 1170. That summer, the unthinkable happened when Henry, the thirty-seven-year-old king whose superhuman vigour was the stuff of legend, fell so seriously ill that rumours of his death flew around France. He recovered, slowly; but the will he had drawn up when he believed he would not survive confirmed his commitment to the distribution of his lands between his sons (and, in practice, his wife) that had been agreed at Montmirail. And then, once restored to health, both Henry and his regime proved able to ride out the international storm unleashed at the end of the year by the murder of Thomas Becket, hacked to death in his own cathedral by knights who believed they were acting on their king's orders.

It took almost two years to emerge from the tempest of outrage and recrimination, but by the summer of 1172 Henry had done public penance for his part in the killing and had at last been freed from the threat of excommunication. The clouds, it seemed, were lifting; and the division of power among Henry's family appeared not simply to be functioning but to be reaching maturity, with the investiture of Richard as Duke of Aquitaine in June and yet another English coronation for his brother Henri in August, this time at Winchester with his young French wife at his side.

Appearances, however, could be deceptive. What Henry had declared his intention to do, and what he had actually done, were two very different things. Perhaps the clerk Walter Map had been right after all to suggest that the king set too much store by his mother Matilda's advice that an unruly hawk might be brought under close control by the proffer of a juicy piece of meat, but only if it were snatched away at the last moment. By the beginning of 1173 Henry's eldest son, now seventeen, and Richard, fifteen, had heard many fine words describing their rights as king and duke, spoken in reverent tones amid a haze of incense in hushed cathedrals. Of the reality of royal and ducal authority, they had seen very little. Perhaps it should not have been surprising that their tirelessly controlling father should find it difficult to hand over the fundamentals, as opposed to the accoutrements, of power. Conflict between fathers and sons had, after all, been a perennial side-effect for the Capetians, too, when they had tried to secure the succession to the French throne by this same method of pre-emptive enthronement. But the thwarted hopes of Henry's sons were mingled with the driving ambition and fiery temper they had inherited from their implacable father. It was a toxic mixture.

The situation began to unravel in February 1173 at what had promised to be a moment of triumph for Henry. He was in the process of negotiating a peace intended to secure the southeastern frontier of his territories, of which the centrepiece was a proposed marriage between his youngest son, six-year-old John, and the daughter and heiress of Count Humbert of Maurienne, a territory that lay east of Provence in the Savoyard Alps. The settlement was proclaimed at a magnificent meeting of Henry's court at Limoges, attended not only by the Count of Maurienne but also by the rival southern powers of the King of Aragon-Barcelona, the King of Navarre, and Count Ramon of Toulouse, against whom Henry had undertaken an imposing but largely unsuccessful military campaign in 1159. On February 25, Count Ramon gave ceremonial expression to the concord he had now concluded with his former enemy by doing homage for Toulouse first to Henry, and then to his eldest son. Young Henri, it seemed, whatever his simmering resentments, had been accorded all due recognition in this gathering of potentates.

But then Count Humbert asked the king what lands the child John would bring to the marriage, to match the riches of his own daughter's inheritance. Chinon, Loudun, and Mirebeau, came the reply: the three castles in Anjou that had been the focus of Henry's conflict with his brother Geoffrey nearly two decades earlier. At this, young Henri exploded in fury. He had been crowned King of England—twice—and invested as Duke of Normandy and Count of Anjou. He had just turned eighteen, already two years older than the age at which his father had taken command of the duchy of Normandy. And yet his father had not handed into his control any of the lands of his inheritance, to which his right had been so publicly and repeatedly proclaimed. Now, the final insult, three of his castles were to be given away to his baby brother. He did not agree. He would not agree. And his father would have to do something about it.

The king was not minded to capitulate in the face of this petulant outburst. Whatever the merits of his son's case, they were outweighed not only by Henry's own reluctance to cede control in any fundamental sense, but also by the fact that young Henri had so far spectacularly failed to prove that he was ready for the responsibility. Quite apart from the questionable judgement revealed by this public foot-stamping, the Young King, as he had come to be known, was engulfed in debt. Though he could, with some measure of justification, argue that this was unavoidable given that he had no lands with which to support his household, such reasoning was badly compromised by the profligacy of his spending on tournaments and banqueting. Two months earlier, according to the chronicler Robert of Torigni, he had held a Christmas feast so extravagant in its conceit and lavish in its execution that one room alone had been filled with 110 knights all named William.

But the bruised amour propre of a vain adolescent took on a more threatening slant in the light of the probability that the Young King's father-in-law, Louis of France, had encouraged or even instigated his demands, and the certainty that he would support them. And the alarm of the Old King—"old" only in relative terms, since Henry was still a few days short of his fortieth birthday, and as remorselessly energetic as ever—was immediately compounded by a private warning from Ramon of Toulouse that Henry's younger sons, Richard and Geoffrey, were conspiring with their brother against him.

Henry responded with characteristic swiftness. On the plausible pretext that he was going hunting, he left Limoges at speed, giving covert orders that his castles in Aquitaine should be put on a war footing. Richard and Geoffrey remained behind in the custody of their mother, while Henry decided that the Young King should travel with him, under close supervision, on his journey north. But when the royal party paused to spend the night at the massive fortress of Chinon, one of the castles in the Loire that had precipitated the confrontation at Limoges, young Henri made his escape silently under cover of darkness in the brief hours while his father slept, and rode furiously for Paris.

It had been entirely foreseeable that Henri would seek to defect to his father-in-law's court, and the Old King's immediate frustration lay not in the fact of his desertion but in his own failure to pre-empt his son's flight. It was a much more brutal shock, however, to learn a few days later that Henri's younger brothers had also made the hurried journey north to join him under Louis's protection. Richard and Geoffrey, at fifteen and fourteen, were still too young to be acting entirely on the basis of independent political calculation, and they had been left in the apparent security of their mother's keeping. There was only one conclusion to be drawn, and it was the most shocking of all: Eleanor, too, was now in open revolt against her husband and king.

One Limousin chronicler, Geoffroi of Vigeois, reports that Eleanor's name had been included with those of her younger sons in Ramon of Toulouse's warning to Henry about the treachery he now faced. If Vigeois is correct, then—given that Henry had left Richard and Geoffrey in Eleanor's care—either the king had not believed the count's warning, or he had calculated that Eleanor would not risk pursuing the conspiracy once its existence had been exposed. Either way, he was profoundly mistaken.

Henry's difficulty in giving credence to his wife's betrayal is mirrored by that of historians in attempting to explain it. Eleanor herself, of course, left no account of her own motives, nor did contemporary chroniclers, who tended to keep themselves at arm's length even from their own narratives of her involvement in the rebellion, shielding themselves behind allusions to hearsay from persons unknown with a constant refrain of "so it is said...." The vacuum of information has been filled, as so often in Eleanor's life, with speculation focusing on her emotional experiences. Just as her personal incompatibility with Louis played a part in the ending of her first marriage, so it has been argued that the private dynamics of her second—which was, after all, a much more potent partnership between two extraordinarily forceful people—lay behind the breach between Eleanor and Henry in 1173. And, as so often with Eleanor, centuries of conjecture have borne fruit in legends of remarkable complexity and persistence. She was violently incensed, so the story goes, by Henry's passion for

a beautiful young woman named Rosamund Clifford, "Fair Rosamund," the "rose of the world." In her jealousy and anger, the queen
roused her sons to rebellion against her unfaithful husband, before
(in a plot twist worthy of this granddaughter of a troubadour) procuring the death by poison of her hated rival for the king's love.

The absence of a single shred of evidence to support this tale—
beyond the fact of Henry's liaison with Rosamund Clifford, who died
in 1176 and was buried at the king's command in a magnificent tomb
at the Oxfordshire abbey of Godstow—need not prevent us from
taking it seriously, in essence if not in detail: it is not the first or last
event in Eleanor's life of which that is true. But a lack of basic plausi-
bility might. Whatever the reality of Eleanor's relationship with her
husband—which is impossible now to recover, any more than we can
know what really happened between Eleanor and her uncle Ramon
of Antioch twenty-five years earlier—there is a banality to the fact
that kings had mistresses, and Eleanor was certainly worldly-wise
enough to know it. There is no incontrovertible evidence that she and
Henry had even seen each other for two years between 1170 and the
Christmas court they held together at Chinon in 1172. Instead, Eleanor had been spending her time engaged in a project which offers
much more fertile ground in explaining her alienation from her husband in the spring of 1173: the rule of her beloved Aquitaine.

There are indications—fleeting, but suggestive nonetheless—
that Eleanor had been seeking to intensify her independence as de
facto ruler of her duchy in the year before the crisis of 1173 began to
unfold. In June 1172 she had received diplomatic visits from the kings
of Navarre and Aragon-Barcelona; the complex process of attempting to stabilise the geopolitics of southern France, in other words,
was one in which she, as well as Henry, had been personally involved.
During 1172 she had also addressed three charters not "to the king's
faithful followers and hers," as she had always done previously, but
"to her own faithful followers" alone. In interpreting such faint traces
of political activity we are reading crumbling runes rather than a
clearly incised script; but even this tentative impression of Eleanor's

increasing self-assertion is significant in a context where—for all her apparent authority in her own duchy—her practical powers were constrained by the fact that she controlled neither the bulk of Aquitaine's revenues, which clinked instead into her husband's coffers, nor the military resources needed to impose order there. In 1171, when the monks of St. Martial's Abbey in Limoges faced a revolt at their nearby town of La Souterraine, it was to Henry—rather than to Eleanor, the duchess on their doorstep—that they appealed for help; and it was Henry, not Eleanor, who sent soldiers to their aid.

The overriding political circumstance, therefore, that shaped Eleanor's actions in 1173 was the fact that she, no less than her sons, had been promised power by her husband and then denied it in practice. Or, at the very least, she had achieved some measure of authority in her own duchy, only to find that the fundamentals of political control still lay beyond her grasp. If her son Henri was brimming with resentment at his father's refusal to relinquish the rights he believed were his due, then Eleanor had no less cause for frustration—and, in fact, much more, since the elaborate diplomacy at Limoges in February 1173, which for a brief instant had seemed such a triumph for Henry, had also represented a dramatic affront to Eleanor's territorial ambitions.

Henry's goals in tackling the intractable rivalries of southern French politics had always been to guarantee the frontiers of his empire, to extend his influence beyond them, and to protect access from the Atlantic port of Bordeaux via Toulouse to the lucrative trade routes of the Mediterranean. In 1159 that had meant waging war on Count Ramon of Toulouse; in 1173 it meant receiving his homage. For Henry, with his steely pragmatism and his absolute capacity to inhabit the present moment, it was a political recalculation so obvious that it did not warrant a second thought. Eleanor, however, did not find it so easy to take this strategic about-turn in her stride. When Henry had led his formidable army against the city of Toulouse in the midsummer heat of 1159, he had done so in the name of his wife's claim to be the rightful heir to the *comté*. Eleanor's

grandmother Philippa, the long-suffering wife of Aquitaine's troubadour duke, had been the only child of Guilhem IV, Count of Toulouse, but—in a scenario that would have been instantly familiar to
Henry's mother, Matilda—she had not been accepted as her father's
successor. The Toulousain inheritance had passed instead in the
male line to Guilhem's younger brother, Ramon IV, whose grandson, Ramon V, now held the title. But the dukes of Aquitaine had
never conceded the legitimacy of this succession, and Eleanor's counter-claim had been pressed at swordpoint first by Louis of France in
1141, and then by Henry in 1159.

Neither campaign had been successful, and by the end of 1172
Henry had concluded that his interests were better served by cul-
tivating Ramon's friendship than by renewing the attempt to blud-
geon the count into submission. In February 1173, Eleanor was
therefore forced to stand by in impotent silence while the husband
she had scarcely seen for two years stormed at his customary speed
into her city of Limoges in order to contract a peace with the man
who had usurped her right to her grandmother's territories. Henry,
meanwhile, gave no hint of doubt or hesitation about the propriety
of his actions; he seems to have suspected nothing awry as Eleanor
watched Ramon kneel before him amid the splendour of his court to
be publicly confirmed in possession of Toulouse.

The form of that ceremony, too, had Henry but recognised it,
supplied yet more grist to the mill of his wife's grievances. Even if
Eleanor could have been persuaded that Ramon was rightfully the
Count of Toulouse, there could be no doubt of the Duke of Aquitaine's claim to the overlordship of the *comté*. In that sense, at least,
Ramon's homage to Henry was unexceptionable, since the king was
also Duke of Aquitaine in his role as Eleanor's husband. But the
homage that Ramon performed that day to Henry and Eleanor's
son, the Young King Henri, was a different matter. True, Henri had
been named heir to England, Normandy, and Anjou; but he had no
claim to Aquitaine, which had been apportioned as the inheritance

of his brother Richard. For Count Ramon to do homage to Henri, in other words, forcefully suggested that Aquitaine was no longer an independent part of Henry's empire but a dependent one, subsumed under the overarching authority of the Anglo-Norman crown. That would have been anathema to Eleanor's ancestors; it was unacceptable to many of her Aquitainian vassals; and there is no reason to think that it was any more tolerable to Eleanor herself.

For all that the devastating rupture of 1173 was precipitated by her son Henri's adolescent posturing, it was Eleanor's grievances that constituted a coherent critique of her husband's strategy over the previous few years. It is understandable, perhaps, that the story of this most charismatic and unconventional of queens has been clouded by an enveloping aura of romance and myth; but if we jettison the presupposition that her estrangement from her husband must have been rooted in emotion, we can find ample grounds for the alienation of a focused political mind. Henry had not delivered the measure of political autonomy he had promised Eleanor or her sons. He had abandoned her claim to Toulouse, a cause for which he, and her first husband before him, had previously been willing to fight. And, in doing so, he had appeared to threaten the autonomy of Aquitaine itself. The triumphant ceremonial at Limoges in February 1173—an unwelcome political ritual performed in the heart of one of Eleanor's own cities—could not have been a more stark reminder of the gulf between her hopes for the duchy and her husband's obliviousness to the aspirations he himself had done so much to foster.

That is not to say that Eleanor's response was either predictable or well judged. Rebellion against one's king—and particularly a king as near-impossible to resist as Henry had proved himself to be—was an intensely dangerous path. But Eleanor had already shown herself to be capable of the apparently unachievable: her almost seamless translation from the crown of France to the crown of England was demonstration enough of that. She had engineered her own escape from one unacceptable royal marriage, and she had proved more than

once that she would not be constrained by fear of the consequences of
her actions. It might seem scarcely credible that she should send her
teenage sons to conspire with her ex-husband against their father;
but it is clear nevertheless that that is what she did. Neither Richard
and Geoffrey, who were still too young to act with any significant
degree of independence, nor the Young King, more of a strutting
peacock than a political thinker, were capable of coordinating such
a threatening coalition between the heirs to Henry's empire and the
King of France. Eleanor was. And it soon became clear quite how
much she was putting at risk in doing so.

There could be no surprise, of course, that Louis of France—
never the wiliest of politicians, but acquiring some greater world-
liness with the advancing years—would take any opportunity to dis-
comfit his rival and destabilise Henry's empire. But the spectacle of
a ruling family imploding into treachery and recrimination caused
horror, at least among Anglo-Norman commentators. It was a "de-
plorable betrayal," one chronicler said; and it served only to feed the
sinister (and deliciously scandalous) tale that Henry's Angevin dynasty was the "Devil's Brood," descended from Melusine, daughter
of Satan himself.

Whatever the outrage it provoked, however, the story of hot-
headed young men resorting to violence and treachery in their
unseemly haste to seize their inheritance was a familiar one to contemporary observers. It was a cause for sorrow, regret, and anger,
but it was far from unprecedented. Louis of France's ill-fated elder
brother Philippe had done little else but provoke their father with his
insolence between his coronation at thirteen and his death two years
later. A closer parallel still was provided by the travails of Robert II,
King of France a century and a half earlier, who had spent the last
six years of his life embroiled in a bitter war with his three sons, in
which the eldest, the young King Hugues, had died at the age of just
eighteen. And there was a ready biblical identification against which
clerical chroniclers could measure Henry's misfortune, in the rebellion of the unhappy Absalom against his father, King David.

The monastic historian William of Newburgh, for example, was in no doubt that young Henri was an "ungrateful son" whose disobedience to his father had "violated the law of nature." Even so, the very fact that his disloyalty could be fitted into the archetype of "the accursed Absalom" meant that the impulses behind it were culturally understood; while the qualities that provoked it—ambition, aggression, unbridled self-assertion—were those which, differently directed, could be seen as proper to a king.

The same could not be said of Eleanor. There were no obvious historical precedents or cultural archetypes to frame her rebellion. When the contemporary chronicler Ralph of Diceto, dean of St. Paul's Cathedral and a learned historian, scoured the annals for past parallels against which to compare the revolt, he compiled more than thirty instances of sons rebelling against their fathers, but not a single case of a queen taking up arms against her husband. Not only that, but the traits Eleanor displayed in resisting Henry were the antithesis of those understood as queenly. A queen was a consort, a helpmeet, an intercessor in the cause of peace and justice. Above all, perhaps, she was doubly bound by a sacred duty to obey her husband—once as a subject, and again as his wife. Eleanor's son Henri, William of Newburgh believed, "had sullied his early years by an indelible stain"; but Eleanor's behaviour threatened the very fabric of society itself. "Man is the head of woman," the Archbishop of Rouen reminded her in some alarm, quoting St. Paul, in a public letter composed on his behalf by the scholar and stylist Peter of Blois. "We know that unless you return to your husband you will be the cause of a general ruin."

But Eleanor had not been cowed by scurrilous rumour in Antioch; she had not acquiesced in the face of a papal prohibition on divorcing her first husband; and she would not back down now. With her sons safely in Paris under the wing of her jubilant ex-husband, she set about mustering military support in Aquitaine, which was readily forthcoming from those lords—Poitevins for the most part—who had always resisted the imposition of central control in the duchy and who had tangled with Henry before: the counts of Angoulême, their allies the Lusignan family, and the Lusignans' cousin Geoffroi de Rancon, at whose side Eleanor had braved the ill-fated ascent of Mount Cadmus a quarter of a century earlier. As she gathered her forces, Louis was assembling an intimidating coalition of allies in support of her sons in Paris. There was Mathieu, Count of Boulogne, who had acquired his title by marrying the daughter of King Stephen and his queen, Mathilde of Boulogne; the count's elder brother Philippe, Count of Flanders; Stephen's nephew Thibaud of Blois; and William, the King of Scots. All saw the unmissable opportunity—together with other defectors in England, Normandy, Brittany, and Anjou—to lay their eager hands on lands they had either forfeited, or never stood a chance of acquiring, under Henry's uncompromising rule.

As her sons prepared to take up arms at the head of this great noble alliance against their father, Eleanor made ready to return for the first time in twenty years to the French court in Paris. It is impossible to know whether she had made a calculated decision to play the odds of this nerve-wracking game, or whether her fearlessness was born of an inability to contemplate the risk of failure. Either way, she was to find that—yet again—she had met her match in Henry. For once, this was a challenge from which she would not emerge unscathed. Before she could reach Paris, at some place and time unknown on the road north from Poitiers, she was captured by her husband's forces—and found to be disguised for her journey in men's clothing, according to the chronicle of Gervase of Canterbury. The story could well be the sensationalised elaboration of a disapproving monk, but at the very least it remains tantalisingly allusive, given that she had figuratively (if not literally) adopted the guise of a man from the moment she rejected her husband's authority.

No tunic and hose, however, could now save her from her fate. By the end of 1173 it was apparent that Henry's military genius, his cool head in a crisis, and his hastily assembled army of ruthlessly professional mercenaries were holding firm against the onslaught of his sons and their allies. That autumn, with the rebel campaign faltering, Henry offered them terms for peace that were financially reward-ing but conceded nothing of the power they craved. Encouraged by Louis, the boys fought on, with sixteen-year-old Richard mounting an impressively stubborn defence of his mother's county of Poitou. By the autumn of 1174, however, it was clear that there was no alter-native but to throw themselves on their father's mercy. Henry loved his sons with "an inordinate love," William of Newburgh believed, and certainly the king was generous in his victory. He exchanged the kiss of peace with his prodigal offspring, and gave them money and noble (if deliberately unfortified) residences in the territories they had claimed, to salve their battered egos. There would be no conces-sion of jurisdiction, but this time they were in no position to argue. Others might accuse them of breaking nature's law, but Henry was prepared to be magnanimous: the treaty concluded at the pretty town of Montlouis in the Loire Valley at the end of September of-fered not simply reconciliation, but reconciliation with honour. Not, however, to Eleanor.

For Henry's captured queen there would be no forgiveness. Her name was not spoken at Montlouis. By then, she was far away in England, where she had already endured months of an imprisonment that would last as long as her husband lived. Revolt had brought her sons chastening experience, and a fresh start with their father. For Eleanor, on the other hand, the rest was impenetrable silence.

NINE

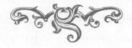

By the Wrath of God, Queen of England

ver since she was thirteen years old, Eleanor had stood at the heart of western European politics. For a decade and a half she had been Queen of France; for two decades more she had been Queen of England. Throughout, she had cherished her rights and responsibilities as Duchess of Aquitaine. She had travelled to Jerusalem and back, and that dramatic voyage had been only the most extraordinary episode in a life lived in constant motion. Above all, perhaps, she had believed in her own agency. Though she could not command her husbands, she had an indomitable will and a tough political mind, and she had always had a choice about how she reacted to the circumstances, however difficult, in which she found herself.

Now, for the first time, she had no choice at all. How can we begin to imagine her response as weeks of captivity became months, and months became years, until it became clear that in this, as in

so many things, Henry would be relentless? Her isolation was such
that imagination is all we have. Even the place of her confinement
is not known for certain, bar the fact that it was in England, where
expenses for her keeping were periodically allowed at the exchequer.
We know nothing of how she spent her days while the years of her
middle age—the time she had hoped to spend ruling her homeland
of Aquitaine—ebbed fruitlessly away. Nor can we be sure how much
she knew about what was happening outside the walls of her prison
(for that is what it was, however comfortable her accommodation).
It is likely that Henry made every effort to restrict her contact with
the outside world; it is equally likely that Eleanor did her utmost to
subvert his orders.

We can only guess, therefore, what news she heard of her sons as
they grew into adulthood without her. Was it a source of distress or
consolation to know that her favourite, Richard, was ruling Aquitaine in her stead, and showing his worth as a soldier and a strategist?
Her sons, at any rate, did not forget her. Henry must have hoped that
her incarceration would serve to coerce their loyalty—although that
was a happy side-effect of a policy rooted in his own rage at the perversion of his wife's betrayal and the intolerable public humiliation it
represented.

If Eleanor was a hostage for her sons' co-operation, her plight did
its work in harnessing Richard to her husband's cause. His first task
as his father's lieutenant in Aquitaine, in command now of the troops
and revenues Eleanor had never been granted for her own government there, was to raze the castles of his recently abandoned allies,
those Poitevin lords who had backed his rebellion. The biting irony
of the campaign did nothing to deter the eighteen-year-old duke
from executing his task with grim efficiency. His next eight years
were spent in the saddle at the head of his soldiers, suppressing a succession of revolts by Aquitainian lords unhappy with Henry's imposing regime and its incarnation in their midst in the person of Richard
himself. There could have been no more rigorous practical training in
the art and science of military command, and it forged Richard into

a leader of such implacable single-mindedness, such nerveless courage and pitiless brutality, that, despite his devotion to his mother's
homeland, he was loathed by many of his vassals there.

His elder brother, Henri, meanwhile, was putting his military
talents to more frivolous use. The Young King's passion was for tournaments—the wild excitement and violent glamour of the mêlée—
which he pursued across France and Flanders at the head of a following largely composed of landless knights, the younger sons of younger
brothers who reaped the rewards of his careless extravagance. He
had neither the application nor the stamina to learn from his father's
attempts to school him in statecraft and the harsh lessons of real,
rather than counterfeit, warfare; but repeated demonstrations of
that fact did nothing to dent his conviction that he was the victim
of outrageous injustice in being kept from the exercise of power. At
first his father placated his tantrums and threats—Henry rendered
indulgent in this, as in no other area of his life, by his love for his son
and his blind determination that Henri would, in time, come to ap-
preciate the scale of his future responsibilities. But by 1183 it had
become starkly apparent that no moment of self-realisation—nor
any concern for his incarcerated mother—would restrain the Young
King from following the dictates of his bloated ego.

By the spring of that year, Aquitaine had emerged as his chosen
battleground. Having failed to persuade his father to hand Normandy or Anjou into his control, Henri had toyed with the idea of
leaving for Jerusalem in a fit of flamboyant pique, before deciding
instead to pick a fight with his younger brother. Richard, in Aquitaine, already had the independence Henri craved; and the hostility of those Aquitainian lords who resented their imperious duke
seemed to offer the Young King a chance to oust his brother from
power, and to supplant him. At an extraordinary gathering of the
royal court at Christmas 1182, with more than a thousand knights
crowding his hall at Caen, the Old King sought, yet again, to broker
a truce by which he might unite his fractured family. But once the
extent of Henri's disloyalty became known—once it was clear that

he was mustering for war at the very moment he pledged his commitment to peace—even Henry had to concede that his heir could be indulged no further. The king summoned troops to the Limousin to fight alongside Richard and his forces, while Henri rallied the rebels of Aquitaine to defy them. Once again—and this time without Eleanor's help—her husband and sons stood on the brink of the abyss.

But this time there would be no reconciliation. At the end of May, after an inconclusive siege of the Young King's encampment at Limoges by his father and brother, Henri fell gravely ill with dysentery. When his doctors realised that he was beyond help, he sent urgently to his father, begging forgiveness and the privilege of a last meeting. But he had abused Henry's trust too many times, and the king, fearing some new treachery, would not go. Henri died on June 11, 1183, at the age of just twenty-eight. The celebrity of this most glamorous and shallow of princes was such that the people of Le Mans kidnapped his corpse en route to its last resting place at Rouen; only under threat of force did they disinter it from a new-made tomb in their cathedral and send the cortege on its way. And with his death, his revolt collapsed, along with his grief-stricken father's plans for the future of his empire.

Eleanor, hearing in faraway England of the loss of the son she had not seen for a decade, was now fifty-nine. It was said that the dying Henri, overwhelmed with remorse and seeking absolution from his absent father, had entreated that his mother should be dealt with less severely for her part in his first mutiny. If the reports were true, his petition may help to explain the shock of Eleanor's appearance at court almost eighteen months later. Dressed in gowns of fur-trimmed samite for which special funds were released from the exchequer, she spent Christmas of 1184 at Windsor with her sons Richard and John and her daughter Matilda, newly returned to England with her husband, Duke Heinrich of Saxony, who had been exiled from Germany by the Emperor Friedrich Barbarossa. But this unexpected show of family unity did not foreshadow any greater liberation for the queen, nor any more general pardon granted by her estranged husband. Eleanor remained in Henry's custody, to be summoned when there was advantage in doing so, and otherwise kept sequestered.

The nature of that advantage became clearly apparent in the spring of 1185, when she was once again called to her husband's side, this time—necessitating her first cross-Channel voyage in more than ten years—in Normandy. The occasion was an unprecedented and startling ceremony in which Richard was required to surrender Aquitaine back into his mother's hands as its rightful duchess. The cause, however, was no sudden apotheosis for Eleanor, but a symptom of new tensions that were wracking her family. Richard was now the king's eldest surviving son, and was expected—not least by himself—to succeed his brother as heir to England, Normandy, and Anjou. Henry did not seek to deny his son this royal inheritance; but he assumed that Richard would in turn cede Aquitaine to his youngest brother, John, who would thereby be provided with the lands he had until now signally lacked. Richard, however, had not fought for his mother's duchy simply to hand it over to a needy sixteen-year-old—especially if what he was offered in exchange was a status so insubstantial, while their father still lived, that it had provoked their dead brother to repeated rebellion.

And by 1184 it was clear that Richard was prepared, yet again, to fight for his right to Aquitaine. In an access of frustration at Richard's recalcitrance, Henry declared that his youngest son should meet fire with fire and take the duchy by force—an outburst of fury rather than a declaration of strategy, given that John had no army and Henry no intention of supplying him with one. But that summer, the young prince did indeed launch a series of plundering raids into Richard's county of Poitou. It was a provocative campaign made possible by an ally whose intervention in this conflict—like his previous participation in the Young King's rebellions—was poisonously damaging to the cause of family harmony.

Geoffrey, the middle of Henry and Eleanor's surviving sons, was, at twenty-five, the ruler of Brittany, the inheritance of his young wife, Constance. He was an able soldier and, like the dead Henri, a brilliant tournament fighter; but his relentless and unprincipled ambition won him as many critics as he had admirers. He was "overflowing with words, smooth as oil," according to the censorious observer Gerald of Wales; a prince "possessed, by his syrupy and persuasive eloquence, of the power of dissolving the apparently indissoluble, able to corrupt two kingdoms with his tongue, of tireless endeavour and a hypocrite in everything." Geoffrey had fought by his eldest brother's side against Henry and Richard at Limoges in 1183; now, with troops from his Breton duchy at his back, he shepherded his youngest brother into an assault on northern Aquitaine in the hope of winning a larger slice of their father's empire for himself.

In the circumstances, Eleanor's sudden emergence from her enforced seclusion just a few months later, at Christmas 1184, becomes a great deal less shocking. That autumn, once news reached the Old King in England that Geoffrey and John were ravaging Poitou while Richard attacked Brittany in retaliation, Henry summoned all three of his unruly sons to his side and knocked their heads together, imposing on them a formal ritual of reconciliation at Westminster before the court moved to Windsor for Christmas. There could be no doubt that their mother's presence during these manoeuvres, and the authority over Aquitaine that she still embodied, prisoner or no, was a significant weapon to be deployed in Henry's campaign to break his sons to his will and keep them from destroying one another.

Just how significant became apparent when winter turned to spring. After renewed sniping and snarling between Richard and Geoffrey, over Normandy this time, Richard was ordered to relinquish Aquitaine into his mother's keeping. And the most extraordinary aspect of the ceremony, which took place in Normandy in April 1185, was not Henry's command, but Richard's compliance. Without Eleanor, an end to the wrangling had been nowhere in sight. Richard would not concede Aquitaine to anyone who threatened his rights as its duke. And Henry would not brook any substantive challenge to his lordship over his domains in the present, or any diminution of his entitlement to determine their future. In that context, the position of a controversial queen became uniquely uncontroversial, an oasis of calm amid a storm of contention. Richard could resign his duchy into his mother's hands because her authority there had always underwritten his, and because the closeness of their relationship offered reassurance for his rights as her heir. Meanwhile, the rights that Henry derived from Eleanor's role as his wife guaranteed his own overlordship of Aquitaine, and his claims on its future.

For Eleanor, this was no moment of political resurrection or practical restitution. She was allowed no initiative, no freedom of movement or action; she was the static fulcrum around which her husband and sons could reorder their unstable relationships. But still, the measured dignity with which she played her part—betraying no public sign of bitterness at the confinement in which she had been kept for ten years—told its own story. At sixty-one, she had lost none of the instinctive political understanding that had always animated her steps through her public life, but there was a new patience, a new appreciation of risk to herself and her sons, behind her acquiescence when grants in Aquitaine were made in her name "with the assent and will of my lord Henry, King of England, and of my sons Richard, Geoffrey and John."

More patience would be required of her yet. Her participation had helped to suppress the nascent conflict of 1184; but her husband and sons could not be kept at peace for long, and their divisions were lovingly fostered by the new King of France, Philippe II, the son and heir for whom Louis had waited so many years that the boy had been nicknamed *Dieudonné*, "God-given." Young Philippe had suffered a life-threatening illness in the autumn of 1179, and Louis, in desperation, had crossed the Channel to pray at the Canterbury shrine of Thomas Becket, whose martyrdom had made him a saint little more than two years after his murder. Louis was accompanied on this pilgrimage by his "most dear brother," King Henry—the two kings finding unlikely common ground at last while the woman they had each married was enduring her protracted imprisonment. But on his way home to France Louis suffered a debilitating stroke. He clung to life for another year, until in September 1180 Philippe found himself in possession of his father's throne at the age of just fifteen.

The new French king had met Henry's sons Henri and Geoffrey when they attended his coronation at Reims, which had taken place, as was customary, during his father's lifetime. His closeness to them was undoubtedly infused with the warmth of personal affection, but it was underpinned by the cold steel of Philippe's implacable ambition to pick apart the English king's empire and fashion the kingdom of France into a great power in its place. Henri was now dead, but when Geoffrey, chafing at the peace imposed on him in 1185, rode into Paris in 1186, Philippe welcomed him with open arms. Geoffrey's capacity to make trouble was extinguished that summer with sudden violence, when he was unhorsed and trampled to death in a tournament mêlée; and at his funeral the French king made an extravagant show of his grief—by one account having to be restrained from casting himself into the open grave in the choir of Paris's new cathedral of Notre-Dame. However, Geoffrey's abrupt exit from the political stage presented Philippe with a new opportunity to disturb Henry's hold on his territories by claiming custody, as overlord of the duchy of Brittany, of Geoffrey's two young daughters and the baby son, Arthur, to whom his widow gave birth seven months after his death.

By June 1187 conflict over Brittany and renewed tensions over the perennially controversial lands of the Vexin, the frontier between Normandy and France, had intensified to the point of open confrontation. Henry and Philippe drew up their armies in battle array at Châteauroux, 150 miles south of Paris; and for two weeks envoys moved between the enemy lines in search of a settlement. Neither the two kings nor the noblemen they commanded were eager to face the indiscriminate dangers of a pitched battle, accustomed as they were to the controlled risks of warfare by siege and raid; and after intense negotiations a two-year truce was agreed. But when Philippe retreated northward to Paris, he carried away an unexpected prize: Henry's son Richard rode with him.

Richard could not have made his disaffection more plainly manifest. Philippe, already at twenty-two a master of the telling political gesture, kept his royal guest constantly at his side. "...every day they ate at the same table and shared the same dish," observed Roger of Howden, a clerk at Henry's court, "and at night the bed did not separate them"—this last a striking public demonstration of political, not sexual, intimacy. The cause of this overt estrangement between the King of England and his eldest surviving son was a familiar and familiarly intractable one: Henry's refusal to make a settlement of the succession that was acceptable to his heir, and his heir's refusal to accept the possibility that his younger brother John might have a claim on their father's territories.

Richard's ostentatious closeness to Philippe did not last, and by the end of the summer he was back in Anjou with his father. But the question of the succession continued to spread its venom. True, other concerns emerged to occupy Richard's attention: in the autumn of 1187 he took the crusader's cross, as his mother had done forty years earlier, to commit himself to the future rescue of Jerusalem (which had just fallen—in a catastrophic reverse for the cause of Christendom—to the Muslim forces of Al-Malik al-Nasir Salah ed-Din Yusuf, known to his enemies in the west as Saladin). But the fact that Richard omitted to consult his father before promising to fight in the Holy Land only served to emphasise the tensions between them, to such an extent that when revolt erupted yet again in Aquitaine in 1188, Henry was suspected of having a hand in encouraging the rebels. With his usual talent for manipulation, Philippe of France worked tirelessly to exploit the divisions between father and son, until at the beginning of 1189, once again, the Angevin dynasty was at war with itself.

By the late spring, Richard and Philippe were in the field together, attacking and overrunning a chain of Henry's castles in Maine. The English king, hamstrung by his fear that Richard would betray him, had succeeded only in alienating his heir to such an extent that Richard now believed the rumours that Henry planned to disinherit him in favour of his youngest and favourite son, John. And Henry, at fifty-six, had at last exhausted the prodigious stores of energy that had kept him in almost constant motion since he had first begun to accumulate his vast territories more than thirty years before. His health had been faltering for months, and, in the oppressive summer heat, he could fight no longer. In his fortress of Chinon, he lay racked with fever, agonised by the failure of his plans. He was unable to forgive the son who would succeed him; and at the last his spirit was broken by the news that even John, the son on whom he had lavished his love, had deserted him. On July 6, 1189, Henry II turned his face to the wall and died.

When the news reached Richard, he rode as hard as he could to meet the cortege that carried his father's corpse a few miles westward from Chinon, across the river Vienne to Fontevraud. It was dusk when the new king stepped into the silence of the abbey church where the royal bier lay. He stood for a moment, looking down for the last time at his father's face. Then he turned on his heel and walked away; and sent word to England that his mother was now a free woman.

TEN

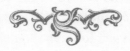

Surpassing Almost All the Queens of This World

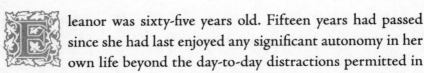leanor was sixty-five years old. Fifteen years had passed since she had last enjoyed any significant autonomy in her own life beyond the day-to-day distractions permitted in her captivity. She was no longer young, by any measure, and she had lost two of her sons while she waited for the liberation of her husband's death. No one who had witnessed her earlier lives as queen first of France and then of England could have been in any doubt of her uncommon calibre, but in the circumstances few could have predicted that she would re-emerge into the political world with an urgency and momentum that would have been remarkable in someone half her age. And she did so with a composure of judgement at which her fortitude in enduring the indignities of her imprisonment had already hinted. The monastic chronicler Gervase of Canterbury, in recounting the tale of the rebellion that had cost her freedom, described the queen as "*prudens femina valde, nobilibus orta natali-*

bus, sed instabilis"—"an extremely astute woman, sprung from noble stock, but unsteady." Unsteady she might have been, once, in her lack of matrimonial loyalty and her willingness to take spectacular risks; but now she brought a judiciously calm control to the business of working to establish her son's regime.

For weeks after his father's death, Richard was occupied in Normandy, stamping out the disorder that he himself had done so much to unleash. And so, along with the order for his mother's release, the new king dispatched to England a command that Eleanor (in the words of the historian Ralph of Diceto) should have "the power of doing whatever she wished in the kingdom." This was not only a stunning reversal of fortune, but a transformation unprecedented even in a life marked out by overwhelming upheaval. Eleanor's years as a queen in France and in England had been spent as a consort, her authority, such as it was, acquired as a satellite of her husband the king. Even in Aquitaine, which was properly her own, she had not controlled the levers of power in the form of money and men. Now, however, she would exercise the power of a king in England. This was not an official regency: her role was not defined or circumscribed in any technical form. Instead, her son had given her the same freedom to command that he himself enjoyed.

That much was clear from Eleanor's rapid progress around the country in the month before Richard's arrival in Portsmouth that August. She travelled "from city to city and castle to castle just as it pleased her," the chronicler Roger of Howden reported, at the head of her "queenly court"—the unusual Latin adjective *"reginalis"* emphasising the rare spectacle of a woman alone at the helm of English government. And the measures she took demonstrated the breadth of her authority. She ordered the dispatch, Howden wrote, of "a body of trustworthy men, both clergy and laity,...throughout all the counties of England" to reform the abuses of local officials, to extract from all free men an oath of loyalty to Richard, and to empty the kingdom's jails—the newly liberated Eleanor remarking with delicate understatement, according to Howden, that "she had learned by experience that confinement is distasteful to mankind, and that it is a most delightful refreshment to the spirits to be set free therefrom."

This was independent action on a scale and of a kind that the Empress Matilda would have viewed with incredulous envy. Yet—unusually for Eleanor, whose career had hardly been uncontroversial—it did not attract critical comment. Her authority, unconstrained though it might be, was so completely identified with that of her son that the fact of her sex was barely noticed: power in the hands of an anointed queen mother, it seems—as opposed to an anointed queen regnant—challenged no fundamental political preconceptions. At sixty-five, moreover, she was an elder stateswoman, not the flighty foreign presence that a queen consort could all too easily appear. And, perversely, the long imprisonment that had been her punishment for rebelling against her husband had turned her into a figurehead for loyalty and unity. The only part she had played in fifteen years of bitter conflict between her sons and their father was to make possible the transient peace settlement of 1185. As a result, she now stood above the fray, uncontaminated by more than a decade of treachery and warfare, and unbendingly committed to the continued existence of her husband's empire under the governance of her son.

For as long as Richard was absent from English soil, Eleanor ruled in his name; and she helped plan the coronation by which he became England's king. In Westminster Abbey on September 13, 1189, the queen mother stood draped in a costly new fur-trimmed gown to watch as her favourite son was touched with holy oil upon the head, breast, and hands in the rite that transformed a man into a monarch. Then, newly dressed in the richest of ceremonial vestments, Richard was crowned with a massive diadem of gold encrusted with precious stones, a crown so heavy that two earls stood by to support its weight.

But this formal inauguration of Richard's reign did not mean that Eleanor could step back into retirement. Instead, she remained by the king's side, noted by the chroniclers as an influential presence in his councils. She was closely involved, for example, in her son's attempt to find a settlement of a viciously protracted dispute between the Archbishop of Canterbury and the monks of his cathedral priory. For eighteen months the monastic community had been barricaded within the priory's walls, kept alive only by the townspeople's gifts of food, while the cathedral itself fell silent and empty. Richard was determined not only to enforce a compromise (an unlikely outcome, it initially seemed, given how much vitriol had already been expended in the debate, but one which he achieved within three months of his coronation) but, crucially, to do so without intervention from Rome; and it was on Eleanor's authority that the pope's legate, Giovanni da Anagni, was detained when he stepped off his ship at Dover in the autumn of 1189 to prevent any possibility of papal meddling.

While Richard was in England, then, his mother was at his right hand, her power unmistakable in the politics, as well as the ceremonial, of his court. But the king remained in England for only seventeen weeks. On December 12, 1189, he took ship for the Continent, where he began raising the men and money needed to launch the crusade to which he had committed himself two years earlier. The scale of his task was almost unimaginably vast, but Richard set about it with irresistible purpose and unprecedented speed. "He put up for sale everything he had," Roger of Howden reported; and by the summer of 1190 he was ready. His father had taken the cross in 1172, as part of his penance for the death of Thomas Becket, but had never set out for the Holy Land. It was in his mother's footsteps, therefore, not his father's, that Richard rode to Vézelay to undertake a perilous journey that Eleanor had completed more than forty years earlier. His starting point and his destination were the same as hers, but, unlike her, he eschewed the overground route across Europe in favour of travelling south to Marseille and on by ship to rendezvous in Sicily with his own huge fleet and that of his crusading ally, Philippe of France.

Once arrived in Sicily, Richard stayed for six months, delayed not only by the closure of the Mediterranean shipping lanes in winter, but by two pressing political problems. The first was the status of his sister Joanna, who had been Queen of Sicily until the death of

her husband, William II, in 1189, and who was now the unwilling
hostage of the new king, William's illegitimate cousin Tancred of
Lecce. A briskly successful assault by Richard's forces on the city
of Messina rapidly secured not only Joanna's freedom but payment of
her dower, a store of gold of a size to gladden the heart of a crusading
king who had already liquidated the assets of the kingdom he had
left behind.

The second problem, meanwhile, required political finesse rather
than the application of force. Richard had been betrothed to Alix,
half-sister of Philippe of France, for more than twenty years; but he
had never shown any particular urgency about the business of marrying her—not least, perhaps, because the two decades she had spent
as his wife-in-waiting at his father's court had given rise to persistent
rumours that Henry himself had made her his mistress. Whatever
her personal entanglements, the French princess had been the plaything of Anglo-French politics for the whole of her adult life—her
betrothal summarily cancelled or abruptly revived by each new sequence of negotiations—and Richard, it transpired, had now tired of
his own part in this diplomatic merry-go-round. He saw a new opportunity to protect the southern frontier of his territories through
an alliance with the Pyrenean kingdom of Navarre, and he had spent
some time in Aquitaine laying the groundwork for a marriage with
Berengaria, daughter of the Navarrese king Sancho VI. Philippe
initially resisted this public slight to his long-suffering sister; but
now—with the crusade already under way, and Richard threatening
to expose Alix's supposed liaison with his father—the French king
had no option but to abandon her cause.

And while Richard negotiated his escape from his former fian-
cée, his mother set off to bring him his new one. Eleanor, who had
spent fifteen years all but immobilised as her husband's captive, now
seemed to have limitless reserves of energy to expend in the service
of her son. In the autumn of 1190 she was in Bordeaux, luxuriat-
ing in the great city of her childhood for the first time since she had
regained her freedom. From there she travelled nearly two hundred

miles south across the Pyrenees to the Navarrese capital of Pamplona, where she was welcomed in great state to the court of King Sancho. There she met her prospective daughter-in-law Berengaria, described from afar as "more prudent than pretty" by the chronicler Richard of Devizes, and more blandly as "a wise maiden, a fine lady, both noble and beautiful" in the first-hand account of Ambroise, a Norman poet in Richard's crusading company.

From Pamplona the two women, with a train of bodyguards and attendants, rode north and east, crossing the Pyrenees once again in order to reach the greater challenge of the western Alpine passes. As the Empress Matilda had discovered before them, a crossing of the Alps in the middle of winter was not to be undertaken lightly. More than a hundred years earlier, when the Emperor Heinrich IV, Matilda's father-in-law, had crossed the Mont Cenis pass in the freezing temperatures of an especially bitter December, his queen and her ladies had been forced to make the descent sitting on sledges improvised out of ox-skins on which they could slide down the steeply treacherous ice. The chroniclers tell us nothing of what Eleanor and Berengaria endured, which suggests that their journey, in less extreme weather, was less dramatically dangerous. Still, it can only have been a relief to reach the foggy and monotonous flatness of the plain of Lombardy.

At Lodi, twenty miles southeast of Milan, the once and future queens met the new German king, Heinrich VI, who had inherited his crown six months earlier when his father, Friedrich Barbarossa, died en route for the Holy Land in the vanguard of the crusade. This encounter necessitated a delicate diplomatic dance, since Heinrich had come to Italy not only for his coronation as Holy Roman Emperor at the hands of the pope, but to claim the throne of Sicily in the name of his wife, Constance, legitimate sister of the dead king William II and aunt of the bastard-born Tancred. And, as both Eleanor and the emperor were well aware, her son was currently a guest and ally—a forcefully imposing one, but an ally nonetheless—at Tancred's court. Eleanor herself, however, skirted elegantly round this impromptu meeting—perhaps assuring Heinrich as she passed that Richard had no interest in staying to defend Sicily when he could be leaving to attack Jerusalem—and rode on to Naples, where she and Berengaria intended to take ship for Messina. Instead, they were required to wait for a few weeks at Brindisi while Richard broke the news to Philippe that he would not, after all, be marrying his sister. When the two women finally disembarked at Messina harbour on March 30, 1191, it was to discover that the King of France had pointedly sailed away a few hours earlier, his former intimacy with the King of England now turned to bitter rancour.

Despite the arrival of the bride, there was no immediate prospect of a royal wedding, since the Church did not allow marriages to be celebrated during the penitential season of Lent. Berengaria therefore joined the travelling establishment of Richard's sister Joanna, the widowed Sicilian queen, when the immense crusading fleet headed eastward to Cyprus on April 10. By then, however, Eleanor was long gone. At sixty-seven, she had needed only three days to recuperate from a journey that had taken her over two mountain ranges and across half of Europe. While Richard set his sights on the Holy Land—a voyage in the course of which he married Berengaria and conquered Cyprus—Eleanor returned, as Ambroise noted, "to look after his land that he had left." And the king knew that it would be in safe hands. Eleanor's status could not have been clearer when, visiting Rome on her way northward through Italy, she intervened with the newly installed Pope Celestine III to secure approval for the consecration of her dead husband's illegitimate son Geoffrey as Archbishop of York. Geoffrey's election to the see had been controversial, and Eleanor's involvement did not damp down the furore; but the fact that she could act with such authority at the papal curia spoke volumes about the power she now wielded.

Quite how much that power was needed had already become obvious in England while Eleanor herself was away. Archbishop Geoffrey was not the only one of Henry II's sons causing trouble there.

For Eleanor's youngest child, John, the knowledge that he was his father's favourite had done nothing to counteract the baleful effects of the fact that he was last in line when it came to the partition of the Angevin territories. The question of what political provision should be made for John had been a cause of repeated familial conflict ever since the rebellion of 1173 that had led to his mother's imprisonment; and his insubstantial title as "lord of Ireland" had provided him with predictably little satisfaction. Richard had now given his brother the Norman county of Mortain and a generous portion of lands and revenues in England, to which John's marriage in the summer of 1189 to the heiress Isabella of Gloucester added still more. But for John—who was clever, insatiably grasping, and implacably narcissistic—it was not enough.

That Richard knew his brother well was clear from the king's insistence, before his departure from Vézelay, that John should swear an oath to stay away from England for three years during his own absence in the Holy Land. Eleanor, too, was under no illusions about John's ambitions, but she disagreed about the best way of containing them. At her urging, the oath was modified to allow Richard's chief minister in England, the Norman-born Guillaume de Longchamp, to decide when and if John should be admitted to the country. In all probability, neither plan would ever have kept him in check; and in practice it took only a matter of months before the cracks began to show.

The catalyst of the crisis was a twofold threat to John's hopes of inheriting his brother's crown: first, the treaty Richard made at Messina with Tancred of Sicily, which named the king's three-year-old nephew, Arthur of Brittany, as his heir presumptive, for the diplomatic purpose of marrying him to one of Tancred's daughters; and, second, Richard's own marriage to Berengaria of Navarre, which promised in time to give him sons of his own. Simultaneously, John was presented with an irresistible opportunity to make his own bid for power in England by the unpopularity of his brother's justiciar

Longchamp, who was fast alienating the great English lords with high-handed exactions that were resented all the more for being imposed by a low-born Norman.

By the summer of 1191 both John and Longchamp were in the field at the head of armed troops. Longchamp laid siege to John's supporters in Lincoln Castle, while John himself seized the nearby royal fortresses at Nottingham and Tickhill in reprisal. But by that time Eleanor had arrived back in Normandy, accompanied by the English-born Archbishop of Rouen, Walter of Coutances, whom Richard had dispatched from Messina with the express task of resolving the hostilities that had erupted in the kingdom he had left behind. Eleanor remained at her manor of Bonneville-sur-Touques, a couple of miles inland from the Norman coast between Caen and Rouen—a station from which she could hope to oversee Richard's domains on both sides of the Channel—while the archbishop sailed for England. There he negotiated a fragile peace, which was reinforced that autumn when Coutances himself took over the justiciar's duties from the discredited Longchamp. In February 1192, however, Eleanor herself took ship for Portsmouth. John's unique capacity to undermine the stability of his brother's kingdom, it transpired, was such that it required his mother's unique authority to curb his excesses.

Her intervention was prompted by information that John—having been thwarted in his attempt to install himself as regent by the arrival of Walter of Coutances—had applied himself instead to conspiring with Philippe of France, who had returned from crusade after less than four months spent in the Holy Land. Philippe's antagonism toward Richard was now unshakeable, and he saw in John's amoral ambition the perfect vehicle for the destabilisation of his enemy's kingdom. He made John a tantalising offer: take the hand in marriage of his sister Alix, Richard's humiliatingly repudiated bride, and receive with her the Angevin lands in France of which Philippe was overlord. John did not hesitate; his existing marriage was conveniently consanguineous and easily cast aside for a prize of this magnitude. He sent word to the coast that a ship should be prepared for his flight to France.

But he had reckoned without his mother. "And who could be so savage or cruel," Richard of Devizes rhetorically inquired, "that this woman could not bend him to her wishes?" Cruelty and savagery were John's stock-in-trade, but even he could not override Eleanor. She was an anointed queen, who spoke with the authority of the absent king. The right to rule Aquitaine was hers as much as it was Richard's. And John himself would need her support to claim the inheritance of which he dreamed if his brother failed to return from the East. Self-interest pure and simple, if nothing else, dictated that he could not afford to defy her completely. And, while the great men of England contemplated the risky business of treading an uncertain path between the demands of loyalty to Richard and the reality that, given the dangers of crusade, John might in fact become king at any moment, Eleanor alone stood above the fray. She was mother to both men, and her insistence that the younger should not rule while the elder still lived had the compelling force not of political partisanship but of unquestionable royal legitimacy.

Eleanor's actions were reported to posterity in acceptably feminine terms. She was, after all, seeking to preserve power for her son, not for herself. "Her maternal heart was moved and pained...," Richard of Devizes wrote; and she succeeded in preventing John from leaving for Paris "through her own tears and the prayers of the nobles." But it is clear nevertheless that her intervention was resolute and decisively authoritative. She convened four great meetings of England's barons in rapid succession, at Windsor, Oxford, London, and Winchester, to bring pressure to bear on her youngest child, that "light-minded youth," as Richard of Devizes called him. Whatever the emotional resonance of any tears she shed at those gatherings, they only lightly veiled the steely threat that John's lands and castles in England would be confiscated if he defected to France. John's ambitions, his greed and his disloyalty, were still on open display; but, thanks to his mother, they were at least temporarily caged.

The bars of that cage, however, were soon to be broken. In the autumn of 1192 Richard agreed to a three-year truce with his enemy Saladin and set sail at last for home, two years and three months since he had turned his horse southward from Vézelay with such expectation. He had not reclaimed Jerusalem from infidel hands, but he had won glory nonetheless, capturing Acre and Ascalon and securing the coast of the Holy Land from Tyre to Jaffa. He had also made enemies. Philippe of France had returned to Europe a year before him, humiliated by the rejection of his sister and smarting at the extent to which Richard had overshadowed him on their joint campaign. And, less obviously but no less significantly, the English king had earned the hatred of Duke Leopold of Austria, who had fought at the siege of Acre with the tattered remnants of the dead Emperor Friedrich's German forces. Leopold had raised his banner next to those of England and France to fly over the defeated city— and Richard's soldiers had torn it down, their king refusing to contemplate the idea that an insignificant third party might have a claim on the spoils of his victory.

Acre was only the first of Richard's triumphs, and in the burning heat of Palestine the hostility of a departed German duke seemed of little moment. A year later, however, it became clear that the incident had cast a long shadow. The returning king reached the island of Corfu in November 1192—too late in the year to pursue his homeward journey by sea even if he could have found a safe port on the western Mediterranean shore that was beyond the considerable reach of Philippe of France and Emperor Heinrich of Germany. Richard can have been in little doubt of the consequences of his breach with Philippe; and Heinrich had been alienated by the English alliance with Tancred of Sicily even before the French king and the German emperor met and made common cause at Milan in late 1191. Richard was a victorious crusader coming home to an empire that had held firm in his absence, thanks in no small part to his remarkable mother. But the profoundly uncomfortable fact of the matter was that his enemies now barred his way. One option remained. Heinrich of Saxony, husband of his sister Matilda, held northeastern Germany in defiance of the emperor, and Richard could hope to find a secure passage home via the northern shipping routes of the Baltic Sea if he made his way through his brother-in-law's lands and under his protection. To get there, however, he first had to pass through the territories of Leopold of Austria.

Compared to the might of France and Germany, the resources of the Austrian duke were limited—which meant that, in the absence of a viable alternative, the route was a risk worth taking. Richard travelled under cover in the guise of a long-bearded pilgrim, attended by only a small handful of servants. But disguise proved difficult to sustain for a king who was accustomed to unquestioned command and expenditure on a scale that attracted attention wherever he went. He was still fifty miles from safety when he was arrested by Duke Leopold's men at a village outside Vienna. By Christmas Day, he was a prisoner in the forbidding fortress of Dürnstein, perched on a craggy rock above the raging waters of the Danube.

This was extraordinary news, and it travelled fast. By December 28 Leopold's lord, Emperor Heinrich, was dictating a letter in delight to Philippe of France. "We know this news will bring you great happiness," he wrote, "…in as much as he is now in our power who has always done his utmost for your annoyance and disturbance." While England waited expectantly for Richard's arrival, Philippe wrote in his turn to the one man among the English king's subjects for whom the revelation that he would not return would be a cause of unalloyed joy. John immediately set off for Paris, where he did homage to King Philippe for Richard's French lands and promised to marry poor discarded Alix. Together, John and Philippe now planned to seize this unexpected moment by launching an invasion of England.

Eleanor, at sixty-nine, might have been forgiven for feeling as tormented by the activities of her living sons as by grief for her dead ones. In the prosecution of her public responsibilities, however, she showed no sign of frustration or exhaustion. And although she worked in close co-operation with the justiciar Walter of Coutances, the monastic chronicler Gervase of Canterbury was in no doubt that orders for the defence of the coast against the threat of a French fleet were given "by the mandate of Queen Eleanor, who," he said, "ruled England at that time."

While the King of France gathered his ships at the port of Wissant in the county of Boulogne, John returned to England to raise a revolt, justifying his insurrection with the spurious claim that Richard was dead. But both invasion and rebellion sputtered into nothing in the face of Eleanor's composed resistance. She knew her youngest son every bit as well as did his elder brother: "My brother John is not the man to win lands by force," Richard supposedly remarked when told of his treachery, "if there is anyone at all to oppose him." And Eleanor was not just anyone. By the end of April John had met such concerted military opposition that he was forced into a truce: its terms permitted him to keep his midland castles at Nottingham and Tickhill but required him to surrender three more—Windsor and Wallingford in the Thames Valley, and the Peak further north—to his mother. At Richard's request, meanwhile, Eleanor secured the election as Archbishop of Canterbury of Hubert Walter, the formidably able Bishop of Salisbury who had been the king's right-hand man on crusade and the first of his subjects to reach him in his German prison. She then addressed herself to the urgent task of raising the staggeringly large ransom—100,000 silver marks—which Emperor Heinrich and Duke Leopold had between them agreed to demand in return for Richard's freedom.

Gold and silver began to pour into St. Paul's Cathedral, where money from a levy of a quarter of the value of the movable goods of both clergy and laity, and treasure and plate from England's churches, was collected in great chests under the seals of Eleanor herself and Walter of Coutances. Eleanor's authority and the depth of the trust confided in her by her son were everywhere apparent in the letter concerning this ransom that Richard sent from the imperial palace at Haguenau, just north of Strasbourg, addressed to "Eleanor, by the grace of God Queen of England, his much-loved mother, and to his justices and all his faithful servants throughout England." The money gathered was, the king ordered, "to be delivered to our mother and such persons as she shall think proper"—an instruction followed by the backhandedly intimidating request that Eleanor should send him a note of the individual sums contributed by his nobles, so that he might know how great were the "thanks" (or something less palatable, reluctant donors might surmise) he owed to each.

Richard was not the only one writing letters. Peter of Blois, the scholar who had once, in the name of an earlier Archbishop of Rouen, berated Eleanor for her rebellion against her husband, now took up his pen in the service of his queen. The letters he composed to be sent to Pope Celestine in Eleanor's name, appealing for the pontiff's help in securing Richard's release, cannot be read as an intimate outpouring of maternal grief. It is possible that they were not even commissioned by the queen; certainly, they were exercises in rhetoric, laced with scriptural quotation, and designed to give the greatest possible emotional and political weight to the argument they made. But their intensely passionate style does serve as a demonstration of the strength of Eleanor's position. The irreproachable and spiritually resonant role of the afflicted mother now underpinned her actions just as much as the culturally unacceptable one of the rebellious wife had undermined her attempt at self-assertion twenty years earlier. One letter begged the pope "to show himself a father to a suffering mother"; the anguish of another draft, meanwhile, explicitly echoed the psalms of King David and his lament for the lost Absalom: "I have lost the staff of my old age and the light of my eyes...Would that I had died for you, my son."

The aged Pope Celestine did not respond to these missives, if they were ever sent, but the diplomatic and military manoeuvres across Europe continued without him. Richard worked hard from his prison quarters to keep his chief captor, the Emperor Heinrich, at a safe distance from Philippe of France, who had failed to instigate revolt in England but had made alarming inroads into eastern Normandy, so that the French flag now flew for the first time over the great frontier stronghold of Gisors. Knowing Philippe as he did, Richard realised that his hope of freedom would be extinguished forever should he one day find himself in a French rather than a German prison. As a result, he was prepared to offer another 50,000 marks of silver, on top of the 100,000 already pledged, to secure a settlement with Heinrich that would keep the emperor away from a conference with Philippe that had been planned for June 1193. "Look to yourself; the devil is loosed," Philippe told John when he heard of this new pact; and John fled to France in fear of his brother's imminent return.

In practice, it took Richard several months more to free himself of his bonds. It was not until December 20, 1193, that Heinrich received a down payment on the king's ransom collected by Eleanor and her advisers that was substantial enough to persuade him to set a date for Richard's release. With the approach of the appointed day—January 17, 1194—the emperor found himself lobbied frantically by Philippe and John with a counterbid: they would pay £1,000 a month into imperial coffers for as long as Richard remained in his custody, or 100,000 silver marks if Heinrich kept him captive until the following autumn (giving them a full campaigning season to further their plans), or 150,000 marks either to hand him over into their control, or at least keep him prisoner for another year. "Behold, how they loved him!" Roger of Howden remarked with withering sarcasm.

While the emperor contemplated this new offer, the ceremony planned for January 17 was cancelled and a new gathering of German princes summoned instead for February 2 to consult on the increasingly convoluted question of Richard's fate. To that meeting, too, came Eleanor, "desirous," said a chronicler in Salzburg, "of freeing the son she especially loved." At almost seventy, she faced yet again the rigours of long-distance travel as she moved eastward across the Low Countries with Walter of Coutances and Guillaume de Longchamp in her train, and with the chests containing the gold and silver of Richard's ransom piled high on heavily guarded baggage carts. She reached Cologne by January 6, and ten days later was reunited with her captive son when she reached Speyer in time to discover the unwelcome news that his formal liberation on January 17 would not, after all, take place. Another journey lay ahead, taking her fifty miles north along the Rhine to Mainz, where the imperial court and the increasingly fretful English delegation assembled at the beginning of February.

The negotiations were "anxious and difficult," Walter of Coutances reported. But the German princes were determined that Heinrich should honour his existing agreement with Richard rather than commit himself to a duplicitous alliance with the dangerously subtle Philippe of France; and Eleanor herself clinched the deal by persuading Richard to surrender the kingdom of England to the emperor in order to receive it back from his hands as an imperial fief. This was a finely calibrated gesture of pragmatic politics—a ritual acknowledgement of the emperor's authority that would oil the wheels of Richard's liberation, but make negligible difference to the reality of his powers once he was free (and efforts were made, in fact, to prevent news of the bargain even reaching England). At last, on February 4, 1194, the archbishops of Mainz and Cologne escorted the king to be delivered from captivity, Roger of Howden noted, "into the hands of his mother Eleanor."

Before their reunion in Germany, mother and son had not seen one another for three years. It had been four years in all since they had been in each other's company for more than a few days. "On the king being set at liberty, all who were present shed tears of joy," Roger of Howden reported; but it was the power of Eleanor's position during Richard's long absence as crusader and captive rather than any display of maternal sentiment that was celebrated during his triumphal journey back to England. She was by his side as he rode first to Cologne, then to Louvain and Brussels. She took ship with him at Antwerp, and with him she landed at the English port of Sandwich on March 13. Together the king and his mother travelled north to give thanks for his safe return at the shrine of St. Thomas Becket at Canterbury, before riding at the head of a glorious cavalcade into London.

Eleanor accompanied Richard to the midland city of Nottingham, too, where the king flexed the military muscles that had stiffened in the confines of his prison by leading an assault on the garrison holding the town's castle in the name of his brother John. It took only two days before the soldiers accepted the reality that their sovereign was back, and surrendered. When Richard then convened a great council to overhaul the administration of his kingdom, the chroniclers named Eleanor first among the great lords who sat with him in the council chamber. And when the king processed into Winchester Cathedral on April 17 to consecrate his return with a ceremony of crown-wearing, richly robed and walking under a silken canopy borne above his head by four earls holding their lances aloft, Eleanor sat in state opposite his throne, surrounded by a constellation of her ladies.

The prominence of the queen mother in this reassertion of kingly power was all the more striking for the fact that Richard's wife, Queen Berengaria, was nowhere to be seen, staying as she was in Poitou after a protracted journey back from Acre via Rome and Marseille. But that prominence made a significant political point, for Eleanor's authority by now was far more than that of a consort. Not only was it sanctioned by, but it had come to buttress Richard's own. Eleanor, after all, had had a consort's share in the sovereign power of the man from whom Richard had inherited his own sovereignty; and the role she had played in securing the integrity of the realm while Richard was detained, voluntarily and involuntarily, so far away had made her an essential focus of unity—the mother of the kingdom as well as the king.

In that role, she had one task left to accomplish. It had to wait until she and Richard had completed their progress around England and had taken ship once more at Portsmouth on May 12 for the Channel crossing to Normandy. They landed, to scenes of wild excitement, at Barfleur, and rode via Bayeux and Caen to Lisieux, Richard moving steadily toward the war zone where his enemy Philippe of France was attempting to annex eastern Normandy town by town and castle by castle. At Lisieux, however, one of Philippe's most valued allies came to kneel at Richard's feet and beg for his grace. The king's brother John had done all he could to support the French advance into the Vexin; his English lands had already been declared forfeit in consequence, and Richard had set a date for judgement to be passed upon him for his treachery. But now John was pleading for forgiveness, and Richard immediately embraced him, dismissing his twenty-seven-year-old brother's repeated betrayals as the actions of an ill-advised child.

This unlikely reconciliation was achieved, Roger of Howden said, "through the mediation of Queen Eleanor." And although there was pragmatism at work on both sides—John's fright at his brother's return finding common ground with Richard's determination to dismantle Philippe's position in Normandy—it seems likely that Eleanor not only engineered her sons' reunion but ensured its success. Her unyielding commitment to the future of their dynasty, as represented by both of her sons, allowed each to trust the assurances of the other, however implausible they might otherwise have seemed in the light of recent history.

Her work was done. Richard advanced at the head of his army to drive back the French king and his troops from the walls of Verneuil. John set about serving his brother with all the conscientiousness he could muster. And Eleanor rode south to the abbey of Fontevraud, on the frontier between Anjou and her own county of Poitou. From there she could keep in close touch with her sons and their concerns, and with her homeland of Aquitaine, while beginning at last to settle into a luxurious retirement.

England no longer needed her, despite the fact that its king was once again absent, back in his military element on campaign against Philippe and against his own rebellious vassals in Touraine and Aquitaine. His administration in England had been left in the fiercely able hands of Hubert Walter, the Archbishop of Canterbury, and Richard himself was close enough to keep a steady stream of missives and directives hurtling across the Channel. Both the kingdom and its justiciar knew that these royal letters would swiftly be followed by the king's royal person should urgent need arise. England's centralised systems of law and administration—which had developed to new heights of sophistication because of Henry II's constant travels around his Continental empire—meant that the kingdom was well suited to government by royal deputy in the temporary absence of the monarch; but its very tractability was what had made it so vulnerable when the king was far away and feared lost for good. A centralised government, when summarily decapitated, could be taken over wholesale—as John had calculated in launching his bid for power in England—by contrast with the piecemeal annexation required to seize control of Normandy, Anjou, or Aquitaine. And that circumstance was what had made Eleanor's role in England so vital and her power so real. Only a royal ruler of unquestioned legitimacy—as Eleanor had been, in embodying the authority of one son against the pretensions of another—could hold together a kingdom that relied for its security on the universal guarantees of royal law.

Now, though, she could rest. She made no move to reclaim the rule of Aquitaine, where Richard emphatically reasserted his control in the summer of 1194. ("The city and citadel of Angoulême we took in a single evening," he told Hubert Walter, before adding, with a casual exaggeration born of supreme confidence, that "in all we captured 300 knights and 40,000 soldiers.") Eleanor had no doubt that his commitment to the duchy was the equal of her own; and she was happy instead to install herself at Fontevraud, a residence replete with material and spiritual comforts, strategically located at the heart of her son's French territories.

For the next five years she remained quietly at the abbey, a revered presence in her own rich apartments within the convent community. She raised no protest when Richard decided, in the autumn of 1196, to secure the southeastern frontier of his lands through an alliance with Ramon VI, Count of Toulouse, son of that Count of Toulouse whose treaty with her husband had helped to spark her ill-fated rebellion in 1173. Perhaps she was prepared now to accept her son's abdication of her own dynastic claim to Toulouse because she identified more closely with his political judgement than she had done with Henry's; perhaps any objections were overcome by the fact that the alliance was sealed by Ramon's marriage to her daughter Joanna, the widowed Queen of Sicily, through whose offspring Eleanor's claim might at last be made good, even if not quite in the way she had hoped. Nor did she demur when Richard named as Count of Poitou his twenty-year-old nephew, Otto, son of his sister Matilda and Heinrich of Saxony, a trusted lieutenant to keep a watchful eye on his treasured maternal inheritance (albeit that this delegation of authority was quickly superseded by Otto's election as King of Germany in 1198). All the evidence suggests that Eleanor was adopting a role akin to that played by her mother-in-law Matilda during her last years at Rouen—an astute observer of international affairs, retired now from the political front line, turning her thoughts increasingly to the needs of her soul while still offering the benefits of her accumulated wisdom to a son whose exceptional abilities she had done so much to foster.

Unlike the empress, however, Eleanor was to be wrenched from the peace of her retreat by sudden and violent tragedy. In March 1199 Richard was in Aquitaine to suppress yet another revolt led by the Count of Angoulême and the Viscount of Limoges. Toward the end of the month he brought his troops to besiege the viscount's castle of Châlus-Chabrol, less than twenty miles southwest of Limoges. The small fortress held a garrison of only forty, of whom just two were trained and armed knights, and Richard was in a relaxed mood as he waited for the castle's inevitable fall. On the evening of March 26, he rode out after supper to inspect the day's progress, protected only by a helmet and shield against the shots of a solitary crossbowman on the ramparts, a bravely ludicrous figure wielding a cooking pan to ward off missiles from below. Richard appreciated the defiant courage of this lone enemy, and cheered good-humouredly as the man loosed his next bolt; but he was too careless of the reality of the threat. He miscalculated the arrow's speed and trajectory by a fraction of a second, and felt the iron barb tear into the flesh of his left shoulder.

The king returned calmly to his tent, giving no public hint of his injury, and tried to wrench out the arrow himself. The wooden shaft broke off in his hand; a surgeon removed the rest, but at an impossible cost. The butchered wound quickly showed signs of infection. As the gangrene spread, Richard knew that death would follow surely and swiftly. By the time the fortress of Châlus fell a few days later, the victory had become an irrelevance. A messenger arrived at Fontevraud, desperate and dishevelled; and Eleanor rode south to watch her son die.

She was at his side when he took his last breath as dusk fell on April 6. She was seventy-five, and had expected her favourite child to attend her burial, not she his. Richard's heart was taken to Rouen, to be interred next to his brother Henri, but his body had less far to go: his cortege retraced his mother's steps back to Fontevraud, where his corpse was laid to rest at his father's feet. But Eleanor would not be there for long to keep vigil over his tomb. Her one remaining son needed her, as his brother had before him.

For all the effort Richard had expended on the present security of his empire, he had exerted himself remarkably little to safeguard the future of his own bloodline. He had one illegitimate son, Philippe of Cognac, but no legitimate offspring to inherit his throne. Not only had his wife, Berengaria, never set foot in the kingdom of which she was queen, but she had spent only a few months of their eight-year marriage with her king; it had been four years since Richard had made time to see her. At forty-one, Richard had been in good health, despite the extra weight his stocky frame was carrying, and perhaps, after the trials of crusade and imprisonment, this superlative soldier had come to believe that he was invulnerable, that the future was his to command. Instead, it now seemed that the future belonged to John, the brother who had served him faithfully since their reconciliation at Lisieux, but who had coveted his throne since before their father's death.

John's inheritance, however, was far from certain. Enemies within and without the Angevin lands could not believe their good fortune as news of Richard's death spread, and they had a rival candidate immediately to hand, in the twelve-year-old form of Arthur of Brittany, son of John's long-dead elder brother Geoffrey. This posed a nice challenge to the nascent principles determining the succession to England's throne: did a younger brother have a greater or lesser claim to the crown than the son of a dead older brother? Even if agreement could have been reached on this elusive theoretical point in English law, the precedents at work in Normandy, Anjou, and Aquitaine would not necessarily support the same conclusion. And, in any event, the practical fact of the matter was that the successful claimant would be identified by the political support he could muster, not simply by the technical merits of his case.

No one knew that better than Eleanor, and there was no question in her mind that the throne belonged to her son rather than her grandson. Arthur's very name emphasised his Breton identity rather than his Angevin heritage. He had been brought up in Brittany under the care of his mother, the duchy's heiress, until the tensions between the Breton regime and Arthur's royal uncle Richard had resulted in 1196 in the boy making a lengthy stay at the court of Philippe of France. There could be little doubt now of how the cards would fall. Philippe launched another invasion of eastern Normandy as soon as he heard of Richard's death; the rebellious lords of Anjou, Maine, and Touraine, led by Guillaume des Roches, declared that Arthur was their king; and the Count of Angoulême and the Viscount of Limoges persisted in the revolt that had claimed Richard's life. Eleanor, meanwhile, made it clear that Arthur, or his advisers on his behalf, had forfeited any claim on a grandmother's loyalty.

Three days after his brother's burial, John arrived at the great fortress of Chinon, where he took possession of the treasury of Anjou, and then rode on ten miles to the west along the banks of the Vienne to take counsel with his mother at Fontevraud. From there he turned his horse northward to Normandy, narrowly escaping capture en route by the French king, who swept into Le Mans with Arthur and the rebel lord Guillaume des Roches only hours after John had left. At Rouen—where there was little sympathy for Philippe or Arthur, enemies to the east and west of the duchy—John was invested with a circlet of golden roses as Duke of Normandy on April 25. After a brief detour to sack Le Mans in punishment for the city's support for his rival, he made for the Norman coast, and by May 27 he had reached Westminster, where he sat in state in the soaring space of the abbey for his coronation as King of England.

It made sense for John to focus his immediate attention on Normandy and England. There he was a known quantity—one viewed with a certain ambivalence, perhaps, after his repeated displays of extravagant duplicity during the years of Richard's long absence, but then again those five years of treachery were now balanced by five more of redemption in his brother's service. In England, certainly, Arthur of Brittany's claims to be Richard's heir had little purchase; and the solemn ceremony at Westminster, which was well attended by the great English lords, gave sacred sanction to John's rights.

Aquitaine, however, was a very different matter. Richard, English-born though he might have been, had become a native Aquitainian duke: enthroned at Poitiers and Limoges at the age of fourteen, he spent years of his life and much of his political energy in the duchy. He made enemies as well as friends there—his death on campaign at Châlus in the heart of Aquitaine was no geographical aberration in his military career—but the fact of his power could not be ignored. John, on the other hand, had last set foot in the duchy fifteen years earlier when he and his brother Geoffrey had plundered Poitou in the attempt to snatch it from Richard's grasp. No less than Arthur of Brittany or Philippe of France, John was an outsider in Aquitaine, and the risk he ran was that he would fast become an irrelevance there.

Not so his mother. Where Richard had depended on Eleanor to embody the authority of the crown in England, John needed her to inhabit the role into which she had been born—that of the ancestral ruler of her own duchy. She had expected to see out her days in the peace of Fontevraud; instead, within three weeks of Richard's death she found herself at the head of an army, accompanying Mercadier—a mercenary captain who had been the king's loyal military lieutenant for a decade and a half, and had been at his side at Châlus—on a campaign to devastate Anjou, beyond the northern border of Aquitaine, in retribution for the support its lords had offered to Arthur. Mercadier led the troops, but Eleanor's presence at his side demonstrated that their ravages were predicated on claims of political legitimacy rather than indiscriminate looting.

Before the end of the month she parted company with Mercadier, leaving to him the further prosecution of the military campaign they had begun in Anjou, and began to move south into Aquitaine, charting a path through the great towns of her duchy—from Poitiers southwestward to Niort, then south to Saint-Jean-d'Angély, westward to the port of La Rochelle, inland again to Saintes, and finally, in the heat of July, south to her city of Bordeaux. As she went she dispensed favours to the great men of Poitou and the Limousin, and privileges to the towns and religious houses she passed along the way. In doing so she marked the duchy yet again as her territory, and sought to bind its people to her side.

That accomplished, she turned north again, travelling two hundred miles to Tours to meet her son's enemy, Philippe of France. It was to be an extraordinary encounter, and not simply because it brought her face to face with the son of her long-ago husband Louis, a man who had caused her own family so much torment. At Tours, Eleanor knelt before the French king to do homage for her duchy of Aquitaine. Sixty-two years after her father's death, there could be no conceivable doubt of her right to her inheritance, but she had never before sworn fealty and done homage to her French overlord. This was a ritual from which women were routinely excluded: the political and military service owed by a vassal, it was assumed, could not be performed by a woman in her own person, and the place of an heiress would therefore naturally be taken by her husband or son. Henry and Richard had both previously offered their homage for Aquitaine on Eleanor's behalf; and young Arthur had already become Philippe's sworn vassal for Brittany, despite the fact that the duchy was the inheritance of his mother, Constance. Why now, at seventy-five, did Eleanor choose to break the mould of feudal ceremony and assert the independence of her rights in Aquitaine?

The gesture was certainly not intended for public effect. We only know that it happened at all thanks to the French chronicler Rigord, since no mention of it survives in English sources. We must assume, therefore, that the meeting took place with the minimum of fanfare, Philippe presumably accepting the fealty of his enemy's mother as a welcome recognition of the authority he was attempting to extend throughout the French kingdom. For Eleanor, however, this was a move in a complex chess game—a stratagem designed to secure the integrity of her duchy and the inheritance of her son in the face of her grandson's challenge.

After all, if she alone, swearing an oath of allegiance in person, was the French king's vassal in possession of Aquitaine, then Philippe would have no right to summon anyone other than Eleanor herself to answer for the rule of the duchy in his court. Having accepted her homage, he could have no straightforward legal basis for intervening in Aquitaine himself, or for promoting alternative claims to its rule, whether from Arthur or John or anyone else. In feudal law, Eleanor now stood as a human shield between the King of France and her homeland. And she immediately set to work to capitalise on her position in order to establish John's stake in Aquitaine's future.

In a document sealed probably that summer, Eleanor formally recognised her son John as her successor in Aquitaine. She had accepted his homage, she declared, and now transferred the allegiance of her vassals to him, "the king their liege," as her own "right heir" and their lord. John, meanwhile, sealed a charter of his own which again recorded his homage to his mother, and went on to acknowledge her authority over him as "*domina*"—"lady," the same title that Matilda had once enjoyed, implying the exercise of female lordship—"of us and of all our lands and possessions." Mother and son were now explicitly locked into a political relationship of mutual support and interdependence. Neither partner, John's charter added, was to give away lands or rights without the other's consent, unless it should be to the Church "for the salvation of our souls." Eleanor had once before exploited the political possibilities of feudal homage, in helping to secure her older son's release from his German prison by suggesting he swear an oath of fealty to the emperor. If that had been a feint, this was a masterstroke—reciprocal recognition between mother and youngest son that simultaneously guaranteed John's rights in Aquitaine and deprived Philippe of the opportunity to assert himself there.

Her duchy, for the moment, was safe, but John's position in Anjou and Maine was much less certain, and likely to depend more on might than on right. Here, however, fortune seemed to be smiling on John. In the autumn of 1199 Guillaume des Roches, Arthur's chief supporter in the region, was persuaded to defect to John's cause, forcing Philippe to the negotiating table; and in January 1200 the two kings came to uneasy terms, by which Philippe formally recognised John as his brother's heir in the Angevin dominions, in return for John's homage and for continued French possession of the parts of eastern Normandy that had already been overrun. As so often before, the treaty was to be concluded with a marriage: this time a union between Philippe's twelve-year-old heir, Louis, and one of John's royal nieces, the daughters of his sister Eleanor and her husband, Alfonso VIII of Castile.

Which niece, however, had not yet been decided—and the task of selecting the bride fell to the girls' apparently indefatigable grandmother. Eleanor had already covered something approaching a thousand miles in her whistlestop political tour around her domains in the summer of 1199. Now, in January 1200, she took to the road once again. In Poitou she was forced to negotiate a passage through the lands of the Lusignans, pacifying their aggression with a grant of the county of La Marche. That political challenge behind her, she then faced the physical test of vertiginous mountain paths as her cavalcade gingerly picked its way over the snow-drifted passes of the Pyrenees and into Navarre. She had been to that kingdom before, a decade earlier, to collect a wife for her beloved older son; but that wife was now a widow, and Eleanor pressed on southward into Castile.

At the elegant Castilian court she was reunited with her daughter Eleanor, who had left her mother behind at Bordeaux more than thirty years earlier to embrace a new life in the country of which she was now queen. This younger Eleanor shared her mother's shrewd intellect as well as her name, and perhaps their meeting offered consolation to both women after the losses of that year: Richard's sudden death had been followed in September by that of his sister Joanna of Sicily and Toulouse, who did not survive the birth of her second child at Rouen in September 1199. The elder Eleanor could also find comfort in meeting her Castilian granddaughters for the first time. Thirteen-year-old Urraca and eleven-year-old Blanca were both accomplished girls, but Eleanor, to the surprise of many observers, chose the younger as the future Queen of France, seeing in her some combination of temperament and talent that would equip her for the Parisian court over which Eleanor herself had presided at an almost equally early age. Urraca was promptly betrothed instead to Afonso, heir to the Portuguese throne, while Blanca prepared herself for the long journey north with her formidable grandmother.

The steepling route through the mountains was easier in the spring warmth, but for the first time the exertion of her travels began to take a perceptible toll on Eleanor. After spending Easter week in Bordeaux, she rode on with her granddaughter as far as the valley of the Loire; but there she gave Blanca into the care of the Archbishop of Bordeaux for the last stage of the route to Normandy. When the little Castilian princess married her French prince, a wedding lavishly celebrated with jousts and feasting, her grandmother was not present to see it. Instead, "wearied by old age and the labours of her long journey," Roger of Howden reported, "Queen Eleanor withdrew to the abbey of Fontevraud and remained there."

She was seventy-six years old; she was ill and she was tired. But still she could not rest completely. Though John had settled one conflict, he lost no time in precipitating another, this time in her duchy of Aquitaine. In the summer of 1200 John celebrated a second wedding—his own, to Isabelle, the young daughter and heiress of the Count of Angoulême. The chroniclers came to believe that John was obsessed with lust for this girl, who was no more than twelve when they married; and there was further scandal to be found in the troublesome detail that John already had a wife, although he had taken care never to obtain a papal dispensation to regularise his first consanguineous marriage to Isabella of Gloucester. But, whatever the gossip, the political fact of the matter was that there was sound strategic sense in an alliance by which John would secure control of the unruly territories of Angoulême that separated Poitiers from Bordeaux.

Or, at least, there would have been, had Isabelle not already been formally betrothed to Hugues de Lusignan, whose lands to the north of the Angoumois had so recently been bolstered by Eleanor's grant of the county of La Marche to the east. This union between two of the most insubordinate dynasties among his vassals was an alarming prospect for John, to which his own impulsive marriage to the child-bride Isabelle put an effective stop. But the cost of curbing this expansion of Lusignan power was the creation of a profoundly dangerous enemy.

Eleanor saw the threat only too clearly, and made strenuous efforts from her sickbed at Fontevraud to counter it. In the early spring of 1201 she achieved an unlikely triumph in securing the compromised allegiance of Aimery, Viscount of Thouars, a powerful but disaffected lord in northwest Poitou, whom John had deprived of the stewardship of Anjou in favour of the defector des Roches, and whose brother Guy had just married Arthur of Brittany's mother, Constance. The letter Eleanor wrote to her son in the wake of Aimery's visit to Fontevraud, advising John on how to handle the viscount's proffer of renewed loyalty, is full of the acute political insight that hard-won experience had brought to her forceful intelligence. "I want to tell you, my very dear son," she began, "that I summoned our cousin Aimery of Thouars to visit me during my illness, and the pleasure of his visit did me good, for he alone of your Poitevin barons has wrought us no injury nor seized unjustly any of your lands. I made him see how wrong and shameful it was for him to stand by and let other barons rend your heritage asunder, and he has promised to do everything he can to bring back to your obedience the lands and castles that some of his friends have seized."

John was not a stupid man—no son of Eleanor and Henry was likely to be—but he had not inherited his mother's strategic brain. Despite his mother's subtle warnings, he treated Hugues de Lusignan with punitive contempt, confiscating La Marche in order to grant the county instead to his new father-in-law, the Count of Angoulême. Lusignan appealed to Philippe as John's overlord, and by the spring of 1202 the renewal of war was inevitable. The French king declared John's lands forfeit and accepted Arthur's homage in his place for all his French territories—including Aquitaine, Philippe proclaimed, "if God grants that either we or he shall acquire it by any means whatsoever." It could hardly have been clearer that John's provocation had dismantled the legal protections Eleanor had so carefully established to shield her homeland from the conflict over the Angevin inheritance.

Yet again Aquitaine and her son stood in need of her help. At seventy-eight, she summoned what reserves of energy she could muster to leave her retreat at Fontevraud once more for the defence of Poitou. She had reached the castle of Mirebeau, fifteen miles north of Poitiers, when the menace that had been implicit in Philippe's edict took concrete form in the shape of her fifteen-year-old grandson, Arthur, marching with Hugues de Lusignan at the head of a force of French soldiers. Thirty years earlier, Mirebeau had been one of the fortresses over which her eldest son, Henri, had gone to war with his father; now it was the place where Eleanor faced a future as a hostage as her family tore itself apart once again. As Arthur's troops

advanced, Eleanor was trapped. She did not panic; nor did she surrender. She had suffered the loss of her freedom before: did she fear
it more or less, now that she had so little time left? While her grandson's forces seized control of the town, she disposed what defences
she had behind the walls of the stone keep, and covertly dispatched a
messenger who slipped silently into the twilight, heading north to Le
Mans, where John was gathering an army of mercenaries.

John had none of his brother's military genius and few decisive military manoeuvres to his name. But this threat to his mother animated
him into sudden and brilliantly resolute action. With the help of the
unlikely pairing of Aimery de Thouars and Guillaume des Roches—
former rivals whose support he would not have had, had it not been for
Eleanor—John led his troops on a forced march of eighty miles in less
than forty-eight hours to arrive at Mirebeau, unheralded and utterly
unexpected, during the night of July 31. As dawn broke they stormed
the town, falling upon Arthur's soldiers while they slept, and seizing
Hugues de Lusignan as he breakfasted on a dish of pigeons. Within
hours Arthur and de Lusignan were John's prisoners, along with all
their men; and Eleanor was safe, and free.

It was the last time she would walk on a public stage. After the
shock of her narrow escape, age and exhaustion caught up with her
at last. She did not press onward from Mirebeau into Poitou, but returned to Fontevraud to rest, and to contemplate the prospect of the
brightness of heaven rather than the storm clouds that were gathering over her son. With the loss of his mother's active support, John
lost, too, the speed of purpose and the maturity of judgement that
he had shown at Mirebeau. Revelling in the glory of his success, he
refused to allow des Roches and the Viscount of Thouars any part
in deciding the fate of the prisoners, many of whom were their countrymen—a mistake that served to confirm John's habit of undermining and alienating allies whom he should instead have nurtured and
exploited. Just two months after Mirebeau, des Roches and Thouars
abandoned him; and within weeks they had wrested Angers from his
control. John tried to forge a new relationship with the Lusignans

in their stead, but it was hardly surprising that his bitterest enemies
met his overtures with dissimulation and disloyalty. At the end of
1202 John once more retreated to Normandy. At Mirebeau, he had
held the keys to Anjou, Maine, Touraine, and Poitou—the heart of
his father's French empire, and the gateway to his mother's duchy—
and he had thrown them away.

Worse was to come. Rumours began to fly concerning the fate
of his nephew and rival, Arthur, who had disappeared as a prisoner
into John's forbidding network of Norman fortresses. Whispers told
of a drunken John, in a sotted rage, stoving in the boy's skull before
dumping the blood-soaked corpse into the Seine. Support for John
was already haemorrhaging because of his paranoiac unreliability, but revulsion at the murder now opened another gushing vein.
Meanwhile, the harrying of Normandy's eastern edge by the French
turned, in the summer of 1203, into a steady advance. Philippe had
never been a warrior in the mode of his lionhearted enemy Richard; the French king was a tense, physically cautious figure, without chivalric glamour or easy camaraderie. But, warrior or no, what
he achieved in the next twelve months was radical, even revolution-
ary, in its effect. On March 6, 1204, Château Gaillard—Richard's
"saucy castle," new-built on a jutting crag overlooking the Seine at
Les Andelys—fell to the French after a six-month siege. The loss of
this supposedly impregnable stronghold served to open the gates of
towns and citadels across Normandy to Philippe, as the duchy's inhabitants realised that John—who had ignominiously retreated to
England in December 1203—would not or could not protect them.
The unthinkable had happened: the Norman dynasty which had
so ruthlessly seized the English crown no longer ruled its Norman
homeland.

Two hundred miles further south, Eleanor retreated into silence.
For the first time in her life, the world that mattered most to her now
was the next one. But, beyond the fact that she took the habit of the
nuns who had welcomed her to their midst at Fontevraud, we know
almost nothing about her last weeks. We cannot tell whether she was

aware, in her final days, of the collapse of her husband's empire in the unsteady hands of her youngest son. All we know is that on March 31, 1204, at the age of eighty, Eleanor of Aquitaine closed her eyes for the last time. She was buried in the abbey which had become a home to her, beside her husband Henry, her son Richard, and her daughter Joanna. The calm with which her graceful effigy held in its hands an open book as it lay alongside theirs marked a cool counterpoint to the violent passions which had fractured her family in life.

And that contrast was a fitting memorial to Eleanor. Always a political creature, she had begun as a charismatically unpredictable force of instinct and will—qualities which the trials of her long in-carceration had tempered with a sophisticated diplomatic sense and what came to be the surest of political touches. The woman whose rebellion against her own husband had once threatened, it seemed, to overturn the natural order of creation had in time become the mother of the English kingdom, and the watchful guardian of her beloved Aquitaine. Eleanor had stood alone to embody the crown in England when its king was feared lost to a German jail; and she became the first woman to kneel in homage to a feudal overlord, to underpin the security of her duchy after six decades as its duchess.

If John needed any reminder of his mother's extraordinary tal-ents, it came in the months after she died. Not only was the fall of Normandy confirmed beyond all possible doubt when Philippe rode into Rouen just eleven weeks after her death, but Poitou, too, began to slip through John's fingers as its towns and lords, bereft now of the protection of their lady, scrambled to offer their allegiance instead to the French king. And in the southwestern stretches of Aquitaine, the troops of Alfonso of Castile were on the march to claim Gascony as the supposed inheritance of his wife, Eleanor's daughter and name-sake.

Jean Sans Terre, they called him; by now, it was no expression of sympathy but a damning verdict on John's catastrophic military losses. Yet this most unlovely King of England did not quite lose all his lands across the sea—and here, too, we might find an echo of

Eleanor's capabilities. Normandy and Anjou, the homelands of the kings who had ruled England for more than a century, were gone. The historian William of Newburgh believed that Normandy had fallen prey to French aggression while King Richard was a prisoner because "the courage of that ancient and most valiant people now languished, since they had neither duke, nor head, nor chief"; and the same could have been said (had William of Newburgh lived to tell the tale) of both Normandy and Anjou under the suspicious and inconstant command of John. But Aquitaine had had a head and a chief—not a duke, but a duchess—for nearly seventy years. And when the dust settled on the debris of John's empire, it was Eleanor's land of Aquitaine—battered and bloody, but still standing—that remained to the English crown.

PART IV

ISABELLA

Iron Lady

1295–1358

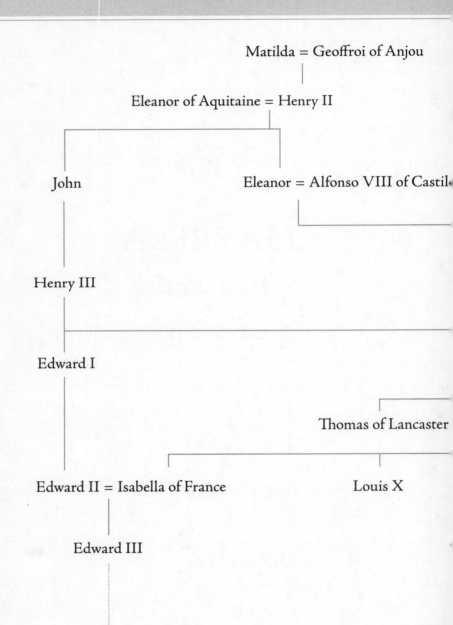

Matilda = Geoffroi of Anjou

Eleanor of Aquitaine = Henry II

John

Eleanor = Alfonso VIII of Castile

Henry III

Edward I

Thomas of Lancaster

Edward II = Isabella of France

Louis X

Edward III

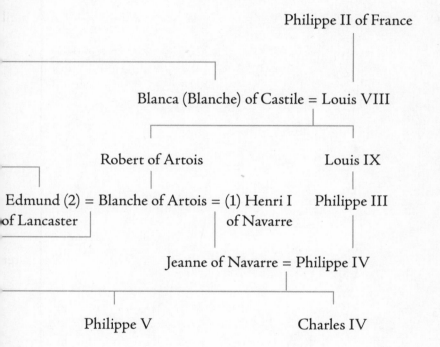

Philippe II of France

Blanca (Blanche) of Castile = Louis VIII

Robert of Artois   Louis IX

Edmund (2) = Blanche of Artois = (1) Henri I   Philippe III
of Lancaster   of Navarre

Jeanne of Navarre = Philippe IV

Philippe V   Charles IV

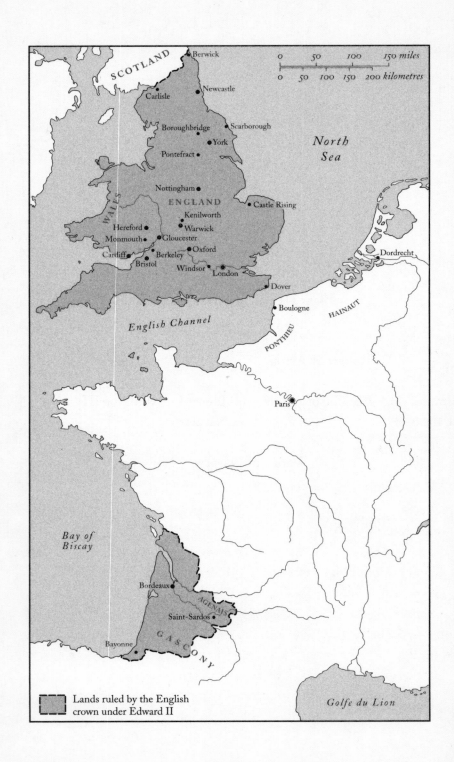

SCOTLAND

Berwick

Carlisle
Newcastle

Boroughbridge
Scarborough

York

Pontefract

North
Sea

Nottingham

ENGLAND

Castle Rising

Kenilworth

WALES

Hereford
Warwick

Monmouth
Gloucester

Cardiff
Berkeley
Oxford

Bristol
Windsor
London

Dover

English Channel

Boulogne
HAINAUT

Dordrecht

PONTHIEU

Paris

Bay of
Biscay

Bordeaux

AGENAIS

Saint-Sardos

GASCONY

Bayonne

Golfe du Lion

Lands ruled by the English
crown under Edward II

ELEVEN

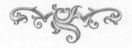

One Man So Loved Another

I t was a cold day in Boulogne, January 25, 1308, when two of Eleanor's descendants met in the cathedral church of Our Lady to exchange their wedding vows.

The bridegroom, King Edward II of England, great-grandson of Eleanor's son John, was a tall and handsome figure, powerfully built and gorgeously dressed. He was a young man, still not quite twenty-four; but his bride, at half his age, was little more than a child. Like Eleanor's granddaughter Blanca, from whom she could trace her descent, this twelve-year-old princess stood before the altar with her royal husband as the living embodiment of an Anglo-French alliance. Isabella of France was the only daughter of the French king Philippe IV, known to his subjects as *"le Bel"*—the Fair—for his statuesque good looks. Despite her youth, it was already clear that Isabella had inherited her father's beauty, and her slight frame was made luminous in the candlelight by a jewelled robe of blue and gold and a crimson mantle lined with yellow.

They were a golden couple, young and strong enough, it seemed, to bear the hopes and expectations that weighed on this marriage. The match had first been proposed a decade earlier, when Isabella was still in the nursery, as a means of bringing peace to yet another conflict over the King of England's rights to Aquitaine and his duty to his predatory overlord, the King of France.

Edward's father, the first King Edward, had harboured ambitions for his role across the Channel worthy of his Norman and Angevin forebears, but the territories he ruled there constituted only a fraction of the empire over which Eleanor's husband and sons had once fought so bitterly. John's loss of Normandy, Anjou, and Poitou had never been reversed, and King Edward, as Duke of Aquitaine, found himself in possession only of the duchy's southwestern province of Gascony, stretching along the Atlantic coast from the great city of Bordeaux to the southerly port of Bayonne.

This first Edward had been a mighty warrior, but fortune had cast military opportunity his way to the west and the north of his kingdom rather than southward across the sea to France. When the native princes of Wales tried to throw off English overlordship, he responded with a full-blown war of conquest, pinning down the principality with a chain of awe-inspiring castles, from Harlech's monolithic grandeur to Caernarfon's polygonal towers, designed in homage to the walls of Constantinople. Meanwhile, in the independent kingdom of Scotland an unexpected succession crisis gave Edward—a wolf invited through the door as arbiter between the rival claims of Robert Bruce and John Balliol—the chance to decide that the Scots, too, deserved the benefit of forcibly imposed English rule. With his energies fully occupied elsewhere, Edward's relations with France remained civil and uncontroversial—until in 1294 Philippe IV seized his moment to occupy Gascony and declare the duchy of Aquitaine forfeit to the French crown.

For three years, England and France fought an unhappy war. The cost to both sides was high in men, money, and, for Edward, political as well as financial capital, since he was simultaneously fighting at full stretch to suppress rebellion in Wales and tenacious resistance in Scotland. Peace, when it came in 1297, was a relief; and it was confirmed in 1299 with the celebration of one wedding—when Edward, at sixty, took Philippe's seventeen-year-old sister, Marguerite, as his second wife—and the promise of another, through the betrothal of little Isabella to the young prince who was heir to the English throne.

Now, in January 1308, that prince was a king. Edward I, indefatigable to the end, had died five months earlier on his way to fight once again in Scotland, leaving his son to succeed him as Edward II. And Isabella was at last old enough to become a wife and a queen. As they stood in the hushed cathedral, it seemed that a new dawn was breaking with the accession of a monarch whom "God had endowed" (said the well-informed anonymous author of the *Vita Edwardi Secundi*, a contemporary Latin account of Edward's life) "with every gift"—including, now, the hand in marriage of the French king's exquisite daughter.

All, however, was not as it seemed. For those who cared to look, there were signs aplenty that the dazzling ceremony at Boulogne glittered with empty artifice rather than political promise. Edward shared his father's name—an unusual Anglo-Saxon throwback, thanks to his grandfather's reverence for the saintly eleventh-century king Edward the Confessor—but in other ways he resembled him little. He was the last-born of his parents' fourteen children, and three older brothers—John, Henry, and Alfonso—had died in turn before they had a chance to try their hand at the business of ruling. Edward alone was left to shoulder responsibility for England's future. And already, before his father's death, he had begun to disappoint.

At six, Edward had been presented with a toy castle, lovingly made and painted in intricate detail by a member of his household. But this military plaything did not shape his tastes as his father might have hoped. Though he grew to be physically strong, a good horseman, and no coward in the face of combat (as he proved in more than

one of his father's campaigns), he did not live and breathe the life
of a soldier as his father had done. He preferred what the *Vita Edwardi Secundi* despairingly called "rustic pursuits"—rowing, swim-
ming, digging ditches, and thatching houses—and the company of
"mechanicals" such as the "buffoons, singers, actors, carters, ditch-
ers, oarsmen, and sailors" with whom he was accused of fraternising
by the unimpressed monastic chronicler Ranulf Higden. These were
not the habits of a king—or, at least, not a king who hoped to win
the respect of his people and the hearts and minds of his war- and
status-obsessed nobility.

Edward was not completely averse to female company, it seems,
since he had an illegitimate son, Adam, who was born before his
marriage to Isabella. But his preference for the unpretentious camaraderie of workingmen, rather than the hierarchical formality of aristocratic society, may nevertheless have been symptomatic of a more
profound inability to "fit" the role into which he had been born. For it
was abundantly clear that the companionship Edward valued above
all was that of one man in particular: a young Gascon named Perrot
de Gabaston, or, as he came to be known in England, Piers Gaveston.

Gaveston and Edward first began to spend time together in 1300,
when Gaveston joined the sixteen-year-old prince's household after
serving for three years as a soldier under the command of Edward's
father. By 1305 they were sufficiently close that, when Edward quarrelled with his father's treasurer that summer, the king manifested
his displeasure not only by stopping his son's allowance but by ban-
ishing Gaveston (along with a few other members of the prince's
household) from Edward's side. This separation was brief, however,
and in May 1306 Gaveston was knighted by his prince, along with
more than 250 other young men, just four days after Edward himself
had received the swordbelt and spurs of knighthood from his father.

By then, the favour in which Gaveston stood with young Edward
was beginning to attract attention. And attention, to Gaveston himself, was like sunlight. By nature—much more so than Edward, the
prince who liked nothing better than to spend his days in the com-

panionable anonymity of physical labour—Gaveston was a peacock, his graceful athleticism constantly on display along with his brittle charisma and his barbed wit. As a result, the deepening of their relationship could not escape public notice, especially since its intensity suggested an affection that went beyond the platonic. "I do not remember to have heard that one man so loved another," observed the author of the *Vita Edwardi Secundi* pointedly. Knights, it was well known, might pledge undying loyalty to one another as brothers in arms, and both biblical and classical tradition offered familiar examples of masculine devotion: "Jonathan cherished David, Achilles loved Patroclus," noted the *Vita*. "But we do not read that they were immoderate." Edward, on the other hand, "was passionately attached to one particular person, whom he cherished above all," Ranulf Higden wrote. And although these chroniclers' verdicts were delivered with the acuity of hindsight, Edward's growing obsession with Gaveston does seem to be the most plausible explanation of steps that were taken in 1307 to separate them.

Gaveston had not endeared himself to old King Edward in the winter of 1306 when, with twenty-one other young knights, he deserted the king's campaign against Robert Bruce to pursue his passion for fighting in the more glamorous arena of the tournament field rather than in the Scottish mud. For that offence he was formally pardoned in January 1307; but only a month later he was banished from England and forbidden to return without the king's express permission. However, the royal treasury was ordered to pay him a generous allowance "for as long as he shall remain in parts beyond the sea during the king's pleasure and waiting recall"—and the unmistakable impression is that this was not so much a punishment for Gaveston as an attempt to remove an overwhelming distraction from the life of the heir to the throne.

It was this—the all-consuming nature of Edward's fascination with Gaveston—that caused such alarm about the prince's conduct, rather than the bare fact that questions might now be raised about his sexuality. Certainly, homosexuality was condemned as sinful by the Church, but so were all sexual acts outside the marriage bed, and some within it, if they were performed for pleasure rather than procreation. Contemporaries might well see some forms of "sodomy" (a word which could be used as a general term for all such sinful sex, as well as in its more specific sense) as more unnatural than others; but then again Edward was not the first of England's rulers to show signs of sexual interest in men as well as women. The Conqueror's son and successor, William Rufus, neither married nor fathered any illegitimate children, and was lambasted by monastic chroniclers for his extravagantly foppish dress, his louche habits, and his irreligiosity. But his stature as a king, in contemporary opinion and that of posterity, was determined not by the fact that his "intimate companions" were male, nor by what the monks saw as the effeminate fashions of his court, but by his considerable judgement as a soldier and a leader.

The problem for Edward, therefore, was a pattern that emerged clearly for the first time with Gaveston's exile in 1307. The fact was that, with Gaveston by his side, Edward was incapable of sustained concentration on government or on war, or on any of the weighty matters that should occupy a king's attention; it was reported that he could scarcely conduct a conversation with anyone else if Gaveston was in the room. "Our king," the *Vita* later lamented, "was incapable of moderate favour, and on account of Piers was said to forget himself...." The solution, thought his father and his magnates, was simple: remove Gaveston, and all would be well. But Edward's obsession was such that separation left him in the grip of a single mania: to secure Gaveston's return.

That much was clear when Edward I died on July 7, 1307, on his way north to Scotland. By the time the new king arrived from London to receive the homage of his magnates at the frontier castle of Carlisle on July 20, messengers had already departed to recall Gaveston from his exile (and he was much nearer at hand to receive them than might have been the case, since he had taken up residence not in Gascony as the old king had stipulated, but just across the Channel in the county of Ponthieu, which the younger Edward had inherited from

his mother in 1290). While the old king's body made its stately way
south to Westminster Abbey, the new king rode north into Scotland
to show his strength and appoint lieutenants there before his return
to London for his father's funeral; and on this journey, at Dumfries
on August 6, Edward declared that Piers Gaveston was to be ele-
vated to the highest rank of the peerage as Earl of Cornwall, a title
and vast estate which had long been held by members of the king's
immediate family. Not only that, but Gaveston would make a royal
marriage: Edward gave him as his bride his young niece, fifteen-year-
old Margaret de Clare, daughter of his sister Joan and the late Earl
of Gloucester.

This glamorous wedding took place only five days after the old
king's burial—indecent haste, perhaps, but then again the speed
with which Edward had already dismissed his father's treasurer, and
promoted others with whom the old king had been at loggerheads,
suggests that defiance rather than deference was uppermost in the
new king's attitude toward his father's memory. Edward himself was
guest of honour at Berkhamsted Castle to witness the ceremony, and
among his personal gifts to the couple were the hundreds of silver
pennies with which the groom and his young bride were glitteringly
showered as they entered the church.

Less than two months later, in the gloom of a Boulogne January, it was Edward's turn to be married. His even younger bride,
the dainty French princess Isabella, did not have to contend with
Gaveston's presence among the cathedral's blue-blooded congregation as she made her vows, since the newly created earl had not
sailed from Dover with the king. But even in absentia Gaveston cast
a long shadow. All those members of the wedding party, French and
English, who concerned themselves with politics knew that he had
remained in London as "keeper of the realm"—in effect, regent of
England. In just six months, this younger son of an obscure Gascon
lord had come a disconcertingly long way.

If Isabella had been shielded from any public display of her husband's devotion to Gaveston during the ceremony that made her a

wife, the same could not be said of the ritual that made her a queen. A month to the day after their wedding, Edward and Isabella walked in magnificent procession from the Palace of Westminster to the neighbouring abbey for their joint coronation. Beneath their feet was a woollen carpet strewn with flowers, and above their heads an embroidered canopy carried aloft on decorated poles by the barons of the Cinque Ports. Before them paced some of the greatest men in England, including the earls of Lancaster, Warwick, Hereford, and Lincoln, carrying the priceless regalia—swords, sceptres, spurs, and robes—with which Edward would shortly be invested. But occupying the position of greatest honour immediately in front of the royal couple—in full view of a crowd so pressingly large that one knight was crushed to death when a wall gave way in the abbey—was Piers Gaveston, "so decked out," noted an eyewitness from nearby St. Paul's, "that he more resembled the god Mars than an ordinary mortal."

The symbolism of Gaveston's role in this most sacred ceremony of kingmaking was as plain to Edward's young queen as it was to every other spectator. It was Gaveston who carried into the church the golden crown of St. Edward the Confessor, a holy relic as well as the physical emblem of the king's authority. Once Edward and Isabella had been anointed, enthroned, and crowned and the shouts of acclamation had rung out, it was Gaveston who held the Confessor's Sword of Mercy as the royal couple re-emerged into the wintry afternoon light. At the coronation feast, Gaveston appeared "more splendidly dressed than the king himself," according to the St. Paul's annalist, in silk of imperial purple embroidered with pearls (as opposed to the mere cloth of gold worn by his fellow earls). And he, not Isabella, sat at Edward's side beneath hanging tapestries that had been specially commissioned for the occasion to depict the heraldic blazons of the happy couple: not the emblems of Edward and Isabella, but "the arms of the king and of Piers Gaveston, Earl of Cornwall."

There could be no mistaking that the king did not stand alone, in either his public or his private life, and that his inseparable companion was not the young woman to whom he had so recently made his vows. No royal bride, playing her part in international diplomacy, would be so naïve as to expect her marriage to be founded on romantic love, or to assume that she would be the only recipient of her husband's attentions. But the unique dignity of her role as the king's anointed consort was a different matter. That, she would take for granted. And, even at twelve years old, Isabella was politically aware enough to object to her public displacement by the man to whom her husband was so slavishly devoted.

Certainly, the little queen's royal uncles who had escorted her to England for the coronation, Louis of Évreux and Charles of Valois, were incensed at her treatment. Offence was piled upon offence: Edward had still not made proper provision for the income and estates Isabella should receive as queen in order that she could support herself and her household with appropriate grandeur; agreement had not been reached about the inheritances her future children would receive; and, most egregiously insulting of all, Edward had given the wedding presents that he and Isabella had received from her father, including jewels and great warhorses, to Gaveston. Louis and Charles walked out of the coronation banquet in disgust and returned to France in a fury, "seeing," the St. Paul's annalist said archly, "that the king frequented Piers's couch more than the queen's."

They were not alone in their objections. By the spring of 1308 Gaveston's place at Edward's side was causing uproar in England as well as at the court of the French king. The nobles had been prepared to tolerate his elevation to their ranks as Earl of Cornwall, but since then their forbearance had been severely tested not only by his place in the limelight at the coronation, but also by the breathtaking arrogance with which he conducted himself among his new peers. At a tournament held at Wallingford in December 1307, Gaveston and his knights had won the day against a company including the earls of Arundel, Hereford, and Surrey. There was no grace in Gaveston's victory, no magnanimity in his physical prowess. Instead, his crowing and condescension made personal enemies of the men he had defeated. "Piers, now Earl of Cornwall, did not wish to remember that he had once been Piers the humble esquire," noted the perceptive author of the *Vita Edwardi Secundi*. "For Piers accounted no one his fellow, no one his peer, save the king alone...His arrogance was intolerable to the barons, and a prime cause of hatred and rancour."

It was not that Gaveston was trying to take the reins of government from Edward's hands. His aims were no more and no less than his own wealth and glory. The weeks he spent as "keeper of the realm" during Edward's absence in France, for example, were not marked by any attempt to pursue a political agenda beyond that of his own self-aggrandisement. That was plenty irritating enough, of course, to generate huge personal animus against this pretentious upstart. But what united the nobles in public defiance of Edward's will was the sense that their king was incapable of addressing the needs of his realm with clear-sighted consistency while his field of vision was obscured by the presence of his favourite. In particular, the English position in Scotland, on which so many lives and so much money had been expended, was in danger of being abandoned without a fight: Edward was showing no signs of interest in pursuing his father's war against Robert Bruce, who was making good use of the free hand he had thereby been given to establish himself as King of Scots in fact as well as in name.

When the English lords assembled for a meeting of parliament at Westminster Abbey in April 1308, their dissatisfaction took concrete form for the first time. For several weeks, both king and barons had been making hurried attempts to arm themselves ahead of the coming storm. And now Henry Lacy, Earl of Lincoln, an old soldier of fifty-eight who had been one of Edward I's right-hand men, stepped forward on behalf of his peers to confront the king. "Homage and the oath of allegiance are more in respect of the crown than in respect of the king's person," argued the document he presented to Edward. "If," therefore, "it should befall that the king is not guided by reason," then his subjects had a duty to act "to reinstate the king in the dignity of the crown"—by force, if necessary. And in this case, of course, the dignity of the crown could only be restored if Gaveston were removed.

If Edward had believed he could hold out against the complaints of his lords, his hopes were dashed when envoys arrived from his wife's father to demand Gaveston's banishment, since the King of France now considered him a mortal enemy. Faced with the double threat of rebellion among the ranks of the English nobility and armed intervention from France, Edward was forced to capitulate. On May 14, 1308, he sought to mollify his father-in-law by endowing his queen, at last, with the northern French counties of Ponthieu and Montreuil. And on May 18 he put his seal to an order that Gaveston should leave England within five weeks, on pain, the Archbishop of Canterbury announced the following day, of excommunication.

For Isabella, this moment shone a rare shaft of light across a landscape of wrecked expectations. Life as England's queen had not, so far, offered much reassurance to a girl raised in one of Europe's most sophisticated courts with a profound sense of the dignity of her station. Like Matilda and Eleanor before her, Isabella had had to embrace the prospect of a new life in an alien land at an age when the comforts of the nursery were not far behind her. Unlike them, she had rapidly discovered that she could depend on her new husband for neither love nor respect. She had been sidelined at her own coronation by a man with whom her husband was publicly and humiliatingly infatuated. Concern for her youth might well have kept Edward away from her bed for some time after their wedding, whatever the circumstances; but his attentions were so ostentatiously engaged elsewhere that he could claim little credit for any such consideration. While Gaveston preened in silks and jewels lavished upon him by the king, Isabella had scarcely been able to maintain her entourage in the state to which she had been accustomed as a princess of France, let alone as the anointed Queen of England. Now, at last, it seemed as though the way was clear for this proud young woman to take her rightful place beside her king—perhaps even to advise and support him, as revered royal wives had done before her.

There was hope, then, for the queen, even as the king's desolation at the loss of his soulmate was plain for all to see. Edward was with Gaveston until the moment he took ship at Bristol for Ireland, his exile having been finagled by the king into an appointment as royal lieutenant there. The last time Gaveston had been forced to leave England by Edward's father, Edward had showered him with gifts including two tourneying outfits in green emblazoned with Gaveston's arms, one in fine linen, the other in velvet embroidered with pearls and piping of silver and gold. This time, his presents were less immediately tangible but infinitely more valuable. Under the terms of his banishment Gaveston had lost his lands as Earl of Cornwall, but Edward insisted that he should keep the title at least, and before he set sail the king granted him estates in England and Gascony on a scale to rival those of which he had been deprived.

His departure left Edward in misery that was equalled only by the relief of his lords and his young queen. But Gaveston's removal did not prove to be the panacea for which they had hoped. True, Edward did now turn his energies to building bridges with his nobles and talking of the urgent need to counter the resurgent Scots—and the earls responded with alacrity to these overtures, desperate as they were for active and purposeful leadership. But by the summer of 1309 it was becoming apparent that these were tactics born of Edward's monomania, not the beginnings of newly focused kingship. Securing the collaboration of his magnates was not the prelude to the Scottish campaign for which they hoped, despite costly preparations now put in train. Instead, it served to bolster Edward's battered authority to the point at which he could secure Gaveston's return— at first in secret when he slipped quietly into the northwestern city of Chester in June, and then in August when he was publicly, if reluctantly, acknowledged by the nobles in parliament.

That the lords were uneasy in their acquiescence was obvious from the grievances about the financial oppressions of his government that they laid before the king as the price of Gaveston's recall. Did the speed with which Edward waved the reforms through suggest that he and his favourite had learned lessons from their separation? The lords must have hoped that it did; but instead Gaveston's reinstatement as Earl of Cornwall proved to be the cue for yet another turn of the merry-go-round. Gaveston himself was not chastened but triumphant at his political resurrection, and his mockery of the serious-minded earls who had tried to expel him from their ranks became still more outrageously insolent. Laughingly, he gave them derisive nicknames—the Earl of Warwick was "Warwick the Dog," the *Vita* reports, with later chroniclers adding "Burst-Belly" for the aging Earl of Lincoln, "Churl" for the Earl of Lancaster, and "Joseph the Jew" for the Earl of Pembroke, "because he was pale and tall." And all the while Edward's officials continued to exact money from his people for a military campaign in Scotland that showed no sign of taking place.

In February 1310 the lords once again came to a parliament armed and angry, to demand that action be taken to deal with the failings of Edward's regime. The king had already sent Gaveston away from court for his own safety while the earls gathered in force, and now Edward had no choice but to give in to their insistence that he appoint a body of twenty-one lords, temporal and spiritual, "to ordain and establish the estate of our household and of our realm." These "Ordainers," as they came to be known, were to rule on Edward's behalf for the next eighteen months, and, although the document to which Edward set his seal asserted that he gave them authority "of our free will," the *Vita* had no doubt of the nature of that freedom: the lords had made it clear that "unless the king granted their demands they would not have him for king, nor keep the fealty that they had sworn to him."

As the Ordainers set to work, Edward embarked on a bold strategy of misdirection. While his lords usurped his government, he would show his worth as king by dealing at last with the catastrophic military situation in Scotland. This plan, it seemed to the beleaguered king, had multiple advantages. He was doing what his subjects had repeatedly demanded, thereby demonstrating that he was capable of defending the realm and its interests as he was required to do by the crown he wore. He was also extricating himself from the shackles the Ordainers had placed upon his authority in London; they might meddle with his administration, but no one, surely, could countermand a king at the head of his troops. Lastly, and most importantly for Edward, he was removing Gaveston from immediate danger. Extraordinary though it might seem, a Scottish battlefield was now a safer prospect for the graceful Earl of Cornwall, able fighter that he was, than an assembly of English peers. For Isabella—who was now fifteen, and having to resign herself once more, with icy restraint, to playing second fiddle in her own marriage—Edward's strategy meant the dubious pleasure of a first visit to the far north of her adopted country in the company of an army led by her husband and his flamboyant lover.

It was an ingenious tactic; but it did not work. It was too late for the king to convince his lords that he intended to emulate his father by hammering the Scots—and, even if he could have persuaded them of his seriousness of purpose, almost none of them were willing to join an army with Gaveston as well as Edward at its head (the only exceptions being the twenty-year-old Earl of Gloucester, Gaveston's brother-in-law, and John de Warenne, Earl of Surrey). A campaign without the military might of the earls at its back was never likely to succeed; and it soon emerged that Robert Bruce and his men would not meet Edward's troops on open ground, but harried them with raids and ambushes amid a ravaged landscape, laid waste by the Scots themselves in order to threaten the English with starvation.

After a fruitless eight months based in the far northeast at the frontier town of Berwick, Edward and Isabella rode south in July 1311, leaving Gaveston, newly named as the king's lieutenant in Scotland, holed up in the Northumbrian fortress of Bamburgh. Back in London at the beginning of August—as Bruce and his soldiers launched devastating raids into northern England, in brutal demonstration of Edward's military failure—the king was confronted by the reforms that had been painstakingly drawn up by the Lords

Ordainer. These forty-one ordinances provided for the detailed supervision of Edward's government—especially the ways in which he
raised money from his subjects, and the ways in which he chose to
spend it—by his nobles, in their capacity as representatives of the
realm. And among these stipulations, to no one's surprise, was the
demand that Piers Gaveston should be exiled from England once
more, this time forever.

Edward may not have been surprised, but he was aghast and enraged at the corner in which he now found himself. He railed against
the appalling presumption of his subjects in seeking to constrain his
sovereignty. But to no effect: and while the Ordainers stood firm,
Edward—with the utter lack of insight that had characterised everything he had done since he inherited his crown—gave the clear-
est demonstration yet of why his lords had been driven to oppose
him. "To satisfy the barons he offered these terms," explained the
Vita: "Whatever has been ordained or decided upon, he said, however much it may redound to my private disadvantage, shall be established at your request and remain in force for ever. But you shall stop
persecuting my brother Piers, and allow him to have the earldom of
Cornwall. The king sought this, time and again, now coaxing them
with flattery, now hurling threats...." What Edward did not see, was
incapable of seeing, was that all but one of the ordinances were concerned not with his "private disadvantage" but with his public duty as
king. Had he only recognised that fact, had he shown any inkling of
the responsibilities as well as the rights of the crown, then the single
provision that should have been a private matter—the one concerning his relationship with Gaveston—need never have been drafted.

But there was no moment of realisation. Instead, confronted with
the reality of civil war as the only possible consequence of his continued resistance, Edward had no option but to concede. The ordinances were proclaimed throughout England, and excommunication
instituted as the penalty for anyone who violated them. And on November 3, Gaveston again sailed into exile.

This time, however, there was nothing strategic about the king's response. He was driven by fury, declaring that his nobles were treating him as though he were an idiot whose household had to be managed by others because of his incapacity. Once again he moved north as soon as he could, to escape the constraints on his freedom of action in London, and as soon as he was free he sent word to Flanders to summon Gaveston back to his side. By the middle of January 1312 they were together again at the great northern city of York, where Edward proclaimed Gaveston's restoration to the earldom of Cornwall, and denounced his exile as unlawful. Now the king was preparing in earnest for war.

And he was not the only one. Here the temperaments and the individual judgements of Edward's most powerful subjects—the men whose foibles Gaveston had so mercilessly mocked—came into play in decisive fashion. Extraordinarily tense though the political world had been ever since Edward's accession, it had been relatively easy until now for the earls to stand united in their demand that the king should expel his favourite and reform his government. But once it became clear that Edward would defy them, the question was no longer what the magnates wanted, but whether they were prepared to take arms against their anointed king to get it. One among the earls was spared this fateful decision. Henry Lacy, Earl of Lincoln and the regime's elder statesman, had died at his London home, Lincoln's Inn in Holborn, on February 5, 1311. His fidelity to the crown and his cultured dignity were a grievous loss in such troubled times; and his death helped to bestow the mantle of leadership on the man who inherited his earldom—his son-in-law, Thomas of Lancaster.

Lancaster, at thirty-four, was a very different proposition from his respected father-in-law. He was acutely conscious of his own pre-eminent position among the English nobility, set apart as he was from his peers both by birth and by the scale of his wealth and power. He was the son of Edmund of Lancaster, Edward I's younger brother, and Blanche of Artois, widow of the King of Navarre and granddaughter of Louis VIII of France—a lineage which made him, uniquely, both the cousin of Edward II and the maternal uncle of the young queen, Isabella. Also uniquely, he held a grand total of five earldoms with lands stretching across England: those of Lancaster, Leicester, and Derby he had inherited from his father, to which his marriage to the heiress Alice Lacy now added the titles and estates of Lincoln and Salisbury. But he did not have the personal stature to match this extraordinary political standing. He was always more aware of his entitlement to demand loyalty than of the qualities needed to inspire it; and his instincts as a loner, aloof and haughty, competed for supremacy with his fierce ambition as a leader.

For now, however, the fact that open conflict could focus on the despised person of Gaveston was enough to hold a tense coalition of magnates together. The Lords Ordainer, with Lancaster now taking a prominent role among them, made arrangements for the security of southern England while dispatching troops northward under the command not only of the intransigent Lancaster himself but also the earls of Pembroke and Surrey, both of whom had previously shown themselves willing to contemplate a more politic engagement with the king and his lover. It was a measure of the extreme caution made necessary by this threatening situation that the task of arresting Gaveston was committed specifically to their careful hands.

Edward and Gaveston, meanwhile, remained for several weeks at York, where Isabella joined them in the second half of February. The length of their stay was occasioned not only by the need to co-ordinate military preparations but also by the fact that Gaveston's wife, the Earl of Gloucester's sister Margaret de Clare, had given birth to a daughter, Joan, on January 12. It was not until February 20 that the countess's churching took place—the ritual of purification that marked her re-emergence into the world after her confinement—and was followed a few days later by the baby's christening, a sumptuous affair on which the king spent lavishly. By then, though she could not yet have known it, Isabella, too, was pregnant.

The timing may simply have been fortuitous. At sixteen, the queen was now mature enough for the prospect of childbirth to be merely commonly, rather than uncommonly, dangerous. If, as seems

likely, a decision had been taken at the time of her wedding that she
was too young to consummate the marriage, such restraint was no
longer physically necessary. But, given the specific circumstances of
Isabella's married life, it is also possible that the start of her sexual
relationship with Edward, and the pregnancy that resulted, were politically inspired. Certainly, the imminent threat of civil war is likely
to have focused the minds of both Edward and Gaveston, his fellow
first-time father, on the advantages of acquiring a legitimate heir.

Advantageous the news may have been, but it did nothing to stop
the conflict. As the earls rode north (claiming, and convincing no
one, that the men they were mustering were gathering to take part in
tournaments), Edward, Gaveston, and Isabella moved ahead of them
to the northeast, Isabella often travelling separately from her husband, and more slowly, perhaps impeded by the early stages of her
pregnancy as well as by the proprieties of queenly travel on rutted
roads amid a large household entourage. Certainly, though, the pressures of their unhappy situation were becoming more intense. At the
end of April Isabella caught up with her husband and Gaveston at
the northeastern fortress of Newcastle, before pushing on another
eight miles without them to the comforting security of Tynemouth
Priory, a Benedictine community nestled within a newly built and
massively fortified curtain wall on a rocky headland overlooking the
North Sea. But both comfort and security vanished in an instant on
May 4, when Edward and Gaveston arrived with a small retinue at
the priory's gate, sweating and breathless from their sudden flight.
The Earl of Lancaster's army had appeared with terrifying speed
outside Newcastle's walls, and the king had left almost everything
behind—weapons, horses, jewels—in his desperation to evade his
cousin's grasp.

They could not rest for long. The next day Edward and Gaveston
put to sea, heading eighty miles down the coast to Scarborough. For
Gaveston, who had recently been ill, this bleak five-day voyage was
a necessary evil to escape the implacable hostility of his enemies.
For Isabella, however, the calculation of risk was very different: her

sex, her station, and her pregnancy would protect her from harm at the hands of the earls, while the danger that she might become their hostage weighed less heavily than the threat to the king's unborn heir posed by the North Sea's unpredictable currents. She therefore hurried south by road, abandoning rich bundles of baggage under guard on the Northumbrian coast to be retrieved at a more propitious moment.

At York she was reunited with her husband, who had left Gaveston safe behind the impregnable walls of Scarborough Castle and ridden west to join her. Unassailable Scarborough's fortifications certainly were, looming as they did from a clifftop three hundred feet above the harbour. But Edward's hopes for Gaveston's safety were soon scattered to the winds. The Ordainers' army, under the command of Pembroke and Surrey, moved swiftly to isolate the headland on which the castle stood, a cordon which in a matter of days formed a stranglehold. True, the besiegers could not reach Gaveston and his men inside the walls, but neither could supplies of food or arms or any other kind of help from his devoted king. In despair, Gaveston accepted terms for his own surrender on May 19. Pembroke and Surrey solemnly swore that they would guarantee their prisoner's safety until August 1. By then, the agreement stipulated, either a peace settlement would be agreed between the king and all his magnates, or Gaveston would be returned to Scarborough, a castle that would be neither re-garrisoned nor re-provisioned in the meantime, to take his chances under renewed siege as if the negotiations had never happened. Edward, who was consulted at York, had no option but to give his assent; and Gaveston began his journey south as a prisoner in the custody of the Earl of Pembroke, Aymer de Valence.

At almost forty, Pembroke was a careful, measured man who had proved a loyal servant to Edward I and to his son, although his loyalty by now was of a kind that Edward II was too short-sighted to recognise. It had been with obvious reluctance that he had been driven to stand against his king—he had even been prepared to argue Edward's case for Gaveston's recall from an earlier exile, in his capacity as an envoy to the pope in the spring of 1309—but a year later his disenchantment with the failings of Edward's rule led him to take his place among his peers as one of the Lords Ordainer. But, as befitted a man who had been intended for a career in the Church until the early death of his elder brother, his newly sworn pledge to ensure Gaveston's safety was for Pembroke a matter of both personal honour and sacred duty, and he treated his prisoner with grace and respect.

On June 9 the two earls, captor and captive, arrived at the village of Deddington in Oxfordshire, where Pembroke found Gaveston comfortable lodgings at the rectory and left him under guard while he rode on another twenty miles to visit his wife at his manor of Bampton. But Pembroke was not the only one of the Lords Ordainer who knew Gaveston's whereabouts on this stately progress southward, and not all of his fellow earls shared Pembroke's serene sense of obligation about the honourable treatment their prisoner was currently enjoying. For some, Gaveston was a renegade who had already made fools of them too often. Was it not obvious that, in order to secure Gaveston's freedom, the king would agree to anything they asked, and then go back on his word as he had done so many times before? The ordinances had already decreed that, if Gaveston breached the terms of his exile, he should be treated "as an enemy of the king and of the kingdom and of his people." And a peace process that set aside this prescription could mean only that the merry-go-round would continue to turn.

Among the earls unhappy with the genteel handling of their prisoner was Guy Beauchamp, the forty-year-old Earl of Warwick. Like Pembroke, he had served Edward I faithfully; unlike Pembroke, he had been quick to voice his opposition to Edward II's failings and Gaveston's role in fostering them. The old king had granted Warwick extensive lands in Scotland as a reward for his military service there, which gave a particularly sharp edge to Warwick's resentment of Edward's disastrous neglect of the English campaign north of the border. He had also been at the old king's bedside when he died, and may have been instructed to resist Gaveston's return from that first, long-ago exile. Certainly, he had been utterly consistent in his determination to remove Gaveston and the provocative distraction he represented. Warwick was a cultured and discriminating man, but something of his tenacious forcefulness is apparent in Gaveston's choice of nickname for him: "Warwick the Dog," the *Vita* reports— an epithet elaborated by later tradition into "the Black Hound of Arden."

In June 1312 Warwick passionately believed that the critical state of English politics demanded more forceful action than the cautious Pembroke had so far shown any sign of undertaking. Hearing that Gaveston had been left, lightly guarded, at Deddington, the earl assembled his retainers in force and rode the twenty-five miles across country from his castle at Warwick. Early in the morning of Saturday, June 10, his men surrounded the rectory where Gaveston was staying; and when they saw how overwhelmingly they were outnumbered, Pembroke's soldiers simply abandoned their arms. "Get up, traitor—you are taken!" the *Vita* has Warwick shout outside Gaveston's window. And Gaveston had no choice but to comply.

"Led forth not as an earl but as a thief," Gaveston was escorted out of Deddington, at first on foot, and then roughly bundled onto a packhorse quite unlike the fine palfreys to which he was accustomed. When they reached Warwick Castle, towering over the town that shared its name, he was cast into a prison cell within the walls of the fortress. Pembroke had treated him with the dignity of a peer, Warwick with all the niceties due to a traitor.

That did not, however, mean that Warwick was confident of his next move. This was the moment at which the unity of the lords would be tested to destruction. They had done so much in the name of the crown against the will of their king—forced reform on his government, issued ordinances in his name, expelled his favourite from England's shores. But could those ordinances now justify the use of lethal force against a man who was not only a peer of the realm, but dearer to the king than the kingdom itself? Could such an execution be lawful, when the king himself, the lawgiver whose responsibility it was to bring justice to his people, would never accept it? Edward had already declared Gaveston's exile unlawful. How, then, could his punishment for breaching its terms be justified? And if an earl could be killed without the sanction of the law, where, then, lay safety for his killers?

Pembroke was clear in his answer. His own honour and integrity depended on fulfilling his guarantee that Gaveston would be kept safe from harm while a settlement was negotiated with the king, and he frantically sought to recover his prisoner. But Warwick, knowing full well the dangers of action, still could not bear to contemplate the risk of inaction: that Edward would yet again put Gaveston's baneful influence before the needs of his country. Collective responsibility—the earls' claim to speak for the "community of the realm"—had so far provided a means by which to restrain the king. Perhaps collective responsibility could now justify Gaveston's death.

More earls on caparisoned warhorses clattered through Warwick Castle's great gates in the days that followed: thirty-six-year-old Humphrey de Bohun, Earl of Hereford and Essex and husband of Edward's sister Elizabeth; twenty-seven-year-old Edmund Fitzalan, Earl of Arundel; and, most powerful of all, Thomas of Lancaster, holder of five earldoms and arbiter, it now seemed, of England's destiny. For days, these lords deliberated while Gaveston waited in the cold and gloom of his cell. They sealed documents promising one another protection from any repercussions that might befall them should Gaveston be executed. Two judges were called in to sentence him to death according to the terms of the ordinances—a legal gloss which could not mask the facts of a case in which the accused had had no properly constituted trial. And the death knell finally sounded when Lancaster at last stepped forward to play out the role of leadership for which his inheritance and his ambition had fitted him. "It was necessary for him to be great who should defend such a deed," explained the *Vita* solemnly. "Hence Thomas, Earl of Lancaster, being of higher birth and more powerful than the rest, took upon himself the peril of the business. . . ."

On Monday, June 19, Gaveston was brought from his prison, blinking and bound in the early morning light, and handed over to the Earl of Lancaster's men. His "martial glory" gone, he was dragged two miles north to Blacklow Hill, which belonged to the estates of Lancaster's nearby castle of Kenilworth. While Warwick remained within the walls of his own fortress, Lancaster, Hereford, and Arundel followed some way behind the procession, the earls' unease made manifest in their physical distance from an execution that bore the hallmarks not of judicial process but of a lynching. A messenger was on hand to relay Lancaster's orders; and at his word a soldier stepped forward and drove his sword into Gaveston's abdomen. Gaveston fell, bleeding, as another man unsheathed a blade to sever his head from his body. Lancaster waited and watched until he saw the head lifted into the air—no trophy, but proof of a job done. Then he turned his horse and rode away.

Gaveston, the preening peacock, was gone at last, his glittering colours faded to black, his mocking voice silenced. But his capacity to make trouble was far from over. The earls had hoped that his removal would free Edward to turn his attention to government, to the war in Scotland, and to the advice of his lords about the needs of his people. Lancaster had been prepared, in the end, to remove him by violence, as a desperate resolution to an intractable problem. But the problem had not gone away. Instead, it had changed in form.

Death did not end Edward's devotion to Gaveston. His mutilated corpse had been left lying on the bloody grass at Blacklow, the embarrassing detritus of a dangerous political act, until it was rescued by a group of Dominican friars and taken to Oxford, where it lay in state at the king's command, embalmed and dressed in cloth of gold, to await burial (since Gaveston, excommunicated by the Archbishop of Canterbury for his breach of the ordinances, could not be interred in consecrated ground until the anathema was revoked). Meanwhile,

Edward's response to his loss was as clear to the author of the *Vita* as it was to the perpetrators of Gaveston's death: "They knew that when the matter came to the king's notice, he would, if he could, proceed to take vengeance."

The earls had begun this conflict united in search of a king who would take responsibility for his realm and offer them leadership. Their unity was now irretrievably fractured: Pembroke was back at the king's side, raging at his former allies who had swept aside his personal promise of safe-conduct to Gaveston (not to mention the possessions he had pledged as a guarantee of his oath). And the consequences of this division ran frighteningly deep. The lords who had Gaveston's blood on their hands—principally Lancaster, the king's cousin and the greatest magnate in England—could not now afford to see their sovereign restored to untrammelled power, however magisterial his rule might conceivably be without the distraction of Gaveston's presence, because Edward, as the *Vita* coolly explains, "had already decided to destroy those who killed Piers." And the manner of that killing—no trial, no hearing before his peers in open court, just a brutal blow on a sunny hillside—had handed the king enough rope to hang them with. No one knew what the future would bring, but there could be little doubt that the scene was set for more turmoil, more violence, and more bloodshed.

One more player remained in the wings, watching and waiting, while she enacted a private drama of her own. On Sunday, November 12, in her brilliantly painted chamber at Windsor Castle—golden stars dancing on green as the Wise and Foolish Virgins played out their parable in the finest pigments—Isabella went into labour. Shortly before six the next morning, she gave birth to a boy. The seventeen-year-old queen had kept her own counsel since the bitter complaints her uncles had relayed to her father in the first unhappy months of her marriage. She had maintained a cool dignity throughout the months and years of following Edward as he followed Gaveston in the fruitless search for sanctuary in his own kingdom. But, in her silence, she had learned a great deal: that her husband had much passion and little judgement; that his understanding of politics was sometimes wilfully obtuse, sometimes hopelessly naïve; and that his nobles were men to be reckoned with. Isabella was still young, but she had a shrewd intellect and a forceful will of her own. And now, with her son in her arms, she held the key that would transform her power as queen.

TWELVE

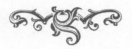

Dearest and Most Powerful

ur King Edward has now reigned six full years," the author of the *Vita* wrote in 1313, "and has till now achieved nothing praiseworthy or memorable, except that by a royal marriage he has raised up for himself a handsome son and heir to the throne." Amid the wreckage of England's hopes, then, Isabella and her baby son embodied Edward's sole accomplishment as king.

The arrival of the new prince—who was named Edward after his English father and grandfather, despite the efforts of a French delegation headed by Isabella's eldest brother, Louis, to suggest Philippe as an alternative—was greeted with wild enthusiasm in the capital. Londoners caroused in the streets, inebriated not only by the free wine flowing from barrels set up at the roadsides but by sheer relief that riotous celebration was overtaking their city, rather than the riotous violence that had threatened to erupt during previous weeks. Then, tense negotiations had been taking place in a desperate attempt to avert all-out war between the king and the earls responsible for Gaveston's death, whose fear for their own safety had taken steel-clad form when they arrived in London at the beginning of September at the head of a formidable army.

Now, at last, God had shown that he was willing to smile again on England and its unhappy monarch. The baby's birth, in providing for the future of the royal line, served to strengthen Edward's hand; he was as yet in no position to impose the vengeance he craved, but a "treaty of peace" was finally patched together on December 20, 1312, under the auspices of envoys from the pope and the French court. The earls of Warwick and Lancaster were to submit to the king's grace and restore to him the jewels and horses Lancaster had seized when Edward and Gaveston fled from Newcastle. In return, the agreement stipulated, Edward would lay aside all rancour arising from Gaveston's death.

The depths of hostility and suspicion that lay behind these ostensibly simple provisions were laid bare by the protracted manoeuvring over their enactment that occupied the uneasy months after the treaty was drawn up. It was hardly surprising that Warwick and Lancaster were reluctant to accept the settlement: Edward had proved many times before that his word was not to be trusted where Gaveston was concerned, and there was ample reason to believe that his offer of forgiveness was entirely disingenuous. Moreover, the treaty as it stood neither mentioned the ordinances, on the authority of which the earls claimed to have acted, nor identified Gaveston as a traitor—and, as such, it gave Warwick and Lancaster no protection in law beyond the offer of the king's grace, fleetingly insubstantial as it was likely to be. Meanwhile, silence on the matter of the ordinances was, for Edward, merely a first step: he sought their revocation, and his own absolution from his oath to maintain them.

By the end of February 1313 Lancaster had finally agreed to return the king's jewels, a dazzling hoard with a value to Edward that went beyond the financial, including as it did not only a golden cup that had been a gift from his mother, but four great rubies, an emerald, and a huge diamond in an enamelled silver box that Gaveston had been carrying when he was captured. But still argument and counterargument continued, while all the time the Scots continued to press home the advantage presented to them by the implosion of English politics. Bruce's violent raids had already exacted thousands of pounds in tribute from the people of Northumberland and Westmorland, and his troops were now plundering the countryside as far south as Yorkshire.

Edward—whose inability to focus on the issues that most exercised his earls had not disappeared with Gaveston's death—chose this moment to announce his departure for Paris. Isabella's father, King Philippe, had invited his daughter and her royal husband to attend the French court for the knighting of his three sons, Isabella's brothers, Louis, Philippe, and Charles. This lavish state visit—undertaken in casual defiance of the ordinances' prescription that the king should not leave the country without the consent of his lords—presented Edward with a characteristically welcome opportunity to absent himself from the scene of conflict at home. But it also marked the emergence of his wife as a political player in her own right. Newly a mother to the heir to the English throne, seventeen-year-old Isabella was returning to her homeland as a queen taking her rightful place beside her husband almost for the first time. Without Gaveston's disturbing presence, Edward and Isabella once again looked every inch the golden couple they had appeared at their wedding five years earlier—and it now seemed possible to hope that, this time, appearances might be matched by reality.

The royal entourage sailed from Dover at dawn on May 23 and made a ceremonial entry into Paris on June 2, before dining with the French king at an elaborately staged banquet that evening. The next day, on the feast of Pentecost, the solemn ritual of knighthood was enacted at the great Gothic cathedral of Notre-Dame (the foundations of which had been laid under the aegis of Louis VII a century and a half earlier, a few years after his divorce from Eleanor of Aquitaine). There Philippe and Edward bestowed the belt and spurs of a knight on Louis, the heir to the French throne—a prince who was already a king, since he had inherited the crown of Navarre from his mother, Jeanne, on her death in 1305. These three kings then made knights of the other young men before them, almost two hundred in all, including Louis's younger brothers, Philippe and Charles, and their cousins Philippe of Valois and Robert of Artois.

Days and nights of celebration followed. The city was a riot of colour, the houses decked in hangings of red, blue, white, black, yellow, and green; there was eating, drinking, and dancing in the streets, with wine flowing from a great fountain around which coiled ornamental mermaids, civet cats, lions, leopards, and other fabulous creatures; and the citizens presented intricate tableaux of popular tales and biblical scenes. On one stage a hundred costumed devils enthusiastically tormented anguished sinners as pitch-black smoke poured from the pit of hell, while, on another, angels sang as souls trooped cheerfully into a brightly painted paradise.

Amid this revelry, kings, queens, and nobles faced a punishingly continuous schedule of feasts and functions. On Tuesday, June 5, it was Edward and Isabella's turn to entertain their hosts at a banquet laid out in richly hung tents beside their lodgings at the abbey of Saint-Germain-des-Prés, with torches blazing ostentatiously in the midday sun while guests were served, in another showy conceit, by attendants on horseback. The following day, Edward returned to Notre-Dame, walking with Philippe and the flower of the French aristocracy on a forty-foot-wide pontoon bridge across the Seine to pledge themselves as crusaders to the future rescue of the Holy Land from the infidel. The day after that, Isabella missed her turn to take the crusaders' cross with the rest of the royal ladies when, after yet another feast, she and Edward overslept—a faux pas which an eye-witness Parisian chronicler treated with amused indulgence, on the grounds that the king could hardly be blamed for tarrying in the bed of such a beautiful wife. (Isabella's failure to wake her notoriously tardy husband may, in fact, have been the result of circumspection rather than the previous night's excesses. When she did finally take the cross two days later, she proved a sceptical crusader-in-prospect, qualifying her commitment by securing a cardinal's promise that she need only set out for the Holy Land if and when her husband did so, and—a crucial proviso, this, for a young woman who luxuriated in her lavish lifestyle—that she would be required to contribute only such sums of money as her own devotion suggested were necessary.)

On June 10 the English king and his queen followed her father to Pontoise, seventeen miles northwest of Paris, where the serious business of diplomacy would take place. There were the usual tensions over Gascony to be tackled, but Philippe was generous in the privileges he granted and the loans he proffered to his son-in-law. The French king's munificence was far from selfless: the weeks of ceremony and celebration had confirmed his own position as the most powerful monarch in western Europe and the champion of Christendom in defence of the Holy Land. But for Edward, too, the visit had been a welcome interruption to the challenges and confrontations he had faced in England, demonstrating the grandeur of his sovereignty and his place among the royal leaders of Europe. And central to that reaffirmation of his authority was Isabella.

Thanks to Isabella, Edward could stand at the heart of the dynastic rituals of the French crown. Thanks to Isabella, he had a son to represent the future of his own dynasty. And, thanks to Isabella, the support he was offered in Paris was unquestioning. No word of criticism, no hint of past scandal or present conflict, attaches itself to *Odouart, roy des Anglois* in the account of the eyewitness chronicler, a Parisian clerk with connections to the royal chancery. Instead, praise is heaped upon Isabella, "the wise and noble lady Isabeau," "the beautiful Isabelot," "the fairest of the fair, even as the sun surpasses the stars."

For Isabella herself, the visit had been a heartening opportunity to see her father, her family, and her childhood home for the first time in five years. The omens of their stay had not all been auspicious: at Pontoise, a fire broke out in the English royal pavilion during the night, destroying many of their possessions and leaving Isabella with a burn to the arm that was to trouble her for many months. Still, she returned to England ready to play the part for which she had been anointed and crowned: to intercede with her husband in the interests of peace and justice, and to support him in his duty to his people.

Not that his people were overly impressed, it had to be said, with the length of time that Edward had chosen to devote to his Parisian progress. The lords had assembled in London in the second week of July in anticipation of a parliament to be held on the king's promised return; but when Edward failed to appear, or even to send word, they dispersed, "weary," the *Vita* says, "of the trouble and expense to which they had been put." It was through gritted teeth that they agreed to reassemble in September. By then, the search for a lasting settlement had become desperate. More than a year had passed since Gaveston's death, and exhaustion had set in among a political community worn down by the accidental strategy of attrition that had been forged out of Edward's stubbornness and his talent for procrastination.

Now Isabella and her family helped make a final push for peace. Just as the threat of French intervention had secured Gaveston's exile in 1308, so now the queen's uncle Louis of Évreux drove forward the negotiations to resolve the consequences of his death. And Isabella herself (together with the young Earl of Gloucester, Gaveston's brother-in-law, who had stayed close to Edward and served as keeper of the realm during his absence in France) stepped forward to mediate between her husband and his nobles. The public intervention of the young queen made it possible for both sides to enter with dignity into a formal ritual of reconciliation, and on October 14 the great lords of England at last knelt before their king in Westminster Hall to submit themselves to his grace and receive his pardon for their part in Gaveston's death. The next day, Edward dined with his cousin Thomas of Lancaster as evidence of their newfound harmony.

But there could be no mistaking that this peace was brittle and tenuous, its limitations exposed by what Edward did not say as much as by what he did. There was still no royal acknowledgement that Gaveston had been a traitor, nor of the force in law of the ordinances by which, the earls claimed, his death had been prescribed. The immediate danger of political conflagration had been averted, but the safety of England's greatest men was left hanging by the slender thread of the king's questionable integrity. And the mistrust behind the public smiles was made manifest all too soon, when Edward began to prepare for a major military campaign against the Scots—a mere six years too late to halt the consolidation of Bruce's power in its tracks.

His army included contingents led by the Earl of Gloucester, who had fought in the abortive campaign led by Edward and Gaveston in 1311; by the Earl of Pembroke, Edward's steadfast ally ever since his promise of safeguard to Gaveston had been so brutally overridden; and by the Earl of Hereford, Edward's brother-in-law, who had followed Lancaster and Warwick in engineering Gaveston's execution but had taken a lead in the search for a settlement, and appeared now to have made his peace with the king. Not present in Edward's company as he moved north in May 1314 were the three other earls responsible for Gaveston's death: Lancaster, Warwick, and Arundel.

These were men who, in other circumstances, would have stood to gain immeasurably from an English triumph in Scotland. Now, however, they knew that victory for Edward north of the border would free his hand to deal with those who had crossed him in England. Meanwhile, an army commanded by Edward seemed a dangerous place to be for men who had every reason to believe that he wanted them dead. The king's forces were huge in number as they marched for Berwick; but, given the absence of these lords from their ranks, the scars of the recent conflict were clear upon them.

Isabella, meanwhile, was immersing herself in her new public role as her husband's adviser and representative. At the end of February 1314 she accompanied the Earl of Gloucester on an embassy to her father in Paris to discuss the affairs of Gascony. The eighteen-year-old queen did not suffer any false modesty in her sense of her own majesty; in England she maintained a household of almost two hundred servants, and she spent money as freely as her extravagant husband. Her entourage and equipment for this, her first return to her French home without Edward, were so extensive that a fleet of twenty-seven ships and thirteen barges was requisitioned to transport the expedition across the Channel. All told, Isabella spent eight weeks in France, leaving costly gifts at holy shrines along her route and hunting with her team of fifteen greyhounds, as well as applying herself to the serious business of assisting Gloucester in his negotiations through her personal intercession with her father.

This embassy meant that she was also present to witness the eruption of a humiliating scandal by which the French court was overwhelmed that spring. Her three sisters-in-law—Marguerite, daughter of the Duke of Burgundy, and Jeanne and Blanche, both descended from a collateral branch of the Burgundian house—had been dangerously indiscreet in dallying with some handsome young knights in their father-in-law's service. The chastity of royal wives was a matter not only of honour and obedience but of dynastic security, and any shadow of suspicion cast on the royal succession was likely to provoke a violent and terrible reckoning. And so it proved: Marguerite and Blanche were convicted of adultery, and Jeanne found guilty of having concealed their liaisons. All three were imprisoned, Marguerite and Blanche in subterranean cells within the forbidding Norman fortress of Château Gaillard, their heads shaved as a mark of their transgression, while their supposed lovers died in excruciating agony, publicly tortured to death for their crimes.

Rumour had it that Isabella had suspected her brothers' wives and had borne witness against them. Whether or not that was so, her poised hauteur certainly marked a stark contrast between her own seriousness of purpose and the recklessness that had precipitated these foolish young women into such appalling suffering.

And, as if to emphasise the gravity of Isabella's royal duties, she had no sooner returned to London than she was preparing to set out once again, this time following the king and his army to Berwick. Travelling sometimes on horseback, sometimes in a covered wooden carriage filled with silk cushions and drawn by three black chargers, she reached Berwick's great walls on June 14, ready to witness from close at hand her husband's inevitable triumph.

Robert Bruce had long avoided meeting an English army in pitched battle. Guerrilla warfare played much more to the Scots' strengths—their intimate knowledge of the terrain over which they moved, and the speed with which they could strike—than the prospect of a set-piece confrontation involving English divisions of well-equipped cavalry and skilled archers that the Scots simply could not match. But in the summer of 1313 Bruce's brother, who was then leading a siege of the strategically vital stronghold of Stirling, thirty miles west of Edinburgh, had accepted the terms of a truce by which the castle's English garrison agreed to surrender if English troops failed to arrive within three leagues (nine miles or so) of Stirling by the next Midsummer's Day, June 24, 1314. While Edward remained mired in conflict with his own lords, that proffer had seemed a good bet, and any English army unlikely to be more than a mirage—until February 1314 when, with an uneasy peace agreed at home, the king suddenly announced his determination to take up the challenge.

By Midsummer's Eve, June 23, the English army was advancing rapidly on Stirling, and Bruce could no longer evade the confrontation he had feared. He drew up his infantry on the north side of the Bannock Burn, a stream flowing through marshy ground into the Forth River a couple of miles from Stirling Castle, while Edward's troops halted to the south of it. The English forces outnumbered Bruce's by a factor of two or three to one. They were better equipped, more experienced, and more highly trained than the Scots footsoldiers. But, by the time battle was joined in earnest on the following day, they were also exhausted by their forced march, struggling with the seeping mud and uncertain footholds of the boggy landscape, and undermined by indecisive and divided leadership.

The earls of Hereford and Gloucester, it emerged on the morning of June 24, were locked in bitter argument over their rival claims on the honour of leading the attack. In the heat of the moment Gloucester dashed forward against the Scots line to prove his mettle with

a sudden assault. It took only an instant for the young earl to be
thrown from his warhorse and hacked to death where he fell in the
blood-churned mud. Hemmed in by the terrain and paralysed by
consternation and confusion, the English ranks collapsed under the
sudden onslaught of the Scots into a scrambling, bloody mêlée.

As Edward watched in horror, his inevitable triumph turned into
an inexorable rout. Panic overwhelmed his despairing troops as the
king fled, surrounded by a bodyguard of knights led by the Earl of
Pembroke, first to Stirling Castle and then, when he was refused
entry to a fortress that the laws of war now ceded to the Scots, eastward to Dunbar, the coast, and safety. Behind him he left men and
horses spitted on pikes, speared with arrows, and dismembered by
swordblows, while others suffocated in the mire or drowned in the
crimson-stained waters of the Forth. When Robert Bruce left the
field, he did so as the unquestioned king of an independent Scotland.
For Edward, defeat was total, and catastrophic.

By the time he rejoined his wife at Berwick, the consequences of
this annihilation were only beginning to become apparent. The Earl
of Gloucester was dead and the Earl of Hereford a prisoner, taken
by the victorious Scots along with the keeper of Edward's privy seal,
his clerks, his archive, and the seal itself. Within weeks, the Scots
were cutting a swathe through northern England, their raids destroying lives and homes throughout Northumberland, Cumbria,
and Durham and deep into Yorkshire and Lancashire, while Robert
Bruce made preparations to dispatch his brother to invade English-
ruled Ireland. And, if God's judgement on Edward's kingship were
not already clear, in the aftermath of military disaster the heavens
opened: torrential rains and a brutal winter destroyed crops in the
ground, and Edward's people began to starve.

Victory for Edward would have meant a chance to free himself
from the shackles of the ordinances and to revenge himself upon the
earls who had killed his beloved Gaveston. Defeat, in a realm harried
from without and decomposing from within, meant the exact opposite. When the king finally laid Gaveston's embalmed body to rest,

on January 2, 1315, at Edward's favourite manor of Langley in Hertfordshire, he did so in the bitter knowledge that power effectively lay in the hands of Gaveston's executioner, Thomas of Lancaster, the great earl without whom northern England could not now be defended against the depredations of the Scots. And Lancaster, it was clear, would insist with every ounce of his strength on keeping the king shackled, since it was the ordinances that vindicated the killing of Gaveston.

Isabella, at not quite twenty, found herself facing the most thankless of tasks: to function as a queen within a profoundly dysfunctional kingdom. The king and his greatest magnate were locked into a mortal enmity that made the normal workings of royal government all but impossible. Isabella might give birth to more royal heirs—as she did to a son, John, in the summer of 1316, and a daughter, Eleanor, two years later. And she might use her symbolic role as intercessor in an attempt to secure the restoration of her husband's power through an accommodation with her uncle of Lancaster. She was, as she had not been during Gaveston's lifetime, the king's companion and his trusted confidante, a loyal spouse and a shrewd political tactician. But, in practice, there was little she or anyone else could do to ameliorate the intractable divisions that now crippled English politics.

Lancaster was an increasingly isolated figure, more estranged than ever from his peers not only by his uncompromising instincts and his lack of political finesse but also by the unpredictable hand of fate. The Earl of Warwick, Lancaster's closest ally and the man with whom he shared ultimate responsibility for Gaveston's death, had sought a prominent role in the direction of Edward's government after the defeat that came to be known as "Bannockburn," after the stream across which it was fought. In August 1315, however, Warwick died at the age of just forty-three, leaving a baby son—named Thomas, after Lancaster himself—as his heir. Some lords positioned themselves much more closely to the king: the Earl of Pembroke remained unwavering in his loyal service to Edward; and the

Earl of Hereford (newly retrieved from Scottish custody in exchange for Robert Bruce's wife, who had been captured by the English in 1306) continued his campaign to efface all memories of his presence at Blacklow Hill through his steadfast support of the king. Others were more wary of Edward, including the Earl of Arundel, who, with Warwick and Lancaster, had refused to fight at Bannockburn. But all, like the rest of the king's subjects, were caught in no-man's-land, trying as best they could to protect their own interests in a country debilitated not only by flood, famine, and the raiding Scots, but by the pernicious stalemate between Lancaster and the king.

As always, the author of the *Vita Edwardi Secundi* was an acute observer of this political paralysis: "... whatever pleases the lord king the earl's servants try to upset; and whatever pleases the earl the king's servants call treachery; and so at the Devil's prompting the familiars of each start meddling, and their lords, by whom the land ought to be defended, are not allowed to rest in harmony." Political division was mirrored in physical distance: Lancaster increasingly kept himself apart from the dangers that lurked in the dark corners of his cousin's court by retreating to his northern strongholds, and sought instead to control Edward from afar, at first through the ordinances, and then, after a treaty concluded at Leake in Nottinghamshire in 1318, through a standing council appointed to govern with the king.

But the inefficacy of these measures, in attempting to build flimsy bridges across chasms of profound mistrust, was obvious in the growing disorder that was engulfing public life. The Earl of Surrey had been struggling for years to escape his loveless and childless marriage to Jeanne of Bar, one of the king's nieces, in order to marry his mistress, the mother of his two sons. Thomas of Lancaster had been among the nobles who supported the Church in rejecting Surrey's plans in 1314; and in 1317—with the king's tacit but obvious support—Surrey retaliated by abducting Lancaster's wife, Alice Lacy. Their marriage had been no more happy or productive than Surrey's, and it seems likely that she colluded in her own kidnapping. But the result of this public humiliation was yet more violence, in the form of a private war between Lancaster and Surrey that raged unchecked across the already disordered countryside of Yorkshire and north Wales.

More trouble, meanwhile, was stirred up by the fate of the earldom of Gloucester after the death of its young lord amid the carnage at Bannockburn. Once it became clear that his widow was not pregnant and that there would be no heir of his body to inherit his title, the earl's rich estates were shared between his three sisters, Eleanor, Margaret, and Elizabeth, whose husbands were precipitated to a startling new eminence by these sudden territorial gains. Margaret, who had once been the unhappy wife of Piers Gaveston, was married in April 1317 to Hugh Audley, and Elizabeth in the same month to Roger Damory—neither man born into the first ranks of the nobility, but both trusted members of Edward's innermost household coterie. Eleanor, the eldest sister, was already married, but her husband, too, fitted this (for Edward) pleasing mould: Hugh Despenser the younger—who had entered Edward's household when both men were in their teens—was the son and namesake of a courtier and confidant of the king whose loyalty had not faltered during the years of Gaveston's dominance.

Now Audley, Damory, and Despenser rose "in the king's shadow," one chronicler remarked bitterly. For Edward, these loyalists within his household offered him the promise of an alternative power base, the prospect of sidestepping (and one day, perhaps, destroying) the lords who had constrained his own authority and killed the man he loved beyond all others. For Audley, Damory, and Despenser, meanwhile, the king's favour presented the chance to enrich and empower themselves to heights of which before they could only have dreamed. This time, it seemed, there would be no second Gaveston: no all-encompassing personal devotion, no exclusive intimacy. But, while his desperate country suffered and starved, Edward spent money like water on men who cared only to advance themselves—and, as he did so, added fuel to the flames of his conflict with the Earl of Lancaster.

It was therefore adding insult to self-inflicted injury when, in the summer of 1318, Edward was publicly accused of being not only a failure as king, but an imposter. That June, a man named John of Powderham walked into the King's Hall in Oxford and announced that he was the rightful King of England. His real father, he said, was not the Exeter tanner who had brought him up but the great warrior Edward I. As a baby he had been substituted for a changeling in his royal cradle by a terrified nurse after suffering an injury in her care; and now he had come to reclaim his inheritance. Edward's first response was to laugh. He welcomed the pretender, the Chronicle of Lanercost records, with a derisive cry of "Welcome, my brother!" But for the queen, struggling to maintain her husband's dignity (and, with it, her own), and acutely conscious of the threatening consequences of Edward's manifest failings, jokes did not come so easily. Proud Isabella was "unspeakably annoyed," the *Vita* notes; and this challenge to a king whose resemblance to his mighty father had never been less apparent ended with Powderham's rotting corpse swinging slowly from a gibbet.

The fact that Isabella was heavily pregnant when Powderham's claim exposed her husband to public ridicule and scurrilous rumour—her daughter Eleanor was born at Woodstock, eight miles from Oxford, in July 1318—cannot have helped her equilibrium. But it did add to the gravitas of any intervention she might make in the discussions between the king and his magnates—and, when the Treaty of Leake was agreed to on August 9, 1318, the queen was first among those credited by the *Vita* with the success of the negotiations.

This settlement was so successful, indeed, that when Edward launched another military assault against the advancing Scots in 1319, his army presented a more united front than at any previous time since his father's death. The English position in the borders had deteriorated so disastrously in the wake of the slaughter at Bannockburn that even the great walled city and castle of Berwick, the spearhead and safeguard of northeastern England, had fallen into Scottish hands in April 1318. The magnates of England who rallied to its defence when Edward mustered his army at Newcastle in

June 1319 included an improbable gathering of earls, including both
Lancaster and Surrey (who had finally settled their private war at
the punishing cost to Surrey of handing over valuable lands to his
enemy), together with Pembroke, Hereford, and Arundel, as well
as Hugh Despenser, Roger Damory, and Hugh Audley, the three
household men who now shared the earldom of Gloucester between
them. This was unity indeed; and Isabella settled herself at a manor-
house just outside York to wait for good news.

It did not come. Instead, the Archbishop of York came galloping
to her gate at the head of a host of armed men quickly gathered from
the city, breathless with alarm and carrying a warning that Sir James
Douglas—one of the most brilliant and brutal soldiers in Scotland,
known as "the Black Douglas" for the fear he inspired as well as for
his dark colouring—was close at hand and planning to seize the English queen as a hostage. Isabella was bundled onto a horse and escorted at speed to York, from where she fled seventy miles southward
to safety behind the massive walls of Nottingham Castle.

Meanwhile, Edward's forces at the siege of Berwick—round
whom Douglas and his men had skirted on their raid into Yorkshire—were faring little better. Lancaster's participation was turning out to be so half-hearted that rumours were flying that he was in
league with the Scots. Though sober assessment suggested that was
unlikely, it was hardly surprising if the earl remained unconvinced
that Bruce's men were his only or even his most dangerous enemy.
As the *Vita* reported, it was painfully obvious that Edward's reconciliation with his cousin was skin-deep at best. "Peace between great
men is to be regarded with suspicion when the eminent princes have
arrived at it not through love but by force," the *Vita*'s author wrote,
with an evidently heavy heart. "When siege had been laid to Berwick
and it seemed that the matter was being pursued to no purpose, the
lord king is said to have uttered some such words as these: 'When
this wretched business is over, we will turn our hands to other matters. For I have not yet forgotten the wrong that was done to my
brother Piers . . .'"

By the beginning of October, Lancaster had withdrawn from the siege and the English army had broken up in disarray: for Edward, it was yet another opportunity squandered. While Lancaster retreated again to the fastness of his castle at Pontefract in West Yorkshire, the king was forced to agree to a two-year truce with the Scots. It was an ignominious retreat ("What best to do, indeed he did not know," remarked one unimpressed northern chronicler)—but it did at least allow him a breathing space in which to embark once again for France. His presence was required there to offer his homage for Gascony to the new king, Philippe V; and for Isabella, the expedition offered a chance to be reunited with her family after years of absence and multiple bereavement.

Her father, Philippe the Fair, had died in November 1314 at the age of just forty-six, a few weeks after suffering a seizure while hunting. Her brother Louis, already King of Navarre, succeeded him as Louis X of France. The new king's disgraced wife, Marguerite, still languished in Château Gaillard; and when she died in August 1315 (an end so convenient and obscure that rumour immediately began to cry murder) Louis remained a widower for a grand total of four days before marrying Clémence, granddaughter of the King of Naples. By the summer of 1316 his new wife was pregnant, and all seemed well in the French royal household at the beginning of June as the young king threw himself into his favourite pastime, a furiously exhausting game of *jeu de paume* ("real" tennis, played on an enclosed court). After the match, sweating and dehydrated, he drained cup after cup of cooled wine—an unwise choice of refreshment which either precipitated a dangerous chill or (as those of a more suspicious nature soon whispered) had been tainted with poison. The result, at least, was incontrovertible: on June 5 the twenty-six-year-old king died, leaving his kingdom in the grip of a sudden succession crisis.

The government of France was temporarily committed into the hands of Louis's brother Philippe while the kingdom waited for the birth of the baby the widowed queen Clémence was carrying. It was a boy, born on November 15, 1316, and christened Jean ("the Posthumous," his subjects called him). But the reign of this king who acquired his crown with his first breath lasted only five days. When the baby died on November 20, the surviving contenders for his throne were his half-sister, Jeanne, Louis's daughter by his tragic first wife—a little girl who was just four years old, and damaged goods because of her mother's publicly confessed adultery—or his uncle Philippe, the adult prince in whose hands power already lay. Realpolitik dictated that there could be no contest between these competing claims; and so, in the absence of any support for little Jeanne's cause, the coronation of Philippe V excluded female heirs from the French succession with an absolute clarity that had eluded Stephen on his similarly pragmatic accession to the English throne nearly two hundred years earlier.

Now Philippe was demanding that his English brother-in-law perform homage for the French territories he ruled, and Isabella was there in June 1320 to watch her husband kneel before her brother in front of the high altar of Amiens Cathedral, a Gothic marvel of riotously painted stonemasonry that lay halfway between Boulogne and Paris. The stalwart Earl of Pembroke had been left as keeper of England when the royal couple took ship at Dover, while Lancaster remained in stubborn isolation behind the massive walls of his fortress at Pontefract. An unsteady peace was holding. Edward's people were still starving, their suffering now compounded by the effects of epidemic disease among their flocks and herds; but at least there were grounds for hope that the king was applying himself to the business of government with a little more purpose. The Bishop of Worcester, writing to the pope during the parliament held at Westminster on Edward and Isabella's return from France, was moved to remark that the king "bore himself splendidly, with prudence and discretion," and that, "contrary to his former habit," he was now "rising early, and presenting a nobler and pleasant countenance to his prelates and lords." "On that account," the bishop added in another optimistic letter to a cardinal at the papal curia, "...there is considerable hope

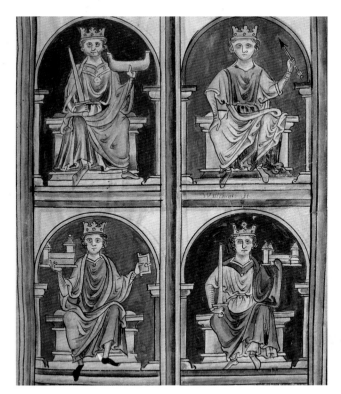

A thirteenth-century illustration of the first four Norman kings: William the Conqueror (top left), his sons William Rufus (top right) and Henry I (bottom left), and Henry's nephew Stephen (bottom right). Stephen holds a sword to show that he was forced to fight for his throne against the claim of Henry's daughter Matilda.

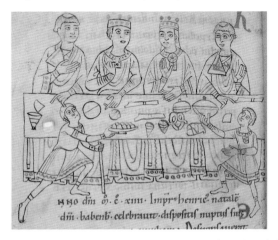

Eleven-year-old Matilda (second from right behind the table) sits beside her first husband, the German Emperor Heinrich V, at their wedding feast in 1114. It was eleven years before she returned to England as the widowed 'Empress Matilda' to be named her father's heir.

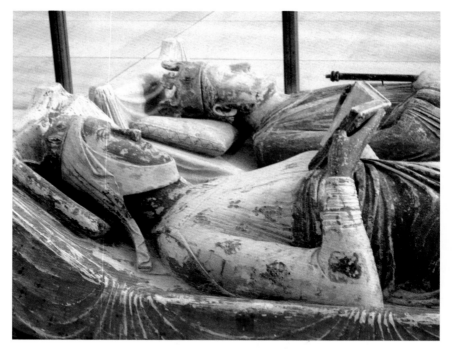

The effigy of Eleanor of Aquitaine lies beside that of her second husband, Matilda's son Henry II of England, in the calm of Fontevraud Abbey – a striking contrast to the turbulence of their marriage.

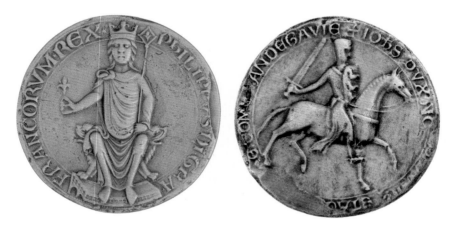

Images of power: the two sides of royal seals show the king with sceptre and sword as judge and warrior – key functions of kingship that a woman could not easily fulfil. On the left is Philippe II of France, son of Eleanor's first husband Louis VII; on the right, John, youngest son of Eleanor and Henry.

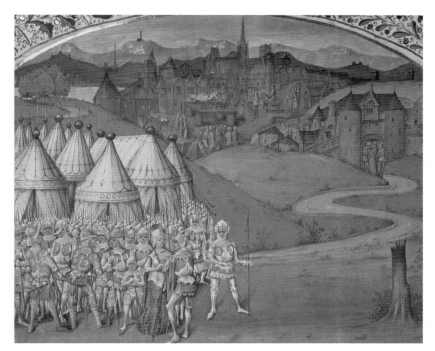

Edward II's queen, Isabella of France, in armour at the head of her troops at Hereford in 1326 – a fourteenth-century image that echoes contemporary depictions of the Amazonian queens of classical myth. In the background her husband's favourite, Hugh Despenser the younger, meets a grisly end on the scaffold.

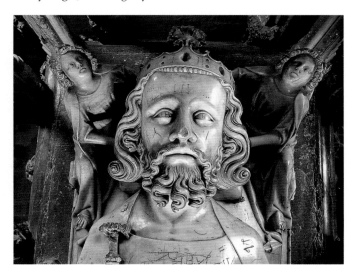

The effigy of Edward II, carved in English alabaster, on his tomb in Gloucester Cathedral.

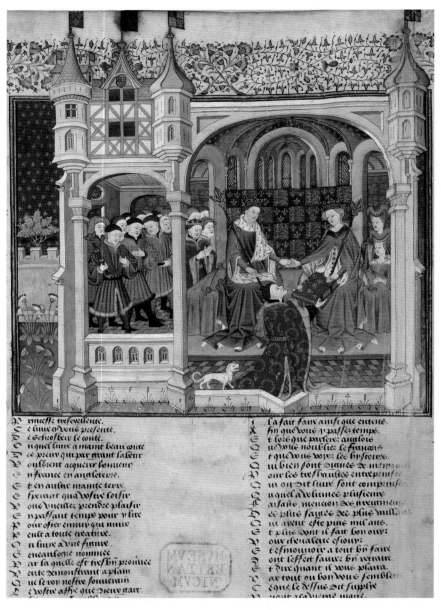

A conventional image of virtuous queenship at odds with Margaret of Anjou's later reputation as Shakespeare's 'She-wolf of France': Margaret sits in a consort's place on the left of her husband, Henry VI, to receive from John Talbot, earl of Shrewsbury, a gift of the book in which this illumination appears.

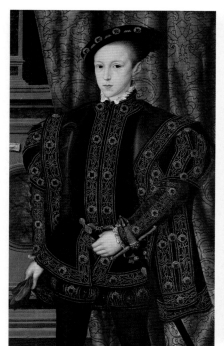
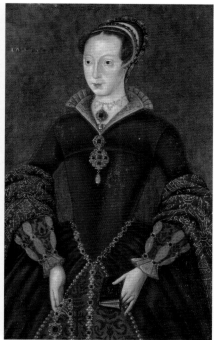

King Edward VI, a slightly built teenager trying to emulate the imposing style of his father Henry VIII; and a posthumous portrait of Edward's cousin Lady Jane Grey.

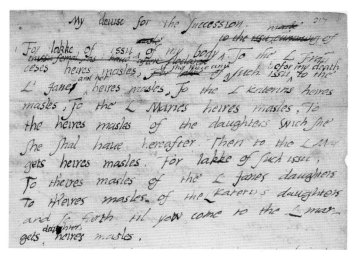

Edward's 'device for the succession', drafted in his own hand, which specified that England's future monarchs should be Protestant and male. During his final illness in 1553, Edward named Jane his heir by changing his bequest of the crown: 'to the L' Janes heires masles' became 'to the L' Janes and her heires masles'.

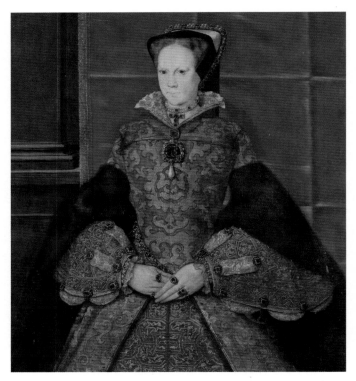

Mary Tudor in 1554, when, according to the outgoing Venetian ambassador Giacomo Soranzo, the queen was 'of low stature, with a red and white complexion, and very thin; … were not her age on the decline she might be called handsome rather than the contrary'.

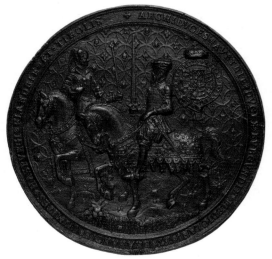

An improvised division of royal labour on the Great Seal of England, 1554: Mary rides ahead, holding the sceptre and looking back at her husband, King Philip, who takes the consort's position on her left with a sword unsheathed in his hand.

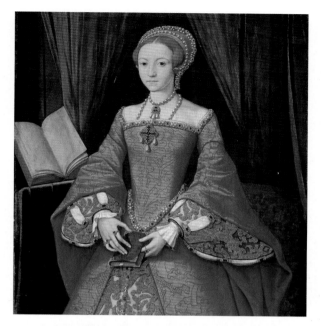

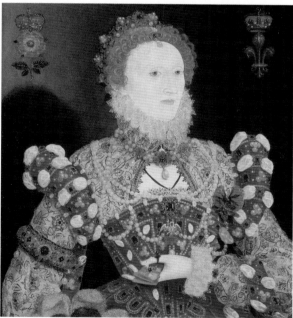

From human being to icon. Top, Elizabeth at thirteen, a study in charismatic self-possession. Below, the queen at forty-two, a stylised figure decked about with symbols: flanked by the Tudor rose, representing the crown of England, and the fleur-de-lys for her claim to France, Elizabeth wears pinned to her bodice an enamelled pelican, a symbol of mystical and selfless motherhood – and therefore of the queen as mother of her people – because it was believed to feed its young with blood pecked from its own breast.

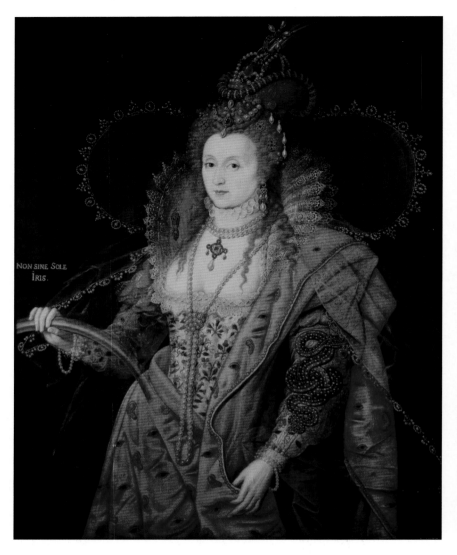

NON SINE SOLE
IRIS.

Apotheosis of an icon: Elizabeth at sixty-six. Goddess-like in her eternal youth, she has a serpent on her sleeve for wisdom, and a rainbow in her hand for the peace and prosperity brought by the sunlight of her majesty, while the eyes and ears on her cloak show that she sees and hears all. The knotted pearls that represent her virginity both emphasise and defend her sexual power. The lesson of this eclectic and densely woven imagery was that, if women were lesser beings and unfit to rule, England's queen was a unique and glorious exception.

of an improvement in his behaviour and a greater possibility of unity and harmony."

But in Edward's train on his visit to France, and by his side when he returned to England, was a man who was about to precipitate the most destructive conflict Edward's fractured rule had yet visited on his kingdom. The younger Hugh Despenser had been appointed chamberlain of the king's household in 1318—an office that had once been held by Piers Gaveston, and which allowed Despenser to spend increasing amounts of his time in Edward's company. There is less suggestion in the surviving sources that Despenser was the object of the king's private passion than there is of Despenser's ravening hunger for all the public power that access to Edward could provide. But that meant merely that he represented a different sort of threat to Edward's subjects—a menacing predator, as opposed to Gaveston's distracting peacock.

And the first prey on which his talons fastened was one of his own brothers-in-law, his coheirs to the earldom of Gloucester. The settlement of the Gloucester estates made in November 1317 had given Despenser vast tracts of land in south Wales, including the lordship of Glamorgan. But it had also served to spur, rather than satisfy, his ambition; and within weeks he had seized more of the dead earl's Welsh properties from Hugh Audley, the husband of his wife's sister, Gaveston's widow, Margaret. Despite Audley's vociferous protests, Edward allowed Despenser to impose a territorial exchange which left Audley holding less valuable lands in the southeast of England and Despenser in unchallenged command of southernmost Wales and the Bristol Channel.

Soon, he set his sights further afield, on the lordship of Gower adjoining Glamorgan to the west, which belonged to a cash-strapped baron named William de Braose. By the time de Braose died in 1320 without a son to succeed him, several of the most powerful landowners in the region were already circling acquisitively in the hope of snapping Gower up at a bargain price, while his daughter's husband, John Mowbray, who was determined to take over the lordship as his father-in-law's heir, immediately took possession of the estates to ward off these challengers. Despenser, however, had other ideas; and in November 1320 he persuaded Edward that Gower should be seized into royal hands.

This was an unambiguous demonstration of Despenser's influence over the king. It was also a mistake. The customary law of the Welsh Marches—the frontier lands between England and the principality of Wales—did not, by long tradition, permit this kind of intrusive royal intervention. And this threat to the legal basis of marcher landholding, together with the manifest certainty that Despenser was now the power behind Edward's throne, was enough to bind together an extraordinary consortium of lords who were prepared to resort to arms to defend themselves against the king and his favourite. John Mowbray, the prospective heir to Gower, was joined by his local rivals for that lordship: the Earl of Hereford, whose loyalty to Edward had been so painstakingly reconstructed after the killing at Blacklow Hill; and a namesake uncle and nephew, Roger Mortimer of Chirk and Roger Mortimer of Wigmore, the latter a major landowner in Ireland as well as in Wales. Also standing alongside them to confront Despenser were his former associates in royal favour, now his deadly rivals, Hugh Audley and Roger Damory. And behind them all loomed a marcher lord with more reason than any to mistrust Edward's intentions: Thomas of Lancaster, whose huge estates made him a neighbour of Despenser in Wales as well as the keeper of the north.

The mortal enmity between Lancaster and the king had been the fault line in English politics for the last ten years. Edward had been unable to take decisive action against his cousin because of the power of Lancaster's earldoms and their function as a bulwark against the Scots. Equally, Lancaster's isolation, both politically and temperamentally, had allowed him to make little headway in consolidating formal checks on the king's authority. Now, however, Edward's increasing indulgence of Despenser's aggression had created a new constituency for Lancaster—one where the competing interests of the marcher lords coalesced into a collective determination to restore the rule of law and free the king from the pernicious influence of Despenser, who was now, the Lanercost chronicler acidly remarked, "as the king's right eye." While Lancaster sought to rally support in the north, his allies began an assault on Despenser's lands in Wales and England, leaving in their wake panic and devastation.

By the end of July, the forces of Hereford, Damory, Audley, and the younger Mortimer—their troops arrayed in liveries of green with the right sleeve yellow—had all converged on London. Once again it was left to the Earl of Pembroke to serve as the voice of loyal reason, pointing out to Edward that he would condemn his kingdom to the horror of civil war if he did not listen to the demands of his lords and send Despenser into exile. And once again, Edward's queen took centre stage in her role as intercessor in the cause of peace. Isabella had given birth for the fourth time only a month earlier, to a daughter, Joan, known as Joan of the Tower because, with armies advancing on the capital, the queen had retreated for her confinement behind the protective walls of London's great fortress. Now Isabella went down on her knees before her husband, playing out the public ritual of queenly intervention so that he could accede to her entreaties in the name of his people without compromising his majesty as king. Her involvement had the desired effect, but it was with a markedly ill grace that Edward capitulated to the appeal of his queen and the advice of his lords and expelled Despenser and his father from England.

The younger Despenser did not go far; and while he prowled the waters of the Channel as a "sea-monster" (the *Vita* says), preying on unsuspecting merchant ships to add to his fleet and his treasure, Edward gave no consideration to his own role in the chain of events that had left him once again cornered by a pack of enraged and fearful lords. Instead, as so often before, his thoughts were all of escape and revenge. And this time it was Isabella who provided the momentary diversion that allowed him to spring the trap.

On October 13 Isabella rode to the gates of Leeds Castle—a

stronghold with mighty defences of stone and water, built on an island in a lake thirty miles from the southeastern port of Dover and the coast of Kent. Her public purpose was a pilgrimage to Canterbury, although Leeds lay off the beaten track that pilgrims usually trod, and her husband, who was also in Kent, was clearly preoccupied not at all with spiritual concerns but entirely with Despenser, who had just made landfall once again, despite the injunctions against him, in the east of the shire on the Isle of Thanet. Nor, in fact, was Isabella's presence at Leeds Castle entirely innocent. Its owner, Bartholomew Badlesmere, had a long history of loyal service at Edward's court, but just three months earlier—with his own alarm at Despenser's belligerence intensified by the fact that his eight-year-old daughter was married to the son and heir of Roger Mortimer of Wigmore—he had suddenly thrown in his lot with the marcher lords. Badlesmere, Edward believed, was not only a traitorous ingrate but a weak link in the rebels' ranks, since his last-minute defection to their cause had done nothing to reconcile him with Thomas of Lancaster, who had furiously objected to Badlesmere's appointment in 1318 as steward of the royal household, an office to which the earl claimed a hereditary right. It seemed possible, therefore, that Badlesmere's castles in Kent could be picked off without precipitating a general mobilisation of the marcher armies; and that feat, should Edward achieve it, would give him a strategic base from which to advance against Lancaster and his confederates.

The appearance of the queen as a pilgrim at Badlesmere's gate—which would normally have been a signal honour, and a welcome opportunity to display the largesse of his hospitality—was therefore laden with unspoken menace. Badlesmere himself was not there, having left the castle with its treasure and garrison in the care of his wife with strict instructions that she was to admit no one—instructions which she followed to the letter, leaving Isabella incensed and without shelter. Her mood was not improved by the knowledge that the castle had been held by her aunt, Edward I's queen Marguerite, until her death in 1318, and should therefore have passed into her own hands as part of her queenly dower, had her husband not chosen instead to grant it to Badlesmere. Irritated and imperious, she ordered her escort to force an entry. Lady Badlesmere responded by giving her archers the signal to shoot. Within minutes, six of the queen's men lay dead.

Perhaps Isabella had been following a script to which she had agreed in advance, or perhaps she had been used as a pawn in a stratagem planned by her husband and his favourite of which she was not fully aware. Either way, her presence at Leeds Castle served to precipitate a vertiginous descent from military posturing into the stark reality of war. Badlesmere's violent reception of Edward's anointed queen was not only an unforgivable insult but out-and-out treason, the king insisted, and he immediately dispatched troops and siege engines to attack the castle. The Mortimers, uncle and nephew, and the Earl of Hereford marched south from Oxford with Badlesmere himself, intending to relieve the small garrison at Leeds; but at Kingston-upon-Thames, southwest of the capital, they halted, stopped in their tracks by news that Lancaster was refusing to join them. The earl saw no reason to lift his sword for a man he despised, a man whose immediate cause had nothing to do with the campaign against Despenser. And while the marcher lords hesitated in consternation before wheeling north to consult their more powerful ally, Lady Badlesmere and the soldiers at Leeds opened the castle gates to throw themselves on the king's mercy.

Ostensibly, Edward had made his point; Badlesmere's castles in the southeast were now his for the taking. But in the wider and deeper conflict within which this was merely a skirmish, the king now had a choice. Lancaster was a unique and uniquely intractable opponent, but the fragility of the coalition gathered around him had just been painfully exposed to public view. If Edward now chose to affirm his commitment to the rule of law, to reassure the lords who had felt the intense threat of Despenser's apparently unbridled self-aggrandisement, he might divide the rebels and re-establish his rule by offering the good government that all his subjects, Lancaster apart, had sought for the last decade.

But Edward had acquired no longer sight, no greater understanding of his own responsibilities, in the years since Gaveston's death. He still sought revenge for the loss of his soulmate and for his own inability to protect him. And now, in this moment, it seemed he had a chance to replay the traumatic events of a decade earlier, but this time in defence of a different favourite and in hope of a different outcome. He did not hesitate. When the defenders of Leeds Castle emerged before him, a sorry sight after two weeks under heavy siege, twelve men were immediately seized and hanged from the walls. And while the corpses kicked and swung, Lady Badlesmere and her young children were sent as prisoners to the Tower.

If execution without trial represented any kind of justice at all, it was the summary justice offered by martial law. Edward's subjects could be under no illusion that once again they faced a stark choice: either fight for the king, or take up arms against him. With a heavy heart, the Earl of Pembroke—now nearing fifty, and wearied by the years he had spent seeking to save the king from himself—summoned his men to Edward's side. With him were Lancaster's old enemy the Earl of Surrey; the Earl of Arundel, who had hitched himself to Despenser's star by marrying his son to Despenser's daughter earlier in the year; and the king's young half-brothers Thomas and Edmund, the sons of Edward I's second marriage to Isabella's aunt Marguerite. As this royal army marched northwestward from London, the rebel lords—who were struggling now to maintain their brittle unity—fell back before its approach.

For once, momentum lay with the king, and it seemed that Edward might carry all before him. At Shrewsbury near the Welsh border in January 1322 the Mortimers surrendered. The faith they had placed in Lancaster's support had been destroyed by the earl's failure to emerge from his fortresses in the north. But if they had hoped that Edward would look with favour on their submission, they were to be bitterly disappointed. Both uncle and nephew were dispatched in chains to London, where they, too, were incarcerated in the Tower. The king pressed on northward, determined now to seize this chance to destroy the man who had killed Gaveston and dismembered his kingdom. Support for Lancaster was ebbing away with every mile he retreated before Edward's advance; and Isabella sent word on her husband's behalf to Andrew Harclay, a veteran of the Scottish war and warden of the western frontier with Scotland, that he should move south to cut off Lancaster's escape.

The earl was still hoping to reach his newly built fortress at Dunstanburgh on the Northumbrian coast, but when his much-diminished army arrived at Boroughbridge in Yorkshire on March 16, they found their way north across the river Ure blocked by Harclay and his men. With Edward's forces not far behind, they had no option but to fight. While Lancaster tried to take the ford across the swollen water at the head of his cavalry, the Earl of Hereford—who had joined Lancaster at Pontefract after the Mortimers' surrender—led an assault on the narrow wooden bridge. But Harclay had stationed soldiers in hiding under the bridge, and one of them speared Hereford from below through a gap in the planks as he tried to cross. His screams as he died in gut-wrenching agony sowed panic among troops who were already buckling under heavy fire from Harclay's archers. Lancaster was forced into retreat; and at daybreak the next morning Harclay's men swarmed across the river to complete their victory.

Lancaster had come to believe that he was untouchable. Cousin to the king, uncle to the queen, an earl five times over, he could stand alone in condemnation of Edward's failings and never fear the consequences of his wrath. Now, as he was escorted south as a prisoner to his own castle at Pontefract, he had time to consider the fate that awaited him: royal revenge, ten years in the making. Hereford was dead; so, too, was Despenser's brother-in-law and Edward's former confidant Roger Damory, who had been fatally wounded a few days earlier. Despenser's other brother-in-law, Hugh Audley, was a prisoner, taken in Lancaster's company at Boroughbridge, as was John Mowbray, whose claim to Gower had served to spark this conflagration, while the Mortimers, kept close in the Tower, awaited trial in London.

Edward's victory was complete. That much was clear to Lancaster on the morning of March 22, when he was brought into Pontefract's great hall to face a hastily assembled tribunal of lords, including the earls of Pembroke, Surrey, and Arundel and Edward's young half-brother the Earl of Kent. An indictment of his crimes was read, reaching backward from the immediate fact of his armed defiance through charges of treasonous communications with the Scots all the way to his seizure of the king's jewels and horses at Newcastle in 1312. The royal pardons he had knelt to receive since then were now worthless, it was obvious, and Lancaster was not allowed to speak in his own defence, beyond a bitterly wry aside which the *Vita* puts into his mouth: "This is a powerful court, and great in authority, where no answer is heard nor any excuse admitted...."

Only one verdict was possible after such a trial. The earl was sentenced, as a traitor, to be hanged and then, while still alive, cut down and beheaded—although the king conceded that he should be spared the gallows in deference to his royal blood (and, according to one chronicler, out of respect for his niece, the queen). This was martial law enacted away from the battlefield, while banners were furled and arms sheathed; and, if it did not closely resemble due judicial process, it was Lancaster himself who had set the precedent by which he was condemned. As the *Vita* observed, "the Earl of Lancaster once cut off Piers Gaveston's head, and now by the king's command the earl himself has lost his head. Thus, perhaps not unjustly, the earl received measure for measure."

And there were unmistakable echoes of Blacklow Hill when Lancaster, dressed in penitential rags, was bundled onto a scrawny mule and led out from Pontefract's great gate, through a freezing downpour of sleet, to a nearby hill. There he was made to kneel with his face turned toward Scotland, the enemy with whom he was accused of conspiring. He bent his head, as if in prayer; and with two or three clumsy strokes, the executioner hacked it from his body. As Edward watched, the severed head was lifted into the air in public demonstration of its owner's fate, before the monks of Pontefract Priory gathered up the bloodstained corpse for burial before the altar of their church.

Unhappy precedent there may have been, but, however shattering the repercussions of Gaveston's death, they could not compare with the shock to the political system that Lancaster's execution represented. Gaveston had been a peer of the realm in name, but not by hereditary right or territorial reach. And, crucially, his death had not been ordered by the king. Now, for the first time since the Conquest, a lord—and not just any lord, but the greatest of them all—had been executed as a traitor. The dreadful penalties that now faced anyone who dared to oppose Edward were rammed home in the minds of his subjects in the days that followed Lancaster's death. Dozens of those who had joined the earl's revolt, lords and knights and squires, met their deaths on gallows erected for the purpose in places where they had once been powerful. John Mowbray was hanged at York on March 23, and his body left suspended in chains to rot under the spring skies. Three weeks later Bartholomew Badlesmere was dragged by a horse through the city of Canterbury and out to a crossroads where he was hanged and then decapitated, his head speared on a pike and set to stare down, hollow-eyed, on the cowed townspeople from the city's east gate. Dozens more—including the sons of Mowbray and Badlesmere—now filled prison cells in royal castles around the country, and rebels' wives and young children were among those who lost their liberty. Even Lancaster's estranged wife, the perennially unfortunate Alice Lacy, and her elderly stepmother, the dowager Countess of Lincoln, were taken into custody.

This was a new and frightening incarnation of a king whose failings had once been those of omission and distraction. The violence was authentically Edward's, the emotional response of a man for whom revenge was no less immediately visceral for having been delayed for a decade. But the thoroughgoing ruthlessness was Despenser's. The favourite and his father had been back at Edward's side since the beginning of March. Two months later, after Boroughbridge and the bloodletting that followed, the elder Despenser was created Earl of Winchester. That title was just the first of the spoils of victory that the two men now began to amass, using threats and force to supplement the royal favour in which they basked.

If Isabella was glad to see her husband restored to the fullness of his power, that joy was rapidly eroded by the realisation of the role Despenser now played in the direction of policy, and of the latitude that Edward was prepared to allow him. She had gone down on her knees to beg for his banishment in 1321—an intervention that represented not personal enmity but her queenly duty in the search for peace, no more and no less. But now it became clear that all those who had sought to broker a settlement between Edward and the rebels were regarded as potential enemies of the new regime. In May 1322 the long-suffering Earl of Pembroke was compelled to swear an extraordinary oath of loyalty to the king "for certain reasons he was given to understand," the royal chancery tersely recorded; and Isabella found herself frozen out of Edward's counsels, while her own properties, it soon emerged, were not immune from the Despensers' covetous glances.

Edward was far from being a simpleton, but his favoured pastimes had always tended toward the obvious diversions of hunting, music, and drinking into the night with the low-born companions who so disconcerted his subjects. Isabella, on the other hand, was more sophisticated in her tastes. Among her possessions was an exquisite chess set, its pieces carved from crystal and jade, that had once belonged to Edward's mother, Eleanor of Castile. And Edward was about to discover just how apt that legacy to his wife had been.

THIRTEEN

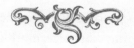

"Someone Has Come Between My Husband and Myself"

Isabella had done everything she could to be the perfect royal wife to a husband who had now demonstrated himself to be incorrigible. She had given him heirs; she had steered him toward the ways of peace and diplomacy; she had sought to reconcile him with his greatest subjects. And her reward was to find herself marginalised and intimidated within her own court.

Of course, as queen she enjoyed protections not available to others who fell victim to Despenser's lust for wealth and power. (Alice Lacy, Lancaster's widow, was threatened in her prison quarters that she would be burned to death unless she surrendered the bulk of her estates into the possession of the favourite and his father, while Despenser's widowed sister-in-law Elizabeth Damory was another victim of a brazen campaign of bullying and blackmail that was as far-reaching as it was lucrative.) Nor did Isabella suffer any of the privations endured by the mass of Edward's people after six long years of famine while Despenser heaped up piles of gold to be deposited with his Florentine bankers. Nevertheless, England's queen was a shrewdly intelligent young woman, still only twenty-seven, with a vigorous sense of her own dignity and the need to secure the future of her royal children, and she was profoundly alarmed at the intensely vulnerable position in which her husband's pliability had now placed her.

She was astute enough to know that there was little she could hope to achieve in the immediate aftermath of Despenser's triumph in the spring of 1322. The king and his favourite were much preoccupied that summer with a renewed campaign against the Scots, who had seized the opportunity presented by the expiry of the latest Anglo-Scottish truce to launch punishing raids into northwest England. Edward gathered an army and marched into Scotland, pushing northward into the highlands. However, the initially buoyant report of the campaign he sent back to the Bishop of Winchester—"we have found no resistance"—proved not to be a harbinger of success but a reflection once again of the Scots' mastery of guerrilla warfare and scorched-earth tactics. By late August Edward's troops were starving and sick, and he was forced to withdraw onto English soil with Bruce in menacing pursuit. The king reached York and safety by the skin of his teeth, but his queen was not quite so lucky.

Isabella had waited once again at Tynemouth Priory, just as she had when her husband and Gaveston had tried to make a stand against Lancaster at Newcastle in 1312. Then, she had made her escape south by road. Now, however, she was cut off on Tynemouth's headland by the advancing Scots, while out at sea Flemish ships patrolled the coast in support of Bruce's army. As the gravity of her situation began to hit home, Edward sent a scrawled order that some of Despenser's men should march to Tynemouth to protect the queen. But Despenser, for Isabella, was an enemy to be feared just as much as the Scots, and she refused point-blank to place her life in the hands of his troops even as she sent panic-stricken appeals for aid. The king dispatched instead a detachment of soldiers "more agreeable than the others"—but by then they found themselves unable to fight their way through the Scots' advance into Yorkshire. Isabella and her entourage were faced with the dreadful realisation that help was not coming. Some of her household squires did what they could to hold the Scots at bay by shoring up the priory's defences before bundling the queen and her attendants on board ship. They made a narrow escape, effected under extreme pressure, which cost the lives of two of her ladies, one lost in the chill waters of the North Sea, the other in premature labour. And by the time the queen reached land and safety at Scarborough, her fear and distrust of Despenser had become an implacable loathing.

Isabella spent Christmas 1322 in the king's company at York, but, as winter gave way to spring, her alienation from her husband and his court became ever more obvious. While Despenser consolidated his hold on Edward's government, enriching both the royal coffers and his own through a combination of acute administrative efficiency and a limitless capacity for extortion, the queen kept quiet, waiting and watching as the fabric of politics was mercilessly shredded. In the spring of 1323 a truce was concluded with the Scots, but not before England had borne the heavy cost of the loss of Andrew Harclay, the hero of Boroughbridge, whom Edward had created Earl of Carlisle in the aftermath of the battle. The debacle of the English campaign in the summer of 1322 had finally convinced Harclay, along with many others in the north, that the defences of his country could only be secured through negotiation with Robert Bruce, rather than through armed confrontation. But when Edward and Despenser found out about Harclay's meetings with Bruce, he was arrested as a traitor, convicted without a hearing, and sentenced to be hanged, drawn, and quartered. By the end of March the pieces of his dismembered corpse had been dispatched around the kingdom, his decomposing head set up on London Bridge, his butchered body on the city walls of Carlisle, Newcastle, Bristol, and Shrewsbury.

With the execution of Harclay, Edward deprived himself of one able lieutenant, and the death of the Earl of Pembroke a year later robbed him of another. Despite the suspicion with which he was regarded by Despenser, Pembroke had continued to give his all in Edward's service, and the circumstances of his death emphasised just how great a loss he was. Having led the search for a settlement with the Scots in the summer of 1323, the fifty-year-old earl collapsed and died in Picardy in June 1324 en route to Paris, where he had been sent as an ambassador to the French court. His aborted mission was an urgent one, for, with war in the north temporarily quieted, another conflict was on the verge of erupting.

France by now had a new king, since Philippe V had died in January 1322 at the age of just thirty, leaving to succeed him only daughters—who, thanks to the precedent established by his own succession, were barred by their sex from wearing the crown. The throne passed instead to his and Isabella's youngest brother, twenty-eight-year-old Charles, who was crowned and anointed as Charles IV. But the change of regime had done nothing to mitigate growing tensions in Gascony between the competing jurisdictions of the French king and the English Duke of Aquitaine. Charles, as was his right, demanded that Edward appear before him in person to do homage for the duchy. But Edward, who had accepted previous invitations to attend the French court for this purpose with such alacrity, this time refused to leave his kingdom, partly because of its dangerously disordered state, and partly because Despenser was reluctant to let go either of the reins of government or of the king whose presence allowed him to hold them. And as hostilities intensified at Saint-Sardos, sixty miles southeast of Bordeaux, it became abundantly clear that Charles was in no mood to compromise. In August 1324 he dispatched an army to seize Gascony from Edward's possession. The English king's lieutenant there, his twenty-two-year-old half-brother, Edmund, Earl of Kent, made a poor fist of the military response; and in September the desperate English were forced to buy themselves breathing space with a six-month truce that left huge territorial gains in the hands of the French.

With Anglo-French relations in deep crisis for the first time in a generation, the foreignness of England's French-born queen was suddenly exposed as never before, and Despenser was quick to take advantage of her vulnerability. In two extraordinary weeks that September, she was systematically stripped of her comforts and resources as queen. First, her lands were confiscated, without warning or compensation. Second, her household was purged when an order was given for the internment of all French subjects in England. In all, Isabella lost the loyal service of twenty-seven of her closest attendants, including her chaplains and her physician. And third, her three younger children—eight-year-old John, six-year-old Eleanor, and three-year-old Joan, who did not yet, like their elder brother, Edward, have households of their own—were removed from her custody and given into the keeping of Despenser's wife and sister.

It was a dangerous as well as distressing moment. Despenser, it seemed, intended to leave Isabella stranded on the political sidelines, bereft of influence and support and rendered powerless by her isolation, while he consolidated his hold over the king to the exclusion of all others. But Despenser, it turned out, was no cool strategist, surveying the playing field with a dispassionately judicious eye. Instead, as he clutched tighter and tighter at the power he had achieved, the panic and paranoia that drove his relentless aggression were ever more apparent.

Enemies, it seemed, were everywhere. England's fortresses were full not just of interned Frenchmen but of incarcerated rebels—and keeping them safely under lock and key was proving harder than Edward and Despenser had anticipated. Lord Berkeley, a Gloucestershire baron who had fought at the Earl of Lancaster's side in 1322, almost escaped from Wallingford Castle in Oxfordshire in January 1323. Eight months later another prisoner, Roger Mortimer of Wigmore, demonstrated with extraordinary daring that the regime had not succeeded in tightening its defences when he escaped from close confinement in the Tower. With the collusion of the fortress's second-in-command, the garrison was stupefied with drugged wine while Mortimer scrambled up a chimney onto the roof, down a rope ladder flung over the massive curtain wall, and across the Thames in a rowing boat before riding headlong for the coast and France. From the French court, where he was welcomed by a French king whose patience with Edward was rapidly running out, Mortimer was suspected by Despenser of planning assassination attempts against his own life and that of the king. Meanwhile, evidence that dissidents within England were using necromancy in an attempt to bring down the government prompted Despenser to complain urgently to the pope that he was threatened by "magical and secret dealings."

The pope gave these supernatural anxieties short shrift—"the Holy Father recommends him to turn to God with his whole heart...no other remedies are necessary," John XXII replied sternly—but clearly loyalty was an increasingly rare and fragile commodity in a kingdom where the functioning of royal power had become so horribly distorted by the toxic combination of Edward's weakness and Despenser's greed and suspicion. But the obsessive concern of both king and favourite to protect themselves against the threat of internal sedition did offer Isabella a glimmer of hope, a slender chance of finding an angle of attack on another flank from which their attention was crucially diverted. The war in Gascony was a disaster that Edward and Despenser could not afford to ignore, and yet their ability to formulate a strategic response to English losses there was compromised by the tensions under which the regime was operating at home. Further fighting to defend the duchy was not an option in the absence of a competent general of proven loyalty, or while Despenser continued to stockpile cash rather than spending it on military operations. But at the same time Edward could not go to France to make peace and do homage for Gascony, since Despenser was unwelcome there and neither king nor favourite was prepared to contemplate the risks of their own separation.

But there was a solution to hand. Was not Isabella, queen of the English king, sister of the French, uniquely placed to resolve this unfortunate dispute? The pope thought so; Charles IV graciously indicated that he would be prepared to receive his sister as Edward's emissary; and Isabella modestly put herself at her husband's disposal. This proud queen had submitted to the indignities heaped upon her with patient dissimulation, so successfully that both the king and Despenser believed that she could be trusted to represent their interests and to return like a loyal lapdog, no matter how harshly she had previously been treated. Or, at least, they had convinced themselves that the danger that she would not do so was the least of the risks with which they found themselves confronted.

On March 9, 1325, therefore, Isabella crossed the Channel from Dover to the port of Wissant outside Boulogne, with an entourage of thirty-one attendants handpicked for their allegiance to the Despenser regime. The queen gave thanks for her safe arrival at the church where she had been married seventeen long years earlier, and then rode on via Pontoise, where she had once stayed in such grandeur with her husband, to Poissy, on the banks of the Seine fifteen miles northwest of Paris. There she was reunited with her brother, King Charles—a warm and emotional meeting, but one that did not presage any dramatic softening of the French stance over Gascony. Ever the publicly dutiful wife, Isabella sent news home to Edward of her painstaking negotiations, which were concluded by the end of the month. In exchange for Edward's homage, to be performed on French soil by August, Charles would confirm the English king's possession of all his French territories save the Gascon lands of the Agenais around Saint-Sardos that French troops had lately overrun, the possession of which would be submitted to formal adjudication in due course. Meanwhile—because of his affection for his sister, the *Vita* explained—the French king also agreed to renew the truce established the previous September.

Isabella had played her part with aplomb. It was hardly a diplomatic breakthrough, but her presence had undoubtedly oiled the wheels of a process from which Edward could not realistically have hoped for more tangible gains. With careful formality, she made a public entry into Paris at the beginning of April, and remained there for the ratification of the treaty in May and her brother's lavish wed-

ding to their cousin, the daughter of Louis of Évreux, in July. But
then, as the weeks went by and Isabella drifted between the royal
palaces and hunting lodges to the west and north of the French capital, making offerings at local shrines and entertaining the great and
good of the French court to dinner, it gradually became clear that she
was making no move to return home.

If Edward was discomfited by his wife's prolonged absence, his
anxiety was offset both by her circumspect demeanour and by the
obvious limitations to her freedom of action. As his consort, she
could represent his wishes to her brother of France; but, as his consort, the only power she could exercise was an extension of his own.
Whether he knew it or not, the legitimacy of his own rule was leach-
ing away as he allowed Despenser to misuse the power of his crown,
but that fact did not mean that legitimate authority would automatically accrue to his wife instead.

And it is also entirely likely that the attention the king paid to
Isabella's movements was limited by his preoccupation with much
more obviously pressing concerns. The moment for the performance
of his homage for Aquitaine was at hand, and on that ceremony depended the safety of the remaining English possessions in Gascony;
but even as preparations were in train for Edward's departure for
France, Despenser and his father frantically sought to dissuade him
from leaving England—for, as the *Vita* sagely remarked, "in the absence of the king they would not know where to live safely." True to
form, Edward succumbed to his favourite's influence, announcing at
Dover on the eve of his embarkation that he found himself indis-
posed and unable to travel.

But the circle still had to be squared and Gascony secured by the
homage that Charles demanded. It was a seemingly intractable dilemma, and a perilous one—until a messenger arrived, fresh from
crossing the Channel, with a proposal for an elegant solution. The
French king, it appeared, would happily receive the homage of Edward's eldest son if he were invested with the duchy of Aquitaine
in his father's stead. Twelve-year-old Prince Edward was already,

conveniently, at Dover with his father; on September 10 he was created Duke of Aquitaine in anticipation of the oath of allegiance he
would offer to his French uncle, and two days later he set sail for
France with an imposing entourage of bishops and lords. And, along
with their young son, the king sent orders to his wife that she should
return immediately to England since her presence at her brother's
court was no longer required by English policy.

It was a double move that made impeccable sense from within
the bunker that Edward's gilded palaces had now become: to bring
a princely pawn into play while retrieving the queen from her position in the front line, all the while allowing Despenser to remain
sheltered at the king's side. But, in their haste and their paranoia,
Edward and Despenser made two mistakes of monumental propor-
tions. They took for granted Isabella's compliance, and they failed to
see the sequence of moves that opened up to her for the first time as
a result of their gambit.

When Prince Edward stepped onto the quay at Wissant on September 14 to be enfolded in his mother's embrace, Isabella's position was transformed at a stroke. With her son at her side, she was
no longer merely an adjunct to her husband's power, a consort who
could be silenced and isolated if she failed to co-operate. Instead,
she stood apart as the mother of the heir to the throne, an anointed
queen who could speak and act for her young son and his people
in the face of the tyranny that her husband's rule had become. The
king had been so focused on his own need to remain in England, on
averting the loss of another favourite and another internal assault
on his own power, that he had failed to recognise the impossibility
of compelling the return of his wife and son once they were beyond
his borders. Isabella, however, had been waiting for her chance; and
now she took it.

When Edward's envoy relayed his command that she should
return to England, he did so in the presence of the French king and
his court, perhaps in the belief that the English queen would not
openly defy her husband. But a public platform suited Isabella's pur-

poses perfectly. "I feel that marriage is a joining together of man and woman...," the *Vita* has her declare, "and someone has come between my husband and myself trying to break this bond. I protest that I will not return until this intruder is removed, but, discarding my marriage garment, shall assume the robes of widowhood and mourning until I am avenged of this Pharisee."

For Edward, her defiance came as a palpable shock. He could not believe that this call for the removal of Despenser—the man who had become his right hand, restoring his power and securing his revenge for the death of Gaveston—had come from his loyal wife. His incredulity as he struggled to comprehend the reality of Isabella's deception is manifest in the *Vita*'s account of his address to his assembled lords in parliament at Westminster that November: "...on her departure she did not seem to anyone to be offended," the king remarked, with a lack of percipience entirely characteristic of his political career. "As she took her leave she saluted all and went away joyfully. But now someone has changed her attitude. Someone has primed her with inventions. For I know that she has not fabricated any affront out of her own head. Yet she says that Hugh Despenser is her adversary and hostile to her...."

Shock, however, was not the reaction of those whom Edward now suspected of involvement in his wife's insubordination. Totally inadequate though his assessment of Isabella's independence of mind might have been, he was not wrong to suppose that she would find allies around her in France. There is no incontrovertible evidence to prove that Isabella and her brother King Charles had worked together behind the scenes to secure her son's presence in France and simultaneously prevent her own return to England, but it is by far the most likely conclusion in the light of their wholly compatible interests and the immediate support Charles gave her once she had made her feelings known. ("The queen has come of her own will, and may freely return if she so wishes. But if she prefers to remain in these parts, she is my sister, and I refuse to expel her.")

Meanwhile, Isabella's self-assertion also made her a figurehead for English as well as French hostility to Edward. And there was plenty of it. There were those even among the handpicked delegation that had accompanied Prince Edward to Paris who preferred, it now transpired, to stay with the queen rather than return to the king—including not only the bishops of Winchester and Norwich but also Edward's own half-brother, the Earl of Kent, whose military failure in Gascony had compounded his own disenchantment with Despenser's role in his brother's regime.

They now joined forces with the exiles who had fled England after the failure of the Earl of Lancaster's rebellion, principal among them Roger Mortimer of Wigmore, the lord who had made such a dramatic escape from the Tower two years earlier. Mortimer was thirty-eight years old, a soldier and politician of hard-won experience gained first as Edward's justiciar in Ireland and later as Despenser's enemy in the Marches of Wales. Isabella had encountered him at her husband's court many times, and in the wake of his incarceration had petitioned Edward to treat Mortimer's imprisoned wife with greater compassion. But he had not been in Paris to greet the queen on her arrival in France, since Edward had made it a condition of Isabella's embassy that his enemies should be expelled from Charles's kingdom before her arrival, and Mortimer had therefore made his way to the county of Hainaut, France's neighbour in the Low Countries to the north.

In December 1325, however, Hainaut's countess Jeanne— a French princess by birth, and first cousin to Isabella and her brother—travelled to Paris for the funeral of her father, Charles of Valois. With her came Roger Mortimer. There is every reason to suppose that Mortimer, just as much as King Charles, had been covertly apprised of Isabella's plans before her public breach with her husband. He was an obvious ally, a man with everything to gain and nothing to lose by supporting the queen's revolt against Despenser's power. Within weeks of their meeting, however, word reached England that, when they were united at last in Paris, Isabella and Mortimer had begun not only a political partnership but a passionate affair.

There is tantalisingly little evidence to document the private dynamics of this charged liaison, but its emotional logic is instantly recognisable. Physical attraction there clearly was: they were almost of an age, Isabella at thirty still a famous beauty, and Mortimer, though his looks are unknown, an athletic and compelling figure. Add to that a combustible combination of forceful temperaments, the aphrodisiac qualities of the power play in which they were caught up, and the depth and breadth of their shared political interests, and it is clear that this was no idle dalliance but an all-consuming personal bond.

That conclusion can only be reinforced by the dangers of the course to which they had now committed themselves. Adultery, for a queen, was sin and treason combined, and Isabella had seen at close hand its grievous effects on her young sisters-in-law and their lovers. Beyond the personal risks were the political ones. By compromising the ground on which she stood as Edward's betrayed wife, she might put in jeopardy the legitimacy of her position as a mother who could speak for the rights of her son. She now chose to wear the becomingly sombre gowns of a widow, in ostentatious expression of her claim that Despenser had destroyed her marriage, but in pursuing a relationship with Mortimer she risked the accusation that she had revealed herself as a scarlet woman.

On the other hand, Mortimer's total identification with her cause also brought her significant practical resources. She could serve as a figurehead and a rallying point for opposition to her husband, but Mortimer was a soldier and could lead an army into battle should confrontation develop into military conflict (as it surely would, for what other choice remained?). He could call on significant lands and loyalties at home. And if their liaison brought opprobrium upon her, it also emphasised the "unnaturalness," to contemporary eyes, of the closeness between Edward and Despenser that had driven her from the marital bed.

Certainly, the affair revealed that—greater tactician than her myopic husband though she undoubtedly was—she was also capable of impulsive behaviour that gave precedence to her immediate inclinations over cautious and far-sighted policy. But her sense of duty had always been inextricably entangled with a profound sense of entitlement, and both were unmistakably in play as she sought to seize her moment amid the political flood tide that she herself had unleashed—fully aware, whatever else she thought she knew, that there were no safe options any more.

The question was what move the queen would make, with her knight at her side and the most valuable pawn of all, her son, under her control. Here for the first time we miss the perceptive commentary of the most acute of contemporary observers, the author of the *Vita Edwardi Secundi*. The single surviving transcript of his narrative stops abruptly at the end of 1325 with the news that "mother and son refused to return to England." This sudden silence, and the absence from the text of any sign of foreknowledge of what was to come, suggests that this wise and humane observer died early in 1326. We are left in the company of other chroniclers—variously interesting and well informed, but few as discerning—to contemplate the choices with which Isabella was now faced.

Her stand so far had been taken against Despenser, his intervention in her marriage and his improper influence with Edward. On those grounds, it was already clear, she would find widespread support in England, as well as among the exiled lords in France. But if she aimed merely at the destruction of Despenser, it had to be said that the precedents of the last twenty years were not good. Edward had shown time and again that he would say whatever his enemies wished to hear, and go back on his word the moment he was able to do so. It was this desperate knowledge that had pushed the Earl of Lancaster to the killing of Gaveston; but that had done no more than condemn the kingdom to a decade of pathological political conflict until the king secured his revenge.

The logic of the position that Isabella had adopted since her son's

arrival in France, meanwhile, dictated that her challenge was in practice aimed as much at her husband as at his favourite. By styling herself a widow, she had thrown off Edward's authority in personal as
well as political terms; and if her husband was now dead to her, her
duty lay with her son, for whose rights and responsibilities she could
claim to speak. To make that challenge real on English soil, however,
she would need an army. Her brother Charles had furnished political
and financial support, and Isabella could also draw on the resources of
her dower lands in Ponthieu and Montreuil. But the prospect of military backing became concrete for the first time in the early months of
1326 thanks to Isabella's cousin Jeanne of Valois and her husband,
Count Guillaume of Hainaut.

A marriage alliance between Hainaut and England, in the youthful shape of the count's eldest daughter and Isabella's son Edward,
had first been proposed six years earlier. Since then, the ebb and flow
of European diplomacy had swept the scheme aside, and, back in
England, King Edward was embroiled in negotiations to secure an
Aragonese princess for his heir. But the enormity of the king's error
in allowing the young prince to escape his grasp meant that Edward
was no longer in a position to dictate his son's future. Now Isabella
and Mortimer revived the plan that young Edward should marry
one of Count Guillaume's daughters—this time one of his younger
girls, Philippa—in an alliance that would bring the queen not only
a daughter-in-law but troops with which her son might claim his
birthright sooner than his father had anticipated.

Too late, Edward could see with horrifying clarity the nature of
the threat that confronted him. In panic, he dispatched letter after
letter across the Channel, to his son ("we are not pleased with you,
and neither for your mother nor for any other ought you to displease
us . . ."), to Isabella's brother King Charles ("if you wished her well,
dearest brother, you would chastise her for this misconduct and
make her demean herself as she ought, for the honour of all those to
whom she belongs"), and to the pope, who obligingly responded—
after a doomed effort to make peace—by weighing in on his behalf,

threatening Charles with excommunication if the French court continued to shelter the adulterous queen and her lover.

This was spiritual instruction with which Charles was happy to comply, in public at least. Isabella and her son were honoured guests at the coronation of Charles's new wife in the jewel-like Sainte Chapelle within the Île de la Cité's royal palace in May 1326, with Mortimer in close attendance upon them; but just two months later the English queen and prince left her brother's court, riding north to her county of Ponthieu. This "expulsion," however, was timed perfectly to enable Charles to defer diplomatically to papal authority while Isabella put the next stage of their plan into action. From Ponthieu she rode eastward to join Mortimer in Hainaut, where he was already working with Count Guillaume to muster and provision a fleet. By September 21 everything was ready. The queen had signed a treaty with Hainaut, promising that her son would marry the count's daughter Philippa; and the bride's dowry had already been assembled, in the form of seven hundred soldiers under the command of the count's brother Jean. With them, filling the hundred or so leased ships that had gathered in Dordrecht harbour, were mercenaries from the Low Countries and Germany, their wages paid out of the revenues of Ponthieu with financial guarantees provided by the King of France. Isabella was on board with her ladies, her son, and the English exiles who had rallied to her cause, Roger Mortimer at their head. And on the morning of September 22, with a fair wind swelling the sails, they set their course for England.

It was an extraordinary journey. This adrenaline-fuelled moment marked the final unravelling of a marriage, just as Eleanor of Aquitaine's revolt against Henry II had done a century and a half earlier. Eleanor had been imprisoned for fifteen years for her pains, and denounced as a threat to the order of all creation. Isabella was— as Eleanor had not been—an adulteress as well as a disloyal wife. And yet, remarkably, her overwhelming defiance of the paradigms of female virtue was not met with the same outrage and vilification. This was a battle over the very nature of legitimate authority; and the greater and preceding sins of her husband meant that Isabella's self-presentation as a wronged queen and a royal mother took precedence over her infidelity and vindicated her rebellion.

That much was clear when, after two days of struggling against the hostile waters of the North Sea, the rebel fleet reached the Suffolk coast on September 24. One of Edward's half-brothers, the Earl of Kent, was already with Isabella, having joined her in Paris. The other, the Earl of Norfolk, had been entrusted with the defence of East Anglia in the name of the king—and he, too, immediately defected to the queen's side. The small force of invaders had not known what to expect when they made landfall, scarcely knowing where they were after the disorientation of a difficult crossing. But as they made cautious progress inland, they discovered, wonderingly, that there was no one to resist them.

The tyrannical regime that Edward and his favourite had imposed on his frightened people was suddenly and silently disintegrating, undermined from within by the reign of terror with which Despenser had sought to make the king's power impregnable. Edward had turned a blind eye to Despenser's bullying and extortion. Worse, much worse, he had allowed his own royal authority to become an instrument of that abuse. And in doing so he had failed to understand that the strength of his crown—the essence of the oath he had sworn at his coronation—lay in protecting his people from unchecked disorder and injustice. For as long as there was no alternative, it was hard to see how an anointed king who had made himself a force for division and oppression could in practice be resisted. But as soon as Isabella appeared—a royal champion acting in the name of the realm and of her son's role as its heir—support for Edward simply melted away.

At news of his wife's arrival, the king had issued urgent orders for his people to muster in defence of his kingdom against an invasion which, unsurprisingly, his proclamations characterised entirely differently: "Roger Mortimer and other traitors and enemies of the king and his realm have entered the realm in force," he declared, "and

have brought with them alien strangers for the purpose of taking the
royal power from the king...." But the bankruptcy of his cause was
everywhere apparent. The musters fizzled out, the sheriffs muttering
excuses, sitting on their hands, or leading the men they recruited to
join the rebels. The royal treasury was filled with thousands of extorted pounds in drifting heaps of gold, but it was slowly dawning on
Edward and Despenser that gold could not save them if its cost had
been counted in forfeited loyalty.

To Isabella, meanwhile, gates were opened, gifts brought, and
service pledged. She rode first to Ipswich, where the citizens proffered a welcome and a loan to support her troops, and then to Bury
St. Edmund's Abbey, where she took possession of more treasure.
Twenty-five miles further west at Cambridge, the support of the
wider Church took concrete form with the arrival of the bishops
of Hereford, Lincoln, Ely, and Durham. At each staging post, she
publicly insisted that fair prices be paid for the supplies her forces
needed; they had come, after all, to rescue Edward's people, not to
pillage them. And all the while Mortimer, in public discreetly maintaining an appropriate distance from the queen, was marshalling
under his disciplined command the growing army of men who rallied to her side.

When news of this triumphal progress reached London, unrest in
the city began to accelerate out of control, and behind the walls of the
Tower Edward and Despenser were gripped by panic. From the start
they had been bound together by obsessional mistrust, the conviction that they were surrounded by enemies intent on their destruction. Now paranoia had created its own reality. With gold packed
heavily into saddlebags, they fled westward on October 2, seeking
the safety of Despenser's strongholds in south Wales, hoping still
that the force of a royal command might bring soldiers to their side.
They had reached Gloucester on October 10 when news came that
the Earl of Lancaster's brother Henry—who had stood aloof from
his brother's revolt four years earlier and had been allowed to inherit a portion of his estates as reward for his loyalty—had ridden

with his men to offer his sword in Isabella's service. This was grim certainty that the ranks of the army for which the king was waiting would be filled only with phantoms. In fear and despair, Edward and Despenser and their handful of guards turned their horses west once again.

Isabella and Mortimer were not far behind. From Oxford, where they were greeted with a gift of a precious silver cup, they rode to the queen's castle at Wallingford. There they issued a proclamation in the name of the queen and the prince which trod the most delicate of political lines: still covering their backs by protesting public loyalty to the king, they called his subjects to arms against Despenser, whom they denounced as "a clear tyrant and enemy of God and the Holy Church, and of our very dear said lord the king and the whole kingdom." Still they had not shed a drop of blood, and as their army grew, the order they brought was thrown into sharp relief by the chaos that was overwhelming London.

Once the king had fled, the capital had declared for his queen; but in her absence the vacuum of power was filled with violent anger at the falling regime, and on October 15 the rioters in the city claimed a significant scalp. The Bishop of Exeter, who as Treasurer of England had been one of Despenser's chief allies in turning Edward's government into a mechanism of financial extortion, rode into the city that day, thinking that he could save his beautiful house, his jewels, and his books from the mob. By the time he realised his mistake, it was too late to turn back. He rode desperately for St. Paul's, hoping to find sanctuary there, but the jeering crowd closed in. He was pulled from his horse, stripped of his armour, and dragged down Ludgate Hill to the great cross in Cheapside, where his head was crudely hacked from his shoulders with a baker's knife.

The bishop's severed head was sent westward to Isabella—a macabre trophy, and an unwelcome reminder of the anarchy that could too easily result from her challenge to her husband's authority. But there was no time to turn back to quiet the capital. Edward and Despenser had reached Wales, where they found a ship at Chepstow to take them to Ireland. But after six days at sea, battling impotently against headwinds that penned them in the Bristol Channel, they were forced to admit defeat and land again at Cardiff. Despenser's father, meanwhile, had been left at Bristol to hold the castle there against the queen's implacable advance. Eight days into a siege by Mortimer's troops, and with no hope of rescue, the garrison capitulated. The elder Despenser was hauled in chains before a tribunal including Mortimer himself, Henry of Lancaster, and the king's half-brothers of Kent and Norfolk. Like the Earl of Lancaster before him, the accused was not permitted to speak in his own defence; unlike Lancaster, he was spared none of the ugly penalties for treason, but was drawn on a hurdle through the streets, hanged from the city gallows, and cut down for decapitation, his head sent on a spear to Winchester, where he had once been earl, and his body fed to the dogs.

By then, the king and the younger Despenser were seven miles north of Cardiff at Caerphilly, seeking shelter in a fortress on which the favourite had lavished part of the extraordinary fortune he had amassed. But now they knew that walls would not save them. At the beginning of November they pressed on twenty-five miles westward to Neath, but, like trapped animals, they had nowhere left to run. They had turned back east when they were caught at last on November 16, bedraggled figures riding in driving rain across open country near Llantrisant, by Henry of Lancaster and his men. Despenser was taken at once to Isabella and Mortimer at the border town of Hereford, tied roughly onto a shambling nag to run the gauntlet of the howling, taunting crowds that lined his route.

His fate was clear. He refused all food and drink, trying to starve himself into oblivion before a more terrible death could find him. He succeeded only in bringing it closer. In Hereford's marketplace on November 24 he was half-carried, almost fainting, before the queen and her lords, who had brought forward his trial for fear he should die on the road to London. They heard a lengthy denunciation of his crimes—to which Despenser was allowed no reply—and watched as he was pulled through the city streets to the walls of the castle for execution. Amid a baying mob, he was stripped of his clothes and hoisted, choking and kicking, by a noose fifty feet into the air. Then the rope was lowered and loosened so that he could see the approach of the executioner's knife that would disembowel and—in a torture added specifically for this intimate companion of the king—castrate him. Beheading, when it came, was a mercy. And, as the crowd sated itself on this bloody spectacle, Isabella and Mortimer knew that the simple part of their task was over.

FOURTEEN

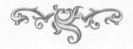

Iron Lady

dward, to whom his wife and her lover had professed such loyalty, was now a prisoner in the keeping of Henry of Lancaster at Monmouth Castle in the borderlands of south Wales. In his person the gulf between the rhetoric and the reality of their invasion was made dangerously real. The practical fact of the matter was that he could not be allowed to regain his liberty, let alone the power of his crown. At the same time, they had rallied the country against Despenser as an enemy of both the kingdom and its king—and the king had now been liberated from his destructive influence.

But seeds had already, carefully, been sown for a process by which Edward's loss of legitimacy could be made explicit. The fruitless days he and Despenser had spent at sea between Chepstow and Cardiff had allowed Isabella and Mortimer to proclaim that Edward had abandoned his realm, and that the young Prince Edward had, "with the assent of the whole community of the realm," been appointed keeper of the kingdom in his father's place. Meanwhile, the Bishop of Hereford had preached a sermon before the queen at Walling-ford, taking as his text a phrase from the Book of Kings—"my head aches"—from which he extrapolated an argument for removing the head of a kingdom altogether if it were found to be diseased.

Now, however, the time had come for action, not argument. And there was no precedent for what had to be done. Never before had a king been unmade. The fact of Stephen's kingship—his consecra-tion and anointing—had stood baldly in the way of Matilda's efforts to assert her own right to the throne, and, though Stephen's heir had been pushed aside to make way for the succession of Matilda's son, Stephen's kingship had been ended only by death. Now Isabella sought to achieve the opposite: to uphold the direct line of succes-sion, but to do so prematurely; to set aside an old king to make way for a new while the former still lived.

She already had the great seal, which had been taken from Edward at Monmouth by the Bishop of Hereford on November 20. While her husband was a prisoner, of course, she and Mortimer could con-trol his public pronouncements, and so it was declared that the king had sent the seal of his own free will "to his consort and son," with orders that they should do "not only what was necessary for right and peace, but also what should please them." This was the same freedom of action that Eleanor of Aquitaine had enjoyed when she ruled Eng-land for her son Richard—"the power of doing whatever she wished in the kingdom." Then, it had been an expression of trust; now, a step on the road to depriving the king of his crown.

The language in which that extraordinary proposition might be couched had, after all, been spoken within months of Edward's acces-sion nearly twenty years earlier: "Homage and the oath of allegiance are more in respect of the crown than in respect of the king's person," his lords had told him in 1308. And now, at a parliament called to meet at Westminster in January 1327, the ways in which the king had forfeited that allegiance were enumerated. Edward "had as good as lost the lands of Gascony and Scotland through bad counsel and bad custody," reported one chronicler, "and likewise through bad counsel he had caused to be slain a great part of the noble blood of the land, to the dishonour and loss of himself, his realm and the whole people, and had done many other astonishing things." In a carefully stage-managed piece of political theatre, the bishops, lords, and selected representatives of the wider realm, with excitable crowds of London-ers gathered outside, declared that they would have Edward's son wear the crown instead of a king whose failings and oppressions were manifest and incorrigible. The Archbishop of Canterbury spoke on the proverbial saw "*vox populi, vox Dei*" ("the voice of the people is the voice of God")—a text that would normally be a contentious propo-sition for a royal administration, now suddenly rendered a valuable political tool. And Prince Edward was ushered forward, a sombre-faced fourteen-year-old, to receive the acclamation of his newly ac-quired subjects.

Still this de facto deposition needed more legitimating ballast. A deputation from parliament led by the bullish Bishop of Hereford rode to Kenilworth in Warwickshire, another of Henry of Lancas-ter's castles, to which the imprisoned king had now been moved. One later account describes Edward, dressed all in black, weeping and fainting when he realised they had come to demand the renunciation of his throne. But in truth we know very little of Edward's emotional reaction to the straits in which he found himself. His responsibili-ties as king had never claimed his full attention; this was the mon-arch, after all, who had offered to agree to anything his lords asked of him if it would secure the presence of Piers Gaveston by his side. Now Gaveston was gone, along with Despenser, the man who had helped Edward to avenge his death. He had neither the resources nor the means to fight on; it may be that he also lacked the will. We cannot know, but we might guess that despair was his overwhelming response as he listened to the bishop's blandishments and threats. At last, on January 20, faced with the utter hopelessness of his cause, Edward was brought to agree that he would resign his crown to his son. Once he had done so, the deputation formally renounced their homage, and the steward of Edward's royal household solemnly

broke his staff of office in two. By the double logic of deposition and
abdication, then, the transformation effected at Edward's coronation
was undone. And at Westminster on February 1, 1327, his son was
anointed and crowned in his stead as King Edward III, a slight figure
in rich red silk amid an abbey ablaze with gold.

From this moment on the decrees of government carried the
authenticating mark "by the king," rather than "by the queen," "by
the queen and the king's firstborn son," or (with nice elision) "by
the queen and her firstborn son," as they had done in the months
since the invasion. But that did not mean the young king was now
ruling his kingdom for himself. Around him stood a formal council,
made up of the great bishops and lords of the realm, with Henry
of Lancaster restored to his brother's lands and named as the "chief
guardian of the king." Behind the council, however, stood Isabella
and Mortimer. Formally, their authority had been superseded by the
coronation and the council; informally, they directed the entire administration. That was not necessarily and inescapably a problem,
given the legitimacy attached to the queen's role as mother of an un-
derage king, and Mortimer's leadership of the army that had ended
the oppressions of the previous regime. But much would depend on
what they did next.

And whatever they chose to do would be done under uniquely
intractable pressure. Never before had England had to contend with
the existence of an ex-king, alive and well in captivity, while a new
king attempted to establish his rule. Isabella's failure to discharge
her matrimonial responsibilities by returning to Edward's side now
that the "intruder" Despenser had been removed had been explained
away by the Bishop of Hereford, chief propagandist of the coup, who
expatiated at length on the violence with which Edward had threatened his wife should he see her again. (He carried a knife with which
to kill her, the bishop declared, and, if that failed, had announced
his intention to dispatch her with his teeth.) But what could not be
so easily remedied was the threat to the nascent regime posed by the
pre-existing claim of the old king as a means of justifying opposi-

tion to the new. Unity had been easy to establish in the heady days of September 1326, when Edward was inseparable from the hated Despenser; but it was much harder to maintain with Despenser dead and Edward deposed through a process of political improvisation and outright invention.

One plot to free Edward had already been foiled by April 1327, when he was moved from Kenilworth sixty miles southwest to Berkeley Castle, a stronghold a couple of miles inland from the Severn estuary that was, in its marshy remoteness, much less easily accessible than Lancaster's midland fortress. It was held by Thomas Berkeley, son of the Lord Berkeley who had rebelled against Edward in 1322, and husband of one of Mortimer's daughters—a much more reassuring custodian, from the point of view of the queen and her lover, than the increasingly powerful and independent-minded Lancaster. There Edward's captivity became closer, to prevent further attempts at rescue, and perhaps less comfortable, in the hope that his robust health might take a convenient turn for the worse in the cold and damp of a less than royally furnished cell.

By the end of the summer, however, it was clear that neither expectation had been fulfilled. Edward remained unhelpfully alive; not only that, but in July a second conspiracy to liberate him had been thwarted, this time by a much narrower margin. Like the first plot, it was the brainchild of a Dominican friar, an order to which Edward had always shown particular favour and devotion—an attachment reciprocated by the friars years earlier in the tending and reverent burial of Gaveston's broken body, and now in these demonstrations of diehard loyalism to a discredited king. This time it seems the conspirators succeeded in releasing Edward from his cell before the breakout was contained and the former king was returned to his prison quarters. But when a third plot was discovered in mid-September, it was obvious just how little hope there was that his continued existence might fade from public consciousness into political irrelevance.

And so, with impeccable and implacable political logic, covert arrangements were put in train that resulted, during the night of September 21, 1327, in the death of the man already known to his former subjects as "Edward, the late king." By its very nature, his end was a grim business that took place in shadows and secrecy. Officially, it was simply reported that he had died—whether by unfortunate accident or a sudden extremity of illness was left disconcertingly unspecified—but the suggestion that natural causes had claimed his life at forty-three in so abrupt a manner, and with such extraordinarily opportune timing, convinced no one. This impulsive and misguided man, who had understood so little about the power he had once wielded, died in an obscurity quite at odds with the royal spotlight in which he had lived—and the vacuum of information about his fate was rapidly filled with swirling dust clouds of rumour, innuendo, and conjecture.

Some of the myth-making about this political murder took the form of unsubtle allusion to the intimate relationships with his favourites that had proved so destructive. Edward was killed, later chroniclers would confidently assert, by a red-hot iron thrust violently into his anus, burning his intestines from the inside without a mark left on his body. Other whispers denied that the killing had taken place at all, and told instead of another corpse buried in his place, while the king himself escaped into exile under an assumed identity. Though these rumours acquired a little traction in the years (and even centuries) that followed, the truth was that such stories formed a familiar accompaniment to politically charged deaths that took place before their time or in mysterious circumstances. Tales already long in circulation included that of the Emperor Heinrich V, Matilda's first husband, who had—so the legend went—faked his own death, substituted another body for his own at his magnificent funeral, and made his way to England to live in penitential poverty as a hermit in Chester. (Nor was he the only royal refugee to do so, according to inventive local tradition; near to his cell, it was said, lived a one-eyed anchorite named Harold who had made his home there after escaping from a battlefield near Hastings.) English folklore had found room for a German emperor: now the German Empire played host to a lost King of England. Edward's tale, as it developed, was Heinrich's in geographical reverse, with the king dodging a counterfeit funeral to arrive in Cologne in the guise of a wandering hermit, before ending his days in religious contemplation near Pavia in Lombardy.

The alchemical quality of Edward's necessarily shadowy death was evident not only in this elaborate afterlife but in the transmutation of his reputation. Even the unlikely figure of Thomas of Lancaster had been transfigured by the shock of his violent end into a candidate for popular sainthood: within weeks of the earl's execution, miracles had been breathlessly reported at his tomb at Pontefract, where his hat and belt were reverently kept as healing relics. Now Edward, too, had his chance to become a political martyr. By the time the chronicler Geoffrey le Baker wrote his venomously partisan account of events some thirty years later, the former king had become a Christlike figure—the description of the lamenting, swooning Edward at Kenilworth is Baker's—whose noble spirit was betrayed and destroyed by those who owed him their loyalty.

Chief among these Judases, of course, was Edward's wife. For Baker, Isabella was Jezebel—a tyrannical and sexually corrupt queen manipulating her husband and son to impose evil on the kingdom—and a "*ferrea virago*," a woman who aped a man, abandoning her feminine virtues, to become as cruel and unyielding as iron. But this vilification of a queen who had been welcomed with open arms in the autumn of 1326—a mother to England's people as well as to its heir, come to rescue the realm from tyranny—was neither instant nor inevitable in the immediate aftermath of Edward's death.

Given the clandestine circumstances in which he died, almost nothing could be known for certain about what exactly had happened or where responsibility lay. Nor has the passage of time made answers any easier to find. Was Isabella the instigator of her husband's murder, or did Mortimer decide that he must be removed? Did one initiate and the other resist, or were they partners in this, as in so much else? In public, the proprieties were carefully observed. The king's corpse was embalmed, and his heart sent in a silver vase to his royal widow. The body lay in state, first at Berkeley, then in the abbey of St. Peter at Gloucester, the coffin draped in cloth of gold embroidered with the arms of England. On December 20 Edward was laid to rest in a ceremony full of elaborate ritual. Isabella and her son knelt before an exquisitely carved and gilded hearse bearing not only the coffin but a fine wooden effigy of the king dressed in royal robes and a copper-gilt crown. Mortimer, too, clad respectfully in black, took his place among the mourners. Then, the following day, the court left Gloucester to spend Christmas at Worcester and to prepare for the young king's marriage to Philippa of Hainaut. Newly arrived in England, she was welcomed into London on Christmas Eve with lavish civic festivities, before travelling north to York for a wedding joyfully celebrated amid a snowstorm in the half-built minster.

Whatever view we take of Isabella's role in her husband's murder, therefore, it has to be noted that his death did not cause a moment's disruption to the part she played in the regime she and Mortimer had created, or to her conduct as a queen and a mother. She had always evinced a conventionally observant piety—but faith, however genuine, might also be as flexible and accommodatingly complex as the person who professed it. Isabella's religious belief had so far proved able to encompass personal and political rebellion against her husband and king, to the point of adultery and deposition; and by September 1327 it was already two years since she had begun to style herself a widow. It is hardly unimaginable, therefore, that Isabella might have brought herself to contemplate the irresistible political imperative of her husband's death, particularly given the depths to which Edward's rule had sunk and the degree of political legitimacy that Isabella's resistance to his oppressions, and her possession of the unquestioned heir to his throne, had conferred on her claim to power. God, after all, had smiled on her actions and vindicated her every move by granting her overwhelming victory.

Much would depend, then, on whether the queen could maintain that legitimacy now that Edward had been removed from the political stage. Whatever happened, the regime over which she and Mortimer presided could not last indefinitely. The young king had just turned fifteen, and, though he had so far been no more than a pawn in the political process, it could not be expected that he would be content to remain forever in the shadow of his mother and her lover. The power that Isabella and Mortimer now enjoyed therefore depended on their continuing claim to be conscientious guardians of the realm until her son was old enough to rule for himself.

But here the limitations of Isabella's worldview, and of her political understanding, were revealed for the first time. She was an intelligent woman, and a political animal through and through, whose acute tactical sense had enabled her to play her hand with masterful skill in the critical moment of 1326. But now it emerged that her overwhelming sense of entitlement—which had driven her resistance to her husband from the moment he had allowed Despenser to displace her from her hard-won position at his side—also prevented her from understanding that constraints on her freedom of action remained, despite the power she had achieved. Of course a royal daughter of France and a Queen of England would expect to command the reverence and enjoy the luxury appropriate to her exalted rank, but the acquisitive arrogance that Isabella now displayed blunted her vision as a ruler in a manner that was alarmingly reminiscent of her feckless husband.

It was indisputable that the queen should retrieve the valuable dower lands, worth £4,500 a year, that had been stripped from her by the rapacious regime she had overthrown. But the award made to Isabella on the day of her son's coronation tripled that already generous endowment. With her new estates worth an astonishing annual sum of 20,000 marks—or £13,333—she enjoyed an income greater even than that of Thomas of Lancaster in his pomp. Among the many properties of which she now took possession were her dead husband's favourite manor of Langley, where Gaveston lay beneath a gilded tomb; Leeds Castle, from the gates of which she had been turned away with such bloody results; Bristol Castle, where the older Despenser had died; and the Earl of Lancaster's fortress at Ponte-fract, which the younger Despenser had seized after Lancaster's execution and which Isabella now appropriated for herself despite the prior claims of the earl's brother Henry. Meanwhile, with a series of cash grants—needed to pay her army of mercenaries as well as to establish her glittering supremacy at her son's new court—she drained the gold that Despenser had stockpiled in the royal treasury.

And she was not alone in her acquisitions. Mortimer's ambition had been no less apparent than Isabella's at the young king's coronation, when his three sons had knelt to receive the order of knighthood dressed in the cloth of gold and furs appropriate to the heirs of an earl. It was no surprise, therefore, to find that title soon among the rewards Mortimer amassed. In the winter of 1326 and during 1327 he accumulated in his possession the great lordships that Despenser had previously held in Wales and the Welsh Marches, together with the estates of his uncle, Roger Mortimer of Chirk (disinheriting his cousin, the heir to Chirk, in the process), as well as the royal office of justiciar of the principality of Wales, to give him power there on a scale of which even Despenser would have been envious. These grants were mirrored by more in Ireland, and in the autumn of 1328 Mortimer was named Earl of March, a new title created especially in his honour, to reflect his extraordinary dominance in the western territories of the young king's realm.

Liberation from the oppressions of Edward II, it was becoming unnervingly clear, had delivered England into the hands of a queen mother determined to enrich herself beyond reason or precedent, and a domineering nobleman who aspired to the status of an uncrowned king, scarcely letting young Edward out of his sight and taking for granted his own right to speak on his behalf. The council, for Isabella and Mortimer, was no more than window-dressing, an irrelevance to the reality of their political control. But they, no less than the dead king and his favourite before them, failed to understand that the process by which they sought to consolidate their own power was also the process by which, piece by piece, they began to forfeit the legitimacy of the authority they claimed.

With alarming speed, cracks began to appear in the fragile façade of unity that still remained as the legacy of their invasion. Doubts were raised about Isabella and Mortimer's capacity to govern not only by the rewards they lavished upon themselves, but also by their handling of the weightiest matters of policy. It had never been likely that the Scots would stand by and watch such violent upheavals in English politics from a gentlemanly distance, and in the summer of 1327 Scottish raids forced the muster of an English army and an advance against them into the northeast. But the English forces were caught ponderously flat-footed by typically agile and elusive Scots manoeuvres, and the teenage king—who had accompanied Mortimer, Lancaster, and his uncles of Kent and Norfolk north on his first military campaign—was almost captured in one daring raid on the English camp. As the exhausted, dispirited soldiers and their bitterly frustrated king made their way disconsolately south, Isabella and Mortimer made the decision to pursue peace in the north rather than war; and in the spring of 1328 a treaty was negotiated to bring a lasting settlement between England and Scotland.

It was not, in itself, a foolish or myopic plan, but it came at a heavy price. England now for the first time formally recognised Scotland as an independent kingdom, and Robert Bruce as its rightful sovereign. The dream that the Scots might be brought under English rule—pursued so ferociously by the first Edward, and never relinquished by the second, no matter how hapless his interventions there—was now abandoned in the name of the third. Not, however, with his consent. When Isabella's seven-year-old daughter, Joan, travelled north to Berwick with her mother in July 1328 to marry Bruce's son and heir, four-year-old David, in fulfilment of the treaty, Edward was not with them. Appalled and angry at the humiliation of the campaign and the subsequent jettisoning of what he saw as his rights over Scotland, the fifteen-year-old king refused to attend the wedding and obstructed his mother's attempt to deliver the Stone of Scone—the sacred sandstone on which Scottish kings were traditionally crowned, which had been captured by Edward I thirty years earlier—back into Scottish hands.

Angry though he might be, the king was still too young to free himself from the enveloping arms of the government which Isabella and Mortimer had created around him. But this breach between mother and son brought widespread condemnation for the first time upon the head of the queen mother and her unofficial consort. The king, it was clear, rejected this policy made in his name. So did his subjects, who called it a *"turpis pax,"* a "shameful peace." Meanwhile, the £20,000 which the Scots agreed to pay in reparation for their raids did little to soothe such discontent, given how rapidly it disappeared into the bottomless pit of Isabella's coffers. And most immediately disquieting for Isabella and Mortimer was the fact that this growing resistance found public voice in the imposing person of Henry of Lancaster.

The wheel, it seemed, was turning full circle. This was not, after all, the first time that humiliation in Scotland had precipitated an Earl of Lancaster into opposition. When parliament met at Salisbury in October 1328—the same tame assembly that ratified Mortimer's elevation to the earldom of March—Lancaster refused to attend, complaining of the failure to prosecute the king's rights in Scotland, the sidelining of the regency council which he himself had been appointed to lead, and the plundering of the royal treasury to the private benefit of Isabella and Mortimer. If this was the reign of the king's father revisited, it was abundantly clear who, this time, might be accused of usurping royal power.

In a process that had become horrifyingly, wearyingly familiar over the previous two decades, division spiralled quickly into armed confrontation. By winter, troops were once again being mustered by England's great nobles, who circled one another warily, trying to find a means to peace while preparing for war. In December Lancaster marched into London at the head of an army, to be joined there by the king's uncles of Kent and Norfolk, who shared his anger at Isabella and Mortimer's appropriation of their nephew's government. But while Lancaster and his allies gathered in the capital, Mortimer's army, accompanied by Isabella and Edward, outflanked them by moving north into the midlands and onto the attack. By January 6 Lancaster's manors in Warwickshire and Leicestershire had been sacked and burned, and his city of Leicester seized by Mortimer in the name of the young king.

In the face of this devastating reprisal, and confronted yet again with the imminent threat of civil war, the earls of Norfolk and Kent decided that discretion was the better part of principled resistance, and abandoned Lancaster to rejoin the court. Realising now that he could not hope to prevail—and also, at almost fifty, finding himself progressively disabled by his failing eyesight—Lancaster surrendered to his king, kneeling in the mud of a January morning to ask his young cousin's forgiveness. His submission saved his life and his lands, albeit at the cost of crippling financial penalties. Thereafter, hobbled by these monetary bonds and by his increasing infirmity, Lancaster was in no further position to resist.

Opposition had reared its head, and it had been crushed. Like Edward II and Despenser before them, Isabella and Mortimer could have chosen to learn lessons from the resistance they faced. Instead, like Edward and Despenser before them, they clung tighter to the power they had achieved. Her son's anger at the Scottish peace might have given Isabella pause for thought; she was an astute woman, after all, and her authority fundamentally depended on his—a fact which made his approach toward adulthood a challengingly complex political phenomenon. Perhaps she had a blind faith that her influence over her son could not be shaken, or perhaps she was simply unable to see the ramifications of long-term strategy when confronted with the pressing imperatives of short-term gain. Perhaps—and unknowably—the dynamics of her relationship with Mortimer obscured any other consideration, political or personal, although it has to be said that Isabella had never before knowingly set her own interests aside.

What is certain, however, is that she and Mortimer now sought to tighten their stranglehold on power with a narcissism and paranoia to rival that of the regime they had destroyed.

The web was drawn ever closer around a king who had shown such unsettling signs of independent thought. Not only had Edward been paraded as the figurehead of military action against Lancaster's revolt, but his household was filled with placemen loyal to his mother and Mortimer. He could trust only a few of the servants around him, notably his secretary, Richard Bury, and his close friend William Montagu, through whom he smuggled a message to tell Pope John XXII that only letters bearing the words *pater sancte* ("holy father") in Edward's own handwriting could be read as genuine communication from the king rather than dictation by those who controlled his government—clearly now against his will.

And Edward was right to be wary. In early 1330, a year after the failure of Lancaster's rebellion, Isabella and Mortimer resolved to flush out any last traces of disloyalty. The king's uncle of Kent had recovered enough of his position after his flirtation with Lancaster to be entrusted in February 1330 with the task of escorting Edward's Queen Philippa—a small, pregnant figure decked out in the finest gold tissue—to her coronation in Westminster Abbey. But a month later Kent was arrested on suspicion of treason. Hedging and vacillation were by this stage second nature to Kent; while in Paris with Isabella before the invasion of 1326, the earl had covered his back by sending covert, panic-tinged messages to England to reassure the king that, despite all appearances to the contrary, he had done nothing that might damage his royal brother's interests. He might now have felt that he had been lucky to escape his entanglement with Lancaster with his head and his estates intact, and yet he chafed at his loss of influence at court and at the dominance of the vauntingly arrogant Mortimer.

So when secret information reached him that the wild rumours were true—that the dead king Edward was still alive and a prisoner in Corfe Castle near the south coast—he responded with alacrity, setting in train plans for his brother's rescue and a counterrevolution to restore him to the throne. But the messages came from agents of Mortimer and Isabella, sent to entrap him; and, having enthusiastically demonstrated his willingness to plot their downfall, Kent was brought before parliament at Winchester in March 1330 to be condemned by letters written in his own hand. On March 19 this son, brother, and uncle of kings, a foolish, vain man brought down by political ambition unmatched by political judgement, was led, shivering in his shirt, out of the gate of Winchester Castle to a scaffold erected beyond its walls. There he stood for long, agonising hours, until the daylight began to fade. Disillusion with the regime that had condemned him was now so widespread and so profound that no one could be found who was willing to spill such royal blood. At last a felon held in the castle's jail agreed to wield the axe in return for a stay on his own execution; and when Kent's severed head was raised, the crowd stood silent and stony-faced.

The circle was almost complete. It seemed, now, that Isabella and Mortimer were unassailable, their limitless power brutally demonstrated in the killing of the king's uncle. But, as Edward II and Despenser had found after the execution of another royal earl, power based on fear, suspicion, and ruthless self-enrichment might prove ephemeral when confronted with a challenge that could call on deep wells of legitimacy and loyalty. Edward II had been overwhelmed by the force of his wife's betrayal; now it was Isabella's turn to experience the sudden shock of rejection by the son in whose name she had deposed his father.

By the autumn of 1330 the Earl of Kent's lands had been parcelled out to supporters of the regime—many of them, with damning predictability, to Mortimer's son and heir. Watches were set on the ports in case of invasion by those allies of the earl who had fled abroad, and everywhere Mortimer's spies multiplied. By the time a parliament was called to meet at Nottingham in October, the fog of rumour and suspicion curled so densely about the court that, when Mortimer and Isabella took up residence in the castle that perched on a sandstone outcrop above the city, they did so with guards re-doubled around them. The seventeen-year-old king, as always, was in their company, but that was no reason to be anything less than watchful. On October 18 Mortimer summoned a number of Ed-ward's household knights, the young king's friend William Montagu first among them, to be interrogated on information that they were plotting against the regime. Mortimer's spies had served him well, in all but one crucial respect: Montagu and his friends were not plot-ting against the king, but with him.

This time Mortimer, though clearly suspicious, was persuaded to let them go, and once their questioning was over they made much play of their public departure from the city. The following night, however, they returned without warning or fanfare, silent this time in the darkness. They gathered, Montagu and two dozen others, at the foot of the castle mound, well away from the torchlit gates and armed guards who both protected the king and imprisoned him. Montagu and his men felt their way into a hidden passageway carved into the rock, a secret which they, but not the garrison above, had learned from a sympathetic townsman. Carefully, with weapons in hand, they made their way up the pitch-dark tunnel, a steeply curving slope punctuated with rough stairs, until they emerged into the heart of the castle. As they had arranged, Edward was waiting to meet them. Mortimer and Isabella were surrounded before they knew what was happening, the queen forced back into her bedchamber, Mortimer struggling in shock and fury to draw his sword against his grim-faced assailants, but quickly disarmed and overpowered. After three years, the rule of Isabella and her consort was over.

Mortimer's fate was not in doubt. The scene had been played out too many times before in the bloodstained years that had been Edward II's legacy to his kingdom: there was the proclamation of evident guilt—in this case, the murder of the last king and the usur-pation of the power of the present one; the sentence of a traitor's death; and then, on November 29, the scaffold at Tyburn. Just a year earlier, Roger Mortimer had styled himself King Arthur at a tournament of extraordinary magnificence where he sat crowned at a Round Table with Isabella playing Guinevere at his side. Now he was stripped of his clothes and strung up from the gallows, a man hanged like a common thief with a lack of ceremony that mocked the hollow vanity of his former pretensions.

For Isabella, Edward's coolly executed coup had a very different outcome. She was, after all, his honoured mother, who had been deplorably diverted from her royal duty to her husband and son by Mortimer's traitorous machinations. For several weeks she was kept under guard at Berkhamsted Castle, twenty-five miles from London, until it became clear whether or not she would accept this revisionist account of her actions—but whatever doubt there might have been was quickly dispelled. Isabella had always been a realist, and she had learned at all costs to protect her own interests ever since the day she had stood at the altar as an uncherished bride twenty-two years earlier. We must assume that she mourned for Mortimer, given the evident intensity of their partnership, but she took care to leave no public traces of her grief. By Christmas she had rejoined her son's court at Windsor Castle, where she remained for the next two years under the most luxurious house arrest Edward could provide. She had formally surrendered her vast estates to her son within a week of Mortimer's death, and a month later she received in return a grant of £3,000 a year to provide for what would be a sumptuously appointed retirement. From 1332 her freedom of movement was gradually restored, and she spent much of her time at Castle Rising—a formidable keep set on top of mighty earthworks a few miles from the sea in northwestern Norfolk—where she maintained a stately household and entertained royal visits from her son and his growing family.

She had discovered, in violent and painful fashion, that the will to power could be its own undoing. But perhaps this royal retirement was vindication of a different kind. The deference and luxury that were her due were now hers without question, and she could claim—albeit by a tortuous route—an extraordinary legacy in the person of her son. Edward had inherited his mother's intelligence; but, more than that, whether by nature or traumatic nurture, he had developed the farsighted political vision that both his parents had lacked. He understood that the power of his crown lay in law, not tyranny; in loyalty, not fear; and in commanding the consent of his realm, not cowing it into compliance. By the time Isabella came to face her last illness in 1358, Edward was thirty years into a reign that would earn him an epitaph as "the flower of kings past, the pattern for kings to come."

By then, the bloody events of her political life were distant memories for the sixty-three-year-old queen. That she had found some form of peace with that past seems a likely reading of her request that she should be buried in the crimson, yellow-lined mantle in which she had been married half a century earlier, with the silver vase containing her husband's heart interred above her own. And perhaps that reconciliation had more to do with the queenship her marriage had brought her than it did with the man she had married. Isabella had fought for her rights as an anointed Queen of England. She had shown—albeit for a brief moment—that female leadership could represent the legitimacy of the crown forcefully enough to depose an anointed king. And her political legacy to her son lay most powerfully in the lessons he learned about the nature of that legitimacy as he watched her do so.

There was one more way in which Isabella continued to shape English politics even after she had accepted her enforced retreat into gilded retirement. Nearly two centuries earlier, Henry II had succeeded to the throne of England as the heir of his remarkable mother, Matilda. His descendant Edward III—who had now come into premature possession of the same crown through the intervention of another formidable woman—was hardly likely, therefore, to accept the wholesale exclusion of the female line that had been adopted across the Channel as an expedient rationalisation for the accession of Isabella's brothers as kings of France. When her last surviving brother, Charles, who had done so much to support her rebellion against her husband, died in 1328, he, too, left only infant daughters, and the great lords of France hailed his cousin Philippe of Valois as their king. But Edward made it his life's work to press the claim to the French throne that he inherited through his mother. Not only had Isabella overthrown a king; she had charted England's course into a war that would last for a hundred years.

PART V

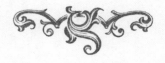

MARGARET

*A Great and Strong
Laboured Woman*

1430–1482

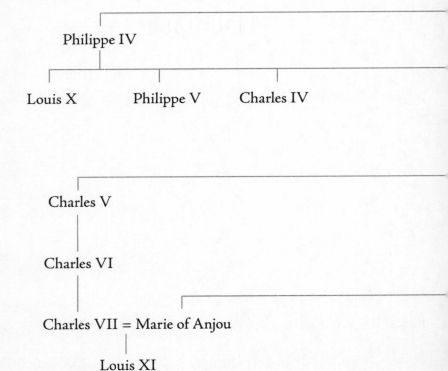

Philippe IV

Louis X   Philippe V   Charles IV

Charles V

Charles VI

Charles VII = Marie of Anjou

Louis XI

MARGARET

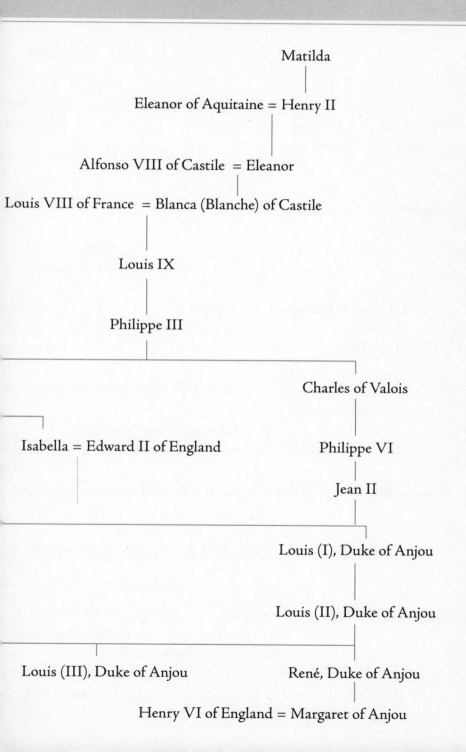

Matilda
|
Eleanor of Aquitaine = Henry II

Alfonso VIII of Castile = Eleanor

Louis VIII of France = Blanca (Blanche) of Castile

Louis IX
|
Philippe III

Charles of Valois

Isabella = Edward II of England

Philippe VI
|
Jean II
|
Louis (I), Duke of Anjou
|
Louis (II), Duke of Anjou

Louis (III), Duke of Anjou

René, Duke of Anjou

Henry VI of England = Margaret of Anjou

THE WARS OF THE ROSES

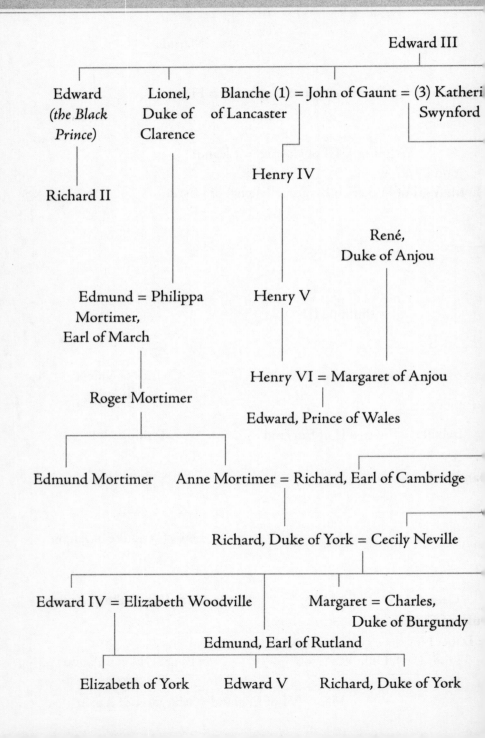

Edward III

Edward (*the Black Prince*)   Lionel, Duke of Clarence   Blanche (1) = John of Gaunt = (3) Katheri of Lancaster   Swynford

Richard II

Henry IV

René, Duke of Anjou

Edmund = Philippa Mortimer, Earl of March   Henry V

Roger Mortimer

Henry VI = Margaret of Anjou

Edward, Prince of Wales

Edmund Mortimer   Anne Mortimer = Richard, Earl of Cambridge

Richard, Duke of York = Cecily Neville

Edward IV = Elizabeth Woodville   Margaret = Charles, Duke of Burgundy

Edmund, Earl of Rutland

Elizabeth of York   Edward V   Richard, Duke of York

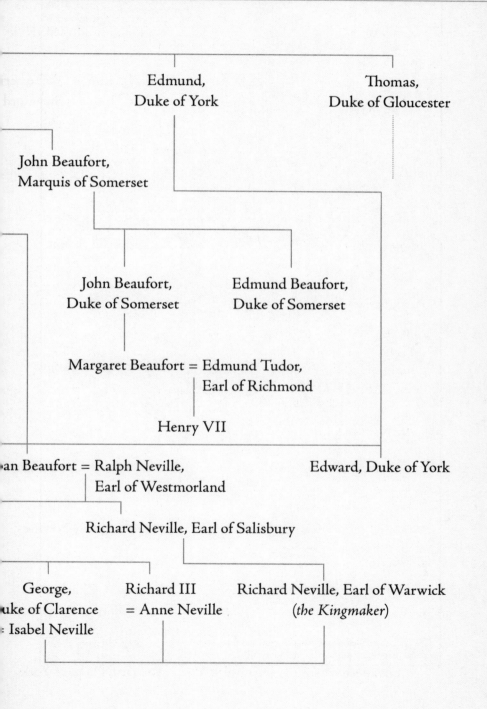

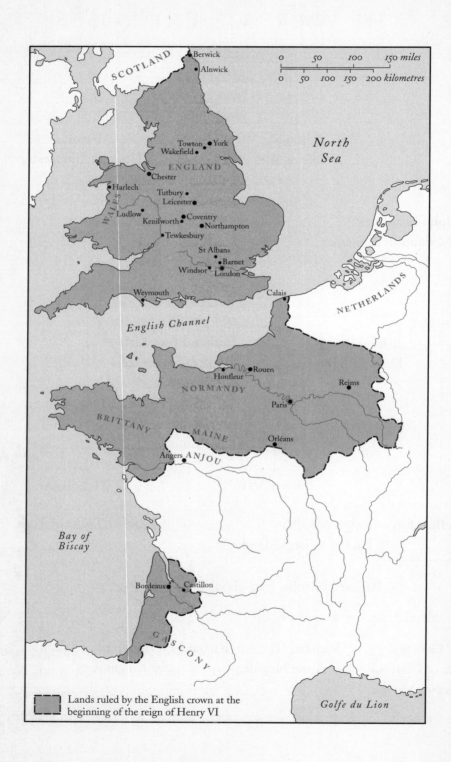

SCOTLAND

Berwick
Alnwick

North
Sea

Towton York
Wakefield

ENGLAND

Chester

Harlech

Tutbury
Leicester

Ludlow

Coventry
Kenilworth
Northampton

Tewkesbury

St Albans
Barnet
Windsor London

WALES

Weymouth

Calais

NETHERLANDS

English Channel

Rouen
Honfleur

NORMANDY

Reims

Paris

BRITTANY

MAINE

Orléans

Angers ANJOU

Bay of
Biscay

Bordeaux Castillon

GASCONY

Golfe du Lion

Lands ruled by the English crown at the
beginning of the reign of Henry VI

0   50   100   150 miles
0   50   100   150   200 kilometres

FIFTEEN

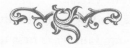

Our Lady Sovereign

argaret of Anjou was not born to be a queen. It was not that she lacked royal blood flowing through her veins: she was directly descended, after all, from Philippe of Valois, the king who had succeeded to the French throne after the deaths of Isabella's brothers. Like Isabella herself, she could trace her line back to Eleanor of Aquitaine and the Empress Matilda; and, through her paternal grandmother, she counted the kings of Aragon among her immediate forebears.

But, while her father, René, was rich in grandly empty titles, he was poor in practical power. Second son of the Duke of Anjou, he styled himself Duke of Lorraine through his marriage to the duchy's heiress, and King of Sicily, Naples, and Jerusalem through his ambitious grandfather's accumulation of paper claims to far-flung crowns. But his wife's right to Lorraine was fiercely contested by the next male heir to the duchy, who inflicted a crushing defeat on René and his army in the summer of 1431. René spent three of the next six years in captivity, only securing his eventual freedom through the payment of a punishing ransom. On his release he set sail for Naples, hoping to win that kingdom in place of the dukedom he had lost; but, four years of fighting later, a disconsolate René was driven out of Italy for good. After the death of his elder brother, he was now Duke of Anjou and Count of Provence, but the resources he had expended in pursuit of his hollow crowns had left him scarcely able to maintain the state of those remaining titles.

Margaret, meanwhile, had been left behind in France along with the rest of the duke's young family, at first under the supervision of their mother, Isabelle of Lorraine, and then—from 1435, when Isabelle made her way to Naples as an advance guard for her imprisoned husband's claims there—of their formidable grandmother, Yolanda of Aragon. By the time René eventually returned home in 1442, twelve-year-old Margaret had learned an extended lesson in how capable a woman could be when called upon to wield authority for an absent husband or son. She had also discovered that neither power nor wealth could be taken for granted. Rights, it seemed, had to be fought for, possession asserted rather than assumed.

Still, the observation that the wearing of a crown did not automatically confer control of a kingdom seemed unlikely to bear directly on Margaret's own experiences. Her marriage was already much discussed, but none of her prospective suitors—the son of the Count of St. Pol, and successively the son and the nephew of the Duke of Burgundy, powerful though they might be—offered her a throne. Nor did the return of her thwarted and impoverished father, a king in insubstantial name only, promise a radical shift in her destiny. But it came all the same, thanks to the war between England and France that had been precipitated by Isabella's claim to the French crown a hundred years before.

Before her death in 1358, Isabella had had the satisfaction of seeing her son Edward III win great victories at Crécy and Poitiers in pursuit of the throne that, he believed, she had bequeathed him. That claim was fiercely disputed by the French, who now elaborated the pragmatic precedent by which Isabella's brothers had become kings of France in place of their infant nieces into a freshly minted "ancient" tradition, the "Salic Law," which formally prohibited female heirs from either taking or transmitting rights to the crown. But despite this French resistance, Edward's military talents were enough to regain control of the great duchy of Aquitaine, restored almost to the glories of its full extent under its Duchess Eleanor centuries earlier.

Edward's triumphs, however, did not last. Less than thirty years after his death, English politics imploded spectacularly under the strain of the paranoid megalomania of his grandson, Richard II. Richard lost his throne and his life to his cousin, Henry of Lancaster, and the French were full of scorn when Henry's son, Henry V, sought to renew the English claim to their kingdom. But their jeers fell silent when this stern young man—scarred by a crossbow bolt taken full in the face amid the maelstrom of battle at the age of just sixteen—crushed the flower of French chivalry into the mud at Agincourt. He proceeded, town by town and castle by castle, to conquer Normandy for the first time since it had slipped through King John's fingers two hundred years earlier. By 1420 Henry was in a position to dictate terms to his bruised and battered opponents, and those terms were that he should marry the French king's daughter Catherine and be recognised as heir to the French throne.

While Henry entered Paris in triumph, the heir he had supplanted—his new brother-in-law, the Dauphin Charles—was forced to withdraw south to the Loire to shelter in the great castles of Anjou under the protection of its widowed duchess, Yolanda of Aragon, whose daughter Marie he married in 1422. But Henry's brightly burning flame was soon consumed by its own ferocity. He died of dysentery at Vincennes, southeast of Paris, at the age of just thirty-five, leaving as his successor a baby son he had never seen. For long years after his death the nobles of England worked together to defend his legacy in the name of this infant king, Henry VI; but during that time the French regrouped, rearmed, and renewed a war that the English had believed they had already won.

In 1429 French military resistance was given overwhelming moral force when—thanks to the unearthly inspiration of a peasant girl named Jeanne d'Arc—the Dauphin Charles was anointed and crowned as King Charles VII at Reims Cathedral, the site where, by hallowed tradition, the monarchs of France were invested with their divinely sanctioned authority. In response, the English lords scrambled to arrange coronations for the boy-king Henry VI on both sides of the Channel, but the improvised ceremonial with which he was crowned King of France in Paris only served to emphasise the solemnity of his rival's consecration. Thereafter, the French began to win territory and fortifications as well as hearts and minds. Paris itself was recaptured in 1436, and by the early 1440s the tide of the war was turning in France's favour, while the English dug in their heels in defence of their increasingly embattled hold on Normandy. It was in this context that young Margaret of Anjou's marriage suddenly became a matter of urgent diplomatic significance.

At the beginning of 1444 the English sought a truce, an honourable breathing space in which they might hope to construct a strategic response to this alarming French resurgence—and no better opportunity to stop the fighting was likely to present itself than their young king's need for a wife. Charles VII was graciously amenable to the unwontedly conciliatory tone of the English approach; but, though he himself had daughters, their hands were not offered in marriage—not because they were King Henry's first cousins (papal dispensation could set aside such entanglements of blood, after all), but because Henry still claimed their father's crown. A bride would have to be found who could embody the cause of peace without loss of face or the necessity of concessions unacceptable to either side.

So it was that all eyes came to alight on Margaret, who turned fourteen while the embassies were mustering in March that year. Her aunt Marie was Charles VII's queen; her grandmother Yolanda had been his greatest support in the darkest days of his disinheritance. And, although her impecunious family could offer England little by way of a dowry—only some cobbled-together cash and her father's meaningless titles to the islands of Mallorca and Minorca—her father, René, was nevertheless a respected figure at the French court, and his duchy of Anjou promised to provide a useful buffer immediately to the south of the beleaguered English duchy of Normandy. It was enough; and this compromise bride served to patch together a compromise treaty—not a permanent peace, but a two-year truce, with the hope of further understanding to come.

On May 24, 1444, Margaret walked in procession into the great church of St. Martin at Tours, her step made heavy by the rich fur-trimmed stuff of her gown, watched by her uncle the king and her aunt the queen, her cousin the dauphin and his Scottish dauphine, and all the great nobles of France. There, before the altar, she met not her husband-to-be, but the man who had represented him on this mission: William de la Pole, the forty-seven-year-old Earl of Suffolk, an intelligent, cultured man of long experience in the war who had risen to become the most influential of Henry VI's noble counsellors. It was Suffolk who placed the golden ring on her finger to symbolise her betrothal (which was as binding as it would have been had Henry himself spoken the vows with her, and needed only the consummation of the marriage to make it indissoluble). And it was Suffolk who led her by the hand to receive the acclamation of the assembled congregation as the new Queen of England.

For six months after the glittering celebrations that followed the ceremony at Tours, Margaret remained with her mother in Anjou, honoured as a queen but, for as long as she remained in her homeland, required to shoulder none of a consort's responsibilities, either political or personal. In November, however, Suffolk—now promoted to the rank of marquis in recognition of his devoted service in securing his king both a peace and a wife—returned to France at the head of a still more lavish delegation to escort her across the Channel. It was five more months before they set sail: time enough to attend the magnificent wedding of her sister Yolande to the son and heir of Antoine de Vaudemont, her father's rival for Lorraine, before taking leave of her parents for the last time. By the time Margaret and her attendants reached Rouen, the capital of English Normandy, she was too unwell—whether victim of an ill-timed infection, or of the unfamiliar pressures of public expectation—to take part in the elaborate procession planned for her entry into the city. It went ahead nonetheless, with her place at its centre taken by Suffolk's wife, Alice Chaucer, in a striking demonstration of the fact that the young queen's role was as yet formulaic rather than functional, her power symbolic rather than real.

Alice Chaucer, at forty, was every inch the equal of her eminent husband, with the quicksilver intelligence of her grandfather, the poet Geoffrey Chaucer, and all the political sophistication of a three-times-married heiress who had acquired her first influential husband at the age of just ten. She was also a new mother—her only son, John, had been born two years earlier—and she welcomed Margaret, a queen young enough to be her daughter, with a kindness that quickly forged a deep-rooted friendship between them. Such comfort was more than welcome to a girl who was not fully restored to health by the time she braved a violently storm-tossed Channel crossing. Two weeks passed after her arrival at the English port of Southampton before she was well enough to travel ten miles to the modestly austere abbey of Titchfield to embark in earnest on the reality of her royal marriage.

This time, the man placing the wedding ring on her finger—a band set with a great ruby from a ring he had worn at his coronation in Paris fourteen years earlier—was not the fatherly figure of the Marquis of Suffolk, but her husband, Henry VI of England. At twenty-three, Henry was eight years her senior; he stood five feet nine, with a physique strong enough to enjoy the hunt in his many royal parks and chases, and in his exquisitely made cloth-of-gold robes he cut an attractive figure. In his face, however, there was none of the grim purpose which had marked out his driven, charismatic father, nor any of the battle scars the older Henry had acquired before he was out of his teens.

This king was seven years older than his father had been when he first led an army in the field, six older than his great-great-grandfather Edward III when he masterminded the coup that overthrew the rule of Isabella and Mortimer; yet Henry still approached the world with a wondering, abstracted air that recalled the simplicity of childhood. His nobles were still—disconcertingly for themselves, as well as for the rest of his subjects—minutely involved in the direction of his government in much the same way as they had been when he was a boy. And, despite the fact that the most pressing of their concerns was the long-drawn-out struggle to protect what was left of his father's conquests in France, the young king showed no flicker of interest in crossing the Channel to take command of his own army—and his lords made no effort to persuade him, perhaps surmising that his art-less presence in the military or diplomatic front line would be more hindrance than help to their efforts. Still, for Margaret at least he was kind and welcoming, not an intimidatingly experienced older man but an innocent so unworldly that he sometimes found himself affronted by the sophisticated manners and supple morals of his own court.

In her husband's reassuringly gentle company the young queen rode to her new capital. There, during the previous summer, it had taken the mayor and aldermen three weeks of heated debate to decide on the colour of the outfits in which they planned to accord her a formal welcome. Now, dressed in their much-discussed blue gowns with scarlet hoods, this august deputation met her at Blackheath on the south side of the Thames on May 28, 1445, and escorted her through the city in an elaborate procession which, over the course of two days, took her past eight specially devised pageants performed on stages constructed along her route. At London Bridge she was greeted by the lavishly gowned and garlanded figure of "Plenty," before "Peace" stepped forward to expound with laboured dignity on the expectations that weighed so heavily on this marriage:

So trusteth your people, with affiance,
Through your grace and high benignity,
'Twixt the realms two, England and France,
Peace shall approach, rest and unite,
Mars set aside, with all his cruelty,
Which too long hath troubled the realms twain,
Biding your comfort in this adversity,
Most Christian princess, our lady sovereign.

It was an onerous responsibility to rest on the slight shoulders of a fifteen-year-old girl, but perhaps a granddaughter schooled by the formidable Yolanda of Aragon expected no less a duty than to be the means of peace between two kingdoms that had fought for a hundred years. Certainly, Margaret did not falter as she was carried in a litter to Westminster Abbey for her coronation, dressed in white damask powdered with gold and a pearl-encrusted circlet resting on her loosened hair, while her subjects cheered, their hearts warmed and their hopes raised by the wine that flowed for this celebratory moment in the city's conduits.

But—as the hangovers faded, the capital settled back into hustling, jostling normality, and the queen set about the task of fulfilling her new role—it gradually became clear that there was nothing simple about what she was required to do. Comforting though it might be to a young bride, King Henry's benevolent vagueness posed an insidious threat to the entire edifice of the government that was conducted in his name. Only the king, after all, had the God-given authority to adjudicate between the competing concerns and opinions of his subjects in order to rule in the interests of the realm as a whole. A king such as Edward II—who had ruled in the interests of Hugh Despenser rather than any approximation of the common good—had found that he might forfeit that authority, with catastrophic consequences. But Henry was not a tyrant. Instead, he simply smiled and nodded and expressed mild amazement at the workings of the world—"St. John, grant mercy!" was a favourite exclamation—before agreeing to whatever proposal was presently placed before him.

The individual authors of such proposals might feel a glow of satisfaction that the king had shown such excellent judgement in endorsing their petitions. Cumulatively, however, this was not judgement; it was failure to rule. That was more obvious at some times than at others. Henry's "decision," for example, to grant the stewardship of his duchy of Cornwall twice over to two lords who were bitter local rivals could hardly be mistaken for considered policy, resulting as it did in the ravages of a private war. But the results of his passive malleability were most perniciously evident on a bigger stage than the increasingly disordered English regions: the monumental theatre of war with France.

While Henry was a child, his nobles had worked together to preserve his father's conquests, their unity of purpose underpinned both by the strength of the English military machine during the 1420s and by the obvious need for collective rule during the king's long minority. It was with some relief that the lords had sought at last to hand over the reins of government when Henry approached adulthood, and precedent encouraged them to assume that he would be waiting impatiently to seize them from their grasp. Instead, to their puzzled consternation, they found the reins dangling limply in his fingers. If a matter hung on the king's personal initiative, nothing happened; if it depended on the petition of an interested party—as was often the case with grants of royal office and revenue—then royal policy lurched indiscriminately, pulled this way and that according to the demands of the latest petitioner to secure access to the apparently infinitely pliable king.

Clearly, he was too "young" to rule without wise advice. ("A saint," wrote his hagiographer; "a natural fool," his subjects muttered in their cups.) And into the breach had stepped the Earl of Suffolk. As steward of the king's household, he could hope to shield the king from the more haphazardly importunate of his subjects, and as a great noble and member of the royal council, he might be able to maintain enough of a consensus among the magnates to keep the ship of state on its course. The war in France had dominated Suffolk's entire life. His father and brother had died fighting under Henry V's command, his father at the siege of Harfleur and his brother as one of the few English casualties at Agincourt. Suffolk himself had fought in France for thirteen years, during which time he had been captured and forced to pay a crippling ransom to secure his freedom; and his wife, Alice, was the widow of his former commander, the Earl of Salisbury, who had been killed by a rogue artillery blast at the siege of Orléans. Suffolk, if anyone, understood by 1445 that, in the absence of a warrior king, a lasting peace was the only way to secure England's possession of Normandy.

What was less clear was how peace should be achieved. The treaty that brought Margaret to England had bought time to consider that question—but not much. By 1445 it was obvious that the French would have to be offered some concrete concession if they were to be induced to come to terms. So, behind closed doors, Suffolk and his colleagues brokered a deal: England would cede to France the county of Maine—which lay between English-held Normandy and French Anjou, and was still, precariously, under English control—in return for a twenty-year extension of the truce. It was not perfect, but it would have to do, and it had the manifest advantages of allowing England time to secure Normandy's borders while at the same time refilling royal coffers that had been emptied by thirty years of constant warfare.

Behind closed doors, too, Margaret lent her voice to the negotiations through which this deal was concluded. The making of peace between her own country and her husband's was after all, as the city of London's pageants had so ponderously emphasised, her raison d'être as England's queen. She had no direct role in the shaping of policy, but the idea that Maine should be a bridge between her husband's lands in Normandy and her father's in Anjou, its surrender into French hands bringing advantage to both sides, cannot have been unwelcome to her. And so she did what she could, as a dutiful

queen should, to facilitate an understanding between her adopted
home and the kingdom of her birth.

There were profound tensions in this role, tensions evident even
in the diplomatic language in which her intercession was couched.
When she wrote to her "very dear uncle of France" to solicit his "good
disposition and inclination...for the good of this peace," she did so
using her formal title as "Queen of France and England"—words
which provocatively encapsulated the essence of the conflict she was
trying to end. But there was at least hope that the truce for which she
and Suffolk were working so assiduously would serve to mitigate the
potentially disastrous effects of her husband's inability to command
his own kingdom.

That hope did not last. The difficulty of enforcing a single, clear
policy in the name of an inert king meant that the truce was followed
by no effective retrenchment in Normandy's defences, while at the
same time the English forces occupying Maine refused to obey the
order to surrender it into French hands. Charles VII was already
well aware that military as well as diplomatic cards were stacked
high in his favour, and this English failure to abide by the terms of
a treaty they had been so desperate to secure gave him legitimate
reason to sweep the agreement aside. In February 1448 his armies
marched into Maine to take by force what the English had promised
him. The county was his within weeks; and in the summer of 1449
Charles turned his attentions to Normandy. It took only two months
for Rouen, the capital of English government in France, to fall. The
English retreat became a rout, and by the summer of 1450 not a foot
of land in Normandy remained in English hands to show that Henry
V's spectacular conquests had ever taken place.

As this disaster unfolded, across the Channel the news was met
with first disbelief, then horror, then finally vitriolic recrimination.
A scapegoat was needed: after all, only evil counsel whispered into
the ear of the innocent king could have engendered such a catastrophe. While the rest of the nobles backed away as surreptitiously as
they could from any suggestion that they had played a part in formu-

lating the failed treaty, Suffolk stood alone, unable to explain away his leading role in its inception. As recently as June 1448 he had been promoted to the rank of duke as reward for his loyal service to the king. Now, on January 22, 1450, he stood before Henry and the lords in parliament to answer for his treason.

This gifted man defended himself with passion and wit, but he was unable to find shelter from the storm which the loss of Normandy had unleashed. In March 1450 he formally submitted to the king's grace and accepted a sentence of five years' banishment from England. For his accusers in parliament, this compromise neatly avoided the risk that a full trial would expose the inconvenient truth that Suffolk had not, in fact, acted alone. But for the king's subjects beyond parliament's walls—furious that thousands of pounds in taxation had been drained from their pockets to pay for a protracted military fiasco—Suffolk's exile was not enough. The rage of the mob had already claimed the life of another of Henry's ministers, the Bishop of Chichester, who had been butchered by mutinous soldiers in Portsmouth a few months earlier. Suffolk was still unscathed when he set sail across the Channel at the end of April, and he believed that he had escaped the worst; but his small ship was intercepted by another, a privateering vessel named the *Nicholas of the Tower*. Its crew staged a mock trial on the deck, declaring that "as the king did not wish to punish these traitors of his own will, nor to govern the aforesaid realm better, they themselves would do it." Then they hacked off the duke's head with a rusty sword, and abandoned his mutilated corpse on the sand at Dover.

It was the beginning of a bloody summer. King, queen, and nobles had gathered for a parliament in the midland city of Leicester when news came of Suffolk's shocking death; and it was less than a month later that more messengers arrived, breathless and sweating in the heat, to report that Henry's discredited government was under attack. Across southeastern England, thousands of his subjects were rising in revolt, spontaneous protest becoming concerted insurrection under the charismatic leadership of a Kentishman known as

Jack Cade. Margaret found herself travelling south amid a tense and armed convoy as her hapless husband rode to his capital, accompanied by an imposing company of his magnates, to issue his royal command that the rebels should disperse. And she was at his side when he retreated back to the safety of his castle at Kenilworth two weeks later, having utterly failed in his purpose.

The rebels swarmed to the south bank of the Thames, and then across London Bridge into the city itself, rallying support as they went with a manifesto that railed against the "false counsel" that had brought King Henry's realm to the brink of ruin: "For his lands are lost, his merchandise is lost, his commons destroyed, the sea is lost, France is lost, himself so poor that he may not pay for his meat nor drink." It was a powerful message, and one that spoke eloquently to the inhabitants of a region that now looked with dread toward the coast, where the triumphant French were seizing their newfound opportunity to raid and plunder with impunity.

But it was the rebels' own violence that proved their undoing. Though Cade held his own judicial hearings in the capital, seeking to demonstrate the legitimacy of his cause, the courtiers and royal officials convicted there who were unlucky enough to fall into the rebels' hands were slaughtered, their severed heads paraded on pikes to the delight of the mob, while houses and workshops were looted and burned. Sympathetic though the Londoners might be to the rebels' demands for reform, they would not stand by while their great city was destroyed. On the night of July 5 a battle was fought on London Bridge between Cade's men, who were expecting to move freely between the city and their commandeered lodgings across the Thames in Southwark, and a cadre of Londoners and loyalists grimly determined to keep them out. After hours of fighting, with death everywhere at hand by water, fire, and sharpened steel, the sun rose on a scene not only of devastation, but of resolution. The revolt was over.

Margaret had a role to play in the long process of restoring order to the chaos-ravaged southeast, since the royal pardon that was dangled as a carrot to induce the rebels to disperse was offered—as was traditional—"by the most humble and persistent supplications, prayers and requests of our most serene and beloved wife and consort the queen." Not that the pardon was enough to save Cade, who died from the injuries he suffered during his eventual arrest on July 12. This inconvenient demise did not prevent the authorities from inflicting the proper penalties on such an egregious traitor: his naked corpse was publicly beheaded outside Newgate prison four days later, and his head then left to rot on a spike overlooking London Bridge, while the pieces of his quartered body were dispatched for macabre display on city walls around the country.

"Normality" had returned. The king's authority was once more unchallenged; its justice was properly tempered by his queen's mercy; and traitors—as Cade's decomposing skull reminded those Londoners who raised their eyes to see it—would meet their just deserts. Still, all was not quite as it should be. The shock of revolt had done nothing to jolt the almost thirty-year-old king into any more active engagement with his responsibilities. The Duke of Suffolk had been taken from his side, but that merely left a vacancy—and one for which there were now, alarmingly, competing candidates. Two of Henry's cousins began to assert their claims to lead his government, and the conflict between them exposed more explicitly than ever the fact that the mild-mannered king was incapable of ruling for himself.

Richard Plantagenet, Duke of York, was by birth and by inheritance the greatest of Henry's magnates. Directly descended in the male line from Edward III, he was the lord of estates that sprawled across England and Wales, and the confidence that this greatness gave him in speaking for the realm was compounded in the specific circumstances of 1450 by the fact that he had left the country in the summer of the previous year to take up an appointment as the king's lieutenant in Ireland. Put simply, responsibility for catastrophe in France and convulsions in England could not be pinned on him because he had not been there when they took place. And the way was therefore clear for him to adopt the people's call for justice, denouncing the "evil counsel" that had led England to disaster and identifying the remedy for the country's ills in the true counsel of the blood royal, as embodied in himself, rather than in the corruption and self-interest of the court.

Edmund Beaufort, Duke of Somerset, meanwhile, was also directly descended in the male line from Edward III (albeit via the controversial marriage of Henry's great-grandfather John of Gaunt, Duke of Lancaster, to his mistress Katherine Swynford, by which their children, the Beauforts, were retrospectively legitimised). This narrow escape from the wrong side of the blanket meant that Beaufort influence was based not on any vast ancestral inheritance but on their proximity of blood to the ruling Lancastrian line and their presence at the Lancastrian court. By contrast with York, Somerset could not have been more intimately involved in the loss of France; he had been the commander who had experienced the abject humiliation of surrendering Rouen in return for a French safe-conduct as English-held Normandy collapsed around him. But he had therefore also been a key agent of policy formulated in the king's name throughout the 1440s, and in 1450 he stepped unhesitatingly into the breach to offer leadership against the turmoil that rebellion was unleashing across the country.

It was this closeness to Henry—personal, physical, and political—that enabled Somerset to win the battle for control of government as 1450 turned into 1451. Devastating though York's criticisms of "court" policy might be (and however much they drew a convenient veil over his own role in the regime before 1449), the intractable fact remained that this "good duke" was not the king. And the king—vague, benign, and blameless—remained the only source of legitimate royal authority. Gradually, then, Somerset pieced back together the kind of consensus among the lords and control of the king's household that had allowed Suffolk to rule before him. But this time York's estrangement from the inner circle of noble counsellors and his explicit criticism of the regime rendered Henry's government more brittle than ever before.

Henry's queen, too, found her place at his side suddenly more uncomfortable than it had been since her arrival in England five years earlier. England's possessions in France were now reduced to two unsteady footholds, one the northern port of Calais, the other the tattered remnants in southwestern Gascony of the once-great duchy of Aquitaine. The peace Margaret had embodied was a distant, devastated memory. For her English subjects, the land of her birth was now a mockingly triumphant enemy, and she had no child to bind her to her new nation. Nor, it appeared, was there any prospect of one. The king and queen were a devoted couple: he, modest and monkish as he was, showed no sign of turning his attentions elsewhere, and she took care to design her life around his, her household travelling with his between the royal palaces at Westminster, Windsor, Sheen, Greenwich, and Eltham. But despite this constant company, by Christmas 1452 the twenty-two-year-old queen had not yet conceived after seven years of married life.

But the early months of 1453 offered new grounds for optimism, both for Margaret and for her adopted country. The Duke of York had been forced to withdraw to his estates after a dangerously tense confrontation with royal forces under the command of the Duke of Somerset at Dartford, just outside London, in 1452. Somerset was now consolidating his control of government by dispatching Henry on a judicial progress around his troubled realm, a display of royal authority that went some way toward calming the jittery nerves of his subjects. News was beginning to filter through that a military expedition sent to Gascony under the command of the Earl of Shrewsbury—a grizzled hero of earlier campaigns in France, known admiringly as the "English Achilles"—was finding unexpected success not only in defending the English position there but in recapturing lost territory, including the rich and strategically crucial port of Bordeaux. When parliament met at Reading in March 1453, there was an unfamiliar outpouring of both enthusiasm for Henry's rule and taxes for his treasury. And by then, Margaret knew that she was pregnant.

God seemed, at last, to be smiling on a beleaguered queen and a beleaguered country. In April sunshine, she travelled—carefully, given the early stage of her pregnancy—to Norfolk to give thanks at Walsingham's famous shrine to the Virgin Mary. Her fellow pilgrims looked on in awe and excitement as a queen took her place in their midst to pay her respects at the Holy House, a replica of the home in Nazareth where the Queen of Heaven had first heard the news of her own miraculous pregnancy from the Archangel Gabriel, and to venerate relics that included a phial of the Virgin's breastmilk. Margaret bestowed on the shrine a gift of a pax—a gold tablet worked with the image of an angel and encrusted with sapphires, rubies, and pearls, for use during mass—to express her gratitude for the child she was now carrying.

Her gift was apparently rich enough to secure the future of her baby, since her pregnancy continued without incident in the summer's heat, and her health remained reassuringly robust. But in all other respects God's favour proved agonisingly transient. On July 17, 1453, the English forces in Gascony, who had done so much to revive the political as well as military prospects of Henry's government, met a French army at Castillon, twenty-five miles east of Bordeaux. Within hours they had been overwhelmed. Their talismanic commander, the sixty-six-year-old Earl of Shrewsbury, was killed, along with thousands of his men; and, almost exactly three hundred years after Eleanor of Aquitaine had first brought her duchy to the English crown, Gascony was lost.

When the dreadful news reached England at the beginning of August, military disaster precipitated political cataclysm. King Henry's always fragile mental faculties suddenly disintegrated. He was "taken and smitten with a frenzy and his wit and reason withdrawn," one contemporary account records with palpable shock. Wit and reason had never been among Henry's most notable attributes, but the newly stark totality of their absence could not now be disguised as the king sat blank and unresponsive, recognising no one, understanding nothing, unable to speak, or even to eat or move without the ministrations of the servants who attended him day and night.

This was not the first time in Henry's reign that he had been incapable of any kind of communication; he had, after all, inherited his throne as a nine-month-old baby. But that incapacity had been both explicable and explicitly temporary. This was different, and it was frightening. Who should—who could?—rule when the king was lost in a catatonic stupor, whether permanently or not no one knew, with the realm reeling from military defeat and a nobility divided against itself?

The answer was no clearer ten weeks into the king's illness, when Margaret gave birth on October 13, the feast day of Edward the Confessor, to a healthy boy who was named Edward in the royal saint's honour. Her husband's pitiful state rendered him oblivious to the arrival of his son, just as he was to everything else. But Margaret had good reason to feel elated. Amid chaos and crisis, she had fulfilled her principal duty as England's queen. She had given the realm an heir, a hope for the future and an anchor amid its present sea of troubles.

She had also presented herself with a dilemma. The infant she held in her arms gave her—as Isabella had discovered before her—a direct stake in the power play that surrounded her. What she had to decide now was how far she would go in using it.

SIXTEEN

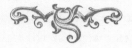

A Great and
Strong Laboured Woman

his was the moment at which Margaret took her first step out of her husband's diminishing shadow to stand on the political stage as a player in her own right, acting under her own independent agency—but the surviving contemporary sources allow us only fragmentary glimpses of her as she did so.

The great tradition of annalistic writing in England—of monastic authors recording the unfolding of God's purpose in the world as it happened, year by year—was stuttering and faltering, to be supplanted eventually, as the fifteenth century gave way to the sixteenth, by the great political propagandists, writing history retrospectively to record the unfolding of God's purpose as their present political masters wished it to be seen. Their depiction of Margaret is so powerful—culminating with lacerating virtuosity in Shakespeare's portrait of the "She-wolf of France"—that it has become almost impossible not to see her through the wrong end of the historical telescope.

Such contemporaneous evidence as we have, however, offers less caricature and more complexity. What is certain is that Margaret's response to her husband's prostration and her son's birth was an immediate decision to advance her own claim to exercise authority on their behalf. In January 1454, when her son was just three months old, a well-informed observer in London reported that "the queen has made a bill of five articles, desiring those articles to be granted; whereof the first is that she desires to have the whole rule of this land"—including, the letter went on, the right to appoint "the chancellor, the treasurer, the privy seal, and all other officers of this land, with sheriffs and all other officers that the king should make," together with the power to "give all the bishoprics of this land, and all other benefices belonging to the king's gift."

This was a dramatic piece of self-assertion—and one which caused political shock waves. Immediate precedent in England offered no support for Margaret's claims to power, since King Henry's mother, Catherine de Valois, had taken no part in the minority government set up to rule during the long years of his childhood. Instead, Queen Catherine had been content to retire from political life after her husband's early death, entertaining herself first by dallying behind closed doors with Edmund Beaufort—then a dashing nineteen-year-old, now the middle-aged Duke of Somerset—and later by marrying an equally gallant but much more obscure Welsh squire named Owen Tudor.

In part, the fact that Margaret was seeking to tread a different path from her royal mother-in-law undoubtedly reflected the difference in the two women's temperaments. Catherine was wilful, wayward, and highly strung; it was through her that the unhappy genetic legacy of her father's mental frailty had been passed on to her son. It was just becoming apparent, meanwhile, that Margaret had inherited the determination and political commitment of the formidable mother and grandmother who had brought her up.

But it was not simply Margaret's character that impelled her to try to take the reins of government. In 1422 the accession of an infant king had been dramatic, but uncontroversial. Without hesitation, all his nobles had united to defend his father's extraordinary military achievements in France and to maintain the security of his English kingdom until Henry should come of age—a task for which Queen Catherine, the sister of Henry's rival for the French throne, was clearly unsuited. In 1453, however, there was no such consensus, and no such clarity. The suppurating damage to the body politic caused by the long-term inadequacies of Henry's rule and the consequent rivalry between the dukes of York and Somerset was laid open to public view by the king's dramatic collapse. The question of who should rule while Henry was incapacitated was so fraught with tension that civil war seemed not only a real but an imminent possibility.

The Duke of York—claiming still to speak for the realm as the greatest of its magnates—arrived in London in November to assert his right to govern on the king's behalf. Now that Henry's catastrophic indisposition could not be concealed, this was a difficult claim to resist. Within weeks, as York took control of the royal council, the Duke of Somerset was arrested and committed to the Tower on the grounds of his allegedly treasonable involvement in the loss of France. His imprisonment did not, however, render him politically impotent: his spies were reported to have infiltrated "every lord's house," and his men were occupying all available lodgings in the streets around the Tower. The rest of the nobility, meanwhile, were gathering arms and men—"all the puissance they can and may"—for the kind of self-protection that might precipitate the collapse into chaos of the entire edifice of government.

In this atmosphere of fear and tension, Margaret's attempt to insist that she should have "the whole rule of this land" need not necessarily be seen as the claim of a damagingly over-assertive woman. She had only to look to her own political education in her native France for the suggestion that she was the obvious candidate to safeguard her husband's kingdom. Positive precedent existed on the southern side of the Channel: Blanca of Castile, the little granddaughter whom Eleanor of Aquitaine had chosen as the bride of Louis VIII of France, had acquitted herself with distinction as regent during the minority of her son Louis IX, and again for the last four years of her life during his later absence on crusade. And this process by which royal women might serve as deputies for their men had been echoed closer to Margaret's home in the commanding roles her mother and grandmother had taken in Anjou and Naples in the absence of her imprisoned father. No doubt the clarity with which women were now excluded from the line of royal succession in France served to simplify this acceptance of female power in a form that was explicitly provisional and temporary, but the idea that an anointed queen—consort to a king, and an embodiment of some of the more restorative and collaborative elements of his God-given authority—might, in time of need, wield power on his behalf had political logic to commend it in an English context too.

But the potentialities of political logic were overwhelmed by the particularities of the political nightmare in which Margaret and her husband's increasingly unnerved subjects found themselves at the end of 1453. She, of course, was not simply a queen but a Frenchwoman, at a time when England—newly redefined in its Englishness by the loss of all its territories in France save the port of Calais—was reeling from a bloody battering at the hands of its French enemies. The birth of her son had rooted her as never before in the political landscape of her husband's kingdom, but the short weeks of his young life had not yet been enough to allow her new persona as an English queen mother to grow to fruition.

Even had her French heritage not made her an object of suspicion, it also had to be said that the very concept of a formal regency was foreign to the recent course of English history. During Henry's childhood, when the authority of the crown could not be exercised by the king in person, government had been conducted instead through the collective responsibility of a noble council under the nominal leadership of the king's uncle, Henry V's youngest brother, Humphrey, Duke of Gloucester, whose official title as "protector, defender and principal councillor" of England notably omitted any suggestion that he might act independently as a regent on behalf of his nephew. And two generations earlier, suspicion about the repercussions of committing authority into the hands of a single powerful individual had similarly circumscribed the formal role of the great John of Gaunt in the minority government of his nephew Richard II.

For Margaret, these already prohibitive circumstances were compounded in 1453 by the fact that the nature of her husband's illness made it difficult for her to obtain any significant hold on the exercise of legitimate royal authority in his stead. In an earlier century, Eleanor of Aquitaine had enjoyed wide-ranging informal powers during her son Richard's absence from England when he was detained elsewhere by the demands of crusade and the bars of a German jail. Isabella of France, meanwhile, had demonstrated a queen's capacity to embody the legitimating power of royal justice and the common good against a king fatally compromised by his own tyranny.

But Henry was not physically absent, nor was he a tyrant. He had never overstepped his powers; instead, he had never properly inhabited them. Margaret's ability to take decisive action was therefore compromised by the fact that her husband was both present and blameless: he had not done anything wrong, even if it was by dint of having not done anything at all. Henry was—technically, at least—an adult; and it was from his supreme authority as king that she derived her complementary capacity as his queen. If she stepped forward into the breach left by his hapless inertia, the identification between her authority and his would serve only to emphasise the "unnaturalness"—and hence illegitimacy—of her self-assertion.

As a result, the one thing on which Henry's nobles could agree, amid this threatening uncertainty, was that the queen's offer to rule over them should be respectfully but firmly declined. Instead, an alternative model—collective noble responsibility for the interests of the realm, the principle that had sustained government during the long years of Henry's childhood—offered both precedent and means by which royal rule could be temporarily approximated. In March 1454 a deputation of lords rode to Windsor and confirmed yet again that, despite three attempts using "all the means and ways that they could think," they could extract "no answer, word nor sign" from their pitifully blank-eyed king. In the absence of any indication that he might imminently recover, it was decided that the best of a handful of bad options would be to allow the Duke of York—who, like Humphrey of Gloucester before him, could claim to be the closest adult male in the line of succession—to lead the newly reconstituted conciliar regime as protector of the realm. And, two weeks before York was formally named to that office, Margaret's five-month-old son was created Prince of Wales and Earl of Chester—a public confirmation of the baby's rights as heir to the throne that served (it seemed from her silent acquiescence, in public at least) to reassure the queen of the regime's loyalty.

York wasted no time in setting about the business of government. At forty-three, encumbered with a chequered political past in this most chequered of political environments, he showed substantial maturity of judgement in realising that power won on the grounds of a claim to speak for the "common weal" of the realm would have to be exercised in explicitly impartial, non-partisan fashion. The protracted strain that Henry's failings had placed on political life at all levels of the political hierarchy was manifesting itself in spiralling disorder across the country. In the north of England in particular, violent rivalry between the two greatest noble families, the Percys and the Nevilles, had all but become a private war. Here York shouldered his newly acquired powers with the utmost seriousness of purpose, working hard on the one hand as a collaborative colleague among his peers in the council chamber, and on the other as the champion of order when, steel in hand, he rode at the head of his troops to quell resistance and recalcitrance in the regions. There was no wholesale purge of the royal household, and those lords who were politically close to the duke soon learned that they could not expect his indiscriminate support in their private vendettas.

But there were limits to what York could do. He could act with self-conscious evenhandedness, but he was still a subject, a private

individual with private interests, not the anointed king. And any sus-
pension of disbelief about the duke's ability to turn the ship of state
from the rocks toward which it was drifting under Henry's motionless hand was undermined by the inconvenient presence of the Duke
of Somerset—the glaring exception to York's policy of inclusion—
who was waiting and watching from behind the Tower's walls for a
chance to strike back against his enemy.

It came with startling suddenness. On Christmas Day 1454, sixteen months after he had last shown any sign of knowing who or
where he was, the king began at last to respond to those around him.
His recovery proved to be as rapid as his collapse. Five days later, Margaret brought their fourteen-month-old son to see his father. Henry
gazed at the toddling prince in wonder and asked his name; "then he
held up his hands and thanked God thereof," a well-informed correspondent reported from the court at Greenwich. "And he said he
never knew him till that time, nor knew not what was said to him,
nor knew not where he had been while he has been sick till now."

The king's return to his senses provoked euphoria both among
his subjects—the Bishop of Winchester and the Prior of Clerken-
well were said to have "wept for joy" after speaking to him for the
first time—and in Henry himself: "He says he is in charity with all
the world, and so he would all the lords were." But, as this artless
optimism made all too clear, the king's senses had never included
any comprehension of the reality of politics, a circumstance which
his restoration to health did nothing to change. Nor, of course, did
it give all of Henry's subjects reason to celebrate. With the king once
more able to walk and talk, the principle of conciliar rule that underpinned the Duke of York's protectorate abruptly evaporated. The
reassertion of Henry's personal rule meant the re-emergence of the
royal household as the centre of political gravity, as well as the renewed influence of the royal kinsman who had led the king's government until the onset of Henry's illness. Somerset was freed from the
Tower at the end of January and declared to be not a traitor but a
"faithful and true liegeman and subject"; and York could only watch

with disillusion and dread as the noble consensus he had so painstakingly nurtured as the bedrock of his power fell away beneath his
feet. On February 9 he was removed from office as protector by the
lords regrouping around their newly revived king; and shortly afterward the duke and his men rode away from the court for the greater
security of his own estates.

This time, however, York's exclusion from government did not,
as it had done in 1451, mean political isolation. The great Neville
family, led by York's brother-in-law Richard Neville, Earl of Salisbury, and Neville's eldest son, another Richard, Earl of Warwick,
had by now concluded that their best chance of protection in their
vicious region-wide feud with the Percys lay in solidarity with York.
The Percys, meanwhile, in a tangled amalgam of cause and consequence, had identified their own best interests with Somerset and
the renaissance of the household regime. As a result, York's renewed
stand-off with the court could no longer be so easily dismissed as
the tantrum of a dissident magnate whose private interests had been
thwarted. Instead, the duke's position was bolstered by the political
and practical force of the Nevilles' support, while at the same time
the court regime was compromised by its increasingly close identification with a partisan faction.

And, this time, the stand-off was quickly broken. Somerset summoned the nobility to a great council meeting at Leicester in May—
an ominous development for York and the Nevilles, who saw in this
move the beginnings of a manoeuvre to destroy them, even before
Somerset left London for Leicester with the king riding happily at
his side at the head of an intimidatingly large body of troops. Counterattack appeared to York to be the best—perhaps last—hope of
defence; and he moved south at speed with his Neville allies and the
biggest army they could muster. On May 22 they intercepted the
heavily armed royal party at St. Albans, twenty miles northwest of
the capital. There it rapidly became clear that the irresistible logic
by which division had become confrontation now dictated that confrontation would become civil war.

York, Salisbury, and Warwick, believing now that only Somerset's permanent removal from Henry's side could secure their own safety, demanded the surrender of "our enemies of approved experience, such as abide and keep themselves under the wing of your Majesty Royal." It was a point on which Somerset and the Percys were hardly likely to capitulate; and for the other nobles in the king's train, whatever their private relationship with Somerset, the horrifying spectacle of three great magnates marching in arms against their monarch was enough to convince them to draw their own swords in Henry's defence.

The first blows were struck at around ten in the morning, when York's troops forced their way into the town of St. Albans. Fighting continued for several hours, with soldiers skirmishing in the narrow streets, trampling bloodstained feet through byres and kitchen gardens, and hacking through wattle-and-daub walls for the purposes of ambush or escape. This was physically confined combat, lacking the unconstrained brutality of the battlefield, and it produced no wholesale slaughter: probably fewer than a hundred men had been killed by the time it became clear that York and the Nevilles had achieved a decisive advantage. But among the dead—almost certainly the victims of a deliberate manhunt rather than the vagaries of war—were the Nevilles' principal enemy, Henry Percy, Earl of Northumberland, and the Duke of Somerset himself.

The king had taken no part in either the abortive attempt at negotiation that had preceded the battle, or the fighting itself, instead sitting haplessly under his banner in the market square while his greatest nobles fought to the death in the streets around him. He had still contrived to be wounded in the mêlée, the unsuspecting victim of an arrow that grazed his neck. But, walk and talk though he might, it was now apparent with unprecedented clarity that Henry was no more than a pawn who, with good intentions and utter malleability, would endorse any views that his current custodians might espouse.

For now, that meant extending his royal grace to York and the Nevilles as they knelt before him, and expressing the magnificently vague hope, it was reported, that "there should no more harm be done." Then the king obediently mounted his horse and rode in procession back to London with the duke he had left the city to oppose. There, on Sunday, May 25, surrounded by York's guards, he sat in state in the Gothic splendour of St. Paul's Cathedral to receive his crown from the duke's hands. It was an imposing demonstration of York's mastery, but also a pointed and very public exhibition of his loyalty. The duke—whose options, like everyone else's, were narrowing as the familiar certainties of the political world began to disintegrate—was staking his future on an attempt to re-create the protectorate that had allowed him to govern England as a loyal servant of the rightful king.

But there was one person at least who no longer recognised this brand of loyalty. Margaret had not accompanied her husband north toward Leicester, and so had been spared the horrifying spectacle of the bloodletting at St. Albans. But her disquiet at the implications of York's victory was manifest. By the time her husband re-entered London's gates in the duke's company, his queen had retreated with their son behind the reassuringly immense walls of the Tower.

Margaret had no history of irreconcilable personal antipathy to York: she had known him since 1445, when he escorted her through Normandy as a fifteen-year-old bride on her way to meet her husband for the first time. Since then she had regularly included the duke and his wife and servants among the recipients of the gifts the queen traditionally distributed each New Year; and during York's earlier estrangement from the court in 1453 his duchess, Cecily Neville, had written to Margaret to appeal for her help in healing a breach that was, she explained, causing the duke "infinite sorrow, unrest of heart and of worldly comfort."

But Margaret had also been close to the Duke of Somerset, whose youthful talent for securing the friendship of French queens had clearly not deserted him. In the autumn of 1451 Margaret had bestowed on him the large annual sum of £100 as a signal (and costly) mark of her favour; and two years later, only a matter of weeks before the duke was incarcerated in the Tower, he had stood godfather to the young Prince Edward. Margaret had acquiesced, then, in York's appointment as protector—at the cost of both Somerset's imprisonment and the failure of her own attempt to rule—but it was evidently not her preferred choice for the disposition of her debilitated husband's government. Still, she was a queen, by venerable tradition an advocate for political harmony, and York's public commitment to her son's rights as Prince of Wales persuaded her to bow to the force of majority opinion among the nobility.

However, Margaret's political compass was radically reset by the events of the early months of 1455. Somerset, newly released from his prison quarters, had come out fighting as the champion of her husband's personal authority. And York, in response, had taken up arms against his king. There could be no doubt where the queen's sympathies lay as she waited for news from St. Albans, or of the horror with which she received word of Somerset's violent death and her husband's capture by the Duke of York. York might protest his fidelity to Henry; but a faithful subject, in Margaret's view, would neither kill the king's chief counsellor nor attempt to subject his sovereign lord to his own will. Henry was no longer immobilised by illness, which surely rendered York's efforts to renew his protectorate wholly illegitimate. Not only that, but York's very identity only served to compound the deep distrust with which the queen now regarded him.

The blood relationship with the royal line of succession on which the duke had dwelt so often in claiming a stake in Henry's government also, in Margaret's eyes, now made him a threat. The king was descended in the male line from the third son of Edward III, York in the male line from the fourth. Through his mother, however, the duke could trace his ancestry back to the second son of Edward III. Until now, it had been unthinkable that this senior claim through the female line could ever be used to challenge the authority of an anointed king. But then again, it had also been unthinkable that two royal dukes should fight to the death at the heads of their armies in the streets of a prosperous English town while the king looked on in dazed bewilderment. And it might easily be noted that a claim through the female line had been the basis on which Henry himself had once been crowned King of France.

York, so far, had uttered no public word that was not scrupulously loyal. But if he was prepared to impose his will at swordpoint on an adult and sentient king, how much—or how little—restraint might he show if it were a question of bowing the knee to Margaret's eighteen-month-old son? The queen's own family history was hardly reassuring. Her father, René, his loyal daughter believed, had been rightfully King of Sicily, Naples, and Jerusalem, but had been unable to claim what was his because of the challenge of dynastic rivals. Now her son's future was at stake, and if her husband was unable to rally his own cause, then it was up to Margaret, his devoted consort, to act in his place.

Her move would have to be made carefully. Treading delicately across this uncertain and unfamiliar ground, Margaret emerged from the Tower to rejoin her husband. A week after the crown-wearing at St. Paul's, king, queen, and prince travelled first to Windsor Castle, and then to Hertford, while York and his allies set about the awkward task of underpinning their renewed power. When parliament met at the Palace of Westminster a month later, surrounded by heavily armed men wearing the colours of York and the Nevilles, public blame for the battle at St. Albans was placed squarely on the shoulders of the dead Duke of Somerset, who was conveniently unable to object; "and nothing done there never after this time to be spoken of," reported a nervous correspondent in the capital. ("After this is read and understood, I pray you burn or break it," he told the recipient of his letter, "for I am loath to write anything of any lord. But I must needs; there is nothing else to write.")

His anxiety was understandable; it was hardly likely that St. Albans could be expunged from the collective memory of the political classes at a stroke of the parliamentary pen. Only a day before the bill was passed, the Earl of Warwick, the younger of the two

Neville earls, had quarrelled openly with another nobleman, Lord
Cromwell, over where responsibility lay for "the steering or moving
of the evil day of St. Albans." And, even though Somerset's death
had removed one bitter personal rivalry from the political equation,
it had done so at a terrible cost. Noblemen were accustomed to the
risks of war, but war fought overseas, with the odds stacked in favour
of the rich and powerful: why kill a lordly enemy, after all, if a large
ransom could be secured by keeping him alive? Now noble English
blood had been spilled by English hands on English soil. There could
be no mistaking the stakes for which this dangerous game was being
played, and the heirs of those who had died might seek revenge, not
reconciliation, as their prize.

That York's de facto ascendancy required some formal validation
to make effective government possible was meanwhile all too evident:
violent disorder continued unchecked across large parts of England
and Wales while the nobility circled one another warily in the capital. Less clear was the means by which that validation should be
achieved. After months of fraught negotiation, the solution on which
parliament settled in November 1455 was that the duke should once
again be installed as protector of the realm, exactly as he had been
in the spring of 1454. But this time the porous edifice of his authority began to crumble from the moment it was established. Despite
reports that "some men are afeared that he is sick again," Henry was
no less capable of ruling for himself that November than he usually
was—which was not saying much, but did, nevertheless, go a long
way toward undermining York's claim to act in his place. Nor was
there any viable consensus among the lords that might serve as ballast for the duke's rule. Instead, York's attempt to impose a controversial financial retrenchment—a wide-ranging act of resumption,
intended to cut royal expenditure and re-establish crown finances on
a sound footing—precipitated his protectorate into crisis after just
three months.

And observers were in no doubt of who was leading the opposition to the duke's rule. "The resumption, men trust, shall forth, if

my lord of York's first power of protectorship stand, and else not, etc.," wrote John Bocking, a servant of the wealthy Norfolk knight Sir John Fastolf, to his master in early February 1456. "The queen is a great and strong laboured woman, for she spares no pain to sue her things to an intent and conclusion to her power." Bocking did not explicitly articulate the link between these two observations, but in such tense times his letter—which might, one never knew, fall into unfriendly hands between London and East Anglia—was already remarkably outspoken. Margaret was not only resisting the implementation of the act of resumption in her own right, but offering her leadership to others at court whose interests were not served by York and his proposals—Bocking's phrase "strong laboured" meaning "much solicited" by those around her.

In other words, having once failed to secure a formal appointment as her husband's regent, Margaret—who was never less than resourceful—had now decided that she already wielded enough authority to take action against the threat that York represented. Her husband wore the crown, and her two-year-old son would do so in future. If both temporarily needed her help in defending their rights—Edward because he was a baby, and Henry because he was scarcely more capable than his son—then she, as Henry's anointed queen, was ready and willing to shoulder the burden. Her success in championing resistance to York's agenda was already evident by February 25, just a fortnight after Bocking's letter, when the duke, faced with rapidly disintegrating support among the nobility for his fledgling regime, resigned as protector. The immediate result was a fraught political impasse: while York did not have enough authority to maintain formal command of Henry's government, neither did anyone else have enough authority to supplant him.

Margaret's work, however, had only just begun. Two months after York's resignation, she left London for her castle at Tutbury in the north midlands, taking her young son with her. But this was no retreat from the forefront of politics. Instead, Margaret was redrafting the rules of engagement. With a regency out of the question, she could acquire no formal stake in council sessions at Westminster; but government rested, too—in the absence of a standing army or professionalised police force under the direct control of the crown—on the practicalities of landed power, and it was these that Margaret now sought to harness for the first time. As she did so, no one could mistake the intensity of purpose or the focused aggression with which her husband's authority would now be defended.

SEVENTEEN

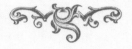

Might and Power

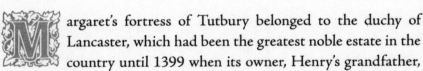argaret's fortress of Tutbury belonged to the duchy of
Lancaster, which had been the greatest noble estate in the
country until 1399 when its owner, Henry's grandfather,
swapped his ducal coronet for the royal crown as King Henry IV.
Among the uses to which the Lancastrian kings had put their private
estates since then had been the endowment of their queens; and as a
result Margaret now held great swathes of the duchy of Lancaster's
lands in the midlands and the north. Together with the estates held
by her son as Earl of Chester and Prince of Wales, the queen could
potentially call on the financial and military resources of a substantial territorial power base with its centre of gravity in the north midlands and the northwest. If the Duke of York chose to use his landed
power to overawe his peers and impose his will on government, then
he might now find that others could do the same.

That, at least, was the implication of the tension-filled stalemate that held during the long hot weeks of the summer of 1456, with the principal protagonists of English politics scattered around the kingdom like pieces on a chessboard. The Duke of York had retreated to his impregnable castle at Sandal in West Yorkshire, and the Earl of Warwick to his midland fortress at Warwick, while Margaret and her son stayed first at Tutbury and then rode northwest to the prince's castle at Chester. King Henry, meanwhile, tended by the members of his household, moved between the city of London and the neighbouring royal palaces of Westminster and Sheen while a council of lords attempted to maintain government in his name, as John Bocking reported in June. But it was clear where the fulcrum of power now lay: "My lord of York is at Sandal still, and waits on the queen, and she upon him."

And by the end of the summer the balance was tipping in Margaret's direction. In late August it was decided—tacitly, but implicitly, at the queen's suggestion—that Henry should join her and their son in the midlands. The king, escorted by his household entourage, arrived in early September at Coventry, the greatest city among the prince's estates, which lay only a few miles from the queen's own imposing castle at Kenilworth in Warwickshire. On September 14 his wife and son came to Coventry to meet him—and there was no mistaking, from the carefully planned pageants with which their triumphal entry into the city was greeted, what Margaret intended her husband's subjects to understand: that royal authority was now vested in the triumvirate of king, queen, and prince, with herself at its centre.

Prophets and evangelists, with St. Edward the Confessor in their midst in a gown of the royallest stuff the city guilds could provide, crowded onto the stage to compare Margaret to the Queen of Heaven ("Like as mankind was gladded by the birth of Jesus, so shall this empire joy the birth of your body . . ."). But it was a model of more than queenly motherhood that this august assemblage of theatrical personages had gathered to provide. The four Cardinal Virtues—Righteousness, Temperance, Strength, and Prudence, the chief qualities of rightful kingship—now pledged their counsel to Margaret in the laborious metre of hastily composed civic verse, and the Nine Worthies then stepped forward to promise her their service ("princess most royal, as to the highest lady that I can imagine"), before the queen's namesake, St. Margaret, took centre stage to slay a dragon in triumphantly heroic style.

Initially at least, the omens, as well as the oratory, seemed promising. At the end of the first week in October a great council gathered in the city. All the leading magnates had been summoned to attend, and most of them complied, including, with some unease, the Duke of York. Most of the nobles still, and with increasing desperation, hoped to find an escape from the horrors of civil war to some form of stability; perhaps the queen's presentation of the royal family as a vehicle for her husband's authority might offer a means to pull back from the precipice that St. Albans had opened up before them. They therefore agreed to the appointment of a new set of officers of state, men who gave Margaret much greater influence over the administration of her husband's government, but were simultaneously acceptable to the majority of his lords. The queen's own chancellor, Laurence Booth, became keeper of the privy seal; the Earl of Shrewsbury, son of the "English Achilles" who had died at Castillon, became treasurer of England; and the king's confessor, William Wainfleet, the scholarly and conscientious Bishop of Winchester, became chancellor.

All the same, the lords would not comply with any attempt to pursue the partisan division that had been so bloodily apparent at St. Albans. If, in Margaret's eyes, the Duke of York's actions that day had proved beyond doubt that he was a traitor, it was not a conclusion that the duke's peers were yet prepared to endorse. The duke was required to swear a public oath declaring his loyalty and obedience, but no further action was taken against him; and when he left Coventry he was said to be "in right good conceit with the king"— Henry's benevolence being, as always, indiscriminate—"but not in great conceit with the queen," an associate of John Bocking reported.

Nevertheless, the practical possibilities afforded to Margaret by her new influence over the machinery of government quickly became apparent in the early months of 1457. At the end of January a formal council was appointed to oversee her three-year-old son's affairs, along with new officials for his household and the administration of his estates. The prince's council included Laurence Booth, the new keeper of the privy seal; Booth's predecessor as Margaret's chancellor, his half-brother William, Archbishop of York; the new treasurer, the Earl of Shrewsbury; and Margaret's chief steward, John, Viscount Beaumont—all of whom were to act as councillors (the patent endorsed in Henry's name declared) "with the approval and agreement of our best-beloved consort the queen." Beaumont was also appointed steward of the prince's lands, while two gentlemen of the king's household, both of them married to ladies-in-waiting in Margaret's own establishment, took over the management of young Edward's finances as his receiver-general and keeper of his great wardrobe.

Piece by piece, Margaret was building a political network that extended her reach within government while reinforcing the territorial power at her disposal through her own and her son's estates. She was making such strides, it seemed, in creating a composite authority to serve as a substitute for her vacuous husband that, when she left Coventry after a second great council meeting that spring, her horse was preceded by the mayor and sheriffs of the city carrying their insignia of office "like as they before time did before the king," the mayor's register noted with some surprise: "And so they did never before the queen till then, for they bore before that time always their servants' maces before the queen."

Margaret might ride with all the trappings of majesty, but there were also signs that the efficacy of her new authority would still be limited. The Duke of York would not simply bow before the queen's influence, as became clear when he refused to attend the second council held at Coventry in March 1457; and for good reason, given that the queen would not accept the need to conciliate a nobleman who had ridden in arms against her husband and might pose a threat to the inheritance of her son. The difficulty for Margaret, meanwhile, was that the unique authority of her husband's crown relied on his ability to provide universal law and representative justice to all of his subjects. If she were now to construct a new form of royal government intended not only to exclude but to destroy the greatest magnate in the country, then she ran the risk that she might undermine the power of the crown itself.

It is not clear, however, that Margaret fully understood the pitfalls of the position she was taking up with such drive and determination. At twenty-six, she was revealing herself to be a political force of relentless energy and unbending will, but she showed less obvious sign of either the tactical shrewdness of her countrywoman Isabella or the fierce intelligence of their mutual ancestor Eleanor. Moreover, her political education had been conducted in France, where kings had acquired their sovereign power by a gradual, attritional process of subjugating great noble domains to the force of their authority (the English-held duchies of Normandy and Aquitaine among them). For Margaret, therefore, steeped as she was in the political traditions of a different kingdom's history, it made perfect sense that the crown might be required to crush an "overmighty" subject—a perspective which served to obscure the fact that, in England, the crown itself might be fatally compromised in the attempt.

But, if there were missteps along the political path she had chosen, it also had to be said that there was quicksand shifting dangerously beneath her feet. The very circumstance that enabled her to act—the fact that she was the king's wife—simultaneously undermined her actions. The more she asserted herself in Henry's stead, the more he appeared an emasculated puppet, his authority ebbing away; and as the reserves of legitimacy on which she could draw gradually diminished, the queen herself became the subject of whispered caricature and contempt.

It was hardly surprising, perhaps, that when her son had been born "people spoke strangely," as one London chronicler reported. After eight childless years of marriage to an unworldly naïf, Margaret's safe delivery of an heir to the throne had been as unexpected as it was convenient. Now, however, more elaborate rumours began to circulate. Little Edward was not the queen's son, some said; others that he was not the king's, or that he had been "changed in the cradle" and was related by blood to neither king nor queen. Gossip about royal changelings was nothing new (as Edward II had discovered); and the fact that the Duke of York had been heir presumptive to Henry's throne before the baby's birth made the young prince an obvious focus for scurrilous speculation among those who sympathised with York's political agenda.

But the language of illegitimacy carried a particular burden of significance amid the power play of 1457. Margaret's political leadership was predicated on her role as wife to the king and mother to his heir—but loyal wives did not customarily supplant their husbands at the head of government. The implication was that unnatural impulses were at work, both inside and outside the royal bedchamber. Margaret might seek to associate herself with the virtuous Queen of Heaven in her attempt to rule through a royal trinity of king, queen, and prince, but the evident fact that she was the prime mover of the three threatened to wreck the whole enterprise on the rocks of her aberrant behaviour as a wife and a woman.

Despite the strides she had made in building a power base at Coventry, the constraints on her ability to rule were publicly exposed at the end of August 1457 by the threat of a French invasion. Danger to the realm required the most authoritative response possible, and that, it became clear, was not the command of the queen. Instead, when king, queen, and lords converged on Westminster, the traditional seat of government, the nobles moved once again to convene a council under Henry's benignly vacant purview. The magnates who were charged by this council with mustering sailors, soldiers, and archers to defend the south coast and the Scottish border included York and the Nevilles, as well as the lords who enjoyed Margaret's trust and those still trying to steer a course between them. And, once this collective mobilisation had seen off the imminent menace of a

French military offensive, an attempt was made to use the same principle of united action to secure internal as well as external peace.

Under the auspices of this council—a fragile simulacrum of the conciliar regimes that had safeguarded England during Henry's childhood and illness—a "loveday" was proposed as a means of settling the conflict within the realm. The holding of a loveday was a familiar element within the grammar of local disputes—a ceremony to enact an arbitrated settlement based on the principles of restorative justice, rather than the winner-takes-all approach of the law courts. Such appeals to mutual interest through mutual concession played a vital part in containing hostilities within local communities. Could the same process now protect the community of the whole realm?

It was a risky business. At the end of January 1458 the lords began to assemble at their lodgings in London, ready to make peace but prepared—just in case—for war, each with hundreds of armed men wearing their badges and liveries. Amid the confined spaces of the city and its suburbs, in an atmosphere that crackled and jumped with tension, friction between these rival bands of soldiers threatened to spark a political conflagration. The mayor and sheriffs nervously set their sentries to watch round the clock, dispatched patrols to walk the main arteries of the city, and outlawed the carrying of weapons inside the gates of the capital.

Their anxiety was well founded. The Duke of York had taken up residence within the graceful walls of Baynard's Castle, his London home, which nestled near Blackfriars Quay at the southwest corner of the city where the Fleet River gave into the Thames, while the young Duke of Somerset, who had been wounded at St. Albans at his dying father's side when he was just nineteen, had found lodgings beyond Ludgate, where Fleet Street and the Strand led westward to the king's palace at Westminster. The Neville earls, Salisbury and Warwick, were, with York, at their townhouses inside the city; the new Earl of Northumberland was with the Duke of Somerset outside London's walls. Those who were charged by the council to forge a peace among the lords therefore had to move uncomfortably be-

tween what amounted to two armed encampments, within and without the city gates; and amid swirling rumours of ambushes and plots,
a dangerous confrontation between the hot-headed Duke of Somerset and the brash Earl of Warwick was only narrowly avoided.

By the middle of March, however, a settlement had been hammered out under the watchful eye of the Archbishop of Canterbury.
York and the Nevilles were to pay some notional financial compensation and offer masses for the souls of the lords killed at St. Albans; in
return, they were to be recognised, along with those who had died, as
the king's loyal subjects. The loveday itself, which would give ceremonial force to this reconciliation, was set for March 25. That morning
the crowds began to gather early, lining the streets that led to the
great cathedral of St. Paul's, its soaring spire reaching into the spring
sky. They were rewarded with an extraordinary sight.

A stately procession made its way through Ludgate toward the cathedral, its participants glittering with gems and cloth of gold rather
than the flashes of steel that had caused such alarm on London's
streets for weeks beforehand. At its head came the youthful figure of
the Duke of Somerset, his gloved hand reluctantly clasped in that of
Richard Neville, the Earl of Salisbury. Next walked Salisbury's son,
the Earl of Warwick, gripping the fingers of Henry Holland, Duke
of Exeter, a close ally of Somerset and the Percy Earl of Northumberland, and most recently Warwick's bitter rival for the captaincy of
Calais. Then came King Henry in solitary majesty, his face beneath
the heavy golden crown almost as full of wonderment as those of his
subjects who had come to watch this unlikely spectacle. And behind
the king, most improbable of all, came the stern-faced Duke of York,
hand in hand with Henry's queen.

For Margaret, it seemed, this was a moment to savour. Here, on
Lady Day—the feast of the Queen of Heaven—the power of the
Queen of England was given full recognition. Under her aegis, the
Duke of York and his allies had been brought to admit culpability
for the bloodshed at St. Albans. No formal role had been available to
her, as the king's wife, in the negotiations that preceded the loveday or

the documents in which the settlement was inscribed, other than the traditional one of intercessor in the cause of peace. The final text of the concord painted an utterly conventional picture of a king moved to mercy by "the great request, cordial desire and entreaties made to us by our dearest and most beloved wife the queen" out of her wish to restore "unity, charity and harmony." But the reality of the loveday told a different story. Behind the inane benevolence of the king stood the unyielding will of his queen, and Margaret, it was clear, was the force with whom York would have to reckon if he made any further attempt to take control of government.

Nevertheless, a closer look at the rictus smiles and strained body language of the procession to St. Paul's suggested that this was likely to be the opening gambit of a new phase of hostilities rather than any kind of resolution. The peace negotiations led by the Archbishop of Canterbury had been well intentioned, and York and the Nevilles had conceded a great deal in their search for security through noble unity. But the form of the settlement tackled symptoms, not causes, of conflict, and in doing so it entrenched division rather than ameliorating it. No attention had been given to the grievances that had driven York and his allies to draw their weapons at St. Albans—principally, the difficulty of securing justice and good government when the king was incapable of ruling. That problem, of course, was profoundly intractable, given that the king remained as incapable as ever, and so mediation had focused on the fighting itself and the deaths that had been its result. But the unhappy effect was to predicate peace on a public demonstration that there were still, three years after the battle, two warring factions among the lords, whose enmity was thereby cast in entirely personal terms. One was led by the Duke of York. And the other—as their symbolic pairing at the loveday made unmistakably clear—was led by the queen.

Margaret was never likely to be satisfied with a gesture of reconciliation that left York in full possession of the resources which had allowed him to challenge the power of her husband's crown in the first place. She knew how to be pragmatic: she took the duke's hand outside the door of St. Paul's with royal condescension, just as she had accepted her failure to secure regency powers during Henry's illness four years earlier. But her goals, and her implacable determination to reach them, did not change, and there is every sign that she welcomed the drawing up of battle lines that the tense political choreography of the loveday quickly came to represent. That summer she retreated to her citadel at Coventry—leaving York and the Nevilles to see how far they could pull the levers of government in London for a few short months—before riding back to the capital in the autumn to sweep them aside. As the animating spirit of the royal trinity of king, queen, and prince, she took control of royal revenues and appointments to royal office—and began to use both to exclude her enemies from power.

How far she might have to go to achieve that end became apparent a few weeks after her return. The need to neutralise the Earl of Warwick—who, as Captain of Calais, commanded the only permanent armed force maintained by the English crown—was especially acute, but the very fact of his command in Calais (which had provided him, among other things, with a lucrative sideline in freebooting raids on Channel shipping) made it especially difficult to remove him from office if he did not wish to be replaced. There was more than one way, however, to eliminate an officer of the crown. Perhaps it was coincidence when, in November 1458, the earl became embroiled in a dangerously violent scuffle at court with men of the royal household, but Warwick himself did not think so. He escaped with his life, but clearly had no intention of exposing himself to the ongoing threat that he might encounter a stiletto in the ribs. Together with his father and the Duke of York, he abandoned the capital to the queen shortly thereafter.

How far Margaret was prepared to go was also rapidly becoming clear. In May 1459 she, too, decamped from London to return to her base at Coventry, taking the king and prince with her and summoning the nobles to assemble for a great council in the city in the following month. When York, Salisbury, and Warwick failed to appear—which was hardly surprising, given that Coventry was a much more threateningly partisan place than the capital they had already left—charges of treason were laid against them. And any doubt of the danger in which they now found themselves was dispelled by the steps the queen was taking to realise the military potential of her estates by distributing her small son's livery badge—a swan wearing a crown as a collar around its elegantly curled neck—to those men of the midlands and northwest who committed themselves to serve her in peace and in war.

It was a strategy that would have been familiar to her French forebears. The duchy of Normandy, after all, was now an indivisible part of the kingdom of France because Philippe II had swept into Rouen at the head of an army, and that had not been the last time a sword had been unsheathed in the French crown's attempt to impose its authority throughout its kingdom. But in England, where the universal force of royal authority and royal law was already well established, this raising of a regional army could only represent a narrowing of royal power into a partial and partisan interest, with all the loss of legitimacy that implied. It was no accident that the only two kings of England who had lost their crowns had also forfeited their subjects' trust in their ability to represent the common good of the whole realm: first Edward II, in his blinkered dependence on Hugh Despenser, and then the paranoid Richard II, who had, like Margaret, sought to raise an army in Cheshire to defend a pale of royal authority in the northwest against the enemies he saw everywhere in his own kingdom.

And Margaret was not even a king. Instead, she was a queen seeking to defend the rights of her cipher of a husband by any means necessary. But her refusal to acknowledge the possibility of any middle ground in this conflict—her insistence that those who would not stand with her against York thereby revealed themselves as enemies of the crown—put such strain on the composite authority through which she was trying to rule that it began to disintegrate. What she was demanding of her husband's subjects was so partisan, so divisive, that the disjuncture between her commanding self and the king and prince from whom she drew her power was ever more exposed.

This fraught relationship between the vestigial power of her husband's royal persona and the female will by which it was now directed became obvious that autumn when political tension ratcheted up into outbreaks of sickening violence. In September the Nevilles set out across country to converge on a rendezvous with York at his fortress of Ludlow in the Welsh borders—the Earl of Warwick fresh from a Channel crossing with a detachment from the Calais garrison riding at his back, and his father, Salisbury, heading south with troops from his Yorkshire stronghold at Middleham. They knew they would have to fight—but not how soon. At Blore Heath in Staffordshire on September 23, Salisbury only narrowly escaped an attempt to intercept him by an army one chronicler described as the "queen's gallants." After four hours of bloody fighting, two thousand men lay dead on the field, among them the gallants' venerable commander, the sixty-one-year-old Lord Audley.

For Margaret, waiting for news five miles away, this was the first experience of the frustrations of female command when political skirmishing became open warfare. Matilda, three centuries before her, had known what it was to be a leader who could not lead in battle—but at least that had meant that her cause, depending as it did on her own claim to the crown, could not be summarily decapitated by a sword-thrust or a stray arrow. Margaret, on the other hand, was secure in the knowledge that her husband and son were protected from the dangers of the mêlée by inanity and infancy respectively—but she, who gave direction and purpose to their cause, could offer their troops neither strategy nor encouragement once the enemy was in sight.

The crown that rested on her husband's head, however, still counted for something. When their forces, regrouped and reinforced after the slaughter at Blore Heath, rode after Salisbury's men toward Ludlow, they did so with royal banners flying high. And when they camped at Ludford Bridge, just below the looming hill on which

York's castle stood, the Calais soldiers began to desert Warwick's command, refusing to fight if it meant taking the field against the king's standard. Salisbury had escaped defeat once, but York could not be confident of doing so again if his forces were melting away. During the night of October 12 he took the decision not to fight but to flee. York himself rode west under cover of darkness and took ship for Ireland, accompanied by his sixteen-year-old son, Edmund, Earl of Rutland, while Salisbury and Warwick set sail for Calais, taking with them York's eldest son, seventeen-year-old Edward, Earl of March.

It was the opportunity for which Margaret had so long been working and waiting. She had mustered an army to defend her husband's crown and her son's inheritance, and her enemies had scattered before her. All that remained, it seemed, was to proclaim them the traitors they were. York's wife, Cecily, and their younger children were placed in the custody of the duchess's sister, the Duchess of Buckingham, whose husband was now emerging as one of Margaret's principal supporters. York's lands and tenants were harried and plundered. And in early December, at the priory of St. Mary in Coventry, a specially summoned parliament declared the Duke of York and his sons, together with the Earl of Salisbury and the Earl of Warwick, to be guilty of treason, and their lands and lives forfeit to the crown.

By this act of attainder, York and his allies were destroyed in law—and yet the unpalatable fact was that they were not there to be destroyed in person. Nor, now, did they have anything left to lose by challenging the very existence of the regime over which Margaret presided. The centrifugal force of spiralling conflict was now so intense that nothing could be taken for granted, other than the certainty that England's future would be decided on a battlefield. And the terrifying truth was that, on a battlefield, anything could happen.

That grim knowledge was etched on the faces of three generations of the Duke of York's family—his sixty-year-old brother-in-law, Salisbury, his thirty-one-year-old nephew, Warwick, and his

own son Edward of March, who had just turned eighteen—as the
three earls set sail to return to the south coast of England in June
1460, their ships full of soldiers recruited once again from the Calais
garrison. This time, however, the earls found themselves welcomed
as champions, not resisted as traitors. Margaret had built herself a
power base in the midlands and the northwest; the heavy cost of that
militarisation, it now transpired, was a haemorrhaging of support for
her cause in the southeast. The people of Kent, Surrey, and Sussex,
and the citizens of London—who, though nervous at the approach of
an army, opened the gates of the capital to the Yorkist lords on July
2—no longer trusted a government led by the queen from her citadel
at Coventry. Instead, they were prepared to give a sympathetic hearing, and practical support, to Yorkist declarations that the crown
had been hijacked and royal justice perverted for partisan ends.

That the city of London should endorse this view of a regime led
by the queen in the name of the king and prince was a startling rejection both of Margaret's claim to exercise power on her husband's
behalf, and of her confrontational strategy. But there would be no
reconsideration of tactics or goals, only an unyielding resolve to
defend the crown against treasonable resistance. When Warwick
and March left London to move north at the head of an army on
July 5, therefore, Margaret's forces marched south from Coventry to
meet them. And once again, the limitations of her position and of
the composite authority she wielded were obvious and inescapable.
She and her six-year-old son remained behind Coventry's city walls,
safe, but helpless to inspire or lead her troops, who were commanded
instead by her loyal supporters the Duke of Buckingham, the Earl of
Shrewsbury, and Viscount Beaumont, while the king rode alongside
them, a docile mascot rather than a royal general.

At Ludford Bridge York's soldiers had refused to take up arms
against their sovereign. But now, just nine months later, when the two
armies met outside the town of Northampton on July 10, Henry's insubstantial presence proved inconsequential rather than talismanic.
The king sat meekly in his tent, sheltering from the pouring rain that

turned the field into a treacherous bog into which his army's artillery
sank, immobilised and useless in the enveloping mud. Warwick and
March seized the advantage, and their soldiers overran the field in
little more than an hour. They had ordered their troops to safeguard
the king and spare the rank and file, so far as was possible, while
concentrating their assault on the lords who commanded the enemy
lines. It was a shrewdly judged tactic for an army claiming to fight
for the common good, and its success was startling. By sundown, the
bloodied, mud-spattered corpses of Buckingham, Shrewsbury, and
Beaumont had been removed for burial; other casualties were few;
and King Henry was riding biddably beside his cousin of March and
the Earl of Warwick on the road south to the Yorkist-held capital.

Pope Pius II was later moved by this passive compliance to describe Henry as "more timorous than a woman, utterly devoid of wit
or spirit." The essence of this papal observation was acute enough,
but its expression much less well considered. With Henry installed
under Yorkist guard in the Bishop of London's palace, and Yorkist
nominees newly appointed to the great offices of state, it was apparent more than ever that the cause of this puppet-king now depended
on his wife—and there was nothing timorous, witless, or unspirited
about Margaret.

The situation she now faced demanded physical endurance and a
more resolute will than ever. Northampton had been a catastrophe:
her husband was lost to her, her chief noble lieutenants slaughtered,
and her base at Coventry under threat as the Duke of York made
preparations to sail from Dublin to Chester at the head of another
army. But a reliably steadfast ally, her husband's half-brother Jasper
Tudor, Earl of Pembroke—one of the two sons of Queen Catherine's
second marriage—remained in control of south and west Wales; the
Earl of Northumberland was mustering men to defend the north of
England against the Yorkists; and the energetic young Duke of Somerset was preparing to return from France, where he had taken refuge
after a bold but unsuccessful attempt to seize Calais from Warwick's

control, in order to raise the southwestern counties for the queen. All was not lost, if she could co-ordinate a rapid counterstrike.

Bundling her son onto horseback to ride pillion with a trusted bodyguard, and taking the saddle with a servant of her own, Margaret headed west from Coventry with a small escort. Her guards were not heavily armed enough to prevent the loss of valuable baggage to thieves along the way, but sometime in September the dishevelled and exhausted party arrived at the gates of Harlech Castle, a massive fortress overlooking the sea from a clifftop on the northern Welsh coast. They were there still, safe behind its formidable walls, when news came that was worse than anything Margaret had yet faced.

On October 10 the Duke of York had ridden into London. Ringing trumpets announced his arrival before his company came into sight. All dressed in livery of white and blue marked with his device of a fetterlock, the duke's men made an imposing spectacle as they escorted their lord through the streets of the capital and out of Ludgate toward the Palace of Westminster. But it was not this show of force that had stopped the breath of those who watched them pass; instead, it was the extraordinary message that could be read in the trappings of the procession. The duke's great sword was carried upright before his horse, just as the king was traditionally attended when he rode among his people. Banners fluttering in the autumn air displayed the arms of Lionel of Clarence, the second son of Edward III from whom York could claim a senior line of royal inheritance to that of Henry himself. And, most unmistakably of all, the royal standard itself now flew above York's head.

After ten years of escalating conflict, ten years in which it had become appallingly clear that there could be no lasting security for York—or peace for England—while Margaret championed the cause of her husband and son against him, the duke had at last come to the frightening conclusion from which he had shrunk for so long. Henry VI, that amiable innocent whose very harmlessness had had such devastating effects, would have to be removed. Amid the echo-

ing magnificence of the great hall at Westminster, where the lords
had gathered for a meeting of parliament, York strode to the dais
and placed his hand on the marble throne, turning to the assembled
peers to await their shout of acclamation.

It did not come. The faces of the nobles before him showed confusion, consternation, and horror. Desperate though they were to find a
way out of the war, a crown on York's head promised only more darkness and bloodshed. After ten years of conflict in which he had taken
such a prominent part, the duke himself was too tarnished a figure
to offer any credible hope of reconciliation or renewal in government.
And, even after everything that had happened, Henry's kingship was
not divisive enough to vindicate York's actions. He was not a tyrant
like Edward II and Richard II, the kings who had previously been
pushed from their thrones because of the threat they posed to the
interests of the subjects they had sworn to protect. Instead, he was an
empty vessel, to whose unassuming mildness still clung a faint aura
of the sanctity of his anointing, and of the divine sanction that his
father's great victories had conferred on his dynasty.

In shock and alarm, the lords retreated into urgent conclave.
Three weeks of tense negotiation followed, in which the Earl of
March, York's eighteen-year-old son, acted as go-between, riding
sombrely between his father at Westminster Palace and the lords
in session at the Black Friars, a monastery built into the southwest
corner of the city walls. Those who were looking for guidance from
God were scarcely reassured when the ornamental crown that hung
in the room at Westminster Abbey where the parliamentary commons sat in debate crashed suddenly to the floor. By October 31,
however, a settlement had at last been reached, and it was promul-
gated with oaths, solemn ceremonial, and public proclamations. By
its terms King Henry VI would keep his throne; but when he died
he would be succeeded not by his son Edward, but by his cousin of
York.

This settlement—a diplomatic homage to the treaty by which
Henry's father had, long ago, been named heir to his defeated enemy,

the French king Charles VI—served its immediate purpose. It was
a compromise which gave due acknowledgement to York's claims,
while allowing his regime to retain the support of the wider political
community by functioning in King Henry's name. Like that earlier
treaty, however, its failure was an inescapable part of its very formulation. Acknowledgement of York's claims meant the disinheritance
of Henry's son—and that meant, in practice, it was no settlement
at all.

For Margaret it was proof of what she had believed ever since
York had first ridden in arms to St. Albans five long years earlier:
that this conflict could be resolved only by the total destruction of
her enemies. Her husband, as usual, was a pawn in the hands of whoever currently had him in their keeping, and he participated with
meek submissiveness in the ceremonies by which the accord was
sealed. The difficulty with which the settlement presented Margaret
therefore lay not simply in its direct attack on her son's position, but
also in its assault on what remained of the composite authority she
had struggled so hard to construct. Henry's increasingly fragile but
still extant claim to legitimacy was now appropriated, along with his
person, by the Yorkist regime, leaving the queen and prince cut adrift
from the crown that had anchored Margaret's claim to rule.

It was no accident that rumours about the irregularity of the
prince's birth now re-emerged with renewed force. For Yorkist partisans, these whispers served the happy double purpose of justifying
York's claim to be Henry's heir and undermining the queen's public
standing through insinuations—damning to a woman as they would
never be to a man—about her private conduct. Margaret responded
with a forceful restatement of her son's rights: a letter to the city
of London written in the seven-year-old prince's name—a habit of
ventriloquism to which she had had to become accustomed during
the fifteen years of her married life—declared him to be "rightfully
and lineally born by descent of the blood royal to inherit the pre-
eminence of this realm." She also attempted to reclaim her husband's
authority by emphasising Henry's plight as a prisoner in need of

rescue, whose acquiescence in the naming of York as his heir was the
result of coercion, not genuine concession.

But she knew, too, that her case depended on the point of a sword,
not legal argument. At the end of November she set sail from Harlech, heading north across iron-grey water to Scotland, to appeal
for help against her enemies in England. Scottish kings were always
eager to make trouble for their southern neighbours, in whatever
form the opportunity presented itself. But the King of Scots in November 1460 was eight years old, his father, James II, having been
killed three months earlier when his own cannon blew up while he
was trying to wrest Roxburgh Castle from its English occupants. In
the matter of royal minorities, as in so much else, the Scots followed
the lead of their French allies, and it was therefore the newly widowed queen mother, Mary of Guelders, who was appointed regent on
behalf of her young son. If Margaret envied the clarity of the Scottish
queen regent's position, she strove not to show it as she petitioned for
men and money while their two boys played.

In England, meanwhile, her loyal lords, led by Jasper Tudor in
the west and the Earl of Northumberland in the north, were massing
the military forces already at their disposal. York knew that he urgently needed to counter this threat before Margaret had the chance
to secure reinforcements from beyond England's borders. Despite
the difficulty of moving armies across country in winter when the
weather was harsh and provisions scarce, the duke set his own forces
in motion. The Earl of Warwick remained in the capital; the Duke of
York's son Edward of March led his troops westward to Wales; and
York himself marched north, in the company of his old ally Salisbury.
What they did not know as they set out on icily rutted roads, their
breath hanging in great clouds around them, was that against all the
odds the Duke of Somerset had succeeded in forging a path from the
southwest—where York had believed he was about to launch an assault on Bristol—to rendezvous with Northumberland in the north.
And when the duke emerged from his castle at Sandal near the town
of Wakefield in Yorkshire on December 30 to encounter his enemy,

it was to face the horrifying realisation that he was both outmanoeuvred and massively outnumbered.

The result was a rout. When the fighting was over, the corpses that lay piled on the cold earth included the Duke of York himself, united in death with his teenage son Edmund, Earl of Rutland. Salisbury, too, lost a son, Thomas, but he had no time to grieve for his lost boy or for York, his brother-in-law and brother in arms; instead, he was taken in chains to Pontefract, where he was killed the following day. Then their four heads were taken to York and set on spikes on the city gates as a terrible warning of the fate of traitors, the duke's mockingly festooned with a paper crown, his pretensions of majesty now as hollow as the sockets of his sightless eyes.

The news, when it reached Margaret more than a hundred miles north in Scotland, was overwhelming. Her greatest enemy was dead. She was no longer a fugitive and a supplicant, driven into exile to beg for help from a fellow queen. Instead, her army held the north of England, and the kingdom lay open to their advance. As soon as she and her son rejoined Somerset and Northumberland and the troops they commanded in early January 1461, they began the long march south, pressing hard for the capital. But the final victory remained to be won—and the journey itself began to reveal the full complexity of the task ahead of them.

Filling the stomachs on which her army marched was no easy task in the dead of winter—and this winter was worse than any England had experienced in decades. Torrential rain all summer long had turned pastures to mud and rotted crops in the ground, so that stores could not be laid down as usual for the cold season, and belts had been tightened even before Margaret's army faced its journey southward. Already by January 12 the soldiers had begun to pillage and plunder the villages and towns through which they passed—violence which the queen and her commanders did little or nothing to restrain, partly because of the pressing need for the troops to eat, and partly because some of the lands which they left ravaged in their wake belonged to the dead Duke of York. Margaret could see the value in such a potent demonstration of the penalties for resistance, as well as the evident necessity for her soldiers to be fed; but she did not foresee the devastating effect of the rumours and reports that flew ahead on the road to London. Her strategy had always been to build territorial power into military might, but the unease that already existed in the southeast about her identification with the midlands and the north had now crystallised into alienation and fear.

When a young gentleman named Clement Paston wrote from London to his elder brother in Norfolk on January 23, it was clear how far the people of the Yorkist-held capital now saw the conflict as a war between north and south. "In this country every man is willing to go with my lords here," he wrote, "and I hope God shall help them, for the people in the north rob and steal and are appointed to pillage all this country, and give away men's goods and livelihoods in all the south country, and that will ask a mischief." And the Earl of Warwick, raising men and munitions in London and across the southeast, was doing what he could to exploit those fears, demanding aid against the "misruled and outrageous people in the north parts" who were "coming toward these parts to the destruction thereof."

His preparations were given a much-needed filip in early February when news broke that Edward of March, now the new Duke of York after his father's death, had won a crushing victory at Mortimer's Cross in the Welsh borders over an army commanded by Jasper Tudor, Earl of Pembroke. Tudor himself had escaped, but his father, Owen—second husband of the late Queen Catherine, and King Henry's stepfather—had been captured and executed after the battle. (At sixty, he had not lost the charms that had won him the hand of a queen: a "mad woman" tenderly washed his severed head and combed his hair, one chronicler reported, and lit a hundred candles to illuminate its resting place on Hereford's market cross.)

Heartened by the knowledge that Edward was heading eastward to join him, Warwick led his troops twenty miles north from London to St. Albans, intending to halt the queen's army in its tracks and hold off any assault on the capital. With him rode King Henry—a token of legitimacy so uncomprehending that his capacity to strike awe into soldiers who stood against him was now, it seemed, long gone. So it proved on February 17 when Margaret's troops, under the aggressively skilful command of the Duke of Somerset, swarmed into the town. For the second time in six years, swords clashed in the streets and the cobbles of the market square were left sticky with blood. But this time Somerset secured his revenge for the defeat that had cost his father his life; this time it was the Yorkists who lost both the battle and the person of the king. Henry was found sitting obediently under a tree and taken to St. Albans Abbey, where his wife and son were waiting to greet him.

Still Margaret had not destroyed her enemies. Warwick survived the encounter at St. Albans but was forced to retreat northward—the pirate captain of Calais feeling the sting of his first military defeat—to join forces with his cousin Edward in the Cotswolds on February 22. But Yorkist hopes now hung by a thread. If Edward and Warwick could get to London before the queen's army, they might still save themselves and their cause, but the capital was four days' forced march away, and Margaret's troops had already advanced to Barnet, just ten miles from the city gates. They marched in any case, in defiance and desperation, placing their faith in their own skill and the support they knew they commanded among the Londoners.

Margaret, meanwhile, seemed to have her pieces poised on the chessboard for one final, inexorable assault. Her husband, feeble though he might be, was back at her side. Her army, in which every soldier wore the badge of her young son, had won two famous victories, and the capital lay before her. And her leadership in the name of the king and prince was amply acknowledged by the deputation the Londoners sent to treat with her army, which was led by three women: the dowager Duchess of Bedford, who had accompanied Margaret on her first journey to England fifteen years earlier; Emma, Lady Scales, who had been a lady-in-waiting in Margaret's household as queen; and the widowed Duchess of Buckingham, who was Prince Edward's godmother.

In the fact of that deputation, however, lay Margaret's problem. Her army desperately needed food and provisions, but the Londoners were not willing simply to open their gates and their stores. The Yorkist sympathies of many of the capital's inhabitants were now compounded by their terror of the rabble of northerners they had heard so much about; they had ample evidence of the devastation Margaret's army had left in its wake on its march south, and of the queen's implacability in pursuit of those who opposed her. The question was whether the queen's wrath could now be staved off by prompt compliance, or whether the city was already doomed by its previous resistance. An exchange of letters between the mayor and the queen produced the unsettlingly vague promise that "the king and queen had no mind to pillage the chief city...but at the same time they did not mean that they would not punish the evildoers." Clearly, Margaret was not, after five years of fighting, about to offer an amnesty to those who had stood against her.

As the city council wrestled with this alarming dilemma, its officers were struggling even to keep order within the city walls. An attempt was made to send carts piled high with food as a placatory offering to the queen's encampment at Barnet, but hostile crowds, enraged by fear and panic, gathered to stop the convoy before it could pass through Cripplegate on the north road out of the city. "That day this place was in an uproar," an Italian observer in London reported—pandemonium which was fuelled by the rumours that had begun to reach the city that the Yorkists were on their way.

Time was running out. Confronted with this violence and disarray, with the urgent need to feed her soldiers, and with the impossibility of forcing her way into a city whose support she needed and whose defences were impregnable, Margaret for once decided that discretion was the better part of valour. Retreating and regrouping had worked for her before, and now she had little choice but to believe that it could do so again. She pulled her army back twenty miles northwestward to Dunstable; and then, knowing that the arrival of the Yorkist army was imminent and that, without provisions and supplies, her troops were in no position to fight, she gave the order to march north. Her army wheeled away from the capital, still looting as it went.

As Margaret retreated, Edward of York and his cousin of Warwick were advancing at speed—and when they reached the capital they could scarcely believe what they found. Overwhelmed with relief at their release from the threat of the queen's vengeance, the Londoners threw open their gates to welcome the Yorkists. Edward, whose cause had seemed lost on his frantic chase across country, now rode into the city unopposed and triumphant. And, extraordinarily, he did so as a king-in-waiting.

York had been Margaret's greatest enemy but not, it turned out, her greatest threat. At eighteen, Edward was everything her ineffectual and distracted husband was not. Unusually tall, strongly built, and jaw-droppingly handsome, he had irresistible charisma, combining easy bonhomie with an imperious will, and a shrewd political brain that had been honed by early experience as his father's trusted lieutenant. Amid the devastation of the Yorkists' military hopes, his precocious skill as a general had been demonstrated in his victory over Jasper Tudor's army at Mortimer's Cross. He was neither the treason-tainted political maverick that his father had been, nor the limp puppet that Henry now was. He looked more like a king than anyone had seen in years, and he could claim technical justification for the sudden suggestion that the crown might in fact be his, since Henry, so the argument went, in "deciding" to rejoin Margaret at St. Albans, had reneged on his oath to recognise York as his heir and in effect resigned his throne.

But the strength of Edward's position went way beyond the theoretical. Margaret's aggressive territorialism had turned southern England into enemy country, and the fact that she had been forced to impersonate the authority of a husband and son who were unable to act for themselves had ended up exposing, rather than concealing, Henry's wretched failure as king. In the eyes of the Londoners at least, Edward offered a fresh start, hope amid a landscape of devastation and chaos; and when on March 4 he processed in state from St. Paul's to the Palace of Westminster to take his seat on the throne that his father had never won, he was followed by thronging crowds who hollered and bellowed their approval.

Nine days later, therefore, when Edward left London at the head of his troops, the ground rules of the conflict had changed dramatically. Both sides—Margaret's army in the north, and Edward's in the south—now had a king to fight for. The unique authority of the crown was so compromised that these two rival monarchs would meet for the first time on equal terms, the last king standing to claim the prize. And so on Palm Sunday, March 29, after a deliberately measured and orderly march north, Edward and Warwick took up position outside Towton, a Yorkshire village only a few miles from the battlefield where the Duke of York and the Earl of Salisbury had died just three months earlier. There they faced an army commanded by the Duke of Somerset and the Earl of Northumberland, who, like Edward and Warwick, had lost their fathers in these wars. Whatever happened at Towton, it promised to be the last act in a political conflict that had become infused with all the emotional resonance and murderous violence of a blood feud.

Margaret, meanwhile, had no choice but to wait, powerless as she was to intervene while her soldiers did their work. This time her husband and son were with her, safe within York's city walls: if Henry now served no purpose in rallying his troops, there was no sense in risking his presence on the battlefield. As she paced restlessly, intent and silent, she had no way of knowing, as hour gave way to hour, that the fighting ten miles away was still relentless. On both sides the order had been given that there would be no quarter, no mercy; and neither side would give way, while the corpses heaped up between them, entangling living feet in the twisted and broken limbs of the dead. For eight hours the slaughter continued, in driving snow that blinded stinging eyes and numbed clumsy fingers, the bitter cold catching each ragged, gasping breath. When some at last turned to run in exhaustion and fear, it was to find their path blocked by the river Wharfe and their final rest in its freezing waters. And all the while, new rivulets of melting snow stained red with blood were snaking through the frozen furrows of the road that led toward York and Margaret.

Blood could not speak; but messengers could, sobbing from their exertions in the cold and the dreadful burden of the news they brought. Thousands upon thousands had died at Towton. And, in the end, it was Margaret's army that had shattered. As the light began to fade, Edward of York stood unchallenged in command of the field, King of England in fact as well as in name. And three muf- fled figures with a handful of guards rode hard on the route north toward Scotland: a grim-faced woman, a bewildered man, and a frightened seven-year-old boy, no longer England's royal family but hunted fugitives.

EIGHTEEN

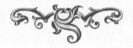

The Queen Sustains Us

dentity had been at the heart of Margaret's difficulties in the long years of struggle for her husband's throne. Henry's inadequacies had left the mantle of kingship hanging limp and empty; and although Margaret had supplied the will and purpose to animate his cause, she could not, as a woman and a wife, simply inhabit the role he had left so damagingly vacant.

Now Margaret had no choice but to watch as those same questions of identity underpinned the creation of a new regime that promised to destroy everything she had ever worked for. The mantle of kingship rested squarely on the broad shoulders of Edward of York. He was forceful, decisive, energetic, magnetic; he promised leadership of a kind England had not experienced since the death of Henry's father forty years earlier. "Words fail me to relate how well the commons love and adore him, as if he were their god," reported an Italian resident in London a fortnight after Edward's victory at Towton. "Thus far, he appears to be a just prince who intends to amend and organise matters otherwise than has been done hitherto...." And when this new king was anointed in Westminster Abbey on June 28—a golden boy in a golden crown—it seemed that God was merely confirming what was already evident in his talents, his actions, and the fact of his victory.

It was not, of course, quite that simple. Although the south of England was agog with expectation and relief at Edward's accession, his newfound authority was much more precarious in the north and west, in the parts of Wales and northern England that Margaret had counted her heartlands. And, crucially, his enemies—Margaret, Henry, and their son, the king's half-brother Jasper Tudor, and the dukes of Somerset and Exeter, who had fled for their lives from the slaughter at Towton—were still at large, despite strenuous efforts to convince observers at home and abroad that they were safely in custody. "I do not believe that, since vain flowers always grow in good news," Prospero di Camulio, the Milanese ambassador at the French court, wrote with some asperity to his duke, Francesco Sforza. "...if the King and Queen of England with the other fugitives are not taken," he added, circumspectly slipping into cipher, "it seems certain that in time fresh disturbances will arise."

Fresh disturbances were certainly Margaret's intention. Unhappy though the comparison might be in the eyes of her adopted countrymen, had not her uncle Charles VII ejected the English from his kingdom of France even after her husband had been crowned in Paris? The accession of a Yorkist king was an illegitimate and therefore temporary interruption to her husband's rights and her son's future inheritance, which she would reclaim with the help of her uncle of France and that of his steadfast allies, her present hosts in Edinburgh.

The price, however, was high. The Scots and the French were fierce guardians of their own interests, not partisans of Margaret's cause. The cost of Scots support was the immediate surrender of the contested border town of Berwick and the promise of the city of Carlisle, if it could be captured. Her hopes for support from her uncle of France were dashed when news reached Scotland of Charles's death on July 22—the very day on which she had written to ask for his help—and the succession of his son, Louis XI, a strategist so subtle he was dubbed "the spider king," who had already as dauphin offered assistance to the Yorkists' cause. Nevertheless, a visit by Margaret to the French court in the spring and summer of 1462 produced a treaty and a loan, albeit on the alarming (and prudently hidden) condition that Calais should be put up as security.

Margaret was working hard and hoping for much, but the longer this intricate diplomatic dance continued, the more uncertain the ground beneath her feet became. The passage of time served only to reinforce Edward's stature as king, and to chip away at what remained of the fragmented authority to which she herself could lay claim. At the first parliament of the new reign, held at Westminster in November 1461, the queen and prince ("Edward *her* son," as the parliamentary proceedings pointedly called him) were attainted of treason on the grounds of offences "committed against her faith and allegiance to our sovereign and liege lord King Edward." Such a description of her actions against a man whose sovereignty she had never acknowledged and would never recognise might well have raised a hollow laugh from Margaret, but this formal denunciation served to give public sanction to what was now an unstoppable flood of venomous innuendo and propaganda.

All the old rumours about the queen's aberrant behaviour had sprung into newly elaborate life in the nerve-wracking weeks before Towton. Gossip in Brussels had it that Margaret had persuaded Henry to abdicate in favour of their son, Prospero di Camulio reported, and that the queen had then poisoned her husband ("at least he has known how to die, if he did not know what to do else") in order to marry the Duke of Somerset. Di Camulio was not convinced by this ornately melodramatic tale, or by Henry's alleged remark that the prince "must be the son of the Holy Spirit"—an observation that was, in any case, altogether too sharp to be plausibly the king's—but he thought them worth recounting nonetheless.

Meanwhile, propagandists for the new regime in England were

offering a more direct political commentary on Margaret's activities. "... it is right a great abusion," one poem in circulation in 1462 argued,

> A woman of a land to be regent—
> Queen Margaret I mean, that ever hath meant
> To govern all England with might and power
> And to destroy the right line was her intent ...
> She and her wicked affinity certain
> Intend utterly to destroy this region;
> For with them is but death and destruction,
> Robbery and vengeance with all rigour.

Long-standing insinuations about the queen's conduct could now be spoken openly. Margaret's self-assertion was illegitimate and reprehensible because she was female, and her intentions toward her adopted country were hostile and destructive. This foreign-born queen was damned twice over, by her birth and by her sex; and her plight now, as a refugee dragging her husband and son between the courts of England's old enemies, dependent on their charity and seeking their aid, only served to emphasise those two dangerous failings.

Nor was the new Yorkist regime slow to underline the point. In March 1462 King Edward wrote to the aldermen of London and other sympathisers with deep purses to ask for their help in resisting a fearsome French invasion by which "the people, the name, the tongue and the blood English" would be wiped out—a scheme to which his "adversary Henry" had been moved "by the malicious and subtle suggestion and enticing of the said malicious woman Margaret, his wife." And rumour fed thirstily on rumour until it was reported that Margaret and Henry would return at the head of an army made up, hydralike, of contingents from Brittany, Burgundy, Scotland, and Spain, with fresh waves of hundreds of thousands more troops sent by the kings of France, Aragon, Denmark, Sicily, Navarre, and Portugal waiting to overwhelm England's shores.

Despite all the wild speculation and Margaret's unrelenting diplomatic efforts, her invasion fleet, when it finally landed on the Northumbrian coast in October 1462, numbered only forty-two ships carrying scarcely more than eight hundred men, the meagre reward of her agreement that summer with Louis XI. Northumberland was friendly country, a stronghold of Percy influence where the new king's authority was tenuous in the extreme, and the great fortresses of Bamburgh, Dunstanburgh, and Alnwick quickly opened their gates to the queen's soldiers. But news came that Edward was marching north at the head of a massive army, and Margaret, knowing that her resources were desperately limited, left garrisons to hold the castles as best they could against Yorkist siege and took ship for a storm-battered retreat to Scotland. A further advance from Berwick in the summer of 1463—Margaret, Henry, and their son at the head of troops provided by the Queen Mother of Scotland—was also quickly rebuffed by forceful Yorkist resistance.

It was devastatingly clear now that, however great the ostensible insecurities of King Edward's regime and however certain Margaret was of the justice of her cause, England was not waiting breathlessly for the chance to rise up in support of Henry VI. His shortcomings, after all, were the same as they had ever been, and the sight of his queen in the company of French or Scottish soldiers was hardly likely to convince the apprehensive inhabitants of northern England that their best interests lay in his restoration. By the autumn of 1463 it was also unhappily apparent that Margaret was not orchestrating the diplomacy in which she was so intensely engaged. Instead—and unsurprisingly, given how few moves she had left to make—she found herself a pawn in others' schemes. She had sailed again to France that summer, after the damp squib of the Scottish campaign, in a determined attempt to shore up the support she had been promised by the slippery Louis XI, but during the autumn and winter her understandings with both France and Scotland collapsed as both kingdoms found themselves persuaded of the superior benefits of dealing with Yorkist England.

Pawn or no, Margaret would never give in. She established herself at her father's castle of Koeur near Saint-Mihiel-en-Bar, 150 miles east of Paris, with her ten-year-old son as always at her side, at the head of a small and impoverished court of loyalists. There they continued their efforts, even submerged as they were in the powerful currents of European politics, and despite the desperate paucity of their resources, both financial and diplomatic; one ill-fated attempt to solicit help from Portugal was hampered by the fact that no one among the little band at Koeur could quite remember the name of the Portuguese king. "…but yet the queen sustains us in meat and drink," Margaret's chancellor John Fortescue reported in December 1464—and in purpose, too, he might have added. "Her highness may do no more to us than she does."

But by then, it seemed, they were lost in political darkness. Back in 1463 Margaret had left Henry in the safekeeping of the Scots, but their treaty with Edward at the end of that year had left her husband a fugitive, a pitiful, lost figure moving from refuge to refuge in northern England. There were grounds for hope that sympathy for his cause might run deep enough in the northern counties to keep him safe, and by the spring of 1464 he was still at liberty. Then, however, such loyalist forces as remained under the command of the Duke of Somerset—who had himself despaired of their chances so much that he had flirted with defection to King Edward's court in 1463—sought to ambush the Earl of Warwick's brother John Neville, Lord Montagu, at Hedgeley Moor a few miles from Alnwick in Northumberland. But Somerset's men were caught in their own trap and put to flight after damaging losses, and at Hexham on May 14 Montagu inflicted the final blow. The duke lost his head the day after the battle, and with this forceful, mercurial man—who was still only twenty-eight and had spent his entire adult life fighting to defend Henry's crown—military resistance on English soil was finally spent.

Montagu found Henry's jewelled and gold-embroidered hat at nearby Bywell Castle, but of the king himself there was no sign.

For twelve more months Henry eked out a wretched existence, constantly moving from place to place with two or three devoted attendants. But at last in July 1465 he was captured near a ford across the river Ribble in Lancashire, and taken under guard to London with his feet tied to the stirrups of his horse. He was treated gently, and his life was in no danger, since there was no advantage to Edward in Henry's death while his wife and son remained at liberty. Much better, the king knew, for his rival for the throne to be an imprisoned fool than a boy growing to manhood in France in the care of his indefatigable mother. And, with Henry under lock and key in the Tower and Margaret and their son in impoverished exile, there seemed little need for serious concern about a revival in the fortunes of this Lancastrian dynasty. "No man living can see far ahead at present in the affairs of England," Prospero di Camulio had written in 1461; but four years later it appeared that some predictions, at least, could be made with confidence.

That, however, was to reckon without the Yorkist regime itself, and the capacity for self-destruction it was already beginning to exhibit. Forged in adversity, the alliance between the young king and his Neville cousins was close and intense, but Edward's relationship with his oldest cousin, Warwick, was beginning to show signs of profound strain. Warwick's pivotal role in the Yorkist campaigns that led to Edward's accession had been rewarded with wide-ranging powers: as well as Captain of Calais, he was now Great Chamberlain and Admiral of England, Warden of the Cinque Ports (the key harbours for trade and defence on the southeastern coast), and—together with his brother Montagu—warden of the borderlands with Scotland in the north. The king had leaned heavily on Warwick in the establishment and defence of his new regime, but Warwick had arrogance and ambition exceeding even his undoubted ability and spectacular wealth, and it was becomingly ominously apparent that he saw himself as the power behind the Yorkist throne by right rather than by royal command.

It was a view of his importance that was shared by many observers. "... they say that every day favours the Earl of Warwick, who seems to me to be everything in this kingdom," the Duke of Milan was told in 1461. Three years later, a similar assessment, more archly expressed, was dispatched to Louis XI. In England, wrote the governor of Abbeville, "they have but two rulers—Monsieur de Warwick, and another, whose name I have forgotten." But Edward himself could not afford to accommodate his cousin's pretensions if he were ever to exercise the untrammelled authority of a legitimate king.

The first indication of a rift between the two men had come in the spring of 1464, when Edward was riding north to meet ambassadors from Scotland in the wake of the defeat of the Duke of Somerset at Hedgeley Moor. On his way, he stopped for a night at Stony Stratford in Buckinghamshire and, early the next morning, went out alone for several hours. On his return, he told his servants that he had been hunting, and retired to bed again to sleep. It was not until four months later that Edward revealed the extraordinary truth: on that May morning he had married in secret, without either consulting or informing his lords and advisers.

Still more astonishing was the identity of his bride. The twenty-two-year-old king had taken as his wife Elizabeth Woodville, a widow five years his senior and already the mother of two young sons, whose first husband, a knight named Sir John Grey, had been killed fighting in Margaret's army against the Earl of Warwick at St. Albans in 1461. It seems likely that this match—not so much politically inappropriate as politically inconceivable—was an impetuous choice precipitated by personal, not political, impulses. Elizabeth, it was rapidly noted, had a steely intelligence to match her exquisite beauty, and had allegedly refused the king's advances unless he married her. But when Edward somewhat sheepishly broke the news of his wedding to his council four months later, the announcement had the supplementary effect of manifesting the king's independence from his cousin of Warwick, who was left embarrassingly marooned in the midst of negotiating a match for Edward with the French king's sister-in-law.

Watching hawkishly from her impecunious little court at Koeur, Margaret was quick to see the significance of this enjoyable humiliation for a long-loathed adversary. "The queen, wife of King Henry, has written to the king here that she is advised that King Edward and the Earl of Warwick have come to very great division and war together," the Milanese ambassador reported from France in February 1465. "She begs the king here to be pleased to give her help so that she may be able to recover her kingdom, or at least allow her to receive assistance from the lords of this kingdom who are willing to afford this...." ("Look how proudly she writes," King Louis observed, with a mixture of amusement and admiration.)

She was right that the disintegrating relationship between Edward and Warwick was a disaster waiting to happen for the Yorkist regime, but the opportunity it afforded her was more complex, more costly, and much slower to materialise than she had hoped in the spring of 1465. Warwick would not lightly loosen his grip on power, and Edward had no wish to alienate his cousin completely. The earl therefore put a brave and graceful face on a marriage he had no choice but to accept as a fait accompli, standing godfather in February 1466 to the king's first child, a daughter named Elizabeth after her mother, and presiding at the magnificent feast held to celebrate the emergence from her confinement of the lovely and unsuitable new queen.

By the summer of 1467, however, Edward's increasingly obdurate refusal to follow Warwick's direction in the conduct of his kingdom's diplomacy was played out on an unforgivingly public stage. Warwick, who had been pressing hard for an alliance with France, left England for Rouen in May to take the lead in negotiations with Louis XI. Edward, meanwhile, was inclining increasingly toward a treaty with France's bitter enemy Philippe of Burgundy, ruler of not only the great duchy of Burgundy on France's eastern border but also the rich territories of Flanders and the Netherlands. And while Warwick was away, Edward remained in London to entertain Duke Philippe's illegitimate son at a sumptuous tournament. When Warwick returned home at the end of June with a deputation of French ambassadors swelling his train, it was to find that Edward was already committed to a Burgundian alliance, and that his own brother George Neville, the Archbishop of York, had been summarily dismissed as England's chancellor. Warwick's pointed and public response was to leave court, riding at the head of his entourage for his estates in the north.

For Margaret, this breach between her two chief enemies represented a chink in the Yorkist armour through which she might hope to strike a fatal blow. That her dreams were not entirely misconceived was evident in the French king's willingness for the first time in years to lend support to an attempted invasion. In June 1468 a small Lancastrian force made landfall in north Wales under the command of Jasper Tudor, who was not only a tireless supporter of his half-brother's cause but had become, in exile, a trusted servant of Louis himself. Only a few weeks passed before Tudor's efforts were repelled and Margaret's hopes dashed; but already, in the alienation between Warwick and Edward and the increasingly unsettled state of Yorkist England, Louis's incisive intelligence had seen the possibility of a different—and an entirely extraordinary—way forward.

More than a year earlier, in February 1467, Louis had been involved in a sharp exchange at dinner with Margaret's brother Jean, who held the title of Duke of Calabria as heir to their father, Duke René. The French king had been generous in his commendation of the Earl of Warwick as a friend to France, which had provoked Duke Jean to vituperative anger, the Milanese ambassador reported: "He was a traitor; he would not suffer any good to be said of him; he only studied to deceive; he was the enemy and the cause of the fall of King Henry and his sister the Queen of England. His Majesty would do better to help his sister to recover her kingdom than to favour the Earl of Warwick; and many other inflated and opprobrious words...." Louis, however, persisted in his praise of Warwick, and the conversation became more heated: "The duke said that, as he was so fond of him, he ought to try and restore his sister in that kingdom, when he would make sure of it as much as he was sure at present and even more so."

These were barbed words spoken on impulse, rendered indistinct in the retelling by the repeated, undifferentiated pronouns; but the apparent suggestion that French favour to the Earl of Warwick and support for the restoration of King Henry and Queen Margaret might not, in spite of everything, be mutually incompatible was a seed that began to germinate. Warwick, after all, had the men and money within England to launch a coup from the very heart of the Yorkist establishment, thereby obviating the need for any French commitment to wholesale military intervention across the Channel; and Henry—as represented by Margaret and her son—had the claim to royal authority that would allow the overthrow of Edward and, with him, the destruction of England's threatening alliance with Burgundy. Three months later, this dinner-table banter had made its way onto the diplomatic agenda, within French counsels at least. When another report was dispatched across the Alps to Milan on May 19, the news from the French court centred on the impending arrival of Warwick's embassy at Rouen and the simultaneous rumours of Edward's intention to agree to a treaty with Burgundy. "If this takes place," the Milanese informants observed, "they have talked of treating with the Earl of Warwick to restore King Henry in England, and the ambassador of the old Queen of England is already here."

What is certain is that—eager though Warwick and Margaret both were to cultivate Louis's support—neither was yet prepared to countenance this bizarre proposal. Yes, Warwick was estranged from his king, and disposed, it seemed increasingly likely, to do something about his growing disaffection. But his plans did not involve the woman who had been responsible for the deaths of his father and brother and whom he had for fifteen years regarded as a mortal enemy. And for Margaret the feeling was entirely mutual.

When Warwick finally made his move, therefore, it was on his own terms, while Margaret and her little band of loyalists at Koeur could do no more than follow the bulletins that reached them via sympathetic eyes and ears in England and at the French king's court. The earl had laid his plans well, convincing Edward that, after a winter spent brooding in his northern strongholds, he was willing to accept a role in royal government that was one of influence rather than control, at the king's right hand rather than pulling his strings. So when Edward made his leisurely way north from London in June 1469, he believed he was faced with a little local difficulty, an eruption of discontent in Yorkshire over taxes he had demanded for an invasion of France which had failed to materialise once the money lay safely in the royal coffers. He had reached the midlands when he heard the chilling news that he faced not a peasant rabble but the might of the Earl of Warwick's army.

The shockwaves of this Yorkist rising against the Yorkist king rippled across Europe. It seemed scarcely credible that the two great architects of King Henry's fall might now face each other across the field of battle. And shock, it appeared, might seal King Edward's fate, since his hurried, urgent attempt to muster troops in his own defence was outmanoeuvred by the carefully planned deployment of Warwick's forces. On July 29 the king set out to meet reinforcements who had already, though he did not know it, been defeated. He was captured on the road and taken under armed guard, icy but impotent in his rage, first to his cousin's castle at Warwick, and then north to the Neville fortress at Middleham.

The initial stage of Warwick's plan—to take control of government by seizing control of the king—had worked, so far as it went. What to do next, however, was less straightforward. Efforts to rule in the name of Henry VI, a king manifestly incompetent to govern for himself, had proved self-defeating and unsustainable, as Warwick well knew. Ruling in the name of King Edward, who was all too obviously neither incapable of making his own decisions nor content to be kept under lock and key, turned out to be impossible. As the country erupted into disorder—which Warwick proved unable to contain on the authority of a king whom the earl himself was holding captive—his options appeared unnervingly limited.

One of his less likely supporters probably had a more creative solution in mind. Extraordinarily, Edward's younger brother George,
Duke of Clarence, had joined Warwick in rebellion against the king,
apparently in pique at Edward's refusal to allow him to marry Isabel,
the elder of Warwick's two daughters, who would one day inherit
all their father's vast territorial riches. On July 11, in an act of open
defiance, Clarence had taken Isabel as his wife at his new father-in-
law's stronghold of Calais, but this was only the first of the benefits
he hoped to receive from the new dispensation in English politics.
The twenty-year-old duke was King Edward's next male heir, Queen
Elizabeth having presented her husband with three daughters in the
five years of their marriage so far, and it seems likely that Clarence—
who was vain, vaultingly ambitious, and profoundly immature—
hoped that Warwick's coup would sweep him to the throne in his
brother's place.

The duke's shallow narcissism, however, was reason enough—
especially in the absence of any arguable case for his right to the
crown—to leave Clarence himself as his scheme's only supporter.
And when at the end of August Lancastrian sympathisers in the far
north seized this unanticipated chance to raise the standard of revolt
in King Henry's name, Warwick found that he had no choice but to
release the other imprisoned King of England, since no one would
answer a call for troops on his own questionable authority while
Edward remained in custody. At that point, with Edward free and
the rebels' heads safely on spikes at York, Warwick discovered that,
having taken the royal genie out of the bottle, he could not easily put
it back.

By mid-October the king had made a triumphal entry into
London, to be greeted by the aldermen and guilds of the city decked
out in their best scarlet and blue. Observers on the Continent had
no idea what to think. "...things there are in the air without it being
possible to form a sound judgement as to what the end will be," the
Milanese ambassador reported from Orléans. "Indeed, His Majesty
is puzzled as well as everyone else." But Louis XI was no more or less

confused than Edward's subjects in London. "I know not what to suppose therein," wrote Sir John Paston from his lodgings in the capital. "The king himself has good language of the lords of Clarence, of Warwick...saying they are his best friends. But his household men have other language, so what shall hastily fall I cannot say."

For five months the cousins circled one another, Edward realising, with epic self-restraint, that he could not bring Warwick to heel until he could be sure of military support to match the earl's own, and Warwick trying to gauge the ramifications of his own inadvertent demonstration that, while Edward remained king, he could not govern without him. The truth was that the earl had few options left to consider. He could take Edward's public magnanimity at face value; or he could take the logic of his own self-assertion to its obvious conclusion. He chose the latter. When the king took the field in March 1470 to quash a "popular" revolt in Lincolnshire, it was to discover that the rebels were wearing the liveries of Warwick and Clarence; and interrogations carried out after the battle revealed that Warwick was now prepared to depose Edward and make Clarence England's king.

Unfortunately for these rebel lords, however, no one else among Edward's subjects was inclined to agree. Warwick's determination to secure his "rightful" place in government and Clarence's vapid self-aggrandisement had taken them far beyond any sustainable conception of legitimate authority. When they found that they could command no support against Edward's advancing army, they fled across the Channel, only to discover that Warwick had tried the loyalty of his faithful Calais garrison one step too far. With the harbour at Calais closed to them, his small party was left adrift at sea. The first son of Clarence and his eighteen-year-old duchess was born, and died, on board ship while they contemplated their fate.

It lay in France. Now, at last, was the moment for King Louis's impossible plan to come to fruition. Edward must be removed from the throne, on that Warwick could finally agree. And the only credible contender to replace him—credible, that is, simply by virtue of the fact that he had already worn the crown for forty years—was the man Warwick's father and brother had died to depose. Still, time had passed, and needs must. There was no way for Warwick but forward. And before him stood his oldest and most determined enemy.

Less than two months after Warwick's small flotilla landed at Honfleur in Normandy, Margaret arrived at the royal palace of Amboise in the company of her son, who, at sixteen, had grown to manhood in exile. He (it had been reported in Milan three years before) was as obsessed with military matters as his father was oblivious to them, talking "of nothing but of cutting off heads or making war, as if he had everything in his hands or was the god of battle or the peaceful possessor of that throne." But Margaret still, as she had always done, made strategy in his name. And she faced an unwelcome choice.

For years her tirelessness in pursuing the rights of her husband and son had been matched only by the hopelessness of her task. Now, suddenly, real help and real hope were within her reach. But to grasp them she had to take the hand of a man she hated, despised, and mistrusted. The more cynically political among her entourage, her chancellor John Fortescue among them, were quick to press the unanswerable logic of the case, but Margaret had been sustained through long years of conflict and isolation by her confidence in the justice of her cause and the impiousness of her enemies, and that was not so easily set aside. King Louis devoted all his attention to this newly honoured but frustratingly uncooperative guest, spending long days patiently closeted with the queen, who "until now," the Milanese envoy noted on June 29, "has shown herself very hard and difficult."

The point on which she would make no concessions was the security of her son. He was crucial to this enterprise, the physical embodiment of the Lancastrian claim and the Lancastrian future, but Margaret had not kept him safe all these years to surrender him into Warwick's dubious clutches. Still, Louis's web, drawn about her in the silken surroundings of Amboise, was irresistible. Without Warwick, the Lancastrian future was nothing but a chimera.

And so on July 22 in the great château of Angers beside the river Loire, the queen and the earl came face to face. When Warwick knelt before her to pledge his renewed allegiance, Margaret's revulsion was such that she kept him on his knees for more than fifteen minutes. But the deal was done. Her son, the Prince of Wales, was to marry Anne, the younger of Warwick's two daughters. Warwick was to take ship immediately for England to restore King Henry to his throne. Only then, once the country was secure, would the queen and prince follow, and the prince would then rule as regent on his father's behalf, with his father-in-law, Warwick, at his right hand in this new Lancastrian government.

With autumn approaching, and Louis keen to set his plan in motion and see the back of his English visitors, there was no time to lose. Warwick landed in the west country on September 13, declaring that he had come with the authority of "the most noble princess Margaret, Queen of England" and that of her son, the prince, to rescue "our most dread sovereign lord, King Henry the Sixth" from the hands of "his great rebel and enemy, Edward, late Earl of March, usurper, oppressor and destroyer of our said sovereign lord and of the noble blood of all the realm of England and of the good, true commons of the same." The man who had done more than anyone else to put this "usurper" on the throne could hardly have taken a more breathtakingly brazen stand, but Warwick did not hesitate. While the earl marched north, Margaret and her son and his new young wife remained at Amboise to wait for the good news.

It was startlingly quick to come. Edward was a perceptive politician and a commanding leader, but he could not free his hands from the the coils in which he now laboured. Six months earlier he had decided to restore the earldom of Northumberland to the Percy family, believing that only the Percys had the depth of support in the far north of England to secure the region against Warwick's now-hostile influence. But in doing so he had to take the earldom away from Warwick's brother, Lord Montagu, whose reward it had been for his role in suppressing Lancastrian resistance in the early 1460s, and whose impeccable loyalty had not faltered even over the previous twelve months when it meant taking up arms against his own brother. Now, however, despite Edward's best efforts to compensate him, Montagu was bitterly disillusioned. How much, the king discovered only when Montagu's advancing troops were within ten miles of his encampment at Doncaster. Shaken messengers delivered the devastating news that Montagu had declared for Edward's enemies and intended not to help but to capture him.

The king's forces were scattered and unprepared, caught between the armies of Warwick and Montagu, and Edward knew that this time he would not have long to live if he were captured. He decided to run, making at speed for the Norfolk coast—narrowly escaping the treacherous tides of the Wash as he did so—and from there found ships to take him to the Netherlands to seek asylum and support in the territories of the Duke of Burgundy. Amid riots in London, Queen Elizabeth, who was heavily pregnant, fled into sanctuary at Westminster Abbey with her three small daughters. As Warwick and his army approached the capital, another of the earl's brothers, the Archbishop of York, seized control of the Tower and conveyed the dishevelled figure of Henry VI from his prison quarters to the lavish apartments the queen had so frantically vacated. And on October 13 Warwick himself carried Henry's train when the crown was ceremonially restored to the bemused king in the magnificent surroundings of St. Paul's.

When the news reached Paris, Louis ordered three days of celebration and thanksgiving at which Margaret and her son—now once again accorded the full estate and majesty of a queen and prince—were guests of honour. The speed of Edward's fall had been greater than Margaret could possibly have hoped, and yet she did not hasten to the coast to take ship for England. The queen herself was in no hurry. After all the reverses, all the bloodshed of the last fifteen years, she would not let her son's feet touch English soil until his security was assured.

And security, in England, was still hard to come by. For all the sumptuous ceremony on the streets of London and Paris, the suddenly restored Lancastrian regime was more patchwork and motley than ever. It rested on paper-thin foundations: returning Lancastrian exiles had to swallow their distaste and distrust to follow the lead of a Yorkist renegade, and Warwick found himself unable to restore their titles and estates without depriving those—himself included—who had benefited from their forfeitures. The position of the Duke of Clarence, the other conspicuous Yorkist cuckoo in this supposedly Lancastrian nest, was becoming particularly invidious. Thwarted and purposeless now that Warwick's conversion to the Lancastrian cause had removed all hope that he might wear the crown himself, he was said to be "held in great suspicion, despite, disdain and hatred with all the lords, noblemen, and other, that were adherents and full partakers with Henry." Henry himself was more confused than ever; the absent prince was still an unknown quantity, his unenviable position as Warwick's new protégé scarcely reassuring for his kingdom's future; and no one yet knew how Margaret's forceful will might sit within a government that was already acutely unstable.

King Louis, meanwhile, was equally reluctant to dispatch the queen and prince into Warwick's care until his own conditions were met—in his case, the fulfilment of Warwick's promise that England would join France in war against Burgundy. It took some time, given how full the earl's hands were already, and the difficulties, political and practical, of imposing the pressures and costs of fighting overseas on a deeply troubled country. But at last, in February 1471, Warwick put his seal to a treaty with France and ordered the Calais garrison to move onto the offensive against Burgundy. Margaret and her son were already at the Norman port of Honfleur, and began to make preparations for their final journey to their recaptured kingdom. Still they were delayed. Every time they put to sea, headwinds drove them back to harbour; and it was not until Easter Sunday, April 14, that the weary royal party stepped ashore at Weymouth in Dorset, where horses were waiting to take them fifteen miles north to rest at the Benedictine abbey at Cerne.

There their world fell apart. The same moment that had convinced them to take ship for England—Warwick's declaration of war on Burgundy—had precipitated a chain of events that had undone everything they thought they knew when they left the coast of Normandy. Back in September, Duke Charles of Burgundy had not given an effusive welcome to the bedraggled figure of the fugitive King Edward on his arrival in Holland. Thanks to the treaty the two men had sealed in happier days, Edward was the duke's brother-in-law; but the duke had no wish to be drawn into all-out war on his behalf, and sent conciliatory messages to the new regime in England through the Duke of Exeter, a Lancastrian loyalist whom he had welcomed to his court after finding him begging in the street as a poverty-stricken exile. But this studied neutrality was no longer an option once Warwick had rebuffed his advances and announced England's support for Louis's war. In February 1471 Edward suddenly found that he had Burgundian money and ships at his disposal; and on March 11, after the same agonising wait for favourable winds that was confining Margaret to the harbour at Honfleur, he set sail for England.

His position—at the head of a small band of fewer than a thousand soldiers driven by storms and by Warwick's defences to land not in Norfolk, as he had hoped, but at Ravenspur in Yorkshire— was intensely dangerous. "It is a difficult matter to go out by the door and then wish to enter by the windows," came the laconic comment of the Milanese ambassador at Beauvais. "They think he will leave his skin there." But the fragility of Warwick's regime was equally apparent. The two greatest northern lords, Warwick's brother Montagu and Henry Percy, Montagu's rival for the earldom of Northumberland, made no move to intercept Edward as he marched south into the midlands. At Coventry, the Duke of Clarence threw himself on his brother's mercy, hoping to save his own skin and salvage his political future from the bonfire of his hopes that his alliance with Warwick had now become. The panic-stricken inhabitants of London, terrified by these bewildering reverses, offered no resistance when Edward rode through their city gates on April 11 to reclaim his crown and meet for the first time his baby son, the new heir to the Yorkist throne who had been born in the abbey sanctuary at Westminster five months earlier.

Two days later, Edward's men were once again on the march, moving ten miles north to Barnet to confront the Lancastrian forces commanded by his cousin of Warwick. A decade earlier, it had been Margaret's unexpected retreat from Barnet that had allowed Edward and Warwick, giddy with euphoria, to sweep into the capital together and unopposed to claim the crown for the Yorkist cause. Now all those old certainties were gone. Next morning, in the early hours of Easter Sunday—just as Margaret's shipmaster was setting his course for the approach to Weymouth harbour—Edward gave the order to attack. The two armies fell on one another in the semi-darkness, shrouded by fog as dense as the confusion of enmities and loyalties at play on the field. Four hours later, fifteen hundred men lay slaughtered. Among them were Lord Montagu, his struggle with his conscience laid bare in the Yorkist badge found on his corpse under his Lancastrian armour, and beside him his brother Warwick, the self-appointed arbiter of England's destiny finally brought to earth by a dagger thrust through his open visor.

Margaret, who had made the safety of her son the touchstone of her political strategy for a decade and a half, had brought him to England on the very day, almost at the very hour, when ten months of intricate preparation to secure his future collapsed into dust. She would not weep for Warwick, but she could not contemplate the ruin of their plans without exhaustion and fear. But all was not lost. Her son was still unharmed; their forces were massing in the southwest; and there might yet be great advantage, once Edward was defeated, in the opportunity to rule without Warwick's oppressive and demanding presence. The queen, the prince, and their military lieutenant, yet another faithful Duke of Somerset—Edmund Beaufort, younger brother of the Somerset who had died at Hexham—pressed on northward toward the Severn estuary, intending to cross into Wales to rendezvous with forces under the command of Jasper Tudor. King Edward, meanwhile, mustered fresh troops of his own and set out to intercept them, proclaiming as he went that death would be the penalty for anyone offering help to "Margaret, calling her queen, which is a Frenchwoman born" or her son.

Confusion and panic reigned. "The world is right queasy," wrote Sir John Paston with impressive understatement, having escaped with his life from Warwick's defeated army at Barnet. Sforza de' Bettini, contemplating from his ambassadorial post in France the difficulty of procuring reliable information to send to his master in Milan, was more forthright. "I wish the country and the people were plunged deep in the sea because of their lack of stability," he said feelingly, "for I feel like one going to the torture when I write about them, and no one ever hears twice alike about English affairs." An Italian resident in Bruges had more patience with the unfolding drama: "King Edward has set out with his power to look for the queen and prince, who had landed and gone to the parts of Wales," he told his father. "We have heard nothing since, although we are greedy for news. There are many who consider the queen's prospects favourable, chiefly because of the death of Warwick, because it is reckoned she ought to have many lords in her favour who intended to resist her because they were enemies of Warwick." The truth, whichever way one looked at it, was that everything now depended on this pell-mell chase across country.

The queen and her army pressed on as hard as they could, but Edward had sent messages ahead to warn the keeper of Gloucester Castle to bar the gates against them. Unable to gain access that way to the bridge across the river Severn, they had no choice but to push on to the next crossing-place, a ford at Tewkesbury. Edward's forces, meanwhile, were bearing down on them, a forced march of thirty-six miles on May 3 bringing them within three miles of Margaret's troops. Early the next morning, it became clear that the queen and prince could not reach their reinforcements in Wales without first confronting their enemy. Yet again, Margaret was left to hurry to the safety of a nearby monastery while her army mustered in battle array. For the first time, however, her beloved son's fate was out of her hands. The seventeen-year-old prince commanded the centre of the Lancastrian army; at last he could put to use the years of military training at Koeur. Today, he would either win his father's crown, or lose his life.

The end, when it came, was quick. First Edward's soldiers broke the Lancastrian vanguard under the Duke of Somerset, who turned and fled to Tewkesbury's great abbey, though sanctuary, in the end, could not save him. And then, amid the carnage of that rout, Edward himself led an assault on the prince's position. Margaret's son died where he fell. The whereabouts of the queen herself were not discovered for three more days, but she did not try to run. She had nowhere to go, and no one left to fight for. She was brought to Edward at Coventry, once her citadel, now a place of humiliation and grief. And when the victorious king made his triumphant entry into London, with trumpets sounding and his loyal lords about him, there was a chariot at the back of the procession in which the queen sat, straight-backed and blank-faced, staring at nothing.

The day after their arrival in the capital, the body of Henry VI was brought out of the Tower. The Londoners were told that their former king had died of "pure displeasure and melancholy" at news of his son's death and the destruction of his cause, but few doubted that his life had been ended on King Edward's orders. There was no advantage, now, in keeping alive a Lancastrian puppet when the whole Lancastrian line could be extinguished. For one night, his corpse was displayed to public view on a bier at St. Paul's, its face uncovered, to forestall seditious rumours of his survival. The next day, it was placed on a barge and rowed twenty miles upriver for burial at the ancient abbey of Chertsey. "And so no one from that stock remained among the living who could claim the crown," one contemporary solemnly noted.

Margaret was forty-one years old, and her life was over. For Edward, and for Louis of France and Charles of Burgundy, manoeu-

vring furiously for advantage in this changed political world, she was
an irrelevance. In June rumours reached France that Margaret, too,
had been assassinated, but Edward was by nature magnanimous
rather than vindictive, and he had no need to pay her the political
compliment of a violent death. Instead she remained a prisoner, at
first in apartments at Windsor Castle and the Tower of London, and
later—the king extending his easy generosity even to this bitterest of
enemies—at Wallingford Castle forty miles west of London, in the
gentler custody of her old friend Alice Chaucer, the dowager Duchess of Suffolk, who had been kind to her when she first left her family
behind to embark on her future as England's queen.

She had been a captive for four years when, in 1475, her fate constituted one of the detailed provisions of a peace treaty agreed at Pic-
quigny between Edward and Louis. By its terms she renounced any
claim she might notionally still have to rights or properties in England, and the French king agreed to ransom her person for a sum of
£10,000. Free, but penniless and purposeless, she went to live quietly
in her father's lands of Anjou. She was at the château of Dampierre,
overlooking the broad meanderings of the Seine, when she fell ill in
the summer heat of 1482. She died on August 25, her end scarcely
noticed by the crowned heads of Europe, and was buried beside her
father beneath the soaring arches of the cathedral at Angers.

Margaret was a woman of will and wit—"more wittier than the
king," noted one chronicler, although that was a backhanded tribute
given the manifest limitations of her foolish, fragile husband. Denied
the formal regency that she might have enjoyed in her French homeland, all her fierce energy was devoted to the task of impersonating,
of reconstituting by other means, the royal will that her husband
was incapable of providing. The magnitude of her role was evident
to those who watched her at work: for Prospero di Camulio in 1461,
for example, the battle of Wakefield was simply "the battle which the
Queen of England fought against the late Duke of York"—a description remarkable in its directness given that Margaret could not, and
did not, set foot on the field of war.

But the magnitude of her role was its own undoing. In stepping forward to champion her husband's cause, she exposed the composite authority she had constructed in his name to public view, and herself to vitriolic disapproval. The harder she fought—and fight hard she did, with an implacable and partisan tenacity—the more obvious were the tensions created by a French queen acting in the place of an incompetent English king. And, little by little, the power she could command fragmented and crumbled away. As an Italian in London noted as the conflict came to its height in 1461, "whoever conquers, the crown of England loses, which is a very great pity...."

That much became evident just eight months after her death. Edward's conquering regime was carefully constructed and authoritatively led, but its roots were not yet deep. In April 1483, shockingly and suddenly, he succumbed to a stroke at the age of just forty, a golden boy bloated into dissolution; and his government collapsed into chaos. The twelve-year-old heir to the throne—the baby boy born to Edward and Elizabeth in the Westminster sanctuary— was deposed and murdered by Edward's youngest brother and most trusted lieutenant, Richard of Gloucester. And the usurpation of Richard III, as the new king called himself, opened the door to a penniless exile named Henry Tudor, Jasper Tudor's nephew, whose mother, Margaret, was the last of Henry VI's Beaufort cousins—a tenuous connection to the royal line, but enough, amid the trauma of 1485, to rally an army. That summer Richard III lost his crown and his life at Bosworth Field, and Henry Tudor took his place as King Henry VII. It was the last act of the drama which had consumed Margaret's life.

PART VI

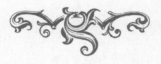

NEW BEGINNINGS

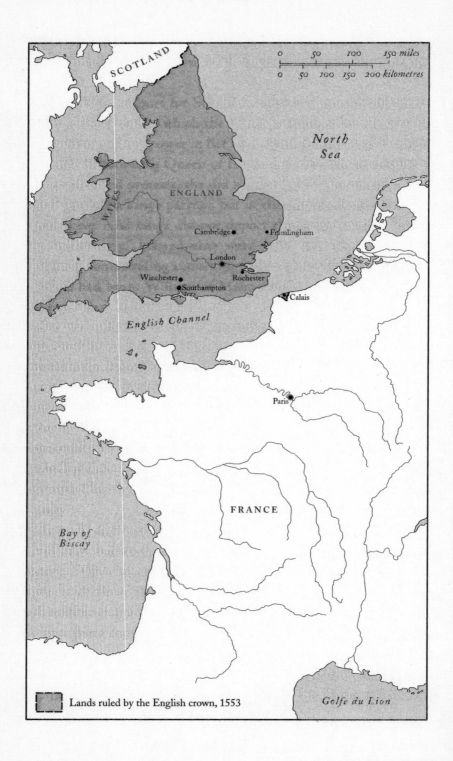

SCOTLAND

North
Sea

ENGLAND

WALES

Cambridge●   ●Framlingham

London
●

Winchester●   ●Rochester
●Southampton

✠Calais

English Channel

Paris
●

FRANCE

Bay of
Biscay

Golfe du Lion

Lands ruled by the English crown, 1553

0   50   100   150 miles

0   50   100   150   200 kilometres

NINETEEN

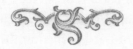

July 6, 1553:
Long Live the Queen

The boy in the bed lay at peace, his breathing stilled, his struggle finished at last. But the men who looked down at the disfigured body knew that theirs had just begun. Now they faced the battle to control the accession of England's first reigning queen.

Their initial task was to stop the news of what had happened from spreading beyond the walls of the bedchamber until the levers of power had been comprehensively secured. The same tactic had been adopted six years earlier when Edward VI's father died; then, deliveries of royal meals had continued for three days to the heavily guarded door behind which lay Henry VIII's monumental corpse, until the person of the new king could be united with his principal councillors and the governmental machine at their disposal to proclaim the start of the new reign as a seamless fait accompli.

In 1553, just as in 1547, the councillors were the strategic architects of the change of regime. The difference now was that the new monarch was their puppet not because he was a child, but because she was a woman: Jane Grey, the chosen vessel through whom Edward's plan for a legitimate, Protestant, and male succession would ultimately be achieved, and through whom the Duke of Northumberland's control of government would meanwhile be upheld. On Sunday, July 9, with the cordon of secrecy still in place around the dead king's darkened chamber at Greenwich, Jane received an enigmatic summons to Syon House, Northumberland's lavish home ten miles west of the capital, "to receive that which had been ordered by the king." On her arrival the bewildered girl was met by the duke and other members of the Privy Council who knelt before her, offering their allegiance and their service to the new Queen of England.

The next day, brightly dressed heralds at last appeared on London's streets to inform Edward's subjects that their king was dead and to proclaim the accession of Queen Jane. As they did so, a flotilla of barges carried the young queen and her hastily assembled royal entourage downriver to the Tower, where she made a ceremonial entry into the monarch's apartments. England's new ruler was a short and slender fifteen-year-old, with auburn hair and freckles powdering her pale complexion, but on this summer afternoon her slight frame was overwhelmed by the trappings of her royal destiny—a heavy gown of green velvet embroidered with gold, a white headdress weighted with jewels, and cumbersome wooden platforms strapped onto her small feet to make her more easily visible to her new subjects.

So began the reign of Queen Jane. Already, however, there were signs that this female repository of royal power might be less passively accommodating than Northumberland had hoped. Jane's discomfort with her new role was more than superficial. She was sharply intelligent and stubbornly principled, and if the duke had assumed that she would be a malleable tool of her cousin's design for the succession, he had begun to be disabused of that presumption from the moment the plan was put into action. At Syon the previous day, her first reaction to the news of Edward's death and her own elevation to his throne had been a storm of grief for her cousin; her second was horror. "The crown is not my right and pleases me not," one of the councillors reported her saying. "The Lady Mary"—the elder of Edward's two sisters—"is the rightful heir." It took all the pressure that Northumberland, her parents, and her new husband, the duke's son Guildford, could muster before she was induced to accept her accession as the will of her Protestant God.

But acquiescence in this did not mean acquiescence in everything. The royal treasures held in the Tower included the crown itself, which the Lord Treasurer attempted to persuade her to try on, saying as he did so, Jane later recounted, that "another also should be made, to crown my husband." The status of a reigning queen's husband was an issue without precedent in England, but special envoys sent by the Holy Roman Emperor Charles V, for example, took it for granted that the accession of Queen Jane Grey meant the simultaneous elevation of King Guildford Dudley. ("...the new king and queen are to be proclaimed this very day," they reported on July 10, before seeking advice from their imperial master about what they should do if they were offered an audience by the council and "the new king.") Jane, however, had other ideas. She had been prevailed upon to accept, reluctantly, that the crown might be hers, but she was certain that it was not her husband's. She would make him a duke, she told her councillors, but not king—a stand which precipitated a furious row with the Duke and Duchess of Northumberland and with eighteen-year-old Guildford himself, who persisted in conducting himself with elaborate ceremonial of a kind that suggested he, too, was England's monarch.

Northumberland had expected a puppet, and was finding instead that Jane was prepared to flex her royal muscles. Jane herself, meanwhile, was wrestling (she later wrote) with "a troubled mind,...infinite grief and displeasure of heart," as she struggled to cope with the shock of a situation in which her father-in-law, her parents, and her husband were foisting royal power upon her, and simultaneously seeking to prevent her from exercising it. Clearly, there were battles ahead. For the moment, however, they would have to wait, overtaken as they rapidly were by battles at hand, since the implementation of Edward's "device for the succession" was not proceeding as smoothly as it might have seemed from within the Tower's royal apartments.

The first indication that all was not well was the silence on London's streets when Jane's queenship was declared. No bells were rung, no bonfires lit, no caps flung into the air. Instead, the news was met with a mixture of puzzlement and resentment under a muffling blanket of fear. The proclamation read out by the heralds that day had detained its listeners for an unusually long time, in part because of the need to explain exactly who the new queen was. If the idea that she might inherit the throne had come as a shock to Jane herself, it was a bolt from the blue for the people who were now required to accept her as their monarch. Emperor Charles V had to ask his envoys to compile a family tree to explain the merits or otherwise of Jane's claim; how much more at sea were her new subjects as they watched their young queen enter the Tower, her long train carried, confusingly, by the mother through whom her right to the crown was said to have come.

Puzzlement, then, at who Jane was, and resentment at who she was not—this being the second issue on which the heralds found themselves expounding at length. The circumstances which had persuaded Edward of her virtues as a candidate for his throne had much less purchase on the hearts and minds of his subjects. Jane's commitment to the evangelical faith which Edward was so desperate to see nurtured and protected in his realm could not be doubted, but few of England's people were as deeply convinced as their king of the doctrinal reformation over which he had presided, and in England's parishes there remained much support still for the old ways of prayer and worship that had been so suddenly prohibited. Not many were prepared to emulate the rebels who had taken up arms for their beliefs in the west country in 1549, but few would see the reformed religion as reason enough to overturn the legitimate line of the royal succession.

What, though, was that legitimate line? The births of Edward's half-sisters, Mary and Elizabeth, had been a matter of public controversy for two decades. There could be no doubt, however, that they were the only surviving children of Henry VIII, and they had been named as his heirs, along with Edward himself, both by parliamentary statute and in the old king's will. Jane's claim, by comparison, seemed a work of invention. No grounds, after all, had been advanced to justify the decision that her right should precede that of her mother. And if the terms of the Act of Succession of 1544 and Henry's will were to be abandoned in order to disinherit Mary and Elizabeth, then—as the imperial envoys noted in some alarm—there were good grounds for arguing that the next heir was not Jane Grey but Mary Stuart, Queen of Scots and Dauphine of France, the granddaughter of Henry's elder sister rather than his younger.

Nevertheless, it was Mary Tudor, daughter of Henry VIII and his first, rejected wife, Katherine of Aragon, who was popularly understood to stand next in line to her brother's throne. Mary had been publicly accepted as heir presumptive to her father during the happy years of her childhood and adolescence, before the catastrophic collapse of her parents' marriage; and, once her brother had become king, she was recognised by politicians and people alike as his heir unless or until he had offspring of his own. Just five months before his death she had been received at court with deferential magnificence, and as recently as April the Duke of Northumberland had offered heraldic recognition of her status as "the second person in the realm" when he "sent her her full arms as Princess of England," the imperial ambassador Jehan Scheyfve reported, "as she used to bear them in the lifetime of her father the late king."

It had been Mary's sex, of course, that had compromised her standing as his heir in her father's eyes, but, given the nature of the improvisation to which Edward had had to commit himself in order to establish his line of Protestant kings, the fact that she was female could hardly be used against her by supporters of Queen Jane. Great play was, however, made of the possibility that Mary might marry "any stranger born out of this realm," as the proclamation of Jane's accession declared, who might then seek "to have the laws and customs of his or their own native country or countries to be practised and put in use within this realm, rather than the laws, statutes and customs here of long time used, whereupon the title of inheritance of all and singular the subjects of this realm do depend, to the peril of conscience and the utter subversion of the common weal of this realm." (Or, as the imperial envoys more laconically put it, "it was stated that the Lady Mary might marry a foreigner and thus stir up trouble in the kingdom and introduce a foreign government.") But it was an argument that seemed unlikely to deal a fatal blow to Mary's claims in the eyes of her prospective subjects. Which, after all, was worse: this hypothetical apocalypse, or the alarming fact that Jane was already married to Guildford Dudley? Dudley was an Englishman, but one through whom the rule of his father, Northumberland—a man much feared and not at all loved by the English people—would, disturbingly, become dynastic rather than merely ministerial.

Neither religion, nor birth, nor the probable direction of government policy therefore provided conclusive reason for the subjects of the English crown to repudiate Mary's right to wear it as her brother's heir. And, as a result, the process of putting his "device" into effect was fraught with tension and danger. That much was clear from the fact that, despite Northumberland's frantic efforts, it proved impossible to contain the seeping of information from inside the royal household about Edward's intentions and his state of health. Jane herself was not aware of her cousin's plans for her future until July 9, three days after his death—although she later said that she had been forewarned by her mother-in-law and dismissed the information as fantastical nonsense—but Ambassador Scheyfve, a watchful presence on the margins of the court, had already learned the details of Edward's "device" five days earlier. When three more imperial envoys arrived to join Scheyfve in London on July 6, they immediately heard the embargoed news that Edward had died that day, despite the council's attempts to persuade them otherwise. ("Sire, the King of England's death is certain," they wrote urgently to the emperor the following morning, adding that, "in answer to our demand for audience, the council have sent to tell us that they will speak to the king about it, fix a time according to his majesty's condition, and let us know some time tomorrow.")

And by then, most damagingly of all for Northumberland and his colleagues, too much information had already reached Mary, the heir they were trying to displace. A tense game of brinkmanship between council and princess had been in play in the last weeks of Edward's illness. Mary had moved to Hunsdon, the Hertfordshire manor that was her closest home to London, in the effort to keep abreast of the rumours emanating from her brother's bedside. She needed to be poised to assert herself as England's queen the moment confirmation came that the king was dead—but not an instant sooner, for fear that she might be denounced as a traitor should she claim the throne before it was vacant. Meanwhile, timing was of the essence, too, for Northumberland: he needed Mary securely under lock and key, but that had to be achieved quietly and calmly, without protest or incident that might precipitate any general convulsion in his current control or his future plans. Much depended on exactly how long the dying boy in the Greenwich bed might cling to life, but the prognostications of his doctors were more art than science, and this calculation—like all the others Northumberland was making—was a finely calibrated risk.

At last, in the first week of July, the duke summoned the princess to her brother's deathbed, sending a message laced with duplicitous reassurance, it seems, that her presence in London was required because she was his heir. By then, however, the sinister whispers escaping from Greenwich's walls had alerted Mary to the danger in which she stood. "She was warned by a friend yesterday that she had better go further away into the country," ran Scheyfve's encrypted report on July 4; and three days later, on the morning after the king's death, when Northumberland finally sent his son Robert Dudley with three hundred armed men to seize Mary at Hunsdon, it was to find the great house empty and his quarry long gone on the dusty road into Norfolk.

At the first hurdle, then, Northumberland's coup had faltered. But the duke saw no reason yet for serious alarm. Mary, after all, was a woman alone. Certainly, she had servants and counsellors within her household and tenants on her estates, but the formidable mechanisms of the Tudor state—the great bureaucracy of government directed by the powerful men of the Privy Council, and the consequent capacity to mobilise strong arms holding stronger weapons—lay under the duke's command. Even Mary's retreat in the direction of the East Anglian coast seemed, in the light of her recent history, to offer Northumberland encouragement as much as disquiet. The princess had lived her entire adult life under intense pressure, both political and emotional, and just three years earlier, as her brother's attempt to force her to give up the Catholic mass began to intensify, she had shown signs of buckling under the strain. In the spring of 1550, exhausted by the confrontation in which she was currently embroiled and frightened by the uncertainty of her future as the Catholic heir to a Protestant king, she had sent secretly to her cousin, the emperor, asking for rescue. Imperial warships appeared off the coast of Essex, waiting to spirit her away; but Mary havered in frantic indecision—according to the imperial secretary, repeatedly asking the agonised question "What will become of me?"—before baulking at the last minute at the tantalising but irreversible prospect of escape.

For Northumberland, it was a heartening precedent: either vacillation or flight on Mary's part would serve his purposes well. And he was not alone in his assessment of the weakness of the princess's position. The French ambassador, Antoine de Noailles, had no hesitation in passing on to his royal master the duke's private assurance "that they had provided so well against the Lady Mary's ever attaining the succession, and that all the lords of the council were so well united, that there is no need for you, Sire, to enter into any doubt on this score." That was, of course, exactly what Henri II wanted to hear, given how little he wished to see the English throne taken by the cousin of his enemy Charles V, and given, too, the enticing prospect that he might press the rival claim of his daughter-in-law Mary Stuart once Mary Tudor was out of the way.

More disturbing for Mary herself was the fact that her own allies were equally unconvinced of her chances of upholding her rights as her brother's heir. "...we see small likelihood of being able to withstand the duke's designs," reported the imperial envoys on the morning after Edward's death. "...it now seems that the Lady Mary's person will be in danger, and her promotion to the crown so difficult as to be well-nigh impossible in the absence of a force large enough to counterbalance that of her enemies.... All the forces of the country are in the duke's hands, and my lady has no hope of raising enough men to face him, nor means of assisting those who may espouse her cause."

Mary, then, was being written off. As a woman, she could not fight for her rights at the head of her own troops. She was also—in a pattern of political interaction that her forebear Matilda would have recognised only too well—declining to follow advice that was offered to her, and finding that her judgement was questioned as a result. Mary had come to the conclusion, Scheyfve and his colleagues told the emperor, that she should proclaim herself queen as soon as Edward's death was confirmed. This was necessary, she believed, partly to stake her claim in so immediate and public a manner that it could not be suppressed without challenge, and partly to raise a standard around which all those who supported her or opposed Northumberland could rally. "My lady has firmly made up her mind that she must act in this manner, and that otherwise she will fall into still greater danger and lose all hope of coming to the throne," the envoys wrote with regretful disapproval, and more than a hint of condescension. "We consider this resolution strange, full of difficulties and danger...." Not only were the military cards stacked high against her, but her plan was hopelessly misconceived because the English would not offer spontaneous support for the claim of a Catholic, "and to proclaim herself without hope of immediate success would only jeopardise those chances that remain to her...."

On this if on nothing else, had they but known it, the governments of England, France, and the Empire were agreed. Mary could not hope to prevail without the backing of imperial troops. Foreign intervention of that kind would compromise her support within England, and in any case (as imperial politicians, but not French or English, were aware), it would not come, because Charles V's military machine was already overcommitted in his Continental campaigns against Henri II. ("Our hands are full with France," he wrote wearily.) His envoys in England were therefore told to do what they could to safeguard the princess's person rather than to press her claim at all costs. The consensus of heavyweight opinion was overwhelming: the first woman to test the bounds of female sovereignty in England would be the reluctant fifteen-year-old in a gilded cage at the Tower, not the thirty-seven-year-old princess contemplating her limited options from the midst of the East Anglian countryside.

That this was a misjudgement on an extravagant scale began to become apparent on the very day Jane was proclaimed queen. That afternoon, an elderly servant of Mary's was ushered into the council chamber, grey with tiredness after the long ride from Norfolk, to present a letter from his lady declaring that the crown was hers and demanding that the council acknowledge her as queen. Northumberland, it was suddenly clear, had failed to remember that the frightened princess who had almost abandoned her country in 1550 was also the resolute woman who had ridden into London eight months later with a train of 130 velvet-clad gentlemen and ladies, every one of them holding a set of rosary beads in ostentatious defiance of her brother's religious laws. And the imperial ambassadors—so confident in the superiority of their diplomatic insight—had utterly misread the dynamics of English politics, of which Mary now showed her mastery. She was the daughter of Henry VIII, the father she idolised despite the abuse and humiliation he had heaped upon her, and she was the rightful heir to her brother's throne. She was not seeking, as the council had assumed she would, "either to flee the realm or to abide there some foreign power." Instead, with the able support of her household officers, she sent letters and messengers flying along the roads of Norfolk and Suffolk and westward into the midlands and the Thames Valley to summon her subjects to their queen's defence.

They answered her call in the thousands. Support for her cause was by no means unanimous, but in eastern England there were many landowners whose sympathies lay with the old religion, who were convinced of her claim to the throne, and who had looked to Mary as the greatest magnate of their region ever since she had been granted estates forfeited by the disgraced Duke of Norfolk six years earlier. As these gentlemen gathered their armed tenants in the deer park of Mary's great moated castle at Framlingham in Suffolk—to which she moved for her muster because its defences were still as formidable as when it was built four hundred years earlier—their confidence in the justice of their mission was palpable.

The same could not be said of their opponents. The Duke of Northumberland was an able man, a shrewd politician, and an experienced soldier, but he was hated by many, and loved by no one other than his wife. Meanwhile, Queen Jane had had no chance to inspire any personal loyalty in the handful of days since she had been so dramatically plucked from aristocratic obscurity. Supporters of the reformed religion, who might have backed the new regime, were torn between fear of Mary's allegiance to Rome and their own loyalty to the lineage of Henry VIII. And in these circumstances—where one side was sustained by deep convictions, both political and religious, and propelled by spontaneous momentum, while the other relied on the conduct of business as usual in the service of radical change imposed entirely from above—the structures of governmental control on which Northumberland's power depended began to disintegrate.

The duke's son, Robert Dudley, was already in the field with three hundred men, pursuing Mary into East Anglia; magistrates and county lieutenants had been warned by Privy Council letters to resist her attempts to "stir and provoke the common people of this realm to rebellion"; and six warships had moved out of the Thames to lie off the Suffolk coast, to preempt any attempt at escape by the princess or invasion by the Empire. But Mary's unexpected resistance meant that more concerted action was needed. Men, horses, and artillery were hastily mustered into an army that marched out of London on Friday, July 12, under the command of the Duke of Northumberland himself, England's finest general, confident still that his soldiers and cannon, backed by the unanimous will of the council, would defeat a challenge for which not a single one of the kingdom's most powerful men had declared his support.

Six days later, as Northumberland approached at last within twenty-five miles of Framlingham, he learned with incredulous horror what lay ahead of him. Mary's forces now counted ten thousand men and rising, more than three times the number of the duke's troops. Still worse was the news of his warships. Contrary winds had forced them into the coast, where Mary's agents had made contact and the crews had defected, putting ashore great guns that were now ranged in defence of her fortress at Framlingham. And when Northumberland retreated to Cambridge in shock at the overwhelming strength of his enemy's position, it was to discover that in his absence his fellow councillors in London had collapsed into panic and recrimination.

Faced with news of the princess's growing power in East Anglia, and increasing resistance, too, in the shires to the west of the capital, the great lords of the council had faced an unpalatable choice: risk everything by following Northumberland onto the battlefield, or attempt to save their skins by declaring for Mary. In the early morning of Wednesday, July 19, their allegiance to Jane was still holding, overwrought and desperately brittle though it now clearly was. By midday, it had broken. A deputation was dispatched to tell the emperor's envoys that, although it had been reported that the whole council had endorsed King Edward's plans for the succession, in fact "only three or four of them had given their willing assent and the rest had been compelled and treated almost as if they were prisoners...." These mistreated unfortunates, now liberated from Northumberland's baleful influence—a good story if they could make it stick—then gathered with the mayor and aldermen at Cheapside in the heart of the capital to proclaim Mary queen.

Jane's proclamation had been greeted with silence. A lone voice daring to speak "certain words of Queen Mary, that she had the right title," had been quickly suppressed, its wretched owner set in the pillory the next morning with his ears sliced off. But now the streets were packed with people brought running by the rumours that were racing through the city. The new proclamation began, and when they heard the name "Mary," the crowd erupted, drowning out everything that followed in a wild explosion of joy and overwhelming relief. "And there was *Te Deum Laudamus*"—the great hymn of thanks for deliverance from danger—"with song and the organs playing and all the bells ringing...," a Londoner named Henry Machyn noted in his diary, "and bonfires and tables in every street, and wine and beer and all, and every street full of bonfires." "Men ran hither and thither," an Italian eyewitness reported in amazement, "bonnets flew into the air, shouts rose higher than the stars, fires were lit on all sides, and all the bells were set to pealing, and from a distance the earth must have looked like Mount Etna." And while the celebrations raged, nervous messengers from the council rode through the night to Framlingham to offer their allegiance and their contrition to Queen Mary.

Just as Edward II and Hugh Despenser had discovered more than two centuries earlier, the imposing edifice of royal government could prove utterly, shockingly insubstantial if the authority it embodied lost its claim to legitimacy. And the issue of legitimacy on this delirious summer night was summed up in Henry Machyn's description of its royal protagonists. Jane, he explained, was "daughter of the Duke of Suffolk," but Mary was "sister of the late king Edward VI and daughter unto the noble king Henry VIII." The Duke of Suffolk himself—as desperate now for his own salvation as he had once been for his daughter's advancement—tore down the cloth of estate that signalled Jane's regal status from above her chair where she sat at dinner in the Tower, saying (the imperial ambassadors were told) "that it was not for her to use it, for her position permitted her not to do so." It was with gratitude that the girl who had reigned for just thirteen days—or nine since her public proclamation—relinquished a crown that she had always believed was Mary's by right. When the news reached Cambridge, the Duke of Northumberland stood in the market square and proclaimed Mary's accession, throwing his hat in the air and, one of his companions later recalled, "so laughed that the tears ran down his cheeks for grief."

Mary's triumph was complete. On August 3, at the head of an imposingly magnificent cavalcade, she rode at last into her cheering capital, a small figure regally dressed in purple velvet and satin "all thick set with goldsmith's work and great pearls." Three weeks later great crowds again thronged the streets of the city, this time to watch Northumberland lose his head on Tower Hill. On the eve of his execution, the duke had renounced the Protestantism for which he had fought, apparently in a vain bid to prove his loyalty and save his life. ("I pray God I, nor no friend of mine, die so," was Jane Grey's shocked response.) Jane herself—*cette pauvre reine*," as the French ambassador called her, "that poor queen"—had returned with relief to her books and the muted clothes recommended by her own unbending faith. She remained in the Tower, condemned as a traitor for accepting the crown, but Mary saw her as a wronged innocent and, as the new imperial ambassador, Simon Renard, reported in frustration, "could not be induced to consent that she should die."

Her enemies thus defeated, it was Mary Tudor who faced the reality—rather than simply, as Northumberland had planned for Jane, the rhetoric—of governing England as its queen. Jane had reigned, fleetingly and powerlessly, her crown acquired only by reluctant submission to the will of others. Mary, meanwhile, had stood alone to resist the plans of the greatest men in the realm. Now she would rule. Her right to wear the crown as her father's daughter and heir had been acclaimed with deep and genuine conviction after the trauma of that July fortnight. But in the exercise of her royal power, the challenges she faced had barely begun.

TWENTY

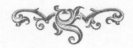

Not of Ladies' Capacity

nlike that of Matilda four hundred years earlier, the legitimacy of Mary's cause had won overwhelming recognition, confronted as she was with a rival who had no advantage of sex or consecration to compete with her lineal right. Like Matilda, however—and Eleanor, Isabella, and Margaret after her—Mary was faced with assumptions embedded deep within the political culture over which she now presided about the conditional nature of female authority and the limitations of female capabilities.

The queen was "of a sex which cannot becomingly take more than a moderate part" in government and public business, the Venetian ambassador to England, Giovanni Michieli, remarked in passing to the doge and senate in 1557. Four years earlier, before he learned of the "device" by which Northumberland's regime planned to place Jane Grey on the throne, "the inferiority of the female sex" had also occurred to Ambassador Scheyfve as one of the "other points which they may raise" to discount Mary as her brother's heir. Even once she had proved the emperor's envoys profoundly wrong in their reading of the crisis and the potential of her leadership, Charles V himself had no doubt, when he wrote to proffer advice three days into her reign, of the constraints which her sex would impose on her rule. "Let her be in all things what she ought to be: a good Englishwoman, and avoid giving the impression that she desires to act on her own authority, letting it be seen that she wishes to have the assistance and consent of the foremost men of the land... You will also point out to her that it will be necessary, in order to be supported in the labour of governing and assisted in matters that are not of ladies' capacity, that she soon contract matrimony with the person who shall appear to her most fit from the above point of view."

Just as in 1141, when Matilda stood on the brink of power, the contradictions implicit in the prospect of a female monarch were precipitated into the open by Mary's extraordinary and unfamiliar situation. No king could have tolerated the proposition that he should not "act on his own authority." For Mary's father, Henry VIII, just as much as for Matilda's father, Henry I, that function—which was simultaneously a right and a responsibility—was the essence of his power. Just a century earlier, the intractable challenges with which Margaret of Anjou had wrestled on behalf of her inert husband had demonstrated how profoundly destructive a king who failed to act on his own authority could be. Yet Mary was being told that for her to do so as queen would be incompatible with being a "good Englishwoman." There are irresistible echoes here of the chronicler's outrage that Matilda should dare, with an "arrogant demeanour instead of the modest gait and bearing proper to the gentle sex," to arrange "everything as she herself thought fit and according to her own arbitrary will."

Mary's situation, however, was significantly different from that of her forebear, and it made possible a significantly different response. Matilda's victory over her rival had been partial and provisional; Mary's was complete. Matilda had had to attempt to call her author-

ity into being through the process of exercising it; Mary could bide
her time before she revealed her hand. Mary, then, had no immediate
need to challenge assumptions on the part of the emperor or her own
subjects that she would need assistance in "matters that are not of
ladies' capacity." She offered no resistance to the suggestion that her
rule would require a husband's help, and three days before her coronation she made a remarkable appeal to the members of her council.
Sinking to her knees before the astonished assembly, she spoke at
length of the providential circumstances of her accession, the duties
of kings and queens, and her determination to fulfil her responsibilities to the glory of God and the benefit of her people. Then she addressed her councillors directly. "She had entrusted her affairs and
person, she said, to them, and wished to adjure them to do their duty
as they were bound by their oaths . . . Her councillors were so deeply
moved that not a single one refrained from tears," the imperial ambassadors reported. "No one knew how to answer, amazed as they
all were by this humble and lowly discourse, so unlike anything ever
heard before in England, and by the queen's great goodness and integrity."

It is hard to know, without access to Mary's thoughts as well as
her words, how much of this public performance was impelled by
conviction and how much by strategy. Certainly, she was intelligent
and highly educated, fluent in four languages and competent in a
fifth, with a "facility and quickness of understanding," the Venetian
ambassador noted with generous condescension, "which compre-
hends whatever is intelligible to others, even to those who are not of
her own sex—a marvellous gift for a woman." At the same time, she
was by temperament profoundly orthodox in ways that went further
than her deeply felt faith, sustained as she had been through twenty
years of uncertainty and suffering by her mother's example of the
female virtues of constancy, piety, duty, and patience.

But whether or not Mary genuinely believed that, as a woman,
she would require help in governing her kingdom, it was unarguably
true, first, that she needed to find a way of managing a council com-

posed of a dangerously unstable mix of her own loyal Catholic servants and those experienced Protestant politicians who had so narrowly extricated themselves from Jane Grey's short-lived regime. As the emperor's ambassadors shrewdly noted, the unaccustomed sight of their queen on her knees appealing for their assistance and their loyalty might well have encouraged some of her lords and ministers to conclude that she was acting out of "timidity and fear"; "but, however that may be," they went on, "it has certainly softened several hearts and turned them away from thoughts of an evil and suspicious nature." In the absence of a male rival embodying a more conventionally commanding model of kingship, Mary was discovering that female "frailties" could on occasion be deployed to politically disarming effect.

The second inescapable truth was that the queen did require a husband—and quickly—if she were to give birth to an heir. As things stood, by her father's will and the act of parliament that had vindicated her own accession to the throne, her next heir was her half-sister Elizabeth. In Mary's eyes, however, Elizabeth was illegitimate, born to Anne Boleyn before the death of Katherine of Aragon, Mary's adored mother and Henry VIII's rightful wife. Elizabeth was also a Protestant, and her current gestures toward Catholicism bore the unmistakable stamp of the princess's political agility rather than any spiritual revelation. For the moment the queen was prepared to treat her sister with gracious magnanimity, but it was an intolerable prospect that her own death should deliver England into heresy and the crown to Anne Boleyn's bastard. A husband, therefore, was a necessity, if not quite for the reasons the emperor had adduced, and, at thirty-seven, Mary had no time to lose.

With her council in harness and the search for a husband in train, the queen's rule had begun—and despite her imperial cousin's advice, the substance, rather than the decorously feminine style, of her decision making revealed Mary's determination that she would indeed "act on her own authority." The first step was her coronation, the moment when God's vindication of her sovereignty was given sacra-

mental form. It was a matter for regret that the parliamentary statute by which her father had declared Mary illegitimate could not be
repealed before this sacred ritual took place, but she could allow no
suggestion that her title to the throne depended on parliamentary
sanction. Kings, after all, called parliaments, rather than the other
way around. Two days before the opening of her first parliament, therefore, Mary was crowned amid the splendour of Westminster Abbey.

For those fluent in the language of royal iconography, the procession in which she made her way from the Tower to the Palace
of Westminster on the eve of the ceremony reflected the complex
novelty of political circumstance in October 1553. Through streets
filled with painstakingly rehearsed pageants, fluttering streamers,
and crowds cheering until they were hoarse, the queen was attended
by the great and the good, servants, nobles, and diplomats, just as a
king would be. But Mary herself adopted the visual style of queens
past, all of whom had acquired their crowns not by right but by marriage. Her slight figure was carried in an open litter lined with the
same dazzling white cloth of gold of which her gown was made, her
auburn hair hanging loose around her shoulders like that of a bride
on her wedding day, in token of the purity and fertility that were the
chief attributes of a royal consort.

Purity and fertility mattered to Mary, too, as a virtuous woman
who hoped for an heir. But for her, unlike the kings' wives who had
set the ceremonial precedents for queenly coronations, those qualities were just two among many she was required to embody as a
female sovereign. And it was a very different example that she followed the next day in the hush of the abbey. Then, she was robed in
crimson like her male predecessors as she received the orb, sceptre,
ring, spurs, and sword that represented the powers of a king. She was
anointed, like a king, on the shoulders, breast, forehead, and temples
(with holy oil specially sent from the Continent, to avoid any possible
contamination from the Protestant practices of her brother's reign).
Finally, the imperial crown of England, not a consort's coronet, was
placed upon her head.

Now that she was a monarch by every measure and every ceremony that her forefathers had enjoyed, Mary could turn her attention to the question of her marriage. But while the queen, her subjects, and her allies were agreed that she needed a husband, it was not so easy to arrive at an acceptable consensus about which particular husband she should take. In retrospect, it was becoming increasingly apparent that being a woman alone had helped her cause in the crisis of the summer: it had been possible for her supporters to unite in hope that she would make the right (as yet unspecified) choice of spouse, rather than finding themselves divided by differences of opinion about one she already had. But now the nettle had to be grasped—and at the heart of the problem was the unresolved question of the balance of authority between husband and wife when the wife wore a crown. If Mary took a husband, would England acquire a king?

That unsettling possibility persuaded many of her subjects that their queen should marry an Englishman, for fear, as the late Duke of Northumberland had warned and the emperor himself now ruminated, that "foreigners, whom the English more than any other nation abhor, would interfere with the government." The leading candidate was Edward Courtenay, Earl of Devon, one of the last remaining representatives of the Plantagenet line through his grandmother, a daughter of Edward IV. The threatening combination of his dangerously royal blood and his parents' closeness to Katherine of Aragon had persuaded Henry VIII to incarcerate Courtenay in the Tower from the age of twelve, but now, at twenty-seven, he reemerged from confinement into the political limelight, hailed as "the flower of the English nobility" and the great white hope of those who wished Mary to marry within the realm.

The extensive support for Courtenay's suit among the queen's household and the council was given public voice on November 16 by an extraordinary parliamentary delegation including many of her greatest nobles and churchmen. On their behalf, the Speaker of the Commons lectured Mary at length on "all the disadvantages, dangers and difficulties that could be imagined or dreamt of in the case of her choosing a foreign husband," Ambassador Renard reported. These ranged from the weighty to the relatively superficial ("the foreigners would wish to lord it over the English; the kingdom would be put to expense in entertaining them"), but in essence boiled down to the threat that England might lose its independence if its queen were subjected to "husbandly tyranny" from abroad.

Mary's response was immediate and unequivocal. Convention had it that the Lord Chancellor should respond to parliament on the sovereign's behalf; but Mary's Lord Chancellor was Bishop Gardiner of Winchester, who was not only her most loyal prelate but Courtenay's most committed advocate. The queen—who had been profoundly irritated by both the tone and content of a homily "so confused, so longwinded and prolific of irrelevant arguments that she was obliged to sit down," she complained to Renard—therefore chose to speak for herself. "Parliament was not accustomed to use such language to the kings of England," she told the unfortunate Speaker trenchantly, "nor was it suitable or respectful that it should do so."

What had roused her anger more than anything in his ill-judged address was the proposition that she should marry one of her own subjects. Mary's views on the sacrament of marriage were as traditional and conservative as the rest of her faith: "She would wholly love and obey him to whom she had given herself, following the divine commandment, and would do nothing against his will," she had told Renard a month earlier. But her views on the majesty of her own sovereign authority were equally traditional and conservative. How could she love and obey a man who was already bound in obedience to her? Only outside her realm would she find a husband whose status was commensurate with her own. And in that case, too, her private duties as a wife could be distinguished clearly from her public responsibilities as England's queen. She would wholly love and obey her husband, she had informed Renard, "but if he wished to encroach in the government of the kingdom she would be unable to permit it."

For twenty years, ever since she had been declared a bastard at the age of seventeen, it had been impossible, in practice, for Mary to marry because of the toxic combination of her potential political significance and her profoundly uncertain status. Now she found herself suddenly transformed into the most eligible woman in Europe, albeit one whose exalted rank meant that few suitors were qualified to seek her hand. Faced with this disconcerting reversal of fortune, her first thought was to look to the cousin who had done so much to sustain her during her long years of internal exile: the widowed Emperor Charles V himself, who had first been proposed as her husband when he was a young man of twenty-two and she a child of six. But at fifty-three, Charles was exhausted and ailing, immobilised by gout, catarrh, and haemorrhoids, and he had no appetite for another marriage. In his place, however, he proposed his son and heir, Philip, who was already ruling Spain on his father's behalf. And by the time Mary responded so angrily to her subjects' representations in favour of an English husband, she had already committed herself to this Spanish match.

Her decision has been seen, by English contemporaries and many historians since, as the defining mistake of her reign. By this account she was, in Ambassador Renard's words, "easily influenced, inexpert in worldly matters and a novice all round," a queen who, in relying too heavily on the support of the emperor and his envoys, badly underestimated the depth of her subjects' objections to a marriage alliance in which she was emotionally overinvolved. Evidence to support this analysis is not difficult to find: Renard's encrypted dispatches repeatedly emphasised how much the queen was "inexperienced in the conduct of public affairs," and Mary herself maintained in her dealings with the emperor the tone of submissive gratitude that she had adopted in the difficult years before her accession to the throne.

In hindsight, certainly, it is clear that her determination to marry Philip had profound and destructive drawbacks. But a similarly retrospective look at the spectacularly disastrous marriages later made by her royal cousin Mary, Queen of Scots, to the lords Darnley and Bothwell might also suggest that, in refusing to marry one of her own subjects, Mary Tudor was prescient rather than myopic. In fact, given the urgency of her need in the autumn of 1553 to find someone who would pass muster as a royal husband, there were compelling reasons for Mary to look favourably on Philip as a suitor. Not least of these was the traditional convergence of geo-political and economic interests between England on the one hand and, on the other, Spain and the Netherlands (both of which territories, thanks to the marriage of Charles V's parents, now formed part of his sprawling empire)—a long-standing alignment disturbed in recent years by religious upheaval in England, but given renewed significance by the imminent union between the Queen of Scotland and the heir to the French crown.

Mary herself was the incarnation of an earlier Anglo-Spanish alliance—and the dynastic heritage she shared with Philip also suggested the possibility of a shared understanding about how the marriage of two monarchs might work. While the history of France had excluded women from the royal succession completely, and that of England had left the issue undecided until that very summer, in the Spanish kingdom of Castile a precedent in favour of female rule had been set by the twelfth-century Queen Urraca, who had succeeded to her father's throne two decades before Matilda attempted to do the same in England. Four centuries later, that precedent had helped to enable Mary's maternal grandmother (and Philip's great-grandmother), Isabella, to wear the crown of Castile in her own right, and to maintain her independent sovereignty throughout her marriage to Ferdinand, the king of neighbouring Aragon. Could Mary and Philip not emulate their illustrious forebears, to the benefit of both their realms?

The queen's resolution that Philip should be her husband need not, therefore, be seen as the emotional choice of a naïve and inexperienced woman in thrall to the land of her mother's birth, nor even simply as a mistake. There were good grounds for thinking that he was the best of the limited choices available to her, all of which were problematic in one way or another. That was not the assessment of her councillors, but they had agendas of their own, many of them mutually incompatible, and concerns, too, about the prospect that the queen might take too independent a view of her own authority. (As the imperial envoys had remarked of the convoluted state of the English court in 1553, Mary had "found matters in such a condition when she came to the throne that she cannot possibly put everything straight, or punish all who have been guilty of something, otherwise she would be left without any vassals at all.")

Meanwhile, Ambassador Renard had every reason to accentuate the queen's dependence on his own judicious advice when he reported events in England to his master in Brussels. And if Mary was happy at times to present herself as a vulnerably innocent woman, there was often advantage in doing so. Her chaste insistence that she had no personal taste for marriage ("she had never felt that which was called love, nor harboured thoughts of voluptuousness") fulfilled valuable political purposes within England. She was married to her kingdom, she was wont to observe with a gesture to her coronation ring, and the accession to the throne of a virgin named Mary had not gone publicly unremarked. Emphasis on her lack of worldly experience also served to justify her resolve that she would only consider a suitor who was personally acceptable to herself. (Courtenay, she maintained, was not—and although she sustained the purity of that verdict by refusing to spend any time with him, she was also proved right very rapidly as his newfound freedom went to his head, revealing alarming deficiencies in his character and judgement.) When, after extensive backstage diplomacy, Philip's proposal was eventually presented at court in November, Mary acted as though the question were new to her, and consulted her council with "becoming modesty, a timid countenance and trembling gestures." But, however convincing her performance, it was her own plan she put to them, and her own plan that prevailed.

It was noticeable, too, that the general insistence on her need for a husband to carry out "the offices which do not properly belong to woman's estate" ("*la profession des dames*," in Renard's elegant cipher) did not include any further specification of what those offices actually were. Ambassador Michieli, for example, in suggesting that her sex required her "to refer many matters to her councillors and ministers," noted without apparent irony that this was also "the custom of other sovereigns." Outside the council chamber, leadership in war was one obvious example of a role that a queen could not easily fulfil; and this division of labour was vividly depicted in the great seal that was cast in 1554 showing the royal couple on horseback, Mary ahead holding the sceptre and looking back at Philip, who rode on her left, the traditional position for a consort, with a great sword unsheathed in his hand. But even this apparently straightforward distinction of function between Mary as a sovereign wife and Philip as her royal husband was fraught with political difficulty, given that the potential benefits of imperial assistance against France and Scotland had to be weighed against the disturbing possibility that England might be drawn into Spain's military quarrels or made subject to its forces.

In fact, the treaty hammered out to give effect to a marriage that was supposedly made necessary by the limitations of the queen's sex went to great lengths to prevent her husband from intervening in the government of her kingdom at all. Here the advantages to Mary of a foreign match were once again apparent: if her councillors believed that she could not govern without a husband's help, it was a principle they were eager to waive if the husband in question were Spanish. Philip would have the title of king in England, but none of the authority. He could assist his wife in the administration of her realm, but only so far as established "laws, privileges and customs" allowed, and he could appoint no officers there. England would take no part in his wars; his wife would not leave her kingdom; and he would have no claim on the throne after her death. Meanwhile, although Philip already had a son by his first, short-lived wife, who would inherit Spain after him, the rich territories of the Netherlands would pass to his future offspring with Mary along with the English crown.

These provisions protected English interests—and the independence of Mary's sovereignty—so effectively that Philip privately vowed that he held himself bound by none of them. Isabella of Castile's example was less welcome, it seemed, to her Spanish great-grandson than it was to her English granddaughter. But while private dissent might salve Philip's pride, it did nothing to prevent the terms of the treaty from passing into English law in parliament in April 1554, along with explicit confirmation that Mary, as "sole queen," should "have and enjoy the crown and sovereignty" in "as large and ample manner and form" after she was married to Philip as she had before. Nor did his objections do anything to compromise the carefully designed ceremonial that attended this momentous royal wedding after his rain-sodden arrival at Southampton on July 20.

Five days later, the weather had not improved when the wedding party assembled at Winchester's ancient cathedral, but the absence of sun was offset by the shining cloth of gold in which bride, groom, and the church's vast interior were all lavishly decked. Philip, at twenty-seven, was a languidly inscrutable figure, large of jaw and elegant of dress, who had resigned himself to his father's plans for this English marriage despite his own profound reservations, both political and personal. His graceful manners betrayed no hint of ungallant thoughts, however, as his bride was escorted to his side, a short, spare woman eleven years his senior, who had once been "more than middling fair," in the Venetian ambassador's forensic assessment, but whose pale face was now lined "more by anxieties than by age." On the eve of the ceremony, the emperor had made his son a king by giving him the kingdom of Naples, to ensure the parity of the eclectically mingled titles by which the couple were proclaimed once their vows had been made: "Philip and Mary, by the grace of God King and Queen of England, France, Naples, Jerusalem and Ireland, Defenders of the Faith, Princes of Spain and Sicily, Archdukes of Austria, Dukes of Milan, Burgundy and Brabant, Counts of Habsburg, Flanders and Tyrol." Their marriage had therefore bestowed on Mary the title of Prince of Spain, just as her husband was

King of England; but on English soil, as on their great seal, Philip's place was on her left, not her right, in subtle ceremonial demonstration that he was her consort, not her sovereign lord.

Mary showed every sign of satisfaction in the marriage she had made. Privately, she was delighted with the courteously attentive husband who would make it possible for her to give her country an heir. Publicly, she had found a spouse whose status outside England was worthy of her own, but whose authority within her realm had been circumscribed almost to nothing. But even as she took her vows, it had already become unsettlingly clear quite how many of her subjects did not share this happy view of her position as a married queen.

For all the uncompromising drafting of her marriage treaty and the legislation that ratified it, for all Mary's careful distinction between her private duty as a wife and her public responsibility as a monarch, everything that her subjects knew about the relative authority of husband and wife served to fuel fears that her marriage to Philip would subject England to Spanish rule. He was now King of England, and kings, they knew, ruled. Queens, in general, did not. Had that been the only issue, had Mary had time to demonstrate that her own sovereignty was English sovereignty, perhaps those anxieties could have been allayed. But from the moment the Spanish match was first publicly broached, it was conflated in the minds of her subjects with another issue that, for Mary, was a matter not of policy but of divinely ordained truth: the restoration of Catholicism in England.

For the last twenty years, successive waves of religious reform had swept over England, leaving in their wake unpredictable eddying currents of change in the faith of the English people. England was not straightforwardly a Protestant country; the collapse of Edward VI's design for a Protestant succession attested to that, and many of Mary's subjects welcomed her commitment to traditional forms of religious practice. Altars were restored, images were retrieved from their hiding places, and the notes of the Latin Mass once more hung

on incense-scented air. Conservative bishops were released from custody, swapping places with the evangelical prelates who had helped
to imprison them, and the statutes that had established the reformed
Edwardian Church were rolled back one by one in parliament. However, the deepest roots of the English Reformation lay not in doctrinal controversy, but in Henry VIII's insistence that the English
Church should have an English head—a matter of jurisdiction that
was given extra political ballast by the determination of the great
landowners to maintain their property rights under English law over
the rich estates they had acquired when England's monasteries were
dissolved. And now the queen's intention to restore the authority of
Rome and her decision to take a Spanish husband were too easily
elided into a double-headed spectre of foreign domination.

As early as the winter of 1553, when news of the queen's proposed
marriage to Philip of Spain began to spread among her subjects, a
conspiracy was under way—encouraged with partisan enthusiasm
by the French ambassador—to defend England's autonomy by removing Mary from the throne. Beyond that, its aims were sketchy.
She might be replaced by Jane Grey, still a prisoner in the Tower,
or perhaps by the queen's rejected suitor Edward Courtenay, better
yet if he were to be married to Mary's sister, Elizabeth. Jane Grey's
father, the Duke of Suffolk, and Courtenay himself were both involved in the plot, but it was entirely characteristic of both men that
lack of competence and loss of nerve rendered them liabilities rather
than leaders of resistance. That left Sir Thomas Wyatt, a gentleman
of Kent, who, alone among the conspirators, had succeeded in raising
three thousand men in his home county. And at the end of January
1554 the scale of the threat that Wyatt's men represented became
unnervingly clear when a London militia sent to confront them at
Rochester was routed, with many troops deserting the militia's ranks
to join the rebels.

Suddenly, the capital itself was in danger. Once again, Mary was
required to show that a queen could lead her people in time of crisis,
and once again she demonstrated her mastery of her role. She would

not leave London (unlike the imperial ambassadors, who wrote with an unmistakable note of panic to ask the emperor if "there is anything to be gained by our staying here longer"), and she would not ask Charles V to send soldiers onto English soil, provocatively counterproductive as that would be. Instead, she rode with her councillors to the Guildhall in the heart of the city to speak to London's citizens.

Six months earlier, she had rallied her supporters against Queen Jane with an address, one eulogising eyewitness said, "of Herculean rather than of womanly daring." Now she combined Tudor charisma with the surest of political touches to denounce Wyatt and to declare her dedication to her realm, playing as she did so on her double identity as a sovereign and a woman. She showed the people her coronation ring, the "spousal ring" signifying her marriage to her kingdom, which never, she told them, left her finger. And she was not only a sovereign wife: "On the word of a prince," she went on, "I cannot tell how naturally the mother loves the child, for I was never the mother of any. But certainly, if a prince and governor may as naturally and earnestly love her subjects as the mother does love the child, then assure yourselves that I, being your lady and mistress, do as earnestly and tenderly love and favour you." When Wyatt's assault finally came, in the night of February 6, the queen stood firm as arrows rattled the windows of the Palace of Westminster. By morning, the revolt had collapsed.

The conspiracy sealed the fate of those who posed a direct threat to Mary's regime. On February 12 Jane Grey was led to the scaffold within the precincts of the Tower, the fortress from which she had not emerged after her proclamation as queen seven months earlier. With extraordinary composure, she admitted her fault in accepting the crown, but "touching the procurement and desire thereof by me or on my behalf," she said, "I do wash my hands in innocency." Her women tied a blindfold over her eyes to shield her from the sight of the axe, and in a moment of terrible pathos she groped for the block, crying, "Where is it? What shall I do?" They guided her gently forward, and, with one final prayer, she knelt to meet her death. It caused little stir among the people who had so briefly—and unexpectedly, on both sides—been her subjects. Edward Courtenay re-entered the Tower on the same day that Jane Grey died. He remained a prisoner for a year before being sent into an exile from which he was never allowed to return. Princess Elizabeth had had the characteristic wit to do nothing other than wait and watch when she learned of Wyatt's plans, but that suspicious inactivity was enough to persuade her sister that she, too, should now be accommodated, temporarily at least, within the Tower's walls.

The events of February 1554 were an emphatic demonstration of both the vulnerabilities and the strengths of Mary's authority. Wyatt himself insisted before he lost his head that he had acted to prevent the queen's marriage from delivering England into "bondage and servitude by aliens and strangers." But the queen herself—plausibly enough, given the identity of the plotters and Wyatt's previous service to her brother's regime—interpreted the rebellion as the work of traitorous Protestants, thereby reinforcing the identification between religious and political anxieties about her government. How complex those anxieties were was indicated by a further statute enacted by the parliament of April 1554, to accompany those concerning the queen's forthcoming marriage: "An act," the rolls of parliament recorded, "declaring that the regal power of this realm is in the queen's majesty as fully and absolutely as ever it was in any her most noble progenitors, kings of this realm." The perceived need for a law to spell out the fact that a female monarch ruled by the same authority as a male might appear to suggest weakness in Mary's position, but there are indications that the act was framed in response to efforts by some of her more fervent Catholic supporters to argue overzealously for the strength of her powers. She was not bound, they said, by any of England's laws made since the Conquest—and could therefore choose to sweep away the entire apparatus of the Reformation at will—because all previous statutes had been made in the name of England's king, while its queen was nowhere mentioned.

Her marriage to Philip therefore exposed her rule to persistent charges that she was handing England into the control of Rome and Spain. Philip's Spanish entourage, who complained of the ceremonial "slights" that indicated his subordinate status as her consort, were presumably unconvinced of the latter, but Mary's concern to honour her husband by associating his name with hers in all her public pronouncements fed sinister suspicions among her English subjects about the extent of his control over their queen. For the Spanish, the lack of a coronation for King Philip was a cause of bitter resentment; for the English, rumours that his coronation was imminent, along with the enhanced authority it was assumed to confer, became a mainstay of propaganda disseminated by those who opposed Mary's policies—and their number was increasing, once the reinstatement of the old heresy laws meant that obdurate Protestants began to die in Catholic flames.

Meanwhile, the queen's decision that she could marry only a man of an equivalent dignity to her own inevitably meant that the husband who her subjects feared was dominating her government could not be constantly at her side. Philip had royal responsibilities outside England, not least his father's wars against France, and although he stayed at Mary's court for thirteen months after their sumptuous wedding, it was another nineteen months after that before he returned. For all the talk of female incapacity, the overriding compulsion behind Mary's marriage had not been the deficiencies of her sex but her need for an heir. Time was already against her, and Philip's absence did nothing to improve her chances of bearing a child.

There was still hope, however, despite the toll taken on her health as well as her looks by the strain under which she had lived for so long. Contemporaries were quick to ascribe the apparent delicacy of her constitution to classically "hysterical" causes: she suffered from "menstruous retention and suffocation of the womb," Ambassador Michieli reported, a condition for which she was regularly bled—resulting, he said, in her characteristic pallor and thinness—and which rendered her vulnerable to bouts of melancholy and weeping.

But it is clear that this, like other aspects of her feminine "weakness," could be useful to Mary when she chose. The queen "had pretended to be ill for the last two days," she told Renard in the autumn of 1553, "but her illness was really the travail that this decision"—her resolution to marry Philip—"had cost her." And she was robust enough to enjoy dancing and hunting and to stand strong against her enemies when her rights were challenged. ("...she is brave and valiant," observed Michieli generously, "unlike other timid and spiritless women....")

Within four months of her wedding, it seemed as though her prayers had been answered. It was not easy to be confident of the early symptoms of pregnancy, and the difficulty was compounded many times over for a woman who had experienced menstrual problems, but by November 28, 1554, the queen had allowed herself to be convinced by her doctors' diagnosis that God had blessed her marriage and her realm. That was the day when papal authority was restored at last in England (her subjects having insisted on prior confirmation that the pope would not disturb their possession of formerly monastic estates)—and, to Mary's joy, it was proclaimed in providential conjunction with the future of the Catholic succession. The queen was "quick with child," the royal letters said, while bells were rung and *Te Deums* sung. Meanwhile, hastily arranged negotiations produced a fraught parliamentary agreement that, in the grudgingly acknowledged interests of stability, Philip would become regent on behalf of the infant heir should Mary not survive the birth of their baby.

By Easter 1555 England expected the arrival of its heir with anxious anticipation. The queen, slowed now by her growing girth, had withdrawn into confinement at Hampton Court, attended by her devoted ladies-in-waiting in warm rooms muffled with rich carpets and tapestries, where an exquisitely carved cradle stood ready beside her bed. On April 30, when word reached London of the birth of a healthy prince, the city erupted in celebration. But it was rumour, running wilder than the bonfires in the streets, and it was quickly denied. May came and went, dates were recalculated. In early July, without fanfare or comment, the queen began receiving visits from male councillors and ambassadors once again, and by the end of the month little doubt remained that she was not, after all, pregnant. God's blessing, it seemed, had been deferred.

Mary was by no means the only woman to have endured a phantom pregnancy. Twenty years earlier the wife of the governor of Calais, who also had a cradle waiting empty, was consolingly reminded that "your ladyship is not the first woman of honour that has overshot or mistaken your time and reckoning." But the political consequences of the queen's failure to produce a child, and the public humiliation to which she was exposed, were much greater than any other woman had to endure. Philip, who had waited in England to be by Mary's side after the delivery that never was, sailed away from Greenwich on August 29, waving his hat in salute to his wife until he was out of view. The Venetian ambassador gave the doge a fulsome account of the "flood of tears" to which the queen gave way once she was alone; how he knew of this emotional collapse remained unexplained, especially since he later admitted that many months had passed since he had been granted the honour of a royal audience. Publicly, it was with a regal grandeur more unfathomable than ever that the queen returned to the hours she spent at her duties and her devotions.

Philip eventually returned to his wife's kingdom for a three-month visit in March 1557, and in January of the following year Mary announced the good news that she was seven months pregnant—"which has given me greater joy than I can express," her husband wrote with formal courtesy, "as it is the one thing in the world I have most desired and which is of the greatest importance for the cause of religion and the welfare of our realm." The queen had waited so long before speaking of her condition, she explained, to be sure that this time she was indeed carrying a baby. But no elaborate preparations were made for her confinement, and although she made a will at the end of March—"thinking myself to be with child," and "foreseeing the great danger which by God's ordinance remain to all women in their travail of children"—she did not go into labour. By May the subject was no longer mentioned.

Despite all her hopes, her marriage had not emulated the success of the union of her grandparents Isabella and Ferdinand. Married at eighteen, Isabella had given birth to six children, while Mary, a bride at thirty-eight, had none. The Catholic monarchs of Aragon and Castile had united their realms to drive out the heathen Moors, but in Mary's kingdom the stench of burning Protestant flesh now served to deepen religious division. And England could look only with envy at the geographical strength achieved by the alliance of the Spanish kingdoms. By the summer of 1557, despite Mary's attempts to act as a peacemaker, England had—as Wyatt and others had feared—been drawn into the Holy Roman Empire's war with France. And in January 1558 the unthinkable news had come that Calais, the garrisoned port that had been the last English foothold on the Continent for the past hundred years, had fallen to the French.

By the spring of that year, a queen alone at the age of forty-two, Mary was resigned to the absence of her husband and facing the certainty that she would not carry an heir. That prospect, Renard had warned after the debacle of her first pregnancy, meant "trouble on so great a scale that the pen can hardly set it down. Certain it is that the order of succession has been so badly decided that the Lady Elizabeth comes next, and that means heresy again, and the true religion overthrown." The queen did not want Elizabeth to inherit her crown, but she could not bring herself to dispose of her half-sister. Mary's own favoured heir was her reliably Catholic cousin Margaret Douglas, the handsome daughter of Henry VIII's elder sister Margaret by her stormy second marriage, to whom she had been close since girlhood. But it could hardly have escaped the queen's attention that, by the precedent of her own victory over Jane Grey, Elizabeth's claim would in turn be irresistible. Mary herself drew an absolute distinction between the legitimacy of her own birth and the bastardy of her sister, but she was enough her father's daughter to know that the power of his bloodline was likely to prevail. All she could hope was that she would live long enough to prevent Elizabeth from uprooting the Catholicism she had so faithfully and forcefully replanted in her kingdom.

In that, too, she would be disappointed. During the summer of 1558 a lethal epidemic of influenza took hold of England. The new disease did not strike quickly, like the plague or the sweat. Instead, protracted, repeated fevers laid thousands low, and many did not rise again from their beds. That autumn, the queen was among them. In the first week of November, knowing by then that she was not expected to survive, she sent to acknowledge Elizabeth as her heir, asking only that her sister should fulfil the terms of her will and maintain "the old religion as the queen has restored it." She held on for ten more days, drifting in and out of consciousness, consoled by visions, she told her closest friend among her ladies, of angelic children singing and playing around her. In the early morning of November 17 mass was celebrated at her bedside before she finally slipped away.

Soon the road north from London to Hatfield, where Mary's sister waited for news, was crowded with the great men of the realm hastening to offer their allegiance to England's new queen.

TWENTY-ONE

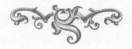

A Queen and by the Same Title a King Also

he was a king's daughter, she was a king's sister, she was a king's wife." Thus far, the Bishop of Winchester's oration at Mary Tudor's funeral a month after her death is strikingly reminiscent of the epitaph of her forebear Matilda, who was lauded four hundred years earlier as the "daughter, wife and mother" of kings. But Mary, unlike Matilda, was not "greatest in her offspring." Instead, as the bishop went on, "she was a queen, and by the same title a king also."

That somewhat ungainly formulation grasped at the heart of the challenge both women faced: to rule in their own right, when every assumption about the exercise of power took it for granted that the crown was shaped to fit a male head. Matilda tried to overcome that presupposition, and failed—not because female rule was expressly prohibited by law or custom in twelfth-century England, but because it proved impossible for her to secure a decisive hold on power when faced with a rival who embodied the conventionally comprehensible authority of male kingship. Mary, the daughter of another powerful King Henry, succeeded in asserting her right to her father's crown, not least because her subjects did not have the option of a plausible male candidate for the throne. But Mary also faced many challenges that Matilda would have recognised as she sought to defend the independence of her own sovereignty, to rule as well as to reign.

The explicit denunciation of women's right to rule that was articulated at this point in the mid-1550s, most famously and heatedly by John Knox, was precipitated by the intersection between religious trauma and political circumstance. Knox, an anglicised Scotsman who had been a royal chaplain at Edward VI's Protestant court, looked on in horror from his Genevan exile as three royal Catholic women worked to hold back the tide of the reformed faith in which he believed so passionately. In the Netherlands, Charles V's sister Mary, dowager Queen of Hungary, served as regent on her imperial brother's behalf. In Scotland, the dowager Queen Marie de Guise governed Knox's native land while her young daughter Mary, Queen of Scots, prepared for her French wedding in Paris. Most egregious of all, Mary Tudor ruled England in her own right, and was setting about the utter destruction of her brother's godly work in Knox's adopted country.

The obvious answer was that this papist tyranny reflected the unholy and unnatural quality of women's "monstrous regiment," "which, among all enormities that this day do abound upon the face of the whole earth, is most detestable and damnable." No woman should be allowed to abrogate the laws of God and nature by wielding power, and those who did—like Mary and her two namesakes, the dowager queens in Scotland and the Netherlands—were "cursed Jezebels." Not even Mary Tudor's worst enemy could seriously accuse her of sexual transgression, but the biblical Jezebel had imposed the idolatrous worship of Baal on God's kingdom of Israel, and it was therefore the English queen's spiritual "fornication and whoredom" that made her "the uttermost of [God']s plagues."

But, however specific the context in which Knox was writing, it was the deeper resonance of his argument that allowed his trumpet to sound. Edward II's queen Isabella, after all, had been named a Jezebel in England long before Christendom had split between Catholics and Protestants. And, as Eleanor of Aquitaine had been reminded when she rebelled against her husband, "man is the head of woman," and she would therefore be "the cause of a general ruin." It was notable, in fact, how limited were the attempts to refute Knox's position. John Aylmer, an evangelical scholar who had been Jane Grey's tutor, answered Knox in 1559 with *An Harbour for Faithful and True Subjects Against the Late Blown Blast Concerning the Government of Women*, but his reasoning differed from Knox's only in extrapolation, rather than foundation. Yes, he agreed, women were "weak in nature, feeble in body, soft in courage, unskilful in practice," and they were subject, as wives, to their husbands; but yet an exceptional woman might be appointed by God's providence to the office of kingship, just as Deborah had been a lone female judge in Old Testament Israel. In any case, Aylmer added, thanks to the role of parliament, government would be conducted not so much by the queen in person as by her male councillors and judges in her name, so "it is not in England so dangerous a matter to have a woman ruler as men take it to be."

The occasion of this somewhat limp rebuttal was the accession of a new, Protestant queen in England, which necessitated a Protestant about-face, executed with undignified haste, on the subject of female rule. Knox himself tried to make up for his own disastrous timing—his fulminations having been published little more than six months before Elizabeth inherited her sister's crown—by writing to the new and clearly affronted queen to explain that he had not meant to include her authority, providentially ordained by God as it was, in his thundering condemnation of all women rulers. Typically, however, he adopted a tone of injured innocence ("I cannot deny the writing of a book against the usurped authority and unjust regiment of women,... but why that... your grace... should be offended at the

author of such a work I can perceive no just occasion"), and could not
resist the opportunity to offer the queen the benefit of his unsolicited
advice ("if thus in God's presence you humble yourself, as in my heart
I glorify God for that rest granted to his afflicted flock within England under you, a weak instrument, so will I with tongue and pen
justify your authority and regiment as the Holy Ghost has justified
the same in Deborah . . .").

Elizabeth was not impressed. When Knox sought to return
from Geneva to Scotland in 1559, she would not let him set foot
on English soil, forcing him to brave the longer and more dangerous North Sea route to Leith. She was happy, however, to adopt the
proffered mantle of a biblical Deborah—a providential exception to
the common lot of women, depicted as a queen in parliament robes
in a Fleet Street pageant at Elizabeth's coronation—knowing as she
did that the alternative was the familiar tag of Jezebel, which would
soon be enthusiastically redeployed against this Protestant queen by
her Catholic enemies. This process of exceptionalism, of Deborah-
fication, by which a woman who exercised authority in ways perceived by an approving observer to be desirable or legitimate could
be excused, or raised above, the limitations of her sex, was familiar
as well as useful. Mary Tudor's bravery in 1553 had been an example, her supporters declared, "of Herculean rather than of womanly
daring," and four centuries earlier King Stephen's wife, Mathilde,
"forgetting the weakness of her sex and a woman's softness," had
borne herself "with the valour of a man."

But the converse of this exceptionalism—the fate of a woman who
exercised authority in ways perceived by a disapproving observer to
be undesirable or illegitimate—was more pervasive and much more
damaging, an infinitely regressive double-bind in which female rulers
were all too easily trapped. Women were soft and weak, hence unfit
to rule; but a woman who showed herself to be strong was not the
equivalent of a man, but a monster, a crime against nature. This was
the essence of the chroniclers' vilification of Matilda, who, with "every
trace of a woman's gentleness removed from her face," conducted her-

self with "insufferable arrogance" rather than the "modest gait and bearing proper to the gentle sex." It offered ammunition against her descendant Isabella as an "iron virago" who aped, rather than emulated, a man. It provided Shakespeare with his portrait of Margaret of Anjou as a "she-wolf," a "tiger's heart wrapp'd in a woman's hide": "Women are soft, mild, pitiful, and flexible; Thou stern, indurate, flinty, rough, remorseless." And it stood at the heart of Knox's portrayal of "that cruel monster Mary," when—with gloriously unacknowledged irony, amid his argument that her rule was monstrous precisely because she was female—he declared that she was "unworthy, by reason of her bloody tyranny, of the name of woman."

How, then, was a woman to rule, to exercise power that was made for male hands, without being sucked into the quicksand? The traditional answer has been that Elizabeth learned from her sister's devastating mistakes to develop a new and uniquely imposing form of queenship. Certainly, she had a cool and capricious intelligence, a silver-tongued capacity to say everything and nothing at the same time, that was very different from the deeply felt, dogmatic certainties by which her sister lived and ruled. Certainly, too, the very English brand of pragmatic Protestantism at which Elizabeth eventually arrived—famously making no windows into men's souls—sought to unite as many of her people as possible around her sovereignty, rather than enforcing divisive spiritual truths with still more divisive violence.

But hindsight—the writing of history in lastingly Protestant England, and the comparison between one queen who ruled for five years and another who ruled for forty-five, not to mention the dazzling effect of Elizabeth's own propaganda—has tended to obscure the extent to which Elizabeth and Mary used the same strategies in representing the force of their female sovereignty. "She was a queen, and by the same title a king also," the Bishop of Winchester said of Mary; "she was a sister to her that by the like title and right is both king and queen at this present of this realm." And both women did speak of themselves as English kings. "Parliament was not accustomed to use such language to the kings of England," Mary admonished her Speaker. Princess Elizabeth, in desperate appeal after Wyatt's rebellion to her sister's royal promise that she should not be condemned without trial, reminded Mary that "the king's word is more than another man's oath." Most famously of all, Elizabeth as queen declared that, though she had "the body of a weak and feeble woman" (a gesture toward the frailties of her sex that she, like Mary, regularly made, although with rather less conviction), she had "the heart and stomach of a king, and of a king of England too."

But these female kings, unlike their male counterparts, were also wife and mother to their kingdom. Elizabeth's reported speech to her parliament in February 1559 echoed Mary's rallying cry to the Londoners at the Guildhall. "I am already bound unto a husband, which is the kingdom of England," Elizabeth told her subjects, and, like her sister before her, showed the "spousal ring" that she had received at her coronation. "And reproach me no more that I have no children; for every one of you, and as many as are English, are my children...." Four years later, she declared to the Commons that "though after my death you may have many stepdames, yet shall you never have any a more natural mother than I mean to be unto you all."

The difference between the two queens—and a huge difference it was—lay in the fact that Elizabeth's coronation ring was not jostling for room on her fingers with a plain gold wedding band such as the one Mary wore. Elizabeth had time and space to consider the marriage that her subjects assumed she would make, in a way that Mary never had. At twenty-five, she had years of potential childbearing ahead of her, and in the meantime she—unlike Mary—had no obvious heir of an unhelpfully different faith hovering unsupportively on the outskirts of her court. The lack of an obvious heir was a cause of anxious unease to her councillors, and her marriage the subject of repeated petitions from her parliaments; Elizabeth was staking a great deal on her own survival, as her subjects fretfully reminded her after she had suffered a dangerous attack of smallpox in 1562. But while she lived, the uncertainty of the succession reinforced her own status as the source of all security for her realm, and she seized this chance to rule as a virgin queen, putting off until a perpetual tomorrow the urgent dilemmas that had been Mary's from the moment of her accession.

And it was as the Virgin Queen that Elizabeth constructed her own answer to those dilemmas. She had witnessed the desperate disadvantages of her sister's Spanish marriage at close hand. Now she observed from a distance the horrifying consequences of the successive marriages of her cousin Mary, Queen of Scots, to her lords Darnley and Bothwell, which set in train the events that led to Mary's deposition, exile, and incarceration in an English prison. Suitors for Elizabeth's hand came and went, and she dallied, diplomatically or otherwise, but would commit to none. Meanwhile, her subjects could enthusiastically agree that the queen should choose a husband, but any candidate in particular always provoked as much dissent as applause. By the late 1570s time had run out. Where Mary's marriage to her kingdom had been compromised by the troubling implications of the fact that she was also wife to a king, for Elizabeth, it was now clear, the union between monarch and realm would transcend metaphor to be both enduring and exclusive.

The courtly compliments continued, but now to Gloriana, a sovereign queen at the centre of a secularised cult replacing the Mariolatry that was forbidden in Protestant England. Elizabeth had begun her reign by clutching the cloak of Deborah around her; now her authority was armoured with a voraciously eclectic array of images, myths, allegories, and symbols. She was king, queen, virgin, wife, mother, and goddess; Diana, Astraea, Phoebe, Juno, Cynthia; the phoenix, eternally rising from the flames, and the pelican, a mystical mother to her people; not only Deborah but also the biblical Judith, whose daring and courage saved Israel from the Assyrians. Elizabeth had used her providential destiny to turn Knox on his head: the fact that a mere woman could rule in such glory demonstrated how special an instrument of God's will this queen really was.

But the power of Elizabeth's image was not an empty shell. The foundation of her authority—like that for which Matilda had fought so hard four centuries before and had succeeded at last in establishing for her son and the generations that followed—was her lineal right, inherited from her imposing father. If she was king as well as queen, a woman with a male heart and male courage, there was one man in particular from whom her power derived: "We hope to rule, govern and keep this our realm," she told her parliament in 1559, "in as good justice, peace and rest, in like wise as the king my father held you in."

"Good justice" mattered too. As Isabella had found two hundred years earlier, legitimacy of action—the reponsibilities as well as the rights of kingship—could consolidate power in unlikely female hands. A French queen consort with her lover by her side, she succeeded in bringing down her husband's tyranny—only to discover, in imposing a tyranny of her own, that the sword she had wielded could turn on her too. Elizabeth, mindful of Knox's charge that her rule was a tyranny by simple virtue (or defect) of her sex, took constant care that her government, however contentious or intractable the matters with which it had to grapple, should plausibly be perceived to represent the "common weal"—and that she herself should be seen as the champion of her people with, as she declared in 1588, "my chiefest strength and safeguard in the loyal hearts and goodwill of my subjects."

That legitimacy could only be maintained, as Margaret of Anjou had so agonisingly discovered, if government were animated by the royal will of the sovereign. However skilled Elizabeth was at procrastination, however little she liked to narrow down the options in front of her, there could be no mistaking that the queen's authority was the animating force by which decisions were made or (often) deferred. "Little man, little man," the almost seventy-year-old queen reproved a councillor who dared to suggest that she must go to bed during what would prove to be her final illness, "the word 'must' is not to be used to princes!" And she drew on what Charles V had called the "assistance and consent of the foremost men of the land" with consummate skill, choosing her councillors well, delegating wisely, and blaming them roundly for decisions—such as the execution of her cousin Mary, Queen of Scots—from which she wished to place herself at an exculpatory distance.

Perhaps more than anything, Elizabeth—like her remarkable ancestor Eleanor of Aquitaine—governed with acumen gained through adversity, albeit that Elizabeth's adversity came much earlier, and in a more profoundly formative manner, than the reverses in Eleanor's extraordinary life. Elizabeth learned watchfulness in the nursery, and only later learned to inhabit the sovereignty to which she might never have come; whereas the lengthy loss of Eleanor's freedom came as a traumatic jolt to a woman who had been a queen since she was thirteen and a great heiress before that. But in both women a quicksilver intelligence and a steely will were skilfully channelled into a public authority of remarkable force.

The glittering carapace of Elizabeth's image owed something, too, to Eleanor. The troubadours of twelfth-century Aquitaine followed Eleanor's route north to Paris, Normandy, and England, bringing with them songs of *fin'amor*, a new form of lyric poetry in which knights pledged themselves to the service of the lady they loved, a figure of remote and wilful allure who was simultaneously idealised and eroticised in their breathless verse. In fact, there is no evidence that Eleanor participated directly in this cult of courtly love, beyond the fact that the poets wrote in lands over which she presided as queen and duchess, but four centuries later Elizabeth was well aware of its political potential. Where her sister Mary had constructed her authority as a female ruler on the foundation of her irreproachable virtue, piety, and sense of duty, Elizabeth was a very different kind of virgin queen. Virtuous, pious, and dutiful, certainly, as occasion demanded, but also worshipped by the devoted knights of her court, who were bound to her by their elaborately declared love, along with their loyalty. ("While your majesty gives me leave to say I love you," the twenty-five-year-old Earl of Essex told the fifty-seven-year-old queen in 1591, "my fortune is, as my affection, unmatchable. If ever you deny me that liberty, you may end my life, but never shake my constancy, for were the sweetness of your nature turned into the greatest bitterness that could be, it is not in your power, as great a queen as you are, to make me love you less.")

This Virgin Queen could do much. She was seductive Venus as well as chaste Diana. She was both a king and a queen, a man's heart in a woman's breast. What Knox had denounced as her "monstrous regiment" had given England the golden age of Gloriana. But the one thing she could not do was the one thing every king saw as the sine qua non of his kingship: to ensure the continuity of his bloodline and the security of his realm by handing on the crown to an heir of his own body. Elizabeth's formidable control of her country's present had been bought at the cost of abdicating her stake in its future.

We are left to wonder: would Matilda—who was, unlike Elizabeth, the mother as well as the daughter of a great King Henry—have exchanged her son's inheritance for the crown she never wore?

NOTE ON SOURCES AND
FURTHER READING

This is the first time I have begun a bibliographic note with a reference to sources online: in the years it has taken to write this book, the extent and quality of historical materials on the Internet has transformed the experience of research. The *Oxford Dictionary of National Biography* (http://www.oxforddnb.com) is a treasure trove of scholarship and insight, available through personal subscription and to members of academic and public libraries; almost every individual mentioned in these pages who was either born in the British Isles or contributed significantly to their history has an entry of their own, complete with extensive bibliographical references. And *British History Online* (http://www.british-history.ac.uk) is a remarkable digital library created by the Institute of Historical Research and the History of Parliament Trust, which makes available an impressive range of printed primary and secondary sources for the history of the British Isles, most free to view, some by personal subscription.

Both sites are an excellent starting point for "Beginnings," the first section of this book. The personalities and politics of the Tudor court can be tracked through the pages of the *ODNB*, while *British History Online* offers access to many important primary sources for the reign of Edward VI—especially, here, the reports of the imperial ambassador Jehan Scheyfve for 1553, which are available in translation in the *Calendar of State Papers, Spain*, vol. 11, ed. R. Tyler (London: HMSO, 1916).

The historiography of the Tudor period is vast and ever expanding. As a starting point, see John Guy's classic *Tudor England* (Oxford: Oxford University Press, 1988), Susan Brigden's *New Worlds, Lost Worlds* (London: Allen Lane, 2000), and *Henry VIII: Man and Monarch*, ed. Susan Doran (London: The British Library, 2009). For the life of Edward VI, see Jennifer Loach's posthumously published *Edward VI*, ed. G. Bernard and P. Williams (New Haven and London: Yale University Press, 1999); Hester Chapman's *The Last Tudor King: A Study of Edward VI* (London: Jonathan Cape, 1958); W. K. Jordan's two volumes, *Edward VI: The Young King* (London: Allen and Unwin, 1968) and *Edward VI: The Threshold of Power* (London: Allen and Unwin, 1970); and Chris Skidmore's biography *Edward VI: The Lost King of England* (London: Weidenfeld and Nicolson, 2007). For the politics of the reign, see Stephen Alford, *Kingship and Politics in the Reign of Edward VI* (Cambridge: Cambridge University Press, 2002), and, on religion, Diarmaid MacCulloch, *Tudor Church Militant: Edward VI and the Protestant Reformation* (London: Allen Lane, 1999), and Eamon Duffy, *The Stripping of the Altars: Traditional Religion in England, 1400–1580* (New Haven and London: Yale University Press, 1992). For Edward's own political journal, see *Literary Remains of King Edward the Sixth*, ed. J. G. Nichols (London: J. B. Nichols and Sons, 1857), and *The Chronicle and Political Papers of King Edward VI*, ed. W. K. Jordan (London: Allen and Unwin, 1966). For masques at Edward's court, see Sydney Anglo, *Spectacle, Pageantry and Early Tudor Policy* (Oxford: The Clarendon Press, 1969), and for his illness, G. Holmes, F. Holmes, and J. McMorrough, "The Death of Young King Edward VI," *New England Journal of Medicine* 345 (2001): 60–62. For discussion of Henry VIII's will and Edward VI's "device" for the succession, see Eric Ives, "Tudor Dynastic Problems Revisited," *Historical Research* 81 (2008): 255–279, and his *Lady Jane Grey: A Tudor Mystery* (Chichester: Wiley-Blackwell, 2009); I hope it will be clear how much I owe to Professor Ives's work, even while my conclusions differ from his.

"Beginnings 2: Long Live the Queen?" draws on a wide variety of sources, including those used in the rest of the book. It opens with Margaret Paston, for whom see *Paston Letters and Papers of the Fifteenth Century*, ed. N. Davis, R. Beadle, and C. Richmond, 3 vols. (Oxford: Early English Text Society, 2004–2005), and my *Blood and Roses: One Family's Struggle and Triumph During the Tumultuous Wars of the Roses* (New York: HarperCollins, 2006). For the history of women in the Middle Ages, invaluable starting points are Henrietta Leyser, *Medieval Women: A Social History of Women in England, 450–1500* (London: Weidenfeld and Nicolson, 1995), and Mavis Mate, *Women in Medieval English Society* (Cambridge: Cambridge University Press, 2000). On the power of the crown in medieval England, see Christine Carpenter, *The Wars of the Roses* (Cambridge: Cambridge University Press, 1997), chapter 2, and Gerald Harriss, *Shaping the Nation: England, 1360–1461* (Oxford: Oxford University Press,

2005), Part I. For the Bayeux Tapestry, see D. M. Wilson, *The Bayeux Tapestry* (London: Thames and Hudson, 1985). John Knox's *First Blast of the Trumpet Against the Monstrous Regiment of Women*, published in Geneva in 1558, can be read in facsimile via participating libraries at *Early English Books Online* (http:// eebo.chadwyck.com) or in *The Works of John Knox*, ed. D. Laing, 6 vols. (Edinburgh: Thomas George Stevenson, 1846–1864). For Thomas Becon's *An Humble Supplication unto God for the Restoring of His Holy Word unto the Church of England*, published at Strasbourg in 1554, see *Early English Books Online* (http:// eebo.chadwyck.com) or *Prayers and Other Pieces of Thomas Becon*, ed. J. Ayre (London: Parker Society, 1844).

For the life of Matilda the chronicle sources are voluminous and fascinating. For Orderic Vitalis, see *The Ecclesiastical History of Orderic Vitalis*, ed. and trans. M. Chibnall, 6 vols. (Oxford: Oxford University Press, 1968–1990). The *Gesta Stephani* is edited and translated by K. R. Potter, with introduction and notes by R. H. C. Davis (Oxford: Oxford University Press, 1976). William of Malmesbury's *Historia Novella* is translated by K. R. Potter and edited by Edmund King (Oxford: Oxford University Press, 1998), and his *Gesta Regum Anglorum* is edited and translated in two volumes by R. A. B. Mynors (Oxford: Oxford University Press, 1998–1999). Henry of Huntingdon's *Historia Anglorum* is edited and translated by Diana Greenway (Oxford: Oxford University Press, 1996; see also her Oxford World's Classics edition, Oxford: Oxford University Press, 2002). The *Gesta Normannorum Ducum of William of Jumièges, Orderic Vitalis and Robert of Torigni* is edited and translated in two volumes by E. M. C. van Houts (Oxford: Oxford University Press, 1992–1995), and the *Anglo-Saxon Chronicle* by M. J. Swanton (London: J. M. Dent, 1996). See also the *Chronicle of John of Worcester*, ed. and trans. P. McGurk, vol. 3 (Oxford: Oxford University Press, 1998). *English Historical Documents, 1042–1189*, ed. D. C. Douglas and G. W. Greenaway (London: Eyre and Spottiswoode, 1968), has extracts from many of these and other contemporary sources, including the writings of Walter Map and Gerald of Wales.

The essential modern work on Matilda is Marjorie Chibnall's *The Empress Matilda* (Oxford: Blackwell, 1991); see also C. Beem, *The Lioness Roared: The Problems of Female Rule in English History* (New York and Basingstoke: Palgrave Macmillan, 2006), chapter 1, and Antonia Fraser, *Boadicea's Chariot: The Warrior Queens* (London: Weidenfeld and Nicolson, 1988), chapter 10. For Henry I, see Judith Green, *Henry I: King of England and Duke of Normandy* (Cambridge: Cambridge University Press, 2006). For the Norman Conquest and its effects (another subject with a vast historiography), see especially George Garnett, *Conquered England: Kingship, Succession and Tenure, 1066–1166* (Oxford: Oxford University Press, 2007). For the civil war, see R. H. C. Davis's lucid *King Stephen* (3rd ed., Harlow: Longman, 1990), which is also the source of the first of the modern quotations given at the beginning of "Matilda 4: Greatest in Her Offspring"; the other is from J. Bradbury, *Stephen and Matilda: The Civil War of 1139–53* (Stroud: Sutton Publishing, 1996). See also *The Anarchy of King Stephen's Reign*, ed. E. King (Oxford: Oxford University Press, 1994); D. Crouch, *The Reign of King Stephen* (Harlow: Longman, 1999); and D. Matthew, *King Stephen* (London: Hambledon and London, 2002). On queenship—in the sense of the rights, powers, and roles of kings' wives, rather than female kings—see Pauline Stafford, *Queen Emma and Queen Edith: Queenship and Women's Power in Eleventh-Century England* (Oxford: Blackwell, 1997), and for Matilda's mother, see L. Huneycutt, *Matilda of Scotland: A Study in Medieval Queenship* (Woodbridge: The Boydell Press, 2003). For Matilda in Germany, see the work of Karl Leyser, "England and the Empire in the Early Twelfth Century" and "Frederick Barbarossa, Henry II and the Hand of St James," in his *Medieval Germany and Its Neighbours, 900–1250* (London: Hambledon Press, 1982), and "The Anglo-Norman Succession, 1120–5," in *Anglo-Norman Studies* 13 (1990), ed. M. Chibnall: 225–241. On the ritual and significance of coronation, see P. E. Schramm, *A History of the English Coronation*, trans. L. G. Wickham Legg (Oxford: The Clarendon Press, 1937). For Matilde of Canossa, see D. Hay, *The Military Leadership of Matilda of Canossa, 1046–1115* (Manchester: Manchester University Press, 2008).

A thorough and helpfully sober overview of Eleanor is provided by R. V. Turner, *Eleanor of Aquitaine: Queen of France, Queen of England* (New Haven and London: Yale University Press, 2009). Not at all sober, but inspiringly lyrical (if requiring of careful treatment), is Amy Kelly, *Eleanor of Aquitaine and the Four Kings* (London: Cassell and Co., 1952). Important essays, especially those by E. A. R. Brown, Marie Hivergneaux, R. V. Turner, James Brundage, Constance Bouchard, Peggy McCracken, and Jane Martindale, are to be found in *Eleanor of Aquitaine: Lord and Lady*, ed. B. Wheeler and J. C. Parsons (New York and Basingstoke: Palgrave Macmillan, 2003). More of Jane Martindale's insights are published in her own collection of essays, *Status, Authority and Regional Power: Aquitaine and France, Ninth to Twelfth Centuries* (Aldershot: Ashgate, 1997), and in her contribution to *King John: New Interpretations*, ed. S. D. Church (Woodbridge: The Boydell Press, 1999); and see the essays by Daniel Callahan, John Gillingham, and Ruth Harvey in *The World of Eleanor of Aquitaine: Literature and Society in Southern France between the Eleventh and Thirteenth Centuries*, ed. C. Léglu and M. Bull (Woodbridge: The Boydell Press, 2005). See also H. G. Richardson, "The Charters and Letters of Eleanor of Aquitaine," *English Historical Review* 74 (1959): 193–213. For Eleanor's second husband, see W. L. Warren, *Henry II* (London: Eyre Methuen, 1973), and *Henry II: New Interpretations*, ed. C. Harper-Bill and N. Vincent (Woodbridge: The Boydell Press, 2007); and for her sons, J. Gillingham, *Richard I* (New Haven and London: Yale University Press, 1999), and W. L. Warren, *King John* (2nd ed., London: Eyre Methuen,

1978). For Eleanor on crusade, see Jonathan Phillips, *The Second Crusade: Extending the Frontiers of Christendom* (New Haven and London: Yale University Press, 2007). For Bernard of Clairvaux, see *The Letters of St Bernard of Clairvaux*, trans. Bruno Scott James (London: Burns Oates, 1953). There is an extensive literature in French on Eleanor's life and career; here I would mention particularly J. Holt, "Aliénor d'Aquitaine, Jean Sans Terre et la Succession de 1199," *Cahiers de Civilisation Médiévale* 29 (1986): 95–100.

Many of the chronicle sources for Eleanor's life are less easily accessible than those for her mother-in-law Matilda. Lengthy extracts from William of Newburgh's *Historia Rerum Anglicarum* and shorter ones from the *Gesta Regis Henrici Secundi* and the writings of Gerald of Wales and Walter Map are printed in translation in *English Historical Documents, 1042–1189*, ed. D. C. Douglas and G. W. Greenaway (London: Eyre and Spottiswoode, 1968). The *Chronicle of Richard of Devizes* is edited and translated by J. T. Appleby (London: Nelson, 1963), and John of Salisbury's *Historia Pontificalis* by Marjorie Chibnall (Oxford: Oxford University Press, 1986). Roger of Howden's chronicle was published in English translation as *The Annals of Roger de Hoveden* by H. T. Riley (London: H. G. Bohn, 1853), and in the original Latin as *Chronica Rogeri de Hovedene* in four volumes by W. Stubbs (London: Rolls Series, 1868–1871). Stubbs also published the original texts of Ralph of Diceto's works in two volumes as *Radulfi de Diceto Decani Lundoniensis Opera Historica* (London: Rolls Series, 1876).

The essential narrative source for the reign of Edward II and Isabella as queen of England is the *Vita Edwardi Secundi*: I have mainly followed the translation by N. Denholm-Young (Oxford: Oxford University Press, 1957), but see also the new edition by Wendy Childs (Oxford: Oxford University Press, 2005). Translated extracts from other contemporary chronicles are included in *English Historical Documents, 1189–1327*, ed. H. Rothwell (London: Eyre and Spottiswoode, 1975). The untranslated text of Geoffrey le Baker's chronicle is published in an edition by E. M. Thompson as *Chronicon Galfridi le Baker de Swynbroke* (London: Rolls Series, 1889); I have also used the *Chronique Métrique de Godefroy de Paris*, ed. J.-A. Buchon (Paris: Verdière, 1827). For the politics of the reign, see R. M. Haines, *King Edward II* (Montreal: McGill-Queen's University Press, 2003); M. McKisack, *The Fourteenth Century* (Oxford: Oxford University Press, 1959); J. R. Maddicott, *Thomas of Lancaster, 1307–22* (Oxford: Oxford University Press, 1970); and N. Fryde, *The Tyranny and Fall of Edward II, 1321–1326* (Cambridge: Cambridge University Press, 1979); also J. S. Hamilton, *Piers Gaveston, Earl of Cornwall* (Detroit: Wayne State University Press, 1988), and *The Reign of Edward II: New Perspectives*, ed. G. Dodd and A. Musson (Woodbridge: York Medieval Press, 2006). For the famine of the early fourteenth century, see W. C. Jordan, *The Great Famine: Northern Europe in the Early Fourteenth Century* (Princeton and Chichester: Princeton University Press, 1996).

For Isabella herself, see H. Johnstone, "Isabella, the She-Wolf of France," *History*, new series 21 (1936–1937): 208–218, and articles by E. A. R. Brown: "The Political Repercussions of Family Ties in the Early Fourteenth Century: The Marriage of Edward II of England and Isabelle of France," *Speculum* 63 (1988): 573–595; "Diplomacy, Adultery and Domestic Politics at the Court of Philip the Fair: Queen Isabelle's Mission to France in 1314," in *Documenting the Past: Essays in Medieval History Presented to G. P. Cuttino*, ed. J. S. Hamilton and P. J. Bradley (Woodbridge: The Boydell Press, 1989), 53–83; and, with N. F. Regalado, "*La Grant Feste*: Philip the Fair's Celebration of the Knighting of His Sons in Paris at Pentecost of 1313," in *City and Spectacle in Medieval Europe*, ed. B. Hanawalt and K. Reyerson (Minneapolis: University of Minnesota Press, 1994), 56–85.

Arguments for Edward II's survival after 1327 have recently been revived and variously updated by Paul Doherty in *Isabella and the Strange Death of Edward II* (London: Constable, 2003), Alison Weir in *Isabella, She-Wolf of France, Queen of England* (London: Jonathan Cape, 2005), and Ian Mortimer in *The Greatest Traitor: The Life of Sir Roger Mortimer, Ruler of England, 1327–1330* (London: Jonathan Cape, 2003), "The Death of Edward II in Berkeley Castle," *English Historical Review* 120 (2005): 1175–1214, and *The Perfect King: The Life of Edward III, Father of the English Nation* (London: Jonathan Cape, 2006). It will be clear that I remain unconvinced; see, for traditions of "undead" kings, M. Evans, *The Death of Kings: Royal Deaths in Medieval England* (London: Hambledon, 2003). Apart from Edward himself and the Emperor Heinrich V, other alleged royal survivors connected to the subjects of this book include Isabella's short-lived nephew Jean the Posthumous, who was "revealed" in 1356 to have been exchanged in his cradle for a baby who died in his place while he grew to manhood as Giannino Baglioni, a merchant banker of Siena; and the Tudor king Edward VI, who was sighted alive and well after 1553, or so rumour had it, in Germany, the Netherlands, Spain, or possibly Denmark: see C. T. Wood, "Where Is John the Posthumous? Or Mahaut of Artois Settles Her Royal Debts," in *Documenting the Past: Essays in Medieval History Presented to G. P. Cuttino*, ed. J. S. Hamilton and P. J. Bradley (Woodbridge: The Boydell Press, 1989), 99–117; and C. Skidmore, *Edward VI: The Lost King of England* (London: Weidenfeld and Nicolson, 2007).

For Margaret, see especially Helen Maurer's *Margaret of Anjou: Queenship and Power in Late Medieval England* (Woodbridge: The Boydell Press, 2003), and J. L. Laynesmith, *The Last Medieval Queens: English Queenship, 1445–1503* (Oxford: Oxford University Press, 2004). For the politics of the period, see J. L. Watts, *Henry VI and the Politics of Kingship* (Cambridge: Cambridge University Press, 1996); R. A. Griffiths, *The Reign of King Henry VI* (London: A. and C. Black, 1981); C. Carpenter, *The Wars of the Roses* (Cambridge: Cambridge University Press, 1997); C. D. Ross, *Edward IV* (London: Eyre Methuen,

1974); C. L. Scofield, *The Life and Reign of Edward IV*, 2 vols. (London: Longmans, Green, and Co., 1923); and my *Blood and Roses* (New York: HarperCollins, 2006). Useful essays include B. Cron, "The Duke of Suffolk, the Angevin Marriage and the Ceding of Maine, 1445," *Journal of Medieval History* 20 (1994): 77–99; D. Dunn, "Margaret of Anjou, Queen Consort of Henry VI: A Reassessment of Her Role, 1445–53," in *Crown, Government and People in the Fifteenth Century*, ed. R. E. Archer (Stroud: Alan Sutton, 1995), 107–143; and J. L. Laynesmith, "Constructing Queenship at Coventry: Pageantry and Politics at Margaret of Anjou's 'Secret Harbour'," in *The Fifteenth Century III: Authority and Subversion*, ed. L. Clark (Woodbridge: The Boydell Press, 2003), 139–149. The principal contemporary sources quoted here are the *Paston Letters and Papers of the Fifteenth Century*, ed. N. Davis, R. Beadle, and C. Richmond, 3 vols. (Oxford: Early English Text Society, 2004–2005), and the *Calendar of State Papers, Milan*, ed. A. B. Hinds (London: HMSO, 1912), available at *British History Online* (http://www.british-history.ac.uk). See also the *Parliament Rolls of Medieval England* (an invaluable new scholarly resource, offering transcriptions of all the surviving rolls of parliaments held between 1275 and 1504, with parallel translation into modern English), available by subscription at *British History Online* (http://www.british-history.ac.uk).

Among the primary sources quoted in "New Beginnings" are the *Calendar of State Papers, Spain*, vols. 11–13, ed. R. Tyler (London: HMSO, 1916–1954), which include the Italian eyewitness account of Mary's proclamation, as well as the dispatches of the imperial ambassadors and letters from Philip of Spain and his entourage in England; and the *Calendar of State Papers, Venice*, vols. 5–6, ed. R. Brown (London: HMSO, 1873–1877), for Giovanni Michieli's remarkable pen-portrait of Mary in 1557, as well as another by his predecessor as ambassador, Giacomo Soranzo, in 1554. Both sources are available at *British History Online* (http://www.british-history.ac.uk), as is the *Diary of Henry Machyn, Citizen and Merchant-Taylor of London*, ed. J. G. Nichols, Camden Society, 42 (London: J. B. Nichols and Son, 1848). See also "The *Vita Mariae Angliae Reginae* of Robert Wingfield of Brantham," ed. and trans. D. MacCulloch, *Camden Miscellany* 28, Camden Society, 4th series, 29 (London: Royal Historical Society, 1984), 181–301; *The Chronicle of Queen Jane, and of Two Years of Queen Mary*, ed. J. G. Nichols, Camden Society, 48 (London: J. B. Nichols and Son, 1850); and *Tudor Royal Proclamations*, ed. P. L. Hughes and J. F. Larkin, 3 vols. (New Haven: Yale University Press, 1964–1969). For John Knox's *First Blast of the Trumpet*, see above, under "Beginnings"; John Aylmer's *An Harbour for Faithful and True Subjects Against the Late Blown Blast Concerning the Government of Women*, published in 1559, can be read at *Early English Books Online* (http://eebo.chadwyck.com).

For Jane Grey and the crisis of 1553, see E. Ives, *Lady Jane Grey: A Tudor*

Mystery (Chichester: Wiley-Blackwell, 2009). For Mary, see the work of J. M. Richards: *Mary Tudor* (Abingdon: Routledge, 2008); "Mary Tudor as 'Sole Quene'?: Gendering Tudor Monarchy," *Historical Journal* 40 (1997): 895–924; and "Mary Tudor: Renaissance Queen of England," in *"High and Mighty Queens" of Early Modern England: Realities and Representations*, ed. C. Levin, D. Barrett-Graves, and J. Eldridge Carney (New York and Basingstoke: Palgrave Macmillan, 2003), 27–44. Also important are C. Beem, *The Lioness Roared: The Problems of Female Rule in English History* (New York and Basingstoke: Palgrave Macmillan, 2006), chapter 2; G. Redworth, "'Matters Impertinent to Women': Male and Female Monarchy under Philip and Mary," *English Historical Review* 112 (1997): 593–613; and E. Russell, "Mary Tudor and Mr Jorkins," *Historical Research* 63 (1990): 263–276. Useful articles on specific moments are A. Whitelock and D. MacCulloch, "Princess Mary's Household and the Succession Crisis, July 1553," *Historical Journal* 50 (2007): 265–287; A. Hunt, "The Monarchical Republic of Mary I," *Historical Journal* 52 (2009): 557–572; and J. D. Alsop, "The Act for the Queen's Regal Power, 1554," *Parliamentary History* 13 (1994): 261–276.

More generally, see D. Loades, *Mary Tudor: A Life* (Oxford: Basil Blackwell, 1989), and his *Mary Tudor: The Tragical History of the First Queen of England* (London: The National Archives, 2006); E. Duffy, *Fires of Faith: Catholic England Under Mary Tudor* (New Haven and London: Yale University Press, 2009); and recent biographies by Anna Whitelock, *Mary Tudor: England's First Queen* (London: Bloomsbury, 2009), and Linda Porter, *Mary Tudor: The First Queen* (London: Portrait, 2007). For the twelfth-century queen Urraca of Castile, see B. F. Reilly, *The Kingdom of León-Castilla under Queen Urraca* (Princeton: Princeton University Press, 1982); and for Isabella of Castile, see J. Edwards, *Ferdinand and Isabella* (Harlow: Pearson Education, 2005). For Eleanor of Aquitaine and courtly love, see R. V. Turner, *Eleanor of Aquitaine, Queen of France, Queen of England* (New Haven and London: Yale University Press, 2009), and Ruth Harvey, "Eleanor of Aquitaine and the Troubadours," in *The World of Eleanor of Aquitaine: Literature and Society in Southern France Between the Eleventh and Thirteenth Centuries*, ed. C. Léglu and M. Bull (Woodbridge: The Boydell Press, 2005), 101–114. As a starting point for the extensive literature on Elizabeth I, see C. Haigh, *Elizabeth I* (2nd ed., London: Longman, 1998); and for the queen's speeches, see *Elizabeth I: Collected Works*, ed. L. S. Marcus, J. Mueller, and M. B. Rose (Chicago and London: Chicago University Press, 2000).

INDEX

Page numbers in *italics* refer to maps.